AMERICAN INDIANS

Answers to Today's Questions

Second Edition, Revised and Enlarged

By Jack Utter

University of Oklahoma Press : Norman

Also by Jack Utter

Wounded Knee & the Ghost Dance Tragedy (Lake Ann, Mich., 1991)

Library of Congress Cataloging-in-Publication Data

Utter, Jack.
    American Indians : answers to today's questions / by Jack Utter.—
2nd ed., rev. and enl.
        p. cm.
    Includes bibliographical references and index.
    ISBN 0–8061–3313–9 (cloth : alk. paper) — ISBN 0–8061–3309–0 (pbk. :
alk. paper)
    1. Indians of North America—Government relations.   2. Indians of
North America—Politics and government.   3. Indians, Treatment of—
United States.   I. Title.

E93 .U48 2001
323.1'197073—dc21

                                                                00–054510

Sketches by Angela Saxon. Computer-drawn maps by Michael Blume.

The paper in this book meets the guidelines for permanence and durability
of the Committee on Production Guidelines for Book Longevity of the
Council on Library Resources, Inc. ∞

1 2 3 4 5 6 7 8 9 10

AMERICAN INDIANS

Answers to Today's Questions

Knowledge is Power.

When combined with wisdom it can mean victory.

One of the axioms developed by
undergraduate and graduate students in my college
course on the history of federal Indian law.
—Jack Utter

CONTENTS

Contents of Part II

THE QUESTIONS

Section C: TREATIES AND AGREEMENTS

SECTION F: WARFARE

Section G: LAND, RESOURCES, AND NON-GAMING ECONOMICS

LIST OF FIGURES (MAPS)

PREFACE

The first edition of this book grew from a desire to counteract ignorance—my own and that of countless other people who, like me, have been uninformed or misinformed on many Indian country issues since we were small children.

Thinking back to the earliest point in my decision to proceed with the original book project, I recall that it occurred one day in the summer of 1991 when I telephoned the public information office of the Bureau of Indian Affairs (BIA) in Washington, D.C. I called because of my frustration in trying to find some particular information on American Indians that was unavailable to me. I had called the BIA earlier that summer, and they had directed me to some question-and-answer booklets and pamphlets, which were available at the University of Arizona's documents library, that the BIA had been publishing from time to time over the past several decades. Although interesting and somewhat useful, these sources lacked sufficient depth, breadth, and references to be of much more than mild anecdotal use in regard to my information needs at the time.

Sharing my thoughts with Evelyn Pickett, a BIA public affairs officer, I mused that if only I had the time and resources, I might employ the BIA's question-and-answer approach to develop an easy-to-read book for people who want substantive, well-referenced, and easily located information on a wide array of Indian country topics.

Evelyn's immediate enthusiasm for such a project caught me a little by surprise. Nonetheless, her reaction was so encouraging that I subsequently shared the idea with John Schultz of National Woodlands Publishing Company. He, too, exhibited a strong interest in the project. After I provided him with a prospectus, John made a commitment to the project and provided the resources necessary to turn the idea into a reality. After a little less than two years, the first edition appeared.

As the new millennium approached, it was time to decide whether to let the book go out of print or produce a second edition. Because John was nearing retirement and his publishing company was reducing its activity, he decided to contact various other publishers to determine if they would be interested in acquiring the rights to produce a second edition. Several responded, but only the University of Oklahoma Press made a commitment to take on the second edition in the way that John, whose company holds the copyright, felt was most appropriate. (I secretly hoped that Oklahoma would come out on top, because my grandparents, parents, and numerous aunts, uncles, and cousins all grew up in Oklahoma. Some also attended the University of Oklahoma [OU]. To me, it seemed a little like keeping the book in the family.) Thus, the second edition of *American Indians: Answers to Today's Questions* is the result of a successful and much appreciated collaboration between this author and my two publishers.

First-time readers with more than a passing interest in American Indians should enjoy this book. For those who are already familiar with the first edition and liked what it had to offer, the second edition is sufficiently "new and improved" to make it worth your while.

PREFACE

to the First Edition

Are American-born Indians who live on reservations citizens of the U.S. or are they not? I recall that, when Ronald Reagan was President, he once told some Russian university students that Indians are not citizens.

F. R., Oklahoma City, Oklahoma
In *Parade Magazine*, July 21, 1991
(Scott 1991)

Ignorance is one of the greatest barriers to understanding between two peoples. If we don't understand each other, if we do not know the culture, the language, or the history of each other, we are unable to see each other as human beings with value and dignity. This is especially true in relations between Indians and non-Indians.

William C. Wantland (1975)
former Attorney General
Seminole Nation of Oklahoma

Apparent in the first quotation—and discussed in the second—is something I call *innocent ignorance*. All of us have it to some degree, whether non-Indian or Indian. Most non-Indians tend to know much less about Native Americans and their culture than the latter know about non-Indians. This is understandable because Euro-American society has so overwhelmingly dominated and intruded upon Native society. A key objective of this book, therefore, is to help fill part of the gap that often exists between public perception and Indian reality.

I began the project by searching out and chronicling common misperceptions about many legal, social, historical, political, and cultural aspects of life for indigenous Americans. Later, help came from numerous people, both Indian and non-Indian, through comments, suggestions, and criticisms, as well as the kind provision of the right reference material at the right time. Ultimately, I endeavored to "stand on the shoulders of giants" to get a better view of the many questions, answers, and other information needed to complete this wide-ranging publication.

A partial list of my "giants" includes such writers and scholars as Felix Cohen, Vine Deloria, Jr., Ruth Underhill, Walter Echo Hawk, D'Arcy McNickle, William Sturtevant, James Mooney, Wilcomb Washburn, Francis Prucha, Tim Giago, Robert Utley, Robert Williams, Jr., Edward Spicer, John Collier, David Getches, Carl Waldman, Alvin Josephy, Jr., Kirke Kickingbird, Sharon O'Brien, Theodore Taylor, David Case, and Charles Wilkinson. Knowledge gained from their works and those of many others, along with government documents and information from non-government organizations, provided the foundation for most of the book. I hope what follows will broaden readers' views and stimulate further inquiry.

ACKNOWLEDGMENTS

I have thought a lot about his part of the book, much more than its length reveals. Although many readers may skip it and move directly to the text, this brief section reflects some of my deeper sentiments surrounding much of the development of the second edition.

TO "ISHI MAN"

In late March 1999, the world's press seized on a short news item coming out of Brazil that told of the establishment of a temporary, six-mile-square reservation in the Amazon rainforest for the protection of a single Indian man. The Brazilian government's National Indian Foundation (NIF) reported that the man appeared to be the last surviving member of an unknown tribe whose people had been victims of "the violent economic occupation of the Amazon."

On the day the news article came out I was giving a guest lecture on federal Indian law to a group of college students at Northern Arizona University (NAU). We discussed the article.

The circumstances of this nameless Indian man in Brazil seemed to us all to mirror those of Ishi, the last of the Yahi people of California, who walked out of the "stone age" and into modern American life in 1911 (see Heizer and Kroeber [1979] and Waterman [1971]). Because of this, one of the students called the lone Brazilian Indian "Ishi Man."

The news article also reported that NIF's agents had tried to make an initial contact with Ishi Man. He responded by shooting an arrow at them.

What has happened to his man's people, and what is now happening to him and thousands of others in South America, Central America, and southern Mexico, is a rerun of what had already taken place in North America from the time of the first European contact through the beginning of the 20th century.

At this writing, Ishi Man's fate remains unknown to me.

TO MY FORMER STUDENTS AT NAU

During 1997 and 1998, I was employed at Northern Arizona University in several capacities relating to the "Navajo Treaty Project." This was a unique commemorative project marking the 130th anniversary of the signing of the Navajo-U.S. Treaty of 1868. The key element of the project involved bringing the original treaty from the National Archives in Washington, D.C., to the NAU campus for a year-long educational exhibit that began on June 1, 1998. No living Navajo had ever seen the original treaty.

In addition to helping coordinate the project under the direction of Dr. Evangeline Parsons Yazzie, I was also assigned the task of teaching several history courses on Federal Indian law, Indian Water Rights, and Indian-U.S. Treaties for the university's Navajo program and the history department.

The time I spent teaching these courses proved to be an unusually rewarding experience. Something seemed to "click" for the students and me, as each class evolved into a special thinking and learning partnership. Perhaps it was due to the atmosphere created by the ongoing Treaty Project. Whatever the cause, we all benefited from being involved in this series of courses, which had never before been jointly offered at NAU. All of the students have graduated or gone on to other endeavors since then, and many are now employed in Indian country—applying much of what we explored and learned.

The students' enthusiasm, effort, and desire for learning in the three subject areas we studied during my visit to NAU in '97 and '98 were, indeed, remarkable. Because much of our learning experience had contributed to the second edition of this book, I have chosen also to dedicate it to my former NAU students.

In alphabetical order, the students—who include people with American Indian, Anglo-American, Anglo-European, Australian Aborigine, and Hispanic heritage—are listed below. Tribal affiliations and non-U.S. countries of residence are indicated where applicable.

Dexter E. Albert (Navajo)
Ettie Anderson (Navajo)
Hollie Anderson (Navajo)
Joelyn Ashley (Navajo & Hopi)

Edlin Bain (Navajo)
Eva Barraza
David Beckley
Delphina Begay (Navajo)

Johnathan D. Begay (Navajo)
Charletta Begaye (Navajo)
Yolanda Benally (Navajo)
Andrea Bia (Navajo)
Erica Bradley (Mescalero Apache)
Lucy Brown (Navajo)
Peterson Brown (Navajo)
Sharon Churchill
Stewart Deats
Edward Dee (Navajo)
Leslie East
Deborah Eriacho (Navajo)
Myron Eriacho (Navajo & Zuni)
Leonard Gilmore (Navajo)
Carol Goldtooth (Navajo)
Andrew Grey (Navajo)
Dawna Holiday (Navajo)
Robert Jacobson
Jason Jennings
Karl Jim (Navajo)
Marvin Jim (Navajo)
Tony Joe (Navajo)
Wahleah Johns (Navajo)
Wenona Johnson (Navajo)
Verdell Kanuho (Navajo)
Elaine L. Kasch (Navajo)
Yvonne Klass (Germany)
Delphina Laughing (Navajo)
Marlene Laughter (Navajo)
Nick Leidig (Narunga, Ngarrindjeri,
    & Romindjeri [Australia])
Beth McCauley
Jon Miller (Navajo)
Debi Nalwood (Navajo)
Gil Nasewytewa (Hopi & Maricopa)
Ramona Antone Nez (Navajo &
    Oneida)
Vernon Nez (Navajo)

Quinzain Orion
Cindy Parrish (Navajo)
Kiyoko Patterson (Navajo)
Irene Pearson (England and Wales)
Gary Pete (Sioux & Navajo)
Robert Price (Mohawk)
Donna Robb (Larrakia [Australia])
Carol Ruben (Nez Perce)
Rolanda Sandoval (Navajo)
Mel Selestewa (Hopi)
April Sewequaptewa (Hopi)
Trudy Shirley (Navajo)
Jeren Smallcanyon (Navajo)
Paulita Smith (Navajo)
Phil Stago, Jr. (White Mountain
    Apache)
Greg Sturtz
Rachael Tanner (Navajo)
Carmen Tsingine (Navajo & Hopi)
LaVonne Tsosie (Navajo)
Lawrence D. Tsosie (Navajo)
Char Tullie (Navajo)
Dr. David P. Van Buren
Ruth VanOtten (Tohono O'odham)
Don Virgil
Cole Wallace
Donovan Watchman (Navajo)
Jarrod Westberg
Raquel Whitehorse (Navajo)
Andrew Wojecki
Dawn Wood (Navajo)
Curt Yazza, Sr. (Navajo)
Donnie Yazzie (Navajo)
Ermalinda Yazzie (Navajo)
Olivia Yazzie (Navajo)
Chee Yazzie-Burnside (Navajo)
Treva C. Yellowhair (Navajo)
Warren Yonnie (Navajo)

Finally, as with the first edition, this book was not the result of an individual effort. John Schultz, the publisher and editor for the first edition, and Joanne Schultz, the coeditor and indexer, continued to provide encouragement, ideas, and assistance that greatly contributed to this new version of the book. In addition, the University of Oklahoma Press, in general, and Ron Chrisman and Jo Ann Reece, in particular, did much to make production of the second edition a rewarding experience—one that should simultaneously serve my interests, those of our readership, and those of the people of the state of Oklahoma, who take great pride in OU and its academic press.

My special friends Merle and Betty Finch, as they have for the 25 years I have know them, continued to inspire and guide me with the wisdom of their nearly 90 years each. Their daughter Margaret Herman and their son-in-law Richard Spence, treasured friends as well, have also been valued advisors.

Most of the individuals, agencies, and organizations who are listed in the acknowledgments for the first edition further contributed to the second in some way. The individuals and entities listed below are acknowledged because of the direct or indirect assistance they have provided me during the research, writing, or production phase of the work on the second edition. I apologize to those who have helped me but who I have inadvertently missed.

My acknowledgment of the following people does not necessarily equal their endorsement of this book.

Pueblo of Acoma
Robert Allan, Esq. (Navajo)
American Indian Law Review
Association on American Indian
    Affairs
Laurita Begay (Navajo)
Dr. Manley Begay (Navajo)
President Kelsey A. Begaye
    (Navajo)
Ailema Benally (Navajo)
Christine C. Benally (Navajo)
Dennis Bowen (Seneca)
Camera Center, Prescott, AZ

Cherokee Nation of Oklahoma
Anna & Tony Cocilovo
Col. Grant Dalgleish
Tammy Decoteau (Dakota)
Vine Deloria, Jr. (Lakota)
Bill Feldmeier
George Finch
Larry Foster (Navajo)
Johnnie Francis (Navajo)
David Getches, Esq.
Leonard Gilmore (Navajo)
Carol Goldtooth and family
    (Navajo)

Tom Gordon
Deborah Gullet
Havasupai Tribe
Congressman J. D. Hayworth
Hualapai Tribe
Senator Daniel K. Inouye
Mike Jackson
Cindy Jarvison (Navajo)
Dr. Robert Johnston
Joe Kee, Jr. (Navajo)
Kirke Kickingbird (Kiowa)
Senator Jon Kyl
Herb Long (Navajo)
Jean Luka, Esq. (Native Hawaiian)
Dr. Dan McCool
Patricia McGee (Yavapai-Prescott)
Robert McNichols
Dr. Nicholas Meyerhofer
Don Mitchell (Yavapai-Prescott)
Donna Mitchell (Yavapai-Prescott)
National Archives
Marjorie Natonabah (Navajo)
Nebraska State Historical Society

Northern Arizona University
Carol Utter Pardue
Dr. Donald Parman
Stanley Paytiamo (Acoma)
Daniel Peterson, M.D.
Prescott College
President Stan Rice, Jr. (Yavapai-
    Prescott)
Sheriff Joe Richards
Professor Ken Roemer
Darrell Russell (Yavapai)
Patricia Slim (Navajo)
Dr. Paul Sneed
Dr. Lula Stago (Navajo)
Arvin Trujillo (Navajo)
University of Oklahoma College of
    Law
Preston P. Van Camp, Esq.
Chad A. Wall
Charles Wilkinson, Esq.
Bennie Williams (Navajo)
Dr. Evangeline Parsons Yazzie
    (Navajo)

ACKNOWLEDGMENTS
TO THE FIRST EDITION

No book, especially one of this nature, is ever an individual effort. Information, encouragement, and assistance in helping me understand Native issues, and in assembling this publication, came from many sources. In the alphabetic list below, I have attempted to recognize those from whom I've learned, or who provided essential assistance in one form or another. Without doubt, some sources have been overlooked, and I sincerely regret any omissions.

I am especially grateful to Joanne Schultz for her untiring effort in reviewing and editing the manuscript, and in compiling the index.

Acknowledgment of individuals, agencies, or organizations does not necessarily equate with endorsements from them.

Administration for Native Americans
Alaska Federation of Natives
Alvin (Tonto Apache)
American Indian Anti-Defamation Council
American Indian Movement
Brian Aranjo
Association on American Indian Affairs
Tina Begay (Apache/Navajo)
Michael Blume
Margery Brown
Senator Ben Nighthorse Campbell (Northern Cheyenne)
Rita and Paco Cantu
Anthony Castillo (Tohono O'odham)
Joseph and Nathan Chasing Horse (Sicangu Lakota)
Congressional Research Service
Argyll Conner (Oklahoma Cherokee) & Dixie Conner
Dennis (Tonto Apache)
Mary Derrick (Navajo)
Merle and Betty Finch
Paula Fleming
Phil Garcia (Laguna)
Gayle Hartmann
Wilson Hunter (Navajo)
Indian Arts and Crafts Board
Indian Country Today (including the Lakota Times)
Indian Health Service
International Indian Treaty Council
Leonard Peltier Defense Committee
Library of Congress
National Anthropological Archives

National Congress of American Indians
National Indian Education Association
National Indian Gaming Commission
National Indian Media Association
National Indian Policy Center
National Indian Youth Council
Native American Rights Fund
Navajo Nation
Agnes Nichols (Chugachmuit Aleut)
Evelyn Pickett (Oklahoma Cherokee)
Bob Robideau (Chippewa) & Paulette D'Auteuil-Robideau
Jackie Rich
Michael Rios (Tohono O'odham)
Dr. John D. Schultz
Jeff Silverman
Smithsonian Institution
Dyanne Stanley (Eastern Cherokee)
Tatanka Oyaté (multi-tribal)
Mililani Trask (Native Hawaiian)
Dr. Brock Tunnicliff
U.S. Bureau of Indian Affairs
U.S. Fish and Wildlife Service
U.S. House Subcommittee on Native American Affairs
U.S. National Park Service
U.S. Senate Select Committee on Indian Affairs
University of Arizona Library and College of Law
Colonel Leon and Jacqueline Utter
Phyllis Utter
Yavapai-Prescott Indian Tribe

INTRODUCTION

This book is not, and was not intended to be, one that will be analyzed by ethereal academicians for decades into the 21st century. It is a book for everyday people with everyday interests and questions about one or more of over one hundred Indian country issues.

Perhaps the two most useful attributes of this book are the accessibility of the information it contains and the Bibliography, which lists many of the best works ever written on the topics discussed in the text. A number of prepublication reviewers have suggested that the Bibliography alone will prove to be of significant ongoing value.

American Indians: Answers to Today's Questions is really meant to be a jumping-off place—an informational starting point from which readers can either learn enough to satisfy their curiosity or take the first steps toward subsequent in-depth research into numerous and often extremely complex subjects. Books like this one are intended to be something like a reader's "combination tool" for learning that is both pleasurable and educational. I hope that the second edition serves that dual purpose.

The amount of material that has been published on the general topic of American Indians is staggering. Any good-sized library is likely to have thousands of books and documents on the subject. Despite this abundance of information, American Indians have been described by some observers as "the unknown minority." Considering the average person's contact with and knowledge about today's Indians, this description would appear to be accurate.

Unfortunately, the majority of Americans have gained their knowledge about Indians from fictional movie and television "westerns" and from history books which frequently limit discussion about Indians to the Indian wars of the 18th and 19th centuries. Relatively few people, for example, have been exposed to enough factual information to know the answers to such basic contemporary questions as:

> Who is an Indian? Who is a Native American? Are Indians
> indeed citizens? What percentage of the population is Indian?
> How many tribes are there? How many reservations are there?
> Do most Indians live on reservations? Does the United States still
> make treaties with Indian tribes? Why are Indian tribes treated
> differently from other groups? Who are the Inuit and Aleut
> people? What is Indian country? What is the primary mission of
> the Bureau of Indian Affairs?

This book does not attempt to "reinvent the wheel" in answering these questions and the many others appearing between its covers. It takes information from various sources and makes that information more readily available to readers. Also, unlike some works that say a lot about a limited number of topics, this project does the opposite by saying a little about a lot of topics. Readers who desire further study are encouraged to obtain more in-depth publications, like many listed in the Bibliography.

The book is divided into three main parts. Part I is the shortest and was composed, in part, as a brief response to the 1992 observance of the Columbus Quincentennial. It also touches on the question of Indian origins. The main purpose of Part I, however, is to help the reader understand why the issue of "discovery" has had so great an impact on American Indians.

Part II contains 156 questions and answers covering a wide array of issues. Descriptive materials consist of maps, photographs, and text relating to contemporary and historical issues. These are distributed throughout the book.

To better comprehend the current relationship between American Indians and the federal government—and where that relationship is apparently headed—it is necessary to have some understanding of its past. To this end, Part III contains a summary history of government policies regarding American Indians, extending from the end of the British colonial period to the present. Collectively, this history and the other segments of the book are designed to provide a broad introduction to many interesting—and sometimes surprising—topics germane to American Indians. A principal goal of this book is to foster new perceptions which will help bring America's image of Native people out of the 19th century.

The basic structure of the second edition of this book has remained almost identical to the first edition. There are, however, a number of additions and modifications, including the following:

1. The addition to Part I of a substantial amount of revealing new material on the *Discovery Doctrine,* and some further information on the debate over the origins of American Indians.
2. A considerable expansion of the "Warfare" section to address new questions asked specifically by Indian and non-Indian readers of the first edition.
3. The updating of all the sections of questions.
4. The addition of another 41 questions and answers.
5. A listing of several useful website locations.
6. The insertion of more informative anecdotes and quotations that various readers of the first edition indicated they wanted more of.
7. The inclusion of a concise section on Indian Gaming.
8. The updating of selected tables and figures.
9. The addition of approximately 300 "new" references to the Bibliography.
10. The expansion of the appendix containing Native Hawaiian information.
11. The development of an entirely new index.

I have also cleared up my former mixed usage of the terms "Native American" and "American Indian." Although I sometimes employed "Native American" in the first edition, over the years I have become increasingly uncomfortable with using it to refer to people who are members of federally recognized tribes and who still have a measure of officially acknowledged sovereignty. The plain truth is that the term "Native American" has no legal association with sovereignty under United States law. In addition, the term has become one of assimilation under U.S. law. (See the answers to questions A-2 and D-6 in the text. For an example of relevant policy assimilation, see the latter part of the answer to question A-16.)

To clarify, the term "Native American" is used to refer to a number of different indigenous peoples from the continental U.S. and the far Pacific Ocean (including the people of one Pacific nation who are not

U.S. citizens). This is collectively demonstrated through such laws as the Native American Languages Act (1990), the Native American Graves Protection and Repatriation Act (1990), and the Native American Programs Act (1975), and their amendments and associated regulations. Therefore, as a teacher of federal Indian law, a supporter of tribal sovereignty, and an opponent of externally imposed assimilation, I join other authors like Lloyd Burton (1991), Rex Lee Jim (1994), Beatrice Medicine (1993), Daniel McCool (1993a), David Wilkins (1997), and the U.S. Bureau of Indian Affairs (2000a) in choosing not to use "Native Americans" when referring solely to the indigenous peoples of the continental United States. "Native American" is generally not socially incorrect; it is only incorrect if issues of sovereignty and verbal or legal assimilation with non-Indian groups are concerns.

Finally, I have always been somewhat intrigued by the following "Introduction" to *The American Heritage Book of Indians* published in the early 1960s—because of who the author is, the nature of his comments, the time in which it was written, and the continuingly timely points it seems to make.

As an interesting test, and without revealing the name of the author, I read the following passage separately to half a dozen friends and acquaintances who are well-informed members of several Arizona and New Mexico Indian tribes. I then asked each in what time period he or she thought it was written. Curiously, most of them said probably within the last few years, and only one guessed as far back as ten years ago. Plus, they all liked most of what the several paragraphs had to say and thought the material would be a good addition to this book. Each of my conferees was quite surprised to find out who wrote the passage and when.

My informal survey tends to underscore the old adage that "the more things change the more they stay the same." The one thing, however, that bothered each of my listeners about the quotation was the possessiveness of the "our Indian people" phraseology found in it. They indicated that this is an ongoing issue for many American Indians who resent the condescension they see in phrases such as this—a condescension, as one of them stated, that has been "fostered by paternalistic missionaries and government officials since the days of first contact" (Parsons Yazzie 2000).

For a subject worked and reworked so often in novels, motion pictures, and television, American Indians remain probably the least understood and most misunderstood Americans of us all.

American Indians defy any single description. They were and are far too individualistic. [In fact, considering all of the hundreds of tribes at once] [t]hey share no common language and [no] common customs. But collectively their history is our history and should be part of our shared and remembered heritage. Yet even their heroes are largely unknown to other Americans, particularly in the eastern states, except perhaps for such figures as Chief Joseph and his Nez Perce warriors of the 1870s, Osceola and his magnificent, betrayed Seminoles of the 1830s, and possibly Sacagawea, the Shoshoni "bird woman" who guided the lost Lewis and Clark expedition through the mountain passes of Montana.

When we forget great contributors to our American history—when we neglect the heroic past of the American Indian—we thereby weaken our own heritage. We need to remember the contributions our forefathers found here and from which they borrowed liberally.

When the Indians controlled the balance of power, the settlers from Europe were forced to consider their views, and to deal with them by treaties and other instruments. The pioneers found that Indians in the Southeast had developed a high civilization with safeguards for insuring peace. A northern extension of that civilization, the League of the Iroquois, inspired Benjamin Franklin to copy it in planning the federation of States.

But when the American Indians lost their power, they were placed on reservations, frequently lands which were strange to them, and the rest of the nation turned its attention to other matters.

Our treatment of Indians during that period still affects the national conscience. We have been hampered—by the history of our relationship with the Indians—in our efforts to develop a fair national policy governing present and future treatment of Indians under their special relationship with the Federal government.

Before we can set out on the road to success, we have to know where we are going, and before we can know that we must determine where we have been in the past. It seems a basic requirement to study the history of our Indian people. America has much to learn about the heritage of our American Indians. Only through this study can we as a nation do what must be done if our treatment of the American Indian is not to be marked down for all time as a national disgrace.

President John F. Kennedy, Introduction to
The American Heritage Book of Indians (Josephy 1961:7)
used with permission.

A Note About Laws And Court Cases Cited In This Book:

Readers who are unfamiliar with the manner in which laws are cited may find the following statement helpful if they wish to learn more about laws referred to in this book. Legislation can be cited in three different ways. For example, the National Environmental Policy Act of 1969 is cited as (1) Public Law (P.L.) 91-190, (2) 83 Stat. 852, or (3) 43 USC 4321. The first citation indicates that the act was the 190th law passed by the 91st Congress. The second tells us that the act is found in Volume 83 of the U.S. Statutes at Large, beginning on page 852. The third citation indicates that the law has been codified in Volume 43 of the U.S. code (USC), beginning at Section 4321. All three methods are correct; they simply allow someone to find them in different sources. The U.S. Code, however, incorporates all amendments to particular laws in the same location with the original law. In this book, you will find laws cited in all of the ways described here.

The names of court cases are italicized. In the Bibliography, information provided after the italicized name of the case will allow interested readers to learn more if they consult with a documents librarian at a library which carries legal reference materials.

PART I

THE DISCOVERY ISSUE

TWO DESCRIPTIONS OF THE FIRST MOMENT:

Thursday, 11 October 1492

The moon, in its third quarter, rose in the east shortly before midnight. I estimate that we were making 9 knots and had gone some 67 1/2 miles between the beginning of night and 2 o'clock in the morning. Then, at two hours after midnight, the Pinta fired a cannon, my prearranged signal for the sighting of land.

Friday, 12 October

At dawn we saw naked people . . .

From the *Log of Christopher Columbus*
In Josephy 1991, p. 13

A few solitary white sails, far out on the blue water, are seen with mysterious awe by the Indian from the Atlantic shore, appearing like huge monsters from the spirit world.

They move toward the land!

From out their sides pour forth a new, unheard-of race. . . .

Henry Howe, 1851
In *Historical Collections of the Great West*

THE AGE OF DISCOVERY

> *Navajo Community College, founded in 1968, was the first institution of higher learning established on an American Indian reservation. Not long after the college was started, its president, Ned Hatathli, was asked what made NCC different. He paused, then said: "We don't teach that Columbus discovered America."*
>
> League of Women Voters, 1976
>
> *Every legal doctrine that today separates and distinguishes American Indians from other Americans traces its conceptual roots back to the Discovery Doctrine.*
>
> Deloria and Lytle 1984, p. 2

"Who *really* discovered America?" The answer to that question may seem obvious since this is a book about American Indians. However, in light of the importance which Euro-Americans placed, centuries ago, on the word "discovery," the reader will find that the question is not trivial. In fact, it lies at the heart of many of the problems which Indians have faced since long before the United States became a nation—and which continue to confront them today.

The 1992 observance of the Columbus Quincentennial might well have helped many Americans understand why Ned Hatathli referred to the discovery issue as he did. Though the voyage of Christopher Columbus was an outstanding navigational achievement, he never set foot on or even saw the North American continent. Nonetheless, he did trace the Central American coast from Honduras to Panama on his last voyage; and he even landed on the northern coast of South America during his third voyage in 1498, thinking it was an island.

Columbus first made landfall on October 12, 1492, on a small island in the Bahamas, southeast of Florida. It was already inhabited by the Taino people. Because he felt he had found an archipelago off the coast of Asia—most likely India—Columbus gave these people the name "Indios," the Spanish word for Indians. Despite the fact that the new lands he encountered were already inhabited, Columbus claimed them for his benefactors, King Ferdinand and Queen Isabella of Spain, who ruled under the blessing of the Pope.

On several occasions during his travels, in what we now call the West Indies, Columbus took his men and Indian scouts on expeditions in search of Japan, which he felt was in the region. Up to the time of his death in Spain, on May 21, 1506, Christopher Columbus was convinced he had reached the fringe of Asia. Though he wasn't first, and he was mistaken about his whereabouts, Columbus stands out as the one man who inaugurated Europe's "Age of Discovery" in the Western Hemisphere, which forever changed Native lifeways in this half of the world.

The distinction of being the first recorded European of the discovery era to walk the shores of North America usually falls to John Cabot. Sailing in the name of Henry VII of England, Cabot reached the far northeast coast of North America on June 24, 1497. When he arrived at Cape Bauld, Newfoundland, he claimed the land for King Henry. Ignoring the Pope, Henry had personally commissioned Cabot to "conquer, occupy, and possess . . . the lands of . . . heathens and infidels," in order to acquire the "dominion, title and jurisdiction of the same." After a hasty exploration of the region, Cabot returned to England in August with three kidnapped Micmac Indians. Unlike Spain's quick response to Columbus' explorations, however, England did not effectively follow through on Cabot's claim for more than a century. It is ironic that John Cabot, whose real name was Giovanni Caboto, was an Italian whose birthplace was Genoa, the reported home city of Columbus.

Though these 15th century explorations took place in what is now called the discovery era, credit for even earlier European landings rightfully goes to the Scandinavian explorers of the 10th and 11th centuries.

VIKINGS AND SKRAELINGS

Adam of Bremen, the German historian, wrote briefly in 1070 A.D. of the Norse voyages to North America that occurred 60 to 80 years earlier. Detailed written descriptions of the Nordic explorations were not available until the Norse "sagas" were first set down in the 1200s. Two of these, the "Saga of Erik the Red" and the "Saga of the

Greenlanders," describe the Vikings' arrival in North America and their early contacts with Native inhabitants.

According to the "Saga of the Greenlanders," Bjarni Herjolfsson first sighted North America (northeast Canada), which the Vikings called "Vinland," in 986 A.D. He had been blown off course while sailing from Iceland to Greenland. Fourteen years later, Lief Ericsson sailed on a westward expedition from Greenland. He eventually landed in Newfoundland where he and his 35 men wintered before their return voyage.

One of the first Viking encounters with the Native inhabitants— to whom the Norsemen referred with the vague term "Skraelings"— was that of Thorvald Ericsson, Leif's brother. About the year 1003, Thorvald led a voyage to Leif's former camp in Newfoundland. Several expeditions were made from the camp over a two-year period. On the final trip, the Vikings found three skin boats upside down on a beach with nine Native men hiding under them. Eight of these men were summarily slaughtered, but one escaped to get help. A small navy of skin boats, bearing numerous warriors, brought a counter-attack. A shower of arrows rained on the Norsemen who were in their own vessels. Thorvald was mortally wounded. Before dying, however, he urged his men to return to Greenland—which they did. Thus ended what is perhaps the earliest-described encounter between Europeans and Native peoples of North America. Other contacts, both violent and peaceful, occurred before the Vikings ultimately quit the Vinland adventures about 1020.

Who were those Native peoples and where did they come from? And, who were the Natives encountered by the Spanish and British hundreds of years later?

THE CONTINUING QUESTION OF THE FIRST INHABITANTS

Other than "Custer Died for Your Sins," *this book* [about traditional views of Indian origins in North America] *has been the most pleasant to write and the most fun to defend. Learning that I did not believe in the Bering Strait theory, the anthropology department at Colorado University, in a series of secretive e-mails, decided*

> *I was a racist reactionary trying to destroy their fictional enterprise and agreed not to invite me to speak to them. . . . Instead of defending me, many of my students decided to call my bluff and went to the libraries and found I was right—no good evidence except the mental illness of the academy exists supporting this theory. Across the board, young professors and graduate students approved the book, and the old guard formed militia movements to protect the tottering bastions of Western knowledge.*
>
> Vine Deloria, Jr., Lakota author and former
> Professor at the University of Colorado.
> From the Preface of his 1997 edition of
> *Red Earth, White Lies*

Like most Indian people of the 19th century and early 20th century, and many still today, Lakota author Vine Deloria, Jr. (1973, 1995, 1997), takes exception to the prevailing dogma of western culture science—particularly anthropology—concerning the origins of the indigenous peoples of the Western Hemisphere. Deloria's primary thesis is that there is value and truth to be found in Native peoples' own traditional knowledge of their origins—if one begins to ascertain how to study and learn from it. Although the jury is still out, there is indeed substance to his general argument, and time has turned up periodic support for some of his positions. Deloria's *Red Earth, White Lies* and an earlier book, *God is Red,* deserve to be read by believers, the uncertain, and non-believers alike. The worst that can happen is an appropriate broadening of one's perspective. The ideas of the "old guard" scientists also deserve to be considered.

In general, many archaeologists believe that nomadic hunters of Asian Mongoloid stock first arrived in North America between 20,000 and 35,000 years ago. Still others believe the earliest arrivals had to have been 40,000 or even 100,000 years ago. Most scientists theorize that prehistoric peoples used the so-called Bering "land bridge" (and perhaps an "ice bridge" and the Aleutian Islands) on migrations to North America. Apparently no one suggests that a massive migration occurred similar to that which took place when the American West was "won." The controversial theory proposes that, over thousands of years, small bands and extended family and tribal groups crossed the land bridge searching for and following the game animals on which they depended for survival.

The Bering Strait, separating Siberia from Alaska, is named after Vitus Bering, a Danish sea captain. He made the first recorded passage through the strait in August 1728, on a voyage of exploration for the Russian Czar, Peter. The strait, roughly 150 feet deep, is only about 50 miles wide at its narrowest point and is bisected by two tiny islands, the Diomedes. The geography allowed Eskimos, in historic times, to cross the strait in their stout skin boats called umiaks. In much earlier times, however, a boat would not have been needed for the crossing.

During the ice ages, ocean levels were lowered because much of the earth's water was tied up in glacial ice. This resulted in exposure of large land areas and creation of a "land bridge" between Asia and North America. The idea of such a bridge of land between Siberia and Alaska conjures up thoughts of a narrow strip of land tenuously connecting the two continents. However, glaciologists and other scientists have proposed that the Bering land bridge was perhaps 1,000 or more miles wide during the last glacial period. (See Figure 1.) This would have perhaps allowed opportunities for land crossings between the continents for those who may have been inclined to make the trek. That is, if glacial ice barriers and subsequent massive swamps did not present insurmountable impediments.

In a logical twist to the Bering land bridge theory, Vine Deloria has presented an overlooked idea. He has written that scientists "cannot tell which way the foot prints were pointing," and it may well be that Asia was populated from the Western Hemisphere (Deloria 1989). This type of provocative speculation continues to stimulate debate on the issue and prevent scientific complacency with a one-way theory of migration, or a single idea of origin.

As the new millennium begins, debate has been rising in the media—and raging within anthropological circles—over the origins and ages of numerous sites of habitation and sets of human remains in North and South America.

There is, for example, an ancient caribou-bone scraper that was found in Alaska and that at least one author has reported is 27,000 years old (Wunder 1994). When one considers that traditional

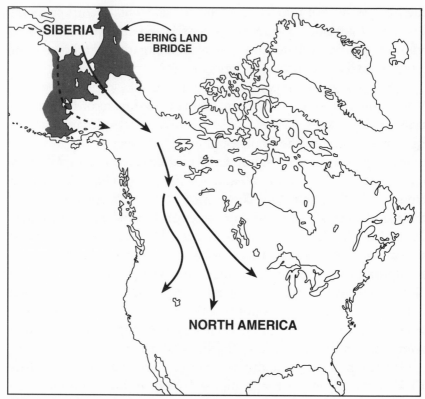

Figure 1. The controversial Bering land bridge migration theory is depicted on the map shown above. Shading represents the area where it is believed the ocean floor was exposed during certain glacial periods, thus allowing theoretical routes of access between Asia and North America. Some observers believe migration may have occurred in either or both directions.

archaeologists would see this as being perhaps 20,000 years older than it should be, according to standard theories, the potential significance of the bone scraper becomes evident.

Then there is the mysterious and highly controversial "Kennewick Man," whose roughly 8,600-year-old, or older, remains were found along the Columbia River in Washington state in 1996 (Fehr-Snyder 2000). The story about who he really is and where he came from remains unclear.

Add to this the intriguing skull, which has been dated at 11,500 years of age, found 200 miles north of Rio de Janeiro, Brazil (Little Eagle 1998). This date predates the Clovis site in New Mexico (traditionally thought to be the oldest in the hemisphere) by 300 years. But the most interesting thing, according to the Sao Paulo anthropologist who has studied the skull, is that the person may have been of Polynesian origin.

There is also the site of a newly dated 12,000-year-old community on the coast of Peru. This suggests to some experts that people may have migrated along the coasts of the Americas instead of crossing a Bering Strait land bridge (Schmid 1998).

Perhaps the most startling of the rash of new revelations is the suggestion by renowned anthropologists Dennis Stanford and Bruce Bradley that the very first inhabitants of North America were non-Indian, and may have come from western Europe (specifically the Iberian peninsula where Spain and Portugal are today) some 15,000 to 18,000 years ago (Murr 1999 and Associated Press 1999a). But the news does not stop there.

Another "ice man" was recently found in a glacier in northern Canada (Republic News Service 1999). It is too early to tell what useful data will be revealed by this discovery, but archaeologists have been analyzing the artifacts associated with the remains.

In the spring of 1999, bones from the skeletal remains of a woman found in the mid-20th century on the Channel Islands, off the coast of California, were radio-carbon tested for the first time with modern equipment (Polakovic 1999). The tests indicated that the bones were probably 13,000 years old—which would make them older than any *human* remains previously tested in the Western Hemisphere.

Recently, Wilkinson (1999, p. 263) reannounced the findings of archaeologist Richard MacNeish, who had discovered evidence of human habitation in Pendejo Cave in southern New Mexico that suggests it may have been occupied as far back as 38,000 years ago.

Finally, a professor from Marquette University has mammoth-bone dates indicating that sites of early human occupancy he has been studying in Wisconsin for many years are up to 13,400 years old (Associated Press 1999b). To archaeologists this date is a revolutionary declaration, because the standard school of thought places the earliest date for human habitation in North America at about 11,200 years ago (the Clovis, New Mexico, site).

There is no doubt that more and more scientific information on the origins of humans on the continent will come to light over the next decade or two, and many of us will be witness to how much more of what Vine Deloria has professed might come to light. As Deloria states in Josephy's *America in 1492*:

> [O]ur knowledge is changing constantly, and a generation from now . . . one might well find that many truisms of today are no longer considered valid, that additional research has thrown new light on some of the puzzling subjects about which today we merely hypothesize [1991, p. 429].

But there are still other "non-scientific" claims about the origins of humankind in the Americas. For example, the Mormon Church and some Jewish scholars (see Glaser 1973) have declared that American Indians—referred to as "Lamanites" by the Mormons—are descendants of a lost tribe of Israel. In contrast, all traditions of North American tribes profess a beginning on the continent. For instance, the Navajo people describe coming from beneath the earth in an area of today's New Mexico, just east of their reservation. The precise time of this origin is unclear, and it is not of great importance in the traditional Navajo view of life.

Though the debate is obviously intensifying, most scientists today persist in the idea that the earliest inhabitants of the continent crossed the Bering land bridge from Siberia. If anyone "discovered" this part of the world, it was the ancestors of these people, or some other ancestors of today's American Indians. When Europeans began arriving, thousands of years later, descendants of the prehistoric pioneers were living throughout the hemisphere and had developed hundreds of distinct cultures. Little did these ancestors of today's Indians realize that "discovery" would become *the* central issue in whether or not they could survive as sovereign peoples, maintaining control of their lives and their land.

THE DOCTRINE OF DISCOVERY

National celebrations of European arrival in the Western Hemisphere cause resentment among many American Indians who are aware of the so-called "doctrine of discovery." This doctrine is the European-invented legal theory upon which all claim to, and acquisition of, Indian lands in North America is ultimately founded.

During the discovery era's fierce international competition for new lands, a need arose for some commonly acknowledged principle by which rights—as between European nations—could be established. The main purpose for developing such a principle was to avoid war over conflicting claims and settlements.

In the earliest years, the competing powers relied directly on grants from the Pope. The prevailing belief, stated by King Duarte of Portugal, was "whatever is possessed by the authority and permission of [the Pope] is understood to be held in a special way and with the permission of almighty God" (Williams 1990, p. 70). But the Pope's international authority was lessening with the growing protestant movement and other world developments. Some more broadly applicable system had to be employed.

Over time, and through many agreements, grants, and charters, the European nations clarified the long-evolving principle that initial *discovery* of lands gave title therein to the government whose subjects, or by whose authority, the discovery was made. This title, ignoring the Native peoples, was good against all other European or civilized (i.e., Christian) governments. It could be secured by possession of the land through the continued presence of the government's citizens or representatives somewhere within the bounds of the claimed area.

The United States officially embraced the discovery doctrine in 1823 through the Supreme Court case of *Johnson v. McIntosh*. The following paragraphs are excerpts from that precedent-setting case in federal Indian law. They begin by addressing the proclaimed superior right of Euro-American governments to sell Indian lands—despite the fact that Indians might claim and be living on them. The last paragraph leaves no doubt as to the U. S. view of the legal effect of European discovery.

> While the different nations of Europe respected the right of the Natives, as occupants, they asserted the ultimate dominion to be in themselves; and claimed and exercised, as a consequence of this ultimate dominion, a power to grant the soil, while yet in possession of the Natives. These grants have been understood by all, to convey a title to the grantees, subject only to the Indian right of occupancy. [For which some form of compensation was usually paid.]

No one of the powers of Europe gave its full assent to this principle, more unequivocally than England. The documents upon this subject are ample and complete.

Thus, all the nations of Europe, who have acquired territory on this continent, have asserted in themselves, and have recognized in others, the exclusive right of the discoverer to appropriate the lands occupied by the Indians. Have the American States rejected or adopted this principle?

By the treaty which concluded the war of our revolution, Great Britain relinquished all claim, not only to the government, but to the "property and territorial rights of the United States," .... By this treaty, the powers of government, and the right to the soil, which had previously been in Great Britain, passed definitely to these States.

The United States, then, have unequivocally acceded to that great and broad rule by which its civilized inhabitants now hold this country. They hold, and assert in themselves, the title by which it was acquired. They maintain, as all others have maintained, that discovery gave an exclusive right to extinguish the Indian title of occupancy, either by purchase or by conquest; and gave also a right to such a degree of sovereignty [over Indians and their land], as the circumstances of the people [of the U. S.] would allow them to exercise.

As the reader should clearly see by the end of this book, many issues which concern American Indians today derive ultimately from the international legal fiction known as the doctrine of discovery. This extremely important and very troubling subject is more thoroughly explored in the following brief essay, which is reproduced from a presentation I made in early 2000 to a special professional audience on the Navajo Reservation (Utter 2000).

THE DISCOVERY DOCTRINE, THE TRIBES, AND THE TRUTH

When most of us first heard, and thought we understood, the term "Discovery Doctrine," we were probably in high school. We were also likely to think the term had its origins with an exceedingly ambitious Italian named Columbus. Many of us may have further imagined Columbus getting together with the king and queen of Spain in the early 1490s to identify and refine some type of international legal theory whereby explorers of the so-called Age of Discovery could justify taking land away from the peoples of any newly "discovered" areas of the world.

As it turns out, such thoughts about when and how the Discovery Doctrine was started, and by whom, were incorrect. In recent years, law professor Robert Williams, Jr. (1990, 1991)—adding greatly to earlier scholarship by Jennings (1975), Washburn (1988), and others—has shown us that we were about 400 years off in our thinking, and that the *legal* doctrine itself was formalized in the late 11th century on starkly prejudiced European religious and cultural biases, and not on any equitable or "just" international laws.

BEGIN AT THE BEGINNING

The Discovery Doctrine was institutionalized through the Christian Crusades of the first several centuries of the second millennium. However, there was an even more distant beginning for the philosophy that is behind the Doctrine—one that reaches back more than 1,800 years before Columbus set sail for the Western Hemisphere.

Aristotle (384 to 322 B.C.), the founder of the science of logic, and one of the most influential philosophical figures in the western world, wrote a number of treatises that profoundly affected the evolution of Western civilization. One of those was *Politics,* which addressed the function and conduct of the "state," or official government. It is the institutionalized superiority of one people over another, as found in the Discovery Doctrine, that we seek to locate the roots of in Aristotle's writings. Moffitt and Sebastian (1996, p.6) have done this very succinctly in the following passage from their revealing book:

> Like all his peers, Aristotle drew a careful distinction between Greeks—real men—and the *barbaroi,* near beasts. A [Greek] was rational; the semi-human barbarian was only emotional, irrational for being only "ruled by his passions." In his *Politics,* . . . Aristotle advanced a dangerous thesis about those who *need* to be ruled by their more rational betters. As "masters," these superior humans

may even properly make slaves of their cultural inferiors. . . . As Aristotle declared (*Politics*, I.2), "barbarian and slave are, by nature, identical." In this world there are but two kinds of men, "that kind which naturally rules, and that which naturally is ruled. . . . [There is the inferior who is meant to provide labor, and he is] by nature, ruled; he is a slave to the superior being. . . . Domesticated animals are, by nature, superior to untamed ones." [The same held true for Aristotle regarding the "civilized" Greeks and the "wild" peoples of the known world.]

Spanish secular and church authorities and legal scholars—recognized today for being the first to apply the Discovery Doctrine to the Western Hemisphere, and for having developed the foundations of modern federal Indian law (Cohen 1942b)—customarily relied on Aristotle's writings (and those of the Church) to justify their actions and adventures in the "New World." Aristotle's ancient writings also provided a philosophical or cultural license for the Spanish and other Europeans, along with their religious license, to justify the displacement, dispossession, and even destruction of other inferiorly perceived peoples—including the Native peoples of North and South America.

An irony arises when we remember that Aristotle was obviously non-Christian—having lived his entire life several hundred years before the time of Christ. Therefore, when he wrote of the "superior" peoples of his time (who he said had superior property rights as well as a natural dominion, in his view, over other groups) he was writing of observed *cultural* differences between peoples, not religious differences. The fact that his "superior" groups were necessarily non-Christian caused some difficulty for the later Christian scholars and church leaders who were looking for revered and time-honored philosophical justifications for a *Christian* religious superiority over non-Christian peoples. They did this by combining their cultural *and* Christian differences into a new worldview.

THE ROLE OF THE CRUSADES

In the year 1095, Pope Urban II of the Roman Catholic Church called for the first Crusade to what is commonly referred to as the Holy Land. The Crusades went on from the 11th through the 13th centuries. The basic justification for the Crusades was that the "heathens and infidels" (the non-Christian peoples) who held Jerusalem and the regions surrounding it could be legally conquered and displaced by Christian European armies acting on orders of the Pope.

Reading the history of the Crusades, and the papal documents developed to justify the actions of the Crusaders, can lead one almost to hear each of the medieval Popes asserting, "I am the vicar of Christ. As such, I have sovereignty over the souls of all humanity, including non-Christians. I therefore declare that non-Christian rulers are unlawful rulers who must bow to the superior rights and superior sovereignty of the Christian cultures of Europe that are endorsed by me." In the 13th century, Pope Innocent the IV did in fact declare that "There is only one right way of life for mankind"; his way. His predecessor, Innocent III (1198–1216), had also determined that the biblical command from Christ to Peter to "feed my sheep" was a mandate for authority over *all* people. He specifically said "the Pope has jurisdiction over all men and power over them in law [if] not in fact" (Williams 1990, p. 45).

The papal trend continued well after the Crusades as, for example, in 1453 when Pope Nicholas the V gave Portugal's king the supposed right to enslave and seize the land and property of "all . . . pagans whatsoever, and all enemies of Christ wheresoever placed." Once again, in 1493, Pope Alexander VI granted to Spain all the world that was not already held or claimed by Christian states. Alexander's generally stated motive was to allow the Spanish to bring heathens "to embrace the Catholic faith and be trained in good morals."

At the end of the 11th century, following the first Crusade, four Euro-Christian states were established in the Holy Land region after the local rulers were defeated. From south to north, they were the Kingdom of Jerusalem (roughly similar to today's Israel), the Countship of Tripoli (covering some of what we know as Lebanon), the Principality of Antioch (in what is now northwestern Syria next to the Mediterranean), and the Countship of Edessa (incorporating an area of Turkey adjacent to today's northern Syria).

Millions of acres of non-Christian lands in the Middle East were summarily taken over and governed by papally sanctioned European rulers because of the perceived and unquestioned "superior culture and superior religion" of the Christian Europeans. Over time, this culturally racist "justification" became a foundation of international law pertaining to lands inhabited by non-Christian peoples, both because of the power of the Pope and because of the large body of legal opinions and theories developed during the Crusades that helped legitimate the taking of lands and property from "infidels."

By the time Columbus carried the Discovery Doctrine to the Western Hemisphere, it was four centuries old and had already been applied to African peoples by the Portuguese, to Baltic peoples by German knights, to the "wild Irish tribesmen" and the "savage" Scottish highlanders by the English, and to others.

Regarding the Irish and Scottish, in the 14th through mid-18th centuries these people differed little from the rural English population. The three groups were even all Catholics, at least in the prereformation era, but the Irish and Scottish were deemed to be the "wrong kind" of Catholics. Their greatest difference with the English, however, was their culture of independent tribes and clans, which contrasted greatly with the English feudal culture and system of government. The English kings and queens could not tolerate this deviation from their "superior" norms of right behavior, culture, and government. They, therefore, eventually conquered and ruled the "deviant" Irish and Scottish peoples.

Thus the Discovery Doctrine was applied to any race of people whose religion and culture varied from a primary Christian European norm. That is why the Doctrine is often referred to as a "culturally racist" precept, as opposed to a biologically racist one—the latter having been applied to peoples who were routinely perceived as biologically inferior to the European conquerors and colonizers. These groups included such well-known victims as "black Africans" and Australian Aborigines.

People who had the "wrong" culture and religion, no matter what their color, were candidates for the Discovery Doctrine. It is this "Doctrine" that has formed the legal basis of the transfer of 97 percent of America from Indian to non-Indian ownership.

THE U.S. ADOPTS THE DOCTRINE

In 1823 the landmark case of *Johnson v. McIntosh* (21 U.S. 543) came before the U.S. Supreme Court. The initial facts of the case are relatively simple. In the early 1770s, the predecessors of Mr. Johnson, an ordinary private citizen, bought some land from the Illinois and Piankashaw tribes in the Illinois region. Some years later, after the U.S. gained independence from the British, the tribes sold the same land to the United States. The federal government later sold that land to the predecessors of Mr. McIntosh, another private citizen.

What the Supreme Court had to decide was who now had valid legal title to the land—Johnson's people, who claimed their title came directly from the tribes; or the McIntosh group, whose title came from the federal government after the U.S. had purchased the land from the tribes. To answer this question, the Court had to decide what title the tribes initially held and whether or not they could sell their land to private parties.

In writing the opinion for the Court, Chief Justice John Marshall found that the Discovery Doctrine had been used by the British and that the U.S., therefore, inherited whatever land rights and control the British had over Indian lands prior to the British loss of the Revolutionary War. Those rights and controls, it was determined, were rather extensive.

In essence, Justice Marshall declared that in the year "1498" (actually 1497), when the Italian explorer Giovanni Caboto (John Cabot) sailed on behalf of Henry the VII of England along the northeastern seaboard of what became the U.S., the British took legal title to their newly "discovered" American lands. He further stated that, at that instant, the sovereignty of the tribes within the territory claimed by the British was automatically and "to a considerable extent, impaired."

In exchange for the reduction of tribal sovereignty and the reduction in tribal property rights through the Discovery Doctrine, Justice Marshall explained that the European powers "found no difficulty in convincing themselves that they made ample compensation to the [Indians] . . . by bestowing on them civilization and Christianity."

What the tribes had left then, according to Marshall, was only a "right of occupancy" in their lands. (This right of occupancy is often referred to as "Indian Title" or "Aboriginal Title.") And, the tribes were all now technically under the superior sovereignty of the British. As the Court further declared, the tribal right of occupancy of their lands could be extinguished by purchase or conquest, and such extinguishment could *only* be done by the "discovering" nation, or its successor.

Thus, with regard to the basic dispute between the Johnson and McIntosh factions, the Johnson group lost. This is because Johnson had bought the land directly from the tribes, and the tribes did not have a right, under the Discovery Doctrine, to sell it to him. They could sell their right of occupancy to the U.S. only and to no one else.

What is perhaps the most revealing language in the opinion, in regard to its strong link to the culturally racist origins of the Discovery Doctrine, is Justice Marshall's explanation of the Court's justification of the Doctrine. Despite the fact that the Doctrine is an apparent injustice against human rights, Chief Justice Marshall stated he would not try to defend the seeming injustice. He did, however, say that the inferior "character and habits of the [Indian] people whose rights have been wrested from them" provide "some excuse, if not justification" for the imposition of the Discovery Doctrine on them. He also said that, "the character and religion of . . . [America's Indian] inhabitants afforded an apology for considering them as a people over whom the superior genius of Europe might claim an ascendancy."

This culturally racist "superior culture and superior religion" conception of the Discovery Doctrine, as formally adopted by the U.S. in the *Johnson v. McIntosh* case of 1823, can be clearly traced all the way back to the first Crusade of 1095, and even further back to the equally arrogant ideas of Aristotle's *Politics*, written in the 4th century B.C.

THE MEANING TO TRIBES TODAY

As Williams (1990, 1991) and others have shown, the Discovery Doctrine provides the foundational principles of modern federal Indian law. It also provides some of the justification for Congressional "plenary" (or near absolute) power over Indian affairs. And, it has always been in the background of such federal policies as assimilation, removal, allotment, forced education, the reservation system, partial termination (e.g., Public Law 280), termination, and relocation.

The idea of the "superiority" of the people and institutions of the larger society over Indian people also underlies the latter-day decisions of the Supreme Court that perpetuate a new kind of termination— "judicial termination."

A partial list of these modern anti-Indian cases includes: the 1977 case of *Rosebud Sioux Tribe v. Knipe* on reservation disestablishment, the 1978 case of *Oliphant v. Suquamish Indian Tribe* on tribal criminal jurisdiction over non-Indians, the 1982 case of *Montana v. U.S.* on treaty interpretation and tribal land control, the 1983 case of *Nevada v. U.S.* on Pyramid Lake water rights, the 1988 case of *Lyng v. Northwest Indian Cemetery Ass'n* on Indian religious freedom, the 1989 case of *Brendale v. Yakima Indian Nation* on tribal land-use zoning powers, the 1990 case of *Duro v. Reina* on tribal criminal jurisdiction over non-member Indians, and the 1998 case of *Alaska v. Native Village of Venetie* on the question of the existence of Indian country in Alaska and of related tribal sovereign powers.

The list of anti-Indian cases goes on, and it will continue to grow until the tribes are reduced to mere remnants of what they are, even today. So, the question arises: What can tribes do? I suggest a new concept of tribal autonomy in "Tribal Independence: A Possible American Model," an article published in the *Native American Law Digest* (Utter 1999).

Specifically, the majority of the founding rules of federal Indian law and policy, starting with the days of "discovery," have always been heavily stacked against the tribes. The long-term message of U.S. policy toward the tribes echoes the old coin toss saying: "heads I win, tails you lose." The only real solution seems to be to literally change the rules. However, any change would obviously have to originate with the tribes themselves.

No one else will do it.

They made us many promises, more than I can remember. . . . They never kept but one: They promised to take our land, and they took it.

Red Cloud
Lakota Sioux Chief

[Additional sources for Part I are: Axtell 1988; Bradford 1973; Ceram 1971; Encyclopedia Britannica 1990; Farb 1968; Getches, Rosenfelt, and Wilkinson 1979; Jennings 1975; League of Women Voters 1976; MacNeish 1971; Mooney 1928; Rouse 1992; Service 1963; Thomas 1899; United States Commission on Civil Rights 1981; Waldman 1985, 2000; Williams 1990; Wrone and Nelson 1973.]

PART II

QUESTIONS & ANSWERS

The issues and the problems that confront Indian people on a day-to-day basis are extremely complex. It takes a lifetime of education to even begin to understand them.

Tim Giago 1991a
Member of the Oglala Lakota Nation and former
publisher of the weekly *Indian Country Today*

INTRODUCTION

For readers who are accustomed to purely historical or ethnological books about American Indians, some of the material in Part II may seem comparatively technical or legalistic. The reason has to do with the contemporary nature of most of the subject matter.

Those who do not experience the phenomenon of everyday life in Indian country cannot have a clear understanding of just how extensively government and laws affect American Indians. Their lives are deeply intertwined in the workings of—and unceasing conflicts among—federal, tribal, state, and local laws and governments (Getches, Wlikinson, and Williams 1998). In the federal area alone, more than 350 treaties have been ratified, more than 5,000 Indian laws passed, more than 2,000 relevant court cases decided, and at least 500 attorneys' general opinions rendered. Thus, any serious effort to discuss widely ranging topics relating to Indian America cannot avoid topics and explanations that are both technical and legalistic.

It is appropriate to ask, "How were the following questions selected?" Some were taken from among the questions most frequently asked of the U.S. Bureau of Indian Affairs (BIA) by the public. Others were developed through the author's own experience, and still more were recommended by reviewers of the first edition of the book and the manuscript of the second edition. The common thread, of course, is that all the questions are relevant to the nation's uncertain concept of American Indian people.

SECTION A: THE INDIAN PEOPLE

> *It should be remembered that aboriginal tribes never considered them-selves "Indians" in a racial sense, but as separate nations.*
>
> Underhill 1974

A-1. *Who is an Indian?**

Before first European contact, the answer to "Who is an Indian?" was easy. Nobody was. "Indian" is a European-derived word and concept. Prior to contact, indigenous people were not Indians but were members of their own socio-political and cultural groups—Lakota, Makah, Yurok, Tlingit, or Chugach, for example, or sub-groups thereof—just as there were Frenchmen, Germans, Englishmen, and Italians in Europe. With the landing of the Europeans, an immediate dichotomy arose that was previously unknown in the hemisphere. Instantly the Native people lost some of their identity when they were all lumped together under a single defining word. The distinction between Native and non-Native peoples resulted in a highly significant legal, political, and social differentiation that remains with us today and is embodied in this first question.

Today in the U.S. there may be 10 to 20 million people with some Indian blood, but only a small percentage identify themselves as being primarily Indian (Russell 1994, Taylor 1984). Also, no single definition of "an Indian" exists—socially, administratively, legislatively, or judicially.

The end purpose of the question "Who is an Indian?" is usually the determining factor in deciding which of the multiple definitions is used (Cohen 1982). For U.S. census purposes, as one example, an Indian is anyone who declares himself or herself to be one. Thus, the concept of *Indian* as used by the Bureau of the Census does not denote a scientific or biological definition but, rather, is an indication of the race with which a person identifies.

*This first of the many questions in the book presents what would seem to be a simple inquiry. However, its answer clearly shows the remarkable complexity of the modern world of American Indians.

Tribal groups, themselves, have differing criteria for who is an Indian of their tribe. The Cherokee of Oklahoma require proof only of descent from a person on the 1906 tribal roll—no matter how small the percentage of Indian blood may be. Other tribes specify one-half, one-fourth, or another degree of blood for membership (Taylor 1984).

From a strictly ethnologic standpoint, if a person is, say, 3/4 Caucasian and 1/4 Indian, that person would normally not be considered an Indian. Yet, for many legal and social purposes, such a person will be an Indian, as might someone with a lesser quantum of Indian blood (Cohen 1982).

Many federal laws and regulations define "Indian," and these various definitions take on great significance when they control the distribution of funds and services or regulate the application of civil and criminal law. As the first of several examples, the BIA *generally* defines an Indian, who is eligible for BIA services, as an individual who is a member of an Indian tribe, band, or community that is "recognized" by the federal government; who lives on "or near" a reservation; and who is of 1/4 or more Indian ancestry (Bureau of Indian Affairs 1987a).

It is necessary, then, to define what "near a reservation" means, in order to know all persons who are defined as "Indians" under BIA social services programs. The BIA has such a definition in Title 25 of the Code of Federal Regulations.

> (r) *Near* [a] *reservation* means those areas or communities adjacent or contiguous to reservations which are designated by the Commissioner [of Indian Affairs] upon recommendations of the local Bureau Superintendent, which recommendation shall be based upon consultation with the tribal governing body of those reservations, as locales appropriate for the extension of financial assistance and/or social services, on the basis of such general criteria as: (1) Number of Indian people native to the reservation residing in the area, (2) a written designation by the tribal governing body that members of their tribe and family members who are Indian residing in the area, are socially, culturally and economically affiliated with their tribe and reservation, (3) geographical proximity of the area to the reservation, and (4) administrative feasibility of providing an adequate level of services to the area.

> The Commissioner shall designate each area and publish the designations in the Federal Register. [1998, Part 20, Subpart A, Section 20.1.]

For the specific purposes of *criminal* jurisdiction, there is no legislative definition of who is an Indian (Hall 1981). A number of court cases have addressed the issue, but the results of their opinions have left later courts with a marked amount of flexibility. Hall (1981, p. 24) quotes from a 1976 federal case in outlining what the courts have said:

> The definition of exactly who is and who is not an Indian is very imprecise. . . . Courts have generally followed the test first discussed in *United States v. Rogers*, 45 U.S. 567 . . . (1845): in order to be considered an Indian, an individual must have some degree of Indian blood and must be recognized as an Indian. . . . In determining whether a person is recognized as an Indian, courts have looked to both recognition by a tribe or society of Indians or by the federal government. . . . [F]ederal cases have held one-fourth to three-eights blood . . . or one-eighth to one-fourth blood . . . is sufficient to be enrolled as a member of a tribe. . . . We find that both Williams and Alvarado [who were one-fourth blood] are of Indian blood and have held themselves out to be Indians. . . . [T]hey are [therefore] Indians within the meaning of 18 U.S.C. Sec. 1153. [Quoted from *United States v. Dodge* (1976), 538 F.2d 770, 786–787.]

Hall (p. 24) continues: "It seems clear that while [tribal] enrollment is the common evidentiary means of establishing Indian status, . . . it is not the only means nor is it necessarily determinative [*United States v. Broncheau*, 597 F.2d 1260, 1263]. . . . Blood quantum, residence, status in the community, reputation as an Indian or non-Indian, all are factors that a court may consider to determine whether a person is an Indian [for purposes of criminal jurisdiction]." (See Flowers 1983 for further discussion of "who is an Indian" for criminal jurisdiction purposes.)

Another definition example relates to the situation where federal assistance is provided for Indian health care education. The definition provided in the Indian Health Care Improvement Act of 1976 is considerably broader than the definition described above for the BIA.

The act defines "an Indian" as anyone who is a member of a "recognized" tribe, with no mention of blood quantum. An individual may also be considered Indian if he or she belongs to a tribe, band, or group that has been terminated since 1940, regardless of whether or not the individual lives on or near a reservation. Another category includes those members of tribes which are recognized now—or may be recognized in the future—by the state in which they reside. In addition, anyone who is a descendant, in the first or second degree, of any of these individuals also qualifies. Eskimos, Aleuts, or other Alaska Natives are considered Indians. Anyone considered by the Secretary of the Interior to be Indian for any purpose qualifies. And, finally, anyone who is determined to be Indian under regulations promulgated by the Secretary of Health and Human Services also is considered to be an Indian.

The Indian Education Act of 1972 employs a relatively broad definition of "Indian." It includes all of the following: people of one-eighth blood ancestry and higher who are members of Indian tribes and groups, residents of state reservations, urban Indians, Indians from "terminated" tribes, and self-identified Indians.

In the Indian Arts and Crafts Act of 1990, "Indian" is defined by Congress, for the purposes of the act, as "any individual who is a member of an Indian tribe, or . . . is certified as an Indian artisan by an Indian tribe." There is no blood quantum requirement. A "tribe" is also defined to include those tribes and Alaska Native villages recognized by the federal government, those formerly recognized, and tribes or groups recognized by a state government when there is no federal recognition.

As indicated above, federal definitions have included Alaska Natives under the broad heading of "Indians" when discussing BIA and other agency programs affecting Indians. Therefore, "Indians" is sometimes employed as a generic term for all Native peoples of the continental United States. At other times, the term refers only to American Indians in the 48 states, while "Alaska Natives" is used to distinguish the Indian, Eskimo, and Aleut people of Alaska.

To avoid the great confusion associated with the question of who is an Indian, Felix S. Cohen (1982)—the renowned chronicler of American Indian Law—suggested that a practical and basic *legal* definition of an Indian would be one which sets two essential qualifications:

(a) some of the individual's ancestors lived in what is now the United States before the first Europeans arrived and (b) the individual is recognized as an Indian by his or her tribe or community.

COMPARATIVE EXAMPLE OF "WHO IS AN INDIAN" FOR SIX FEDERAL PURPOSES, REGARDING MEMBERS OF THE FEDERALLY RECOGNIZED HOPI TRIBE OF ARIZONA AND THE STATE RECOGNIZED GABRIELINO-TONGVA (G.T.) TRIBE OF CALIFORNIA

	"Indian" for these purposes					
	Census Bureau Indian Count	BIA Services	Indian Arts & Crafts Authenti- cation	Regulations Re: Obtaining Eagle Feathers for Religion	Administr. for Native Americans Programs	BIA Hiring Preference
Blood degree						
4/4 Hopi	YES	YES	YES	YES	YES	YES
1/4 Hopi	YES	YES	YES	YES	YES	YES
1/8 Hopi	YES	NO	MAYBE	NO	YES	MAYBE
4/4 G. T.	YES	NO	YES	NO	YES	YES
2/4 G. T.	YES	NO	YES	NO	YES	YES
1/4 G. T.	YES	NO	YES	NO	YES	NO

A-2. *Who is a Native American?* (See also questions A-3, A-5, and D-6.)

> *I am an American Indian . . .*
>> N. Scott Momaday (Kiowa), Pulitzer prize-winning author
>>> (1991, p. 14)
>
> *I am . . . not a "Native American."*
>> Rex Lee Jim (Navajo), (1994, p. 6).

The term, "Native American," came into usage in the 1960's to denote the groups served by the Bureau of Indian Affairs: American Indians and Alaska Natives (Indians, Eskimos and Aleuts of Alaska). Later the term also included Native Hawaiians and Pacific Islanders in some Federal programs. It, therefore, came into disfavor among some Indian groups. The preferred term is American Indian.

The Eskimos [Inuit] and Aleuts in Alaska are culturally distinct groups and are sensitive about being included under the "Indian" designation. They prefer, "Alaska Native."

Bureau of Indian Affairs 2000a

Taken as a whole, [General] Crook's command was a fine organiza-tion, and its officers, four-fifths of whom were <u>native Americans</u> and West Pointers, were fully in sympathy with the ardor of the men.

From a dispatch by a reporter who accompanied
Gen. George Crook's 1,000-man army to the
Bighorn River country of Montana, where in
June 1876, the General suffered an embarrassing defeat at the
hands of Crazy Horse and Sitting Bull, one week before
Lt. Col. George A. Custer met his end
(Vaughn 1956, p. 29–30, emphasis added).

In the broadest sense, anyone born in the Americas is a Native American (Burton 1991). Nonetheless, the term "Native American" is widely recognized as meaning a person who is of a tribe or people indigenous to the United States. It is most frequently applied to American Indians in the 48 coterminous states, but it also includes Alaska's three ethnological groups—Indians, Eskimos, and Aleuts. (Eskimos are also called Inuit.)

The Native American Languages Act (1990, sec. 2902) states: "The term 'Native American' means Indian, Native Hawaiian, or Native American Pacific Islander." The term "Indian" includes people who are ethnologically considered as American Indian, Inuit, or Aleut. "Native American Pacific Islander" includes "any descendent of the aboriginal people of any island in the Pacific Ocean that is a territory or possession of the United States."

The federal government, through the U.S. Department of Health and Human Services, has included a further definition for "Native Americans" within its regulations for the Native American Programs Act of 1975. That definition lists the groups referenced above, and clarifies that the term "Native American Pacific Islanders," includes American Samoan Natives and the indigenous peoples of Guam (Chamorros), the Commonwealth of the Northern Marians, and the Republic of Palau (Administration for Native Americans 1991a & b; Luka 2000). Guam is a U.S. territory, as is American Samoa. The Commonwealth of the Northern Mariana Islands is a commonwealth of the United States, much like Puerto Rico. The Republic of Palau, however, is an independent country. It gained independence from U.S. trust territory status on October 1, 1994. (To learn more on the Pacific islands under U.S. jurisdiction, contact the Interior Department Office of Insular Affairs [www.doi.oia].)

To summarize, under various U.S. laws and regulations, "Native Americans" include:

> Indians, Inuits, and Aleuts (All three groups are "Indians" under United States law. *Tribal* sovereignty does not extend beyond these groups. In other words, only the term "Indian," not "Native American," has a legal association with tribal sovereignty under U.S. law.)
> Native Hawaiians
> American Samoans
> Chamorros of Guam
> Native peoples of the Commonwealth of the Northern Mariana Islands
> Native peoples of the Republic of Palau (These people are not U.S. citizens, but are residents of a former U.S. Pacific island trust territory. They have their own sovereignty as citizens of an independent country, but they do not exercise any "tribal" sovereignty under U.S. law.)

A-3. *How do American Indians view themselves in the context of the larger society?*

Over the past two decades, a number of Indian acquaintances have made it clear to the author that they see themselves as tribal members first, Indians second, and Americans third. Even so, they are aware of being all three at once. They have also stated that this view is widely held in Indian country. Social scientists and the courts have referred to this understandable phenomenon as "community consciousness" (Weatherhead 1980; *Mashpee Tribe v. New Seabury Corp.* 1979).

A few non-Indians have suggested that this attitude, at first glance, may seem "unpatriotic." Actually, it tends to show an extraordinary patriotism that does not break faith with ancestral nations, centuries or millennia older than the U.S., and that expands to embrace additional allegiances. In addition, one of the conceptual requirements of tribalism long recognized by the U.S. government is that tribes are "distinct political communities" and the "members owe immediate allegiance to their . . . tribes" (U.S. Department of the Interior 1894, p. 664).

A-4. *What are the earliest origins of the word "Indian?"*
"Indian" is a Europeanized word ultimately derived from the ancient Sanskrit term "sindhu," which means river; specifically the sacred "Indus" river (Oxford English Dictionary 1971). Sanskrit is the holy language of Hinduism.

> *Who were the "naked people" Columbus and his men observed at dawn on that autumn day five hundred years ago? Columbus, the first ethnographer in the New World, tells us a few things about them. They were broad in the forehead, straight and well proportioned. They were friendly and bore gifts to their visitors. They were skilled boat-builders and boatmen. They painted their faces and their bodies. They made clothes and hammocks out of cotton. They lived in sturdy houses. They had dogs. And they too lived their daily lives in the element of language; they traded in words and names. We do not know what name or names they conferred upon their seafaring guests, but on October 17, on the sixth day of his sojourn among them, Columbus referred to them in his log as "Indios"* [Momaday 1991, p. 14].

The word "Indian" is obviously the English version of the Spanish word "Indios." Prior to 1492, the Spanish applied the term exclusively to the peoples inhabiting all the lands east of the lower Indus River (which flows through present-day Pakistan), and west of the Bay of Bengal which runs along the eastern coast of India. Thus, the land province trending east south-eastward of the lower Indus River eventually came to be known as "India." Because Columbus thought that he had arrived off the great eastern fringe of India, he named the people he encountered "Indios."

Rex Lee Jim (1994, p. 6–7), Navajo author, philosopher, and educator, has contemplated the term "Indian" and has offered us this analysis:

> The clanship system in Navajo culture has provided me with hours of storytelling with my grandfathers. One of them used to say, *"The sacred begins at the tip of your tongue. Be careful when speaking. You create the world around you with your words."* It is only right then that . . . [we] Indian people recreate [our] world—the past, the present, and the future.
>
> American Indians have been ordained by the Holy People with the power to choose. They must begin once again to exercise that power to choose. . . .
>
> The Italian explorer Christopher Columbus simply verified [by using the name Indios] what Indians already knew when he described them as *un gente que vive en dios—a people who lived in God.* [Making his choice for the sacred, Rex Lee Jim selects *en dios* as the root for *Indios,* and he then goes on to declare:]
>
> I am an American Indian . . .*

---

*There is something in Mr. Jim's discussion that goes beyond words. It is not unlike what seems to be the underlying attitude of Indian authors like Vine Deloria, Jr. (Lakota), David Wilkins (Lumbee), or Robert Williams, Jr. (Lumbee) in many of their publications. It could be described as "constructive resistance." This seems to be an essential element of the ongoing efforts toward tribal survival.

A-5. *How do the major "Native American" groups generally differ?*
According to the contentious Asian migration theory, the parent stock of today's Indians is considered to have migrated to North American thousands of years before those of the Aleuts and Eskimos (Sutton 1985). The Aleuts are thought to have come second, and the Eskimos most recently, but still in prehistoric times. Distinct cultural, linguistic, and genetic differences exist between American Indians, as one group, and Eskimos and Aleuts as another.

In the lower 48 states, all of the indigenous people are of *Indian* heritage. In Alaska, the Indian people are grouped into two main classifications: (1) the Athapaskan tribes, e.g., Ahtna, Koyukon, Kutchin, Tanana, etc., of interior Alaska, and (2) the southeast coastal tribes—Eyak, Tlingit, Haida, and Tsimshian (Waldman 1985).

Eskimos and *Aleuts* differ from each other, both genetically and by their unrelated languages, but they developed comparable sea-hunting cultures. The similarities are considered by some to be greater than the differences (Bureau of Indian Affairs 1966; Damas 1984).

PHOTO COURTESY OF THE SMITHSONIAN INSTITUTION

More often than not, the word "Indian" conjures up images similar to this photograph of a Kiowa chief from the central plains, circa 1870s. Lone Wolf was nationally known for fighting the White Man—but more in the courts than on the battlefield. In the famous U.S. Supreme Court case of *Lone Wolf v. Hitchcock* (1903), he was unsuccessful in his efforts to get the U.S. government to uphold treaties it had made with the Kiowa and Comanche tribes.

Eskimos (or Inuit) are generally people of far northern, western, and southern Alaska. They have traditionally lived along the coasts of the Bering Sea, Arctic Ocean, and Gulf of Alaska, as well as up some of the rivers that flow into these waters, and on the islands of St. Lawrence, Nunivak, and Kodiak. (See Damas 1984.)

Aleuts are the traditional people of the western Alaska Peninsula and the Aleutian chain of islands. They were the first Alaska Natives to come under non-Native domination when Russian fur traders began to enslave them in the mid-1700s. They suffered greatly under early Russian domination and are estimated to have lost as much as 80 percent of their population to disease and violence by the end of the 18th century (Bureau of Indian Affairs 1966; Arnold 1976). Most Pacific Eskimos (i.e., those of southern Alaska) are now called Aleuts.

Native Hawaiians, also considered to be Native Americans, are descendants of the Polynesians who migrated to the Hawaiian Island chain many centuries ago. In at least two pieces of federal legislation regarding education and health care (respectively, Title IV of the Elementary and Secondary Education Act amendments of 1988 and the Native Hawaiian Health Care Act of 1988), Congress has defined a Native Hawaiian as being "a descendant of the aboriginal people, who, prior to 1778 [the year of first European contact], occupied and exercised sovereignty in the area that now comprises the State of Hawaii, as evidenced by: (i) genealogical records, (ii) Kapuna (elders) or Kam'aina (long-term community residents) verification, or (iii) birth records of the state of Hawaii."

Houghton (1989) wrote a law journal article supporting the recognition of legal "Indian status" for Native Hawaiians. He suggested this be done under the general laws which recognize the political existence of the three other major Native American groups. A majority of Native Hawaiians disagrees with Houghton's "Indian" approach to resolving the lingering questions of their legal status (Trask 1992).

For further discussion on Native Hawaiians, refer to Appendix 1 for a summary of basic Hawaiian issues.

PHOTO COURTESY OF THE SMITHSONIAN INSTITUTION

An Eskimo, or "Inuit" woman from Alaska territory, 1908. Considered "Indian" under broadly applicable federal law, the Inuit are ethnologically distinct from Indians, as are the Aleut people of Alaska. Also, the sociopolitical organization of the Inuit and Aleut people was based not on tribes but on small groups of extended families. Today it is largely based on a corporate model, following passage of the Alaska Native Claims Settlement Act (1971). Photo by F.H. Nowell.

A-6. What is the Indian population of the United States?*

1990 Census Numbers

In 1990, through the Census Bureau's system of self-identifying, there were 1,959,234 individuals identified as Indians, including Alaska

*When the second edition went to press, the final 2000 census data were not yet available. Nonetheless, there were estimates and projections of population. Those figures were used in the answers for A-6, A-7, and A-8.

For the latest population information, search the government's internet Web site at www.census.gov or call the census bureau's statistical information staff, population division, at (301) 457-2422.

Be aware that the government's figures for "American Indian, Eskimo, and Aleut" includes "foreign born" individuals who self-identify as part of this population. (This could include, for example, North American indians who immigrated from Mexico and Canada.) For the year 2000, the "foreign born" category was estimated to have been 158,000 people, or just over 6 percent of the total population of "American Indians."

Natives. This was 0.8 percent of the total U.S. population of 248,709,873. The "Indian" population broke down ethnologically to 23,797 Aleuts, 57,152 Eskimos, and 1,878,285 Indians.

Census 2000 Estimates

The total U.S. population estimate for all races in the year 2000 was 275,306,000. The "American Indian, Eskimo, and Aleut" population was estimated to be 2,433,000. That amounts to just under 0.9 percent of the total. No further breakdown estimates were provided, except median age (27.7), average age (30.5), male (49.5 percent), and female (50.5 percent).

A-7. *What is the Indian population in each of the 50 states and Washington, D.C.?* (See question A-6 for census update information.)

CENSUS 2000 ESTIMATES IN THOUSANDS

State	Total Population of State	Indian & Alaska Native Population	Percent of State's Total
Alabama	4,451	16	0.4
Alaska	653	95	14.5
Arizona	4,798	262	5.4
Arkansas	2,631	14	0.6
California	32,521	292	0.9
Colorado	4,168	37	0.9
Connecticut	3,284	8	0.2
Delaware	768	2	0.3
Florida	15,233	51	0.3
Georgia	7,875	17	0.2
Hawaii	1,257	6	0.5
Idaho	1,347	17	1.2
Illinois	12,051	26	0.2
Indiana	6,045	15	0.2
Iowa	2,900	9	0.3
Kansas	2,668	24	0.9

CENSUS 2000 ESTIMATES IN THOUSANDS (continued)

State	Total Population of State	Indian & Alaska Native Population	Percent of State's Total
Kentucky	3,995	6	0.2
Louisiana	4,425	19	0.4
Maine	1,259	6	0.5
Maryland	5,275	16	0.3
Massachusetts	6,199	14	0.2
Michigan	9,769	60	0.6
Minnesota	4,830	58	1.2
Mississippi	2,816	9	0.3
Missouri	5,540	21	0.4
Montana	950	57	6.0
Nebraska	1,705	15	0.9
Nevada	1,871	31	1.6
New Hampshire	1,224	2	0.2
New Jersey	8,178	20	0.2
New Mexico	1,860	165	8.9
New York	18,146	73	0.4
North Carolina	7,777	94	1.2
North Dakota	662	30	4.5
Ohio	11,319	22	0.2
Oklahoma	3,373	270	8.0
Oregon	3,397	46	1.4
Pennsylvania	12,202	17	0.1
Rhode Island	998	5	0.5
South Carolina	3,858	9	0.2
South Dakota	777	60	7.7
Tennessee	5,657	12	0.2
Texas	20,119	95	0.5
Utah	2,207	30	1.4
Vermont	617	1	0.2
Virginia	6,997	19	0.3
Washington	5,858	100	1.7
Washington, D.C.	523	2	0.2
West Virginia	1,841	2	0.1
Wisconsin	5,236	46	0.9
Wyoming	525	11	2.0

A-8. *Is the Indian population increasing or is it decreasing?*

It is definitely on the increase. One hundred years ago the U.S. Indian population hit an all-time low of about 250,000. The 1990 census count was 1,959,234. The 2000 census estimate was 2,433,000. These numbers represent increases of 37.9 percent and 58.5 percent respectively over the 1,420,400 Indians counted in 1980. Part of the increase in recent decades has been attributed to a greater willingness of people to identify themselves as Indians.

The numbers of full-bloods among American Indians are increasing in some tribes and decreasing in others. For example, among the Kaw Tribe of Oklahoma (formerly known as the Kansa), only six full-bloods remained in 1991, and all of them have since passed away; yet there are many thousands more Navajo full-bloods than there were in the last century. This is primarily because the Navajos have been relatively isolated from large non-Indian populations in the past and because their population has increased greatly since the late-1800s.

American Indian population projections from the U.S. Census Bureau for the years 2005 and 2010 are 2,624,000 and 2,821,000, respectively. The total U.S. population for 2005 and 2010 is estimated at 287,715,000 and 299,821,000.

A-9. *How many Indians live on reservations?*

The 1990 census reported that 437,431 Indians—or 22.3 percent of the total—lived on legally designated reservations or associated trust lands. Another 10.2 percent (200,789) lived within "Tribal Jurisdiction Statistical Areas," which are former reservation areas in the state of Oklahoma where tribes retain certain types of tribal jurisdiction. (Although the numbers will change with the 2000 Census data, the percentages are not expected to vary greatly.

In Alaska, except for one small reservation in the far southeastern part of the state (Annette Island Reserve), there are no designated Indian reservations. Therefore, for census purposes, "Alaska Native Village Statistical Areas" have been identified by the Bureau of the Census. They coincide with living areas of tribes, bands, clans, groups, villages, communities, or associations that have been recognized in some way by the federal government. The Native people in these Statistical Areas made up 2.4 percent of the total U.S. Indian population in 1990, or 47,244 individuals. They accounted for 55 percent of the population of Alaska Natives.

One last population statistic is that for "Tribal Designated Statistical Areas." These are home areas delineated by tribes outside of Oklahoma who do not have reservations. They accounted for 2.7 percent of the Indian population in 1990, or 53,644 people. Therefore, a total of 1,220,126 Indian people—or 62.3 percent of all Indians—resided *outside* all official categories of Indian areas identified by the Census Bureau.

A-10. *How many non-Indians live on reservations?* **(See question A-6 for census update information.)**

The total population (all races) for reservations and trust lands in 1990 was 808,163. Subtracting Indian residents left a population of 370,732 non-Indians, or 45.9 percent of the total, on average. (This percentage is not expected to vary significantly with 2000 census data.) But the range of percentages of non-Indians on Indian lands varies widely from a low of less than 1 percent to as high as 100 percent in isolated situations.

Various reasons account for the large percentage of non-Indian residents. Inter-marriage is responsible for some of the non-Indian count, as is non-Indian employment or certain land-leasing programs. The most notorious reason, however, is the "allotment system" established by the government in 1887 and rigorously pursued into the 1930s. Under this system, many tribes' lands within legally established reservation boundaries were divided up by government agents and assigned to individual Indians. Left-over "excess" lands, amounting to millions of acres, were sold to non-Indians. The exterior boundaries of many of these "allotted" reservations have remained the same. Ownership of these allotted and excess lands has gone partially or primarily to non-Indian settlers, their descendants, and successors, who make up much of the non-Indian population on allotted reservations. The Flathead Reservation of western Montana is typical. There, the Indian population in 1990 was 5,130; but non-Indians (living on what is now private, non-Indian land within the original and still valid boundaries of the reservation) accounted for another 16,129 people, or 76 percent of the residents. An example from the other end of the scale comes from Jemez Pueblo in New Mexico—99.3 percent of the Pueblo's 1,750 residents in 1990 were Indian.

A-11. *Do many Indians live in urban areas?*

Yes. Most Indians, like most other Americans, live in what the Census Bureau defines as urban or suburban settings. At least 50 metropolitan areas in the United States have Indian populations ranging in size from 4,000 to 90,000 individuals. These 50 areas, alone, were home to 740,000 self-identified Indian people in 1990. Listed below, in alphabetical order, are the 25 U.S. "metropolitan statistical areas" with the highest Indian populations. Their relative rankings, as to Indian numbers, are also given. (Data are from the 1990 census.)

AMERICAN INDIANS LIVING IN URBAN AREAS, 1990

Metropolitan Statistical Area	1990 Indian Population (Includes Alaska Natives)	Ranking
Albuquerque, NM	16,296	14
Anchorage, AK	14,569	16
Chicago, IL–into IN & WI	15,758	15
Dallas–Ft. Worth, TX	18,972	11
Denver, CO	13,884	17
Detroit, MI	17,961	12
Fort Smith, AR–into OK	9,054	22
Houston–Galveston, TX	11,029	21
Los Angeles–Anaheim–Riverside, CA	87,487	1
Milwaukee–Racine, WI	8,522	23

AMERICAN INDIANS LIVING IN URBAN AREAS, 1990
(continued)

Metropolitan Statistical Area	1990 Indian Population (Includes Alaska Natives)	Ranking
Minneapolis–St. Paul, MN–into WI	23,956	8
New York, NY–into Long Island, NJ & CT	46,191	3
Oklahoma City, OK	45,720	4
Philadelphia, PA–into NJ, DE, & MD	11,307	19
Phoenix, AZ	38,017	6
Portland, OR–into Vancouver, WA	13,603	18
Sacramento, CA	17,021	13
Salt Lake City–Ogden, UT	8,337	25
San Diego, CA	20,066	10
San Francisco–Oakland–San Jose, CA	40,847	5
Seattle–Tacoma, WA	32,071	7
Tucson, AZ	20,330	9
Tulsa, OK	48,196	2
Washington, DC–into VA & MD	11,036	20
Yakima, WA	8,405	24

A-12. *What was the Native population of the Americas in 1492?*
Several 20th century researchers attempted to estimate what the aboriginal population of the Western Hemisphere was on the eve of Columbus' arrival. Much of their work has been summarized and critiqued by Denevan (1976), who opens page one of his informative book as follows.

> How many Indians were there? No one will ever know, but can't we at least agree on where there were few or many? Apparently not yet, for on few questions of history do so many authorities continue to differ so greatly. The reasons for attempting to know are numerous and important. It would not be an overstatement to hold that almost every major investigation of pre-Columbian

cultural evolution and ecology, of the European conquest, and of colonial social and economic history must ultimately raise the question of Indian numbers. Thus the effort to determine those numbers continues, and as the quality of the research improves, the trend is toward acceptance of the higher numbers.

Denevan compiled a table of population estimates from five noted researchers who published their data between 1924 and 1966. The table is reproduced here in slightly modified form.

SOME ESTIMATES OF ABORIGINAL AMERICAN POPULATION, CA. 1492

	Kroeber (1939)	Rosenblat (1954)	Steward (1949)	Sapper (1924)	Dobyns (1966)
	(in millions)				
North America	0.9	1.0	1.0	2.0–3.5	9.8–12.3
Mexico	3.2	4.5	4.5	12.0–15.0	30.0–37.5
Central America	0.1	0.8	0.7	5.0–6.0	10.8–13.5
Caribbean	0.2	0.3	0.2	3.0–4.0	0.4–0.6
Andes	3.0	4.8	6.1	12.0–15.0	30.0–37.5
Lowland South America	1.0	2.0	2.9	3.0–5.0	9.0–11.2
Hemisphere Total	8.4	13.4	15.5	37.0–48.5	90.0–112.6

Denevan believes it is reasonable to estimate that somewhere between 50 and 100 million Natives inhabited the Western Hemisphere at the time Columbus arrived. He points out, however, that Magnus Morner, a respected expert, calculates the number to have been 33 million. The controversy continues through more recent works by writers like Churchill (1997), Henige (1998), Stannard (1992), Stiffarm and Lane (1992), and Thornton (1987).

A-13. *Was military conflict the greatest single reason Native population declined during the conquest era?*

Apparently not. It seems most historians believe that introduced disease was the major killer of American Indians. At least one researcher, however, believes that too much emphasis has been put on the impact of disease (Henige 1998). Even so, disease obviously devastated many tribes. Single epidemics often reduced Indian communities by half or more, and many tribes were completely wiped out in a matter of decades (Denevan 1976).

In 1837, for example, smallpox swept through a 1600-member Mandan tribe in the upper plains. Only 31 people survived (Capps 1973). Smallpox was the most notorious killer, but other, newly introduced diseases also became common causes of mortality. Among them were measles, whopping cough, chicken pox, bubonic plague, typhus, diphtheria, amoebic dysentery, influenza, and parasitic worms (Denevan 1976). Surviving tribes which had been exposed longest began to develop some resistance to new diseases by the 17th century.

Ever since I can remember, I have loved the Whites. . . . I was always ready to die for them, Which they cannot deny. I have Never Called a White Man a Dog, but to day, I do Pronounce them to be a set of Black harted Dogs . . . them that I always considered as Brothers, has turned Out to be My Worst enemies. . . . I do not fear Death my friends. You know it, but to die with my face rotten, that even the Wolves will shrink with horror at seeing Me, and say to themselves, that is the 4 Bears the Friend of Whites—

Listen well what I have to say, as it will be the last time you will hear Me. think of . . . all [who are] Dead or Dying, with their faces all rotten, caused by those dogs the whites, think of all that My friends, and rise all together and Not leave one of them alive. The 4 Bears will act his Part.

Mandan chief Four Bears, from a speech he
gave to Arikara and Mandan people on the
day he died from smallpox, July 30, 1837
Calloway 1996, p. 68–69

Nondisease factors contributing to population decline included military conflict, mistreatment, starvation or malnutrition, depression and loss of vigor or will to live, and exportation into slavery. Shoemaker (1999) discusses the reverse trend in her book on American Indian population recovery in the 20th century.

A-14. What is "The Indian Problem" mentioned so often in U.S. history books and government documents through the 1960s?

> *There is, I insist, no problem as created by the Indian himself. Every problem that exists today in regard to the Native population is due to the white man's cast of mind, which is unable, at least reluctant, to seek understanding and achieve adjustment in a new and significant environment in which it has so recently come.*
>
> Luther Standing Bear, 1933
> quoted in Worton 1974, p. 121

"The Indian Problem" is a term of antiquity that, with its various phrasings, predates the establishment of the United States by centuries. In fact, it goes right back to the time of first European contacts with American Indians during the 1490s and early-1500s.

The term's meaning has changed over time; but, as long as there was a frontier, one description covered all frontier settings: "How were the newly arrived immigrants to deal with the Native inhabitants of the land?" (Deloria and Lytle 1984).

At the earliest stages of addressing "the Indian problem," the primary issue, as the Spanish identified it, was whether or not the Indians were fully human. If so, what rights did Indians have that should be respected by the "civilized" nations of the world? Decisions made one way or another would obviously have profound effects on Indian policy.

There were those, like Gonzalo Fernández de Oviedo y Valdez, who could be counted among supporters of the less-than-human argument. Oviedo was a royal officer, notary, and historian in the West Indies whose many official duties included the branding of Native slaves—for which he was paid a small amount of gold for each Indian branded. Oviedo's opinion is made evident in the following quotation from one of his histories, written in the early 1500s, and decrying the Indians and their culture.

> Their marriages are not a sacrament but a sacrilege. They are idolatrous, libidinous, and commit sodomy. Their chief desire is to eat, drink, worship heathen idols, and commit bestial obscenities. What could one expect from a people whose skulls are so thick and hard that the Spaniards had to take care in fighting not to strike [an Indian] on the head lest their swords be blunted? [Williams 1990, p. 94.]

On the other side of the argument were men like the Dominican scholar Franciscus de Victoria (or Vitoria), whose advice on royal policy as it related to Indian affairs was sought by the Spanish king. In 1532, Victoria delivered a lecture titled "On the Indians Lately Discovered" in which he established three main points that were later partially adopted by Spain and other nations which colonized North America. Cohen (1942b) and Williams (1990) describe Victoria's three points in the following manner:

1. The Native inhabitants of the Americas possess natural legal rights as free and rational people. ("Rational" was frequently equated with "human.")
2. The Pope's grant to Spain of title to the Americas was baseless and could not affect the inherent rights of Indian inhabitants.
3. Only transgressions by the Indians against the Spaniards' natural rights to travel, trade, and "sojourn" in the Indians' lands could justify a war against the Indians and the taking of their property through the right of conquest. (This was often interpreted by Spaniards in the New World—that is, by those who even bothered to consider it—to mean that any objections to their activities by Native peoples justified Spanish retaliation.)

Victoria's discourse did not halt the injustices and atrocities committed against the indigenous peoples. Nonetheless, it served to temper official hemispheric policies toward Natives (as bad as some of these policies were) in the early stages of policy development.

> On the Indian question[,] . . . As Indians were transformed from "lords of the soil" to "poor children of the forest," so the nature of the threat they posed to the United States changed from a military to a moral one. . . . Nineteenth-century Americans had to account, in moral terms, for the fact that the nation was built on the graves of Indians.
>
> Susan Scheckel (1998, p. 4–5.)

By the time the United States became a nation, the Indian tribes were generally considered to be impediments to civilization and "the Indian problem," as the U.S. government generally interpreted it, had two facets: (1) how to best develop trade with the Indians and (2) how to most effectively obtain their land for national expansion. This early characterization of the problem evolved over the next two centuries to include: how best to (a) remove the tribes from the settled parts of the country, (b) conquer them, (c) establish and keep them on reservations and away from American society, (d) take their reservation lands away, (e) extinguish their culture and absorb them within American society, (f) reorganize them for renewed self-government, (g) terminate their self-government, and (h) establish opportunities for Indian tribes to determine for themselves what their futures should be.

Alvin M. Josephy, Jr. (1968), in *The Indian Heritage of America,* wrote about "the Indian problem." What he penned was appropriate for the times and warrants repeating—especially considering recent adverse decisions in the U.S. Supreme Court relative to freedom of religion for Indians and, potentially, other Americans. (See *Lyng v. Northwest Indian Cemetery Protective Association* 1988, and *Oregon v. Smith* 1990, as well as the Religious Freedom Restoration Act of 1993, which was the response by Congress to these two cases.)

> [The] Indian has survived, still posing to the white conqueror a
> challenge that not all non-Indians, particularly in the United
> States, wish happily to tolerate, even, indeed, if they understand
> it: acceptance of the right to be an Indian. That right suggests, at
> heart, the right to be different, which in the United States runs
> counter to a traditional drive of the dominant society. Ideally, the
> American Dream in the United States offers equal opportunities
> to all persons; but in practice the opportunities imply a goal of
> sameness, and the Indians, clinging to what seems right and best
> for them, have instinctively resisted imposed measures by non-
> Indians designed to make them give up what they want to keep
> and adopt what they have no desire to acquire. That has been—
> and continues to be—the core of the so-called "Indian problem"
> in the United States, which many Indians characteristically refer
> to as "the white man's problem." [Emphasis added.]

From the present author's point of view, two important points
should be made. First, employing the generic term "the White
man" to distinguish Indians from the rest of American society is no
longer sufficiently inclusive—for the U.S. is fast becoming a nation
where racial minorities will make up the majority. Secondly, to very
generally characterize part of what might be called "the Indian
problem" of today, one could reasonably say the non-Indian views
it from a somewhat benign position and describes the problem as
being one of *clarifying* existing Indian rights. The Indian, on the
other hand, would justifiably view the problem as being one of
having to rigorously *defend* existing Indian rights and actively
reclaim past rights.

There are further important economic aspects to the "Indian
problem," that have been part of the continuing fallout from the
massive collision of "capitalism" with "tribalism" that began in 1492.
High school courses in economics teach us that of the three basic
elements of economic production (land, labor, and capital), land is
always the first among them. Land, of course, includes not only its
surface area but the resources on or beneath the land.

Steve Cornell (1988) thoughtfully and plainly discussed an
often understated but essential element of the on-going "Indian
problem": the American economy's demand for an aggressive pursuit of tribal lands and resources. Cornell describes how American

Indian societies had a *relationship* with their homelands that helped provide their personal and cultural identities and a sense of membership in their communities. Cornell (p. 40) then declares

> that relationship was at odds with the market; capital accumulation could not proceed until land was set free of the encompassing restraints of [the Indians'] social relations and cultural conception. The incorporation of Indian resources [into the economy] required either a fundamental transformation of Native American societies or their removal from the scene. . . .
>
> Thus "the Indian Problem": how to gain access to Indian resources. Of course, there was more to Indian affairs than this. For federal and state authorities, for policymakers and philanthropists, Indian-White relations were more complex than so simple a statement implies. For them "the Indian problem" was variously one of protecting the frontiers from the Indians; protecting the Indians from the unscrupulous; keeping peace among Indians themselves; promoting Euro-American civilization; negotiating treaties and land cessions; distributing education, Christianity, food, annuities, and other odds and ends among the tribes; and coping with the many persons and interests making claims to some part of the Indian business. But all these aspects of Indian-White relations were in one way or another derivative of their essence: U.S. expansion over Indian lands and consequent Indian resistance.

Today Indian gaming is seen by troubled non-Indian policy makers (and competitors in the powerful American gaming industry) as the new "Indian problem." But, again, it is Indian resources—now the money and political influence of the successful gaming tribes—that the outsiders envy and seek to claim. If the past is a template of the future, then they will eventually succeed.

A-15. *What about the "Black Indians?"*

There is a growing interest in this issue, which is succinctly summarized in the title of a book by Katz (1997): *Black Indians: A Hidden Heritage.* Many thousands of people in the U.S. (and the rest of the Western Hemisphere) have mixed Black-and-Indian ancestry. However, there are not many historical or contemporary sources of information on the topic and the lives and histories of the "Black Indians."

Still, there are some useful sources, including another book by William Katz (1996), *The Black West: A Documentary and Pictorial History of the African American Role in the Westward Expansion of the United States*; Kenneth W. Porter's *The Black Seminoles: History of a Freedom-Seeking People* (1996); another Seminole title, *A Brief History of Seminole-Negro Scouts* by Thomas A. Britten (1999); Jack D. Forbes's *Africans and Native Americans: The Language of Race and the Evolution of Red-Black Peoples* (1993); and finally, a book originally written in 1915 by Annie Heloise Abel (1992a), *The American Indian as Slaveholder and Seccessionist.*

Several years ago, the "Black Native American Association" (BNAA) was started in Oakland, California. Their website, www.bnaa.org, has an extensive listing of useful internet links. Another similar organization is the "Black Indians and Intertribal Native Americans Association." They, too, have a website (http:// hometown.aol.com/blkindians/blackindians.html), but it is easier to reach them through a link with the BNAA site.

*Author's note: One of the clan relatives of Radmilla Cody, a recent Miss Navajo Nation, asked me this question. Radmilla is a dynamic and talented young woman whose father was black and whose mother was Navajo. She was raised mostly by her grandmother on the reservation. She is a Navajo speaker, a competent sheepherder, a good orator, an accomplished singer, and college educated. And, she proudly acknowledges the two heritages that she represents.

Ms. Cody and other celebrities with African American and Indian heritage (like professional golfer Tiger Woods) have brought the rarely discussed issue of "Black Indians" into the public arena.

A-16. *What were "the year" and "the century" of reconciliation?*
They began in South Dakota when publisher Tim Giago and other
Indian leaders urged Governor George Mickelson to pronounce 1990,
the centennial of the Wounded Knee massacre, as a year of reconciliation between Indians and non-Indians within the state. The governor embraced the idea and enthusiastically made the designation.
The "year" concept has since been expanded to a declared "century"
of reconciliation in South Dakota, where frequent animosity between
non-Indians and Indians, as well as among different factions of
Indians, has been an unfortunate reality since the mid-1800s.

A step similar to the highly commendable one taken in South
Dakota was taken in the U.S. Congress in the form of a resolution for
a national year of reconciliation. The resolution, which passed both
houses, speaks for itself and is reproduced below. It was introduced
by members of the South Dakota delegation and their House and
Senate supporters. President Bush signed the resolution into effect
on May 11, 1992. It became one of the official counter balances to the
Columbus Quincentennial.

102d CONGRESS
1st SESSION

S. J. RES. 222

JOINT RESOLUTION

To designate 1992 as the "Year of Reconciliation Between American
Indians and non-Indians."

Whereas 1992 will be recognized as the quincentennial anniversary of
the arrival of Christopher Columbus to this continent;

Whereas this 500th anniversary offers an opportunity for the United States
to honor the indigenous peoples of this continent;

Whereas strife between American Indian and non-Indian cultures is of
grave concern to the people of the United States;

Whereas in the past, improvement in cultural understanding has been
achieved by individuals who have striven to understand the differences between cultures and to educate others;

Whereas a national effort to develop trust and respect between American
Indians and non-Indians must include participation from the private
and public sectors, churches and church associations, the Federal

---

Government, Tribal governments and State governments, individuals, communities, and community organizations;

Whereas mutual trust and respect provides a sound basis for constructive change, given a shared commitment to achieving the goals of equal opportunity, social justice and economic prosperity; and

Whereas the celebration of our cultural differences can lead to a new respect for American Indians and their culture among non-Indians: Now, therefore, be it

Resolved by the Senate and House of Representatives of the United States of America in Congress assembled,

That 1992 is designated as the "Year of Reconciliation Between American Indians and non-Indians." The President is authorized and requested to issue a proclamation calling upon the people of the United States, both Indian and non-Indian, to lay aside fears and mistrust of one another, to build friendships, to join together and take part in shared cultural activities, and to strive towards mutual respect and understanding.

This pattern of national recognition has continued in the form of the annual presidential proclamation of "National American Indian Heritage Month." The core provision from the November 1, 1997, proclamation by President Clinton is reprinted below. It is followed by the President's 1999 proclamation, which is reproduced in full.

The government-to-government relationship *between the Tribes and the United States embodies the fundamental American belief that people of widely varied and diverse cultural backgrounds can join together to build a great country. Such greatness can be sustained, however, only so long as we honor the ideals and principles upon which America is founded and abide by our commitments to all our people. In recognition of America's moral and legal obligations to American Indians and Alaska Natives, and in light of* the special trust relationship *between tribal governments and the Government of the United States, we celebrate National American Indian Heritage Month.* [Emphasis added.]

From President Clinton's 1997 proclamation
of American Indian Heritage Month

THE WHITE HOUSE

NATIONAL AMERICAN INDIAN HERITAGE MONTH, 1999

- - - - -

BY THE PRESIDENT OF THE UNITED STATES OF AMERICA

A PROCLAMATION

Ours is a nation inextricably linked to the histories of the many peoples who first inhabited this great land. Everywhere around us are reminders of the legacy of America's first inhabitants. Their history speaks to us through the names of our cities, lakes, and rivers; the food on our tables; the magnificent ruins of ancient communities; and, most important, the lives of the people who retain the cultural, spiritual, linguistic, and kinship bonds that have existed for millennia.

As we reflect on the heritage of American Indians, Alaska Natives, and Native Hawaiians, we also reaffirm our commitment to fostering a prosperous future for native youth and children. At the foundation of these efforts is our work to provide a quality education to all Native American children. In particular, we have sought significantly increased funding to support Bureau of Indian Affairs school construction and 1,000 new teachers for American Indian youth. My 1998 Executive order on American Indian and Alaska Native Education sets goals to improve high school completion rates and improve performance in reading and mathematics. And we are working to get computers into every classroom and to expand the use of educational technology.

We are also seeking ways to empower Native American communities and help them prosper. My Administration is expanding consultation and collaborative decision-making with tribal governments to promote self-determination. We also support tribal government economic development initiatives, particularly those that increase or enhance the infrastructure necessary for long-term economic growth. My New Markets Initiative seeks to leverage public and private investment to boost economic development in areas that have not shared in our recent national prosperity. In July, I visited the Pine Ridge Reservation of the Oglala Sioux, as part of my New Markets Tour, to explore opportunities for economic development in Indian Country.

Among the most serious barriers to economic growth facing tribal communities is a lack of housing, physical infrastructure, and essential services. My Administration is working with tribal leaders to build and renovate affordable housing on tribal lands, bring quality drinking water to economically distressed Indian communities, and improve public safety. We are moving to assist tribal governments in developing the physical infrastructure needed for economic development, including roads, fiber-optic cabling, and electric power lines.

In working together to shape a brighter future for Indian Country, we must not lose sight of the rich history of Native Americans. Just weeks ago, the Smithsonian Institution broke ground on the National Mall for the National Museum of the American Indian. This wonderful facility will preserve and celebrate the art, history, and culture of America's indigenous peoples. It is also fitting that the first U.S. dollar coin of the new millennium will bear the likeness of Sacajawea and her infant son—an image that captures the importance of our shared history.

NOW, THEREFORE, I, WILLIAM J. CLINTON, President of the United States of America, by virtue of the authority vested in me by the Constitution and laws of the United States, do hereby proclaim November 1999 as National American Indian Heritage Month. I urge all Americans, as well as their elected representatives at the Federal, State, local, and tribal levels, to observe this month with appropriate programs, ceremonies, and activities.

IN WITNESS WHEREOF, I have hereunto set my hand this first day of November, in the year of our Lord nineteen hundred and ninety-nine, and of the Independence of the United States of America the two hundred and twenty-fourth.

WILLIAM J. CLINTON

In an effort to be "politically correct" and also to be as many things to as many people as possible, the 1999 proclamation creates confusion. On the BIA's internet page announcing the 1999 proclamation, the agency referred to *"Native American* Heritage Month" (emphasis added), though the official White House title for the event was American Indian Heritage Month. The BIA obviously noticed that in the White House staff's zeal to include another indigenous group, Native Hawaiians had been added to the proclamation. Native Hawaiians are *not* American Indians, and do not currently have a federally recognized right to "self-determination," which is mentioned in the third paragraph of the proclamation.

Also, noticeably absent in the 1999 proclamation, when compared to the quoted paragraph from the 1997 version, is any mention of the "government-to-government relationship" or "the special trust relationship." This is because Native Hawaiians do not have such a relationship with the United States, as of early 2001. (See Appendix 1 for more information on the legal status and related struggles of Native Hawaiians.) By combining as part of a "Native American" group those who are not American Indians, as was done in the 1999 proclamation, there is a legally necessary (and perhaps suspicious) watering down, or actual elimination, of the "government-to-government" and "trust" relationship language that is applicable to federally recognized "Indian Tribes," and that all but one of the other officially recognized "Native American" groups do not have. Native Hawaiians, American Samoans, the Chamorros of Guam, and the Native people of the Commonwealth of the Northern Mariana Islands do not now have separate tribal governments that are federally recognized. Oddly, the Native people of the Republic of Palau, though not citizens of the U.S., are defined as "Native Americans" under the Native American Programs Act of 1975 and its amendments and regulations. As citizens of an *independent* country, the "Native Americans" of Palau *do* have a government-to-government relationship with the U.S. through their own government and its "Compact of Free Association" with the United States. (See the answers to Questions A-1 and A-2.) Their relationship with the U.S., however, is that of a "foreign" nation. Federally recognized Indian tribes, on the other hand, are described as "domestic dependent nations" under U.S. law (*Cherokee Nation v. Georgia* 1831).

As the "melting pot" philosophy of America continues to expand, the "watering down" that is visible between the 1997 and 1999 proclamations for American Indian Heritage Month may affect the future through adverse administrative decrees and federal legislation. It is already an easily identifiable trend in the U.S. Supreme Court's anti-sovereignty rulings in a number of its Indian cases. [For citations to relevant cases, see page 18. See also, Johnson and Martinis (1995) on "Chief Justice Rehnquist and the Indian Cases."]

SECTION B: INDIAN TRIBES

> By a "tribe" we understand a body of Indians of the same or similar race, united in community under one leadership or government, and inhabiting a particular though sometimes ill-defined territory. . . .
>
> U.S. Supreme Court
> In *Montoya v. United States* 1901, p. 266

B-1. *What defines an Indian tribe?*

The term "tribe" is commonly used in two senses—an ethnological sense and an official political sense. Distinguishing between them is important because the latter has far-reaching legal consequences.

Before the federal government developed official definitions for an Indian tribe, the term was purely ethnologic. A tribe was a group of indigenous people, bound together by blood ties, who were socially, politically, and religiously organized according to the tenets of their own culture, who lived together, occupying a definite territory, and who spoke a common language or dialect.

Originally, the question of official political delineations by non-Indians arose in connection with treaty relations. It was necessary to determine which groups were tribal political entities in order to negotiate treaties of peace or land acquisition on a government-to-government basis. Later, federal legislation to regulate Indian affairs, to allow claims for Indian depredations, to permit claims by Indians against the government, and to protect Indian property and other rights required determinations of which groups were affected by particular statutes (Cohen 1982).

Establishment of the Indian reservation system and the placement of tribes on reservations sometimes created new tribal identities. On some reservations, two or three ethnologically autonomous tribes were placed together and had to form a new political identity to deal with the U.S. government. Occasionally this led to a great tribal stress or even warfare with the U.S., e.g., the Modoc War of 1873. In still other cases, a tribe might be broken up and spread over two or more reservations (e.g., the Chiricahua Apaches) to be politically absorbed into the "tribe" established for the particular reservation.

Today, after centuries of cultural and political interference by Euro-Americans, the term "tribe" might apply to a distinct group within an Indian village or community, the entire community, or a large number of communities. It might also refer to several different groups or villages speaking different languages but sharing a common government, or a widely scattered number of villages with a common language but no common government (Taylor 1984).

Legally, no universal definition for the generic term "tribe" exists in the U.S. Constitution, federal statutes, or regulations. Nonetheless, the term is specifically found in the Constitution, in hundreds of statutes, in hundreds of treaties, and in numerous regulations. In most instances, a question of a tribe's political existence can now be resolved by reference to a treaty, legislative agreement, statute, or executive order of the President "recognizing" the tribe at some time in the past. In other cases, the definition of "tribe" will depend in part on the context and the purpose for which the term is used (Cohen 1982). Occasionally, a court may find that there have been sufficient dealings by agents of the federal government (such as the BIA) with an Indian group that, over time, the group became "recognized" as a tribe. This type of ruling has to be consistent with the overall intent of Congress in its broad constitutional authority over Indian affairs.

Canby (1998, p. 3–4) has provided a reasonable, contemporary, and concise definition to keep in mind as a basic initial response to the question of "What is an Indian tribe?" He writes: "At the most general level, a tribe is simply a group of Indians that has been recognized as constituting a distinct and historically continuous political entity for at least some governmental purposes." Canby further notes: "The key problem with this definition lies in the word 'recognized.' Recognized by whom? The answer is that recognition may come from many directions, and the sufficiency of any given recognition is likely to depend upon the purpose for which tribal status is asserted." By far, the most significant and valuable recognition is that of the U.S. government.

B-2. *What is the significance of federal "recognition" of an Indian tribe?*

As an international example of what intergovernmental "recognition" means, recall that with the break-up of the Soviet Union in 1991, a number of the former republics declared their independence and immediately sought to obtain diplomatic "recognition" by other nations of the world, including the United States. Once granted by a nation, initially through a formal declaration, this recognition becomes the official acceptance of one nation by another as a fellow sovereign government. It is the starting point for an ongoing government-to-government relationship.

This international form of recognition is the historic foundation of our federal government's recognition of Indian tribes. It is a legacy from early colonial days when tribes were considered entirely independent nations with whom inter-governmental relations and appropriate "foreign affairs" were to be observed and maintained. In its earliest years, the U.S. adopted this same policy from the precedent set by the British. But, by the early 1800s, all of the remaining independent Indian nations east of the Mississippi were subdued—through disease, conquest, pacification, and assimilation—and became "domestic dependent nations," as declared by the U.S. Supreme Court in 1831 (*Cherokee Nation v. Georgia*). Without realizing it, the other tribes which eventually came under U.S. jurisdiction as the country expanded also inherited dependent nation status. This occurred once they were recognized as tribes by the U.S. government through treaty negotiations or other official interactions. Recognized tribes, therefore, became semi-sovereign political entities whose level of self-government has varied over the years according to the policies of Congress, in addition to the effects of Supreme Court decisions.

Under regulations first published in 1978, the Bureau of Indian Affairs can administratively "acknowledge" the existence of an Indian tribe. Acknowledgment is essentially the same as recognition. Perhaps because of its international flavor, however, the term "recognition" seems to be left mostly to use by Congress and the President. (The BIA regulations can be located on the Internet at www.doi.gov/bia/acknowl.html, or in Title 25 of the Code of Federal Regulations, Parts 82 and 83.)

Recognition or acknowledgment really have the same effect. They establish that a tribe exists as a unique political entity which has a formal relationship with the United States government—a relationship that is ultimately traceable to the Indian Commerce Clause and the Treaty Clause of the U.S. Constitution (Art. I, Sec. 8, Cl. 3 and Art. II, Sec. 2, Cl. 2, respectively). Recognition also establishes that a recognized tribe has certain inherent rights and powers of self-government and is entitled to specific benefits and services enumerated in various federal laws. Further, rights reserved or granted to tribes by treaties, executive orders of the President, or special acts of Congress, or rights verified through the judicial process, may be available to the tribe and its members. Finally, recognition also means that a tribe becomes subject to the extremely broad powers that Congress has in dealing with Indian tribes. For example, Congress has the power to unilaterally terminate the legal existence, and extinguish the reservation, of any federally recognized tribe. This fact demonstrates the ultimately precarious legal environment in which all federally recognized tribes exist.

> *THE CONGRESS shall have Power . . .*
> *To regulate Commerce with foreign Nations, and among the several States, and with the Indian Tribes;*
>
> U.S. Constitution Art. I, Sec. 8, Cl., 3
>
> *[THE PRESIDENT] shall have Power, by and with the Advice and Consent of the Senate, to make Treaties, provided two thirds of the Senators present concur;*
>
> Art. II, Sec. 2, Cl. 2

B-3. *How many tribes have federal recognition?*

As of January 2000, the official BIA count of politically recognized Indian tribes was 558. According to the Bureau of Indian Affairs (2000), this number includes 329 "tribal entities" in the lower 48 states, which are described as Indian tribes, bands, villages, communities, and pueblos. (For the official federal list, which names only 555 tribes at this writing because it is not regularly updated, check the BIA website at www.doi.gov/bia/tribes/telist.) The remaining 229 recognized entities are in Alaska.

The number for Alaska is slightly misleading, however. Though this number includes all of the politically recognized tribes, communities, bands, clans and villages, perhaps 300 more "Native Entities" in Alaska are "eligible to receive services from the United States Bureau of Indian Affairs" (Office of the Federal Register 1988). The difference is that, at present, these additional bands, villages, and communities, though eligible to receive services, are not politically recognized. The main reason for this exception is that Congress has passed certain laws which apply only to Alaska Natives and their special circumstances. These laws make Native groups eligible for certain BIA programs even though they may not be officially recognized as tribes or may not be able to prove their historical existence as tribes. Absence of historical documentation on a number of Alaska groups would make it very difficult, if not impossible, for them to comply with such a requirement.

For additional information on the number of federally recognized tribes, contact the BIA's Division of Tribal Government Services at (202) 208-2475.

B-4. *Are any tribes not officially recognized by the federal government?*

Yes. Even though the great majority of ethnologically identifiable tribes in the U.S. are officially recognized by the federal government, some are not. Perhaps as many as 150 or more tribal entities are not recognized (O'Brien 1989, Bureau of Indian Affairs 2000). Reasons have varied. A few Indian groups which never made war on the U.S. may never have had the opportunity to get recognition through the treaty process. Others were so physically or socially isolated that nobody outside the local area ever officially noticed them. And, there were those who chose to keep to themselves and avoid contact with the United States, sometimes for fear of hostilities. Then there are tribes which once had been federally recognized but whose recognized status was terminated by Congress. In at least 20 instances, tribes are recognized by the states in which they reside, in the absence of federal recognition, and some may be satisfied to retain this status.

Nonetheless, a significant number of the Indian groups currently not recognized by the federal government desire recognition. Roughly 100 self-identified Indian tribes, at this writing, have active petitions for acknowledgment as "tribes" before the Secretary of the Interior. Some will be successful in the long and tedious process and some will not, the latter because they do not meet the regulatory requirements. At this time, two of the most recent tribes to be successful with their requests for Congressional recognition or their petitions for acknowledgment by the Interior Department are the Match-E-Be-Nash-She-Wish Band of Potawatomi Indians of Michigan (August 1999) and the Snoqualmie Indian Tribe of Washington (October 1999).

Generally, unless an Indian group currently desiring federal recognition can gain independent acknowledgment of its tribal status from Congress, it must comply with the Interior Department's petition process. The steps to be taken are set forth in Title 25 of the Code of Federal Regulations (CFR), Part 83, "Procedures for Establishing That An American Indian Group Exists As An Indian Tribe." These procedures are summarized in Appendix 2.

Members of some of the recognized tribes have asked Congress to reform the process of conferring recognition. They claim the administrative procedures: (1) are too burdensome with respect to documentation requirements, (2) are too costly to comply with (up to $500,000 for genealogical and historical research), (3) take far too long (up to a decade or more), and (4) are controlled by recognized tribes who want to keep other legitimate Indian groups from sharing in governmental privileges. In 1991, Senator John McCain of Arizona introduced a bill to transfer administrative authority for tribal recognition from the BIA to an independent commission. The BIA, which did not support the senator's idea, has since instituted some mild reforms to the procedures. Representatives of a number of recognized tribes have said the BIA's rules should be maintained to keep the process "respectable" (Lick 1991). However, in 2000 the Congress was considering a new tribal recognition process that mirrors the earlier McCain proposal. The process was developed as part of Senate Bill G11, known as "The Indian Federal Recognition Administrative Procedures Act" (Stokes 2000a).

B-5. *What benefits and services are available to federally recognized tribes?*

The two main federal agencies which provide benefits and services to recognized Indian tribes are the Bureau of Indian Affairs (BIA) and the Indian Health Service (IHS). The BIA is a unit of the U.S. Department of the Interior and the IHS is a branch of the U.S. Department of Health and Human Services (USDHHS). Major benefits and services provided by these agencies include, but are not limited to, the following: medical and dental care, grants and programs for education, housing programs, aid in developing tribal governments and courts, resource management, and other services based upon tribal needs and interests. Some of the latter range from police protection and other law enforcement activities to economic development. With the federal government's policy of self-determination for tribes, a policy which has been evolving since the 1960s, numerous federal agencies have joined with tribal governments in providing services and benefits, just as they do with government entities like cities, counties, and states. To describe all the specific agencies and programs involved would require a separate book, such as that developed by Roger Walke (1991). The major players, including those within the USDI and USDHHS, are within the Departments of Agriculture, Education, Housing and Urban Development, Justice, Labor, and Transportation. The Environmental Protection Agency has also expanded its consultation and assistance roles in Indian country.

B-6. *What responsibility or accountability comes with federal recognition of an Indian tribe?*

A recognized tribe has a responsibility to provide some level of formalized government for its people—one that identifies and responds to the people's needs and goals as prescribed by the tribe's culture, laws, and capabilities, and by applicable federal law. This tribal government role can be much like that of other governments in the American system, be they local, state, or even the federal government. Frequently, larger tribes' activities involve programs relating to law enforcement, education, health care, employment, emergency services, transportation, housing, environmental protection, tribal courts, land and resource management, taxation, and social services. At the same time, these and less comprehensive tribal governments are often delimited by, and must remain consistent with, the many federal laws and regulations pertaining to Indian tribes. Among such laws are those affecting Indian government organization, disbursement of grants and other funds, the major crimes acts, civil rights legislation, and laws relating to Indian lands and other properties held in trust by the federal government.

B-7. *How is tribal membership determined?*

In the past, the federal government was directly involved in membership requirements of federally recognized tribes. Federal officials decided, on a person-by-person basis, who was to be considered a member. The determinations, theoretically, were made through "good faith" evaluations. Today it is generally the tribes which define who is and who is not a member—though Congress ultimately has authority to intervene. Tribal decisions on membership, however, are still influenced by past and present federal policies.

A formalized enrollment process exists for each tribe and is administered by the BIA or the tribe. The process varies among tribes but it is typically established by a tribal constitution, tribal law, or a separate tribal roll document approved by the federal government. Sophisticated methods of electronic record-keeping are often used.

As a caveat, the legal aspects of present-day tribal enrollment are entirely inconsistent with traditional concepts of tribal membership (Deloria 1974a). This concerns some Indian people so much that they refuse to participate in the official "federally sponsored" tribal enrollment process. A representative sentiment is: "This is not our way. We never determined who our people were through numbers and lists. These are rules of our colonizers . . . I will not comply with them" (Churchill 1991, p. 12, quoting Leonard Peltier, Ojibwa-Sioux).

Cohen (1982) reports that the courts have consistently declared one of an Indian tribe's most fundamental powers is that of determining its own membership. A tribe may grant, deny, revoke, and qualify membership. Specific requirements may be established by custom, written law, treaty with the U.S., or intertribal agreement.

No single set of criteria exists which establishes tribal membership. Some tribes accept relationship through the mother, and others through the father, while many accept a tribal tie through either parent. The requirements concerning blood quantum also vary. In some instances, only a trace of Indian blood is required. Determining factors are those of (1) being a direct descendant of a previously or currently enrolled tribal member of Indian heritage and (2) being able to document this relationship adequately. Other tribes require one-half or more Indian blood, and some may have a rule that a tribal member must have been born on the tribe's reservation. For some tribes, adoption is another method of obtaining membership. This latter method may or may not lead to eligibility for tribal or federal government services, depending on the laws of the tribes and the Indian heritage of the adopted individual.

An excellent example of tribal membership rules appears in the Navajo Tribal Code and is reproduced in Appendix 3.

B-8. *What are the basic consequences of tribal membership?*

Official tribal membership is highly significant in a cultural sense. In addition, it is almost always a prerequisite for an Indian who needs to make use of the education, training, health, and other assistance programs offered by tribal, state, or federal governments. Membership may bring the individual under tribal jurisdiction for certain criminal and civil matters. It can also make him or her subject to certain federal criminal jurisdiction not otherwise applicable, though enrollment is less critical in this area. In other words, federal criminal jurisdiction may apply if the individual concerned is not an enrolled tribal member but is found by the court to be "an Indian."

Tribal membership allows qualified individuals to take advantage of the preferences which the Bureau of Indian Affairs, the Indian Health Service, and the tribes have toward the hiring of Indians. Verifiable state or federal tribal membership also allows a person to legally produce and sell "Indian made" arts, crafts, and related products in accordance with the Indian Arts and Crafts Act of 1990 (discussed in a later section). Under this act, non-enrolled or non-authenticated artists and craftspersons—as well as museums and retailers—which knowingly misrepresent "Indian made items" are subject to substantial criminal penalties.

Finally, payments to tribal members under statute and treaty depend on enrollment, as do tribal voting rights and the capacity to be an elected tribal official. In addition, direct assignments of tribal lands to individuals for living areas and for certain economic purposes can be made only to enrolled members (Park 1975).

B-9. *How does a federally recognized tribe officially acknowledge the membership of its citizens?*

The one mandatory means of recognition is the official tribal membership rolls. These are maintained by the individual tribal governments and copies are provided to the BIA. Many tribes have tribal identification cards that look much like a driver's license. Also, when individuals need to document that they are enrolled tribal members for some official purpose, such as eligibility for Indian scholarships or "Indian preference" in employment, their tribe usually provides them with a document that is most often referred to as a "CDB" or "CDIB." These are acronyms for "Certificate of Degree of Indian Blood." The process that tribal members go through to obtain a CDIB is somewhat similar to the process of obtaining official transcripts from a high school or college, except that the tribal member usually has to be present at the time the CDIB is issued. The BIA also sometimes issues CDIBs, depending on the circumstances.

A straightforward example of one CDIB appears below, slightly modified from the original. CDIB forms vary from tribe to tribe.

[Navajo Nation Seal]

THE NAVAJO NATION

KELSEY A. BEGAYE   TAYLOR McKENZIE, M.D.
PRESIDENT   VICE PRESIDENT

UNACCEPTABLE IF ALTERED

CERTIFICATE OF NAVAJO INDIAN BLOOD

PART A (To be used if applicant is enrolled)

_____ Mosi _____
AGENCY

_____ 2/1/00 _____
DATE

I certify that __John Doe Smith__ is listed on the Navajo Indian Census Roll, dated _____, which is an official record of this office as being of __4/4__ degree Navajo Indian blood, with Roll Number __–0–__ , date of birth __2/1/00__ .

RECORDED: ___[Date]___

_____ [Signature] _____
VITAL STATISTICS MANAGER
VST/

THE INFORMATION CONTAINED ON THIS DOCUMENT HAS BEEN TAKEN FROM THE OFFICIAL TRIBAL ROLL OF THE NAVAJO NATION.

VITAL RECORDS & TRIBAL ENROLLMENT PROGRAM
THE NAVAJO NATION • ARIZONA

B-10. *What are the largest and smallest Indian tribes in the U.S.?*

Officially, the largest Indian tribe in the U.S. is the Navajo Nation. In fact, it is the largest single tribe in the Western Hemisphere. The Indian population of the Navajo *Reservation* (including members of other tribes) is estimated to be 160,000. A tribal official recently quoted this number to the author but said it may change significantly after the 2000 census data are available. The same official stated that a recent low estimate of the total Navajo population, on and off the reservation, was 200,000 but the number of people who qualify for enrollment may be as high as 215,000 or greater. The disparity is because not all Navajos are registered with the Nation, and many have moved to different regions of the country.

The Oklahoma Cherokee Nation, with about 140,000 officially enrolled members, is closest in population to the Navajo. It is note-worthy that the Oklahoma Cherokees no longer have a reservation. They were forced to relinquish it when Oklahoma became a state in 1907.

Determining the Indian population by tribe—as opposed to reser-vation—is difficult. During the 1990 census, for example, the Census Bureau counted tribal memberships for the first time. The Census Bureau has done this again in the 2000 census. But, as is always the case with the census, these are not official tribal enrollment numbers.

In the table which follows, population data for the largest tribes are at variance with those presented above because of the way the census counts were made. The Census Bureau counts as "Indian" everyone who says he or she is Indian, and then the individual is asked for tribal affiliation. There were 542 tribes counted in the 1990 census, but two of them—Cherokee and Navajo—made up 25 percent of the total number of Indians counted. Although the Cherokee tribe is listed as the largest, its official enrollment is less than the Navajo, and Cherokee tribal officials acknowledge the Navajo as the largest tribe. Tribes listed in the table are those which the Census Bureau identifies as the largest American Indian tribes. Tribal enrollment numbers are often notably smaller. Updated tribal numbers may be available from the Census Bureau's website at www.census.gov.

The second most populated *reservation* in the U.S., with respect to Indians, is Pine Ridge, of the Oglala Lakota (Sioux) Nation. In 1990,

LARGEST AMERICAN INDIAN TRIBES
(as identified in the 1990 Census, through self-reporting)

Cherokee	308,132	Tlingit	13,925	Ottawa	7,522
Navajo	219,198	Seminole	13,797	Ute	7,273
Chippewa	103,826	Athapaskans	13,738	Colville	7,140
Sioux	103,255	Cheyenne	11,456	Yuman	7,128
Choctaw	82,299	Comanche	11,322	Winnebago	6,920
Pueblo	52,939	Paiute	11,142	Arapaho	6,350
Apache	50,051	Salish	10,246	Shawnee	6,179
Iroquois	49,038	Yaqui	9,931	Assiniboine	5,274
Lumbee	48,444	Osage	9,527	Pomo	4,766
Creek	43,550	Kiowa	9,421	Sac and Fox	4,517
Blackfoot	32,234	Delaware	9,321	Miami	4,477
Canadian/		Shoshone	9,215	Yurok	4,296
Latin American	22,379	Crow	8,588	Omaha	4,143
Chickasaw	20,631	Cree	8,290	Nez Perce	4,113
Potawatomi	16,763	Yakima	7,850	Eastern tribes	3,928
Tohono O'odham	16,041	Houma	7,810		
Pima	14,431	Menominee	7,543		

some 11,182 Indian residents comprised 91.7 percent of the reservation's total population. This percentage may have changed slightly since the 1990 census.

Determining the smallest tribe is difficult. It is likely to be one of several California *rancheria* groups which have half-a-dozen or fewer members. For example, Buena Vista Rancheria near Sacramento, had only one tribal resident listed with the BIA in recent years. Other tiny tribal acreages in California and elsewhere have no residents.

B-11. *What is a "terminated" tribe?*

"Termination" is used to describe a specific policy toward Indian affairs, the popularity for which peaked in Congress in 1953 and resulted in the infamous House Concurrent Resolution 108. Simply stated, the policy goal of HCR 108 was to end the federally recognized status of Indian tribes and their trust relationship with the United States "as rapidly as possible." Many of the policy's naive but sometimes well-intentioned supporters were convinced they were finally going to solve "the Indian problem" through yet another form of forced assimilation—making the Indian people become just like "other citizens."

Approximately 100 Indian tribes, bands, and rancherias were thus "terminated," i.e., their official recognition as tribes ended; their special relationship with the federal government ended; they were fully subjected to state laws; and their lands were converted to private ownership, being sold in most instances. Stated another way, between 1953 and 1968 the U.S. terminated the legal existence of just over 100 tribes. After termination, these former tribes' members were no longer legally considered to be "Indians" under most, but not all, U.S. laws.

With no formalized tribal organization, tribal lands, federal health care services, BIA education programs, or other benefits (except for frequently inadequate investments or short-lived monetary settlements), these people were set adrift. Generally, the results were disastrous.

Government enthusiasm for termination began to wane in the late 1960s. Many of the terminated tribes then began scratching and clawing their way back up through the bureaucracy to "recognized" status. The Ponca Tribe of Nebraska is among the terminated tribes to regain federal recognition. This occurred on October 31, 1990—only 37 years after the termination resolution was passed by Congress!

B-12. *What is the President's official policy toward American Indian tribes?*

First, some background. Presidents historically played a much more direct and active role in Indian affairs than is the case today. Nonetheless, in modern times the president does set the tone of the administration. If the president is perceived as being favorable toward Indian causes, as was President Lyndon B. Johnson, then the executive branch tends to adopt this positive attitude. However, if the president is uninterested (as were Eisenhower and Carter), or even hostile (as was Reagan), the executive branch will also tend to reflect an indifferent attitude (Deloria and Lytle 1984).

On April 29, 1994, President Clinton issued his administration's first major official policy on American Indians in a memorandum to heads of executive departments and agencies. It is reproduced in full below. This policy memorandum was issued immediately after the President made a historic speech at the White House to 300 elected representatives from tribes throughout the U.S. That speech, made at a truly unique gathering (which also included the cabinet), warrants review for its historical value if nothing else. (See the BIA's *Indian News*; vol. 18, no. 4 [May 13, 1994].)

President Clinton's policy statements are the latest in a series of relatively positive White House policies that began with Lyndon Johnson (1968) in his historic special address to Congress on "The Forgotten American." The views (as taken from public documents and statements issued during their respective presidencies) of six other recent U.S. presidents, beginning with Lyndon Johnson, follow here (from Thompson 1996, p. 197–200). There is hope that Indian policy under future presidents will be even more enlightened than that of their predecessors.

GOVERNMENT-TO-GOVERNMENT RELATIONS WITH NATIVE AMERICAN TRIBAL GOVERNMENTS

Memorandum for the Heads of Executive Departments and Agencies

The United States Government has a unique legal relationship with Native American tribal governments as set forth in the Constitution of the United States, treaties, statutes, and court decisions. As executive departments and agencies undertake activities affecting Native American tribal rights or trust resources, such activities should be implemented in a knowledgeable, sensitive manner respectful of tribal sovereignty. Today, as part of an historic meeting, I am outlining principles that executive departments and agencies, including every component bureau and office, are to follow in their interactions with Native American tribal governments. The purpose of these principles is to clarify our responsibility to ensure that the Federal Government operates within a government-to-government relationship with federally recognized Native American tribes. I am strongly committed to building a more effective day-to-day working relationship reflecting respect for the rights of self-government due the sovereign tribal governments.

In order to ensure that the rights of sovereign tribal governments are fully respected, executive branch activities shall be guided by the following:

(a) The head of each executive department and agency shall be responsible for ensuring that the department or agency operates within a government-to-government relationship with federally recognized tribal governments.

(b) Each executive department and agency shall consult, to the greatest extent practicable and to the extent permitted by law, with tribal governments prior to taking actions that affect federally recognized tribal governments. All such consultations are to be open and candid so that all interested parties may evaluate for themselves the potential impact of relevant proposals.

(c) Each executive department and agency shall assess the impact of Federal Government plans, projects, programs, and activities on tribal trust resources and assure that tribal government rights and concerns are considered during the development of such plans, projects, programs, and activities.

(d) Each executive department and agency shall take appropriate steps to remove any procedural impediments to working directly and effectively with tribal governments on activities that affect the trust property and/or governmental rights of the tribes.

(e) Each executive department and agency shall work cooperatively with the other Federal departments and agencies to enlist their interest and support in cooperative efforts, where appropriate, to accomplish the goals of this memorandum.

(f) Each executive department and agency shall apply the requirements of Executive Orders Nos. 12875 ("Enhancing the Intergovernmental Partnership") and 12866 ("Regulatory Planning and

Review") to design solutions and tailor Federal programs, in appropriate circumstances, to address specific or unique needs of tribal communities.

The head of each executive department and agency shall ensure that the department or agency's bureaus and components are fully aware of this memorandum, through publication or other means, and that they are in compliance with its requirements.

This memorandum is intended only to improve the internal management of the executive branch and is not intended to, and does not, create any right to administrative or judicial review, or any other right or benefit or trust responsibility, substantive or procedural, enforceable by a party against the United States, its agencies or instrumentalities, its officers or employees, or any other person.

The Director of the Office of Management and Budget is authorized and directed to publish this memorandum in the <u>Federal Register</u>.

(Signed) WILLIAM J. CLINTON, April 29, 1994

The greatest hope for Indian progress lies in the emergence of Indian leadership and initiative in solving Indian problems. Indians must have a voice in making the plans and decisions in programs which are important to their daily life. . . . (W)e must pledge to respect fully the dignity and uniqueness of the Indian citizen. That means part-nership—not paternalism. We must affirm the right of the first Americans to remain Indians while exercising their rights as Ameri-cans. We must affirm their freedom to choice and self-determination.

Lyndon B. Johnson (presidency: 1963–1969),
From his 1968–1969 Public Papers, I:335

The first Americans—the Indians—are the most deprived and most isolated minority group in our nation. On virtually every scale of measurement—employment, income, education, health—the condi-tion of the Indian people ranks at the bottom. This condition is the heritage of centuries of injustice. From the time of their first contact with European settlers, the American Indians have been oppressed and brutalized, deprived of their ancestral lands and denied the opportunity to control their own destiny. Even the Federal programs which are intended to meet their needs have frequently proven to be ineffective and demeaning. . . . This then must be the goal of any new national policy toward the Indian people: to strengthen the Indian's sense of autonomy without threatening his sense of community. We must assure the Indian that he can assume control of his own life without being separated involuntarily from the tribal group. And we must make it clear that Indians can become independent of Federal control without being cut off from Federal concern and Federal support. . . . The Indians of America need Federal assistance—this much has long been clear. What has not always been clear, however, is that the Federal government needs Indian energies and Indian leadership if its assistance is to be effective in improving the conditions of Indian life.

Richard M. Nixon (presidency: 1969–1974),
Special message on Indian Affairs, July 8, 1970

No domestic matter has given me greater pride than my administration's record of turning about the discrimination and neglect that all Indians faced for so many years. In January of 1975, I signed the Indian Self-Determination Act, a magna carta for Indian people. Today, we recognize Indian tribal governments, including those in Oklahoma, as vital government organizations, in their own right. . . . In a few minutes, I will sign a Presidential proclamation declaring October 10 to 16 as Native American Awareness Week. The administration's support for Indian programs is not just rhetoric. We back up our words with action. . . . There are one million American Indian citizens, and some may say this is a very small minority. I count American Indian people, however, not in numbers but in the honored place that they hold in our multicultured society and in the future of our Nation. The 215 million of us are keenly concerned with the one million. The welfare and the progress of Native Americans is high on the agenda of the American conscience.

Gerald R. Ford (presidency: 1974–1977), Remarks made in
Lawton, Oklahoma, upon signing a proclamation for the
observance of Native American Awareness Week, October 8, 1976

The Federal Government has a special responsibility to Native Americans, and I intend to continue to exercise this responsibility fairly and sensitively. My Administration will continue to seek negotiated settlements to difficult conflicts over land, water, and other resources and will ensure that the trust relationship and self-determination principles continue to guide Indian policy. There are difficult conflicts which occasionally divide Indian and non-Indian citizens of this country. We will seek to exercise leadership to resolve these problems equitably and compassionately.

Jimmy Carter (presidency: 1977–1981),
State of the Union Address, January 23, 1979

Let me tell you just a little something about the American Indian in our land. We have provided millions of acres of land for what are called preservations, or reservations, I should say. They, from the beginning, announced that they wanted to maintain their way of life, as they had always lived there in the desert and the plains and so forth. And we set up these reservations so they could, and have a Bureau of Indian Affairs to help take care of them. At the same time, we provide education for them—schools on the reservations. And they're free also to leave the reservations and be American citizens among the rest of us, and many do. Some still prefer, however, that early way of life. And we've done everything we can to meet their demands as to how they want to live. Maybe we made a mistake. Maybe we should not have humored them in that wanting to stay in that kind of primitive lifestyle. Maybe we should have said, "No, come join us; be citizens along with the rest of us." As I say, many have; many have been very successful. . . . And you'd be surprised; some of them became very wealthy because some of those reservations were overlaying great pools of oil, and you can get very rich pumping oil. And so, I don't know what their complaint might be.

Ronald Reagan (presidency: 1981–1989),
Statement made in a question-and-answer session with students
and faculty at Moscow State University, May 31, 1988

I take pride in acknowledging and reaffirming the existence and durability of our unique government-to-government relationship. . . . the concept of forced termination and excessive dependency on the

> *Federal Government must now be relegated, once and for all, to the history books. Today we move forward toward a permanent relationship of understanding and trust, a relationship in which the tribes of the nation sit in positions of dependent sovereignty along with the other governments that compose the family that is America.*
>
> George Bush (presidency: 1989–1993),
> Statement for National Flag Day, June 14, 1991

In 1998 President Clinton put more force behind his general views by issuing two important executive orders on the topics of (1) requiring federal agencies to consult with tribes on administrative actions that may affect them (E.O. 13084, May 14) and (2) significantly improving Indian education (E.O. 13096, August 6). These powerful directives will remain "official" federal executive branch policy until modified or revoked by a later president. However, even if they remain unchanged, their future strength will depend on support by successive presidents.

As a presidential candidate in the 2000 election, George W. Bush, stated: "My view is that state law reigns supreme when it comes to Indians, whether it be gambling or any other issue" (from a campaign speech in New York, October 1999).

B-13. *Who are the Five Civilized Tribes and how did they get their name?*

The Oklahoma Indian nations referred to as the Five Civilized Tribes are the Creek, Choctaw, Chickasaw, Cherokee, and Seminole. Their ancestral lands covered a broad area of the southeastern U.S., east of the Mississippi River. Of the five, the Seminole tribe did not come into existence until the latter part of the 1700s. At that time, White pressure forced a fusion of smaller groups of resisting Creeks, Apalachicolas, Alabamas, and others into a tribal alliance which was identified separately by the federal government (Spicer 1969; Worton 1974).

During the late-1700s and early-1800s, in a political and social attempt to cope with overwhelming White encroachment, all five tribes adopted many of the customs and institutions of the settlers in their original homelands. These new lifeways included Christianity, individual land holdings, routine farming and stock raising, formal schooling, town living, Euro-American housing, road building, written constitutions, formal legal codes, and even Black slavery. Therefore, they were called "civilized" by their White neighbors and the national government.

This effort to stave off what proved to be the inevitable worked only so long. All the tribes were eventually forced to give up their lands during the 1820s to 1840s and move to reservations in the Indian territory west of the Mississippi. However, some of their tribesmen managed to stay behind in small and often isolated communities.

B-14. *Who are the Six Nations?*

The Six Nations constitute the Iroquois League, or Confederacy, of the Senecas, Mohawks, Onondagas, Cayugas, Oneidas, and Tuscaroras. They refer to themselves as the Haudenosaunee, or "People of the Longhouse." Their primary homelands are in central and western New York state. Before 1722, the Iroquois League consisted of the Five Nations, a name which some people have confused with the Five Civilized Tribes. In that year, the Tuscaroras joined the League after migrating north from the Carolinas where colonists and colonial militia had brought military actions against them (Spicer 1969; Jennings 1984).

Farb (1968) provided an overview of Iroquois constitutional government which suggested a significant resemblance to the United Nations. In the mid-1700s, the sophisticated political organization and powerful confederacy of the Iroquois strongly impressed several future revolutionaries like Benjamin Franklin and others. They went on to formulate the United States' first national government under the Articles of Confederation and borrowed at least some of their ideas from experiences with the Iroquois (Grinde 1977; Larabee 1961). One of the great traits of the Iroquois has been their tenacity in clinging to important aspects of their culture and self-government in the face of fierce and continual opposition and repression over the centuries. The same can be said for most of the other surviving tribes.

SECTION C: TREATIES AND AGREEMENTS

> *The words "treaty" and "nation" are words of our own language, selected in our diplomatic and legislative proceedings, by ourselves, having each a definite and well understood meaning. We have applied them to the other nations of the earth. They are applied to all in the same sense.*
>
> Chief Justice John Marshall, of the U.S. Supreme Court,
> in *Worcester v. Georgia* (1832, p. 60)

C-1. *What is a treaty?*

The word "treaty" has more than one meaning. Under the principles of international law, the term broadly refers to any agreement, compact, alliance, convention, act, or contract between two or more independent nations with a view to the public welfare. This would include agreed-to terms of peace, alliance, boundary establishment, trade, or other issues of mutual interest. Such a treaty would normally be "formally signed by commissioners properly authorized and solemnly ratified by the . . . sovereigns or the supreme power of each state" (Black's Law Dictionary 1990). Specific means of ratification vary widely among nations and between agreements. Also, there is no set form for treaties. Most, however, including Indian-U.S. treaties, usually contain five elements: (1) a preamble, (2) terms and conditions, (3) provisos (special conditions, usually referring to some time in the future), (4) consideration (the exchange of something of value), and (5) signatures, seals, and marks (Kickingbird, et al. 1980).

Under the United States Constitution, technical application of the term "treaty" is more restrictive than in international law. It refers to those international agreements concluded by the President with the advice and consent of the Senate, provided it is ratified by "two thirds of the Senators present" (Article II, Sec. 2, Cl. 2, U.S. Constitution). These are commonly referred to as "Article II treaties," which are binding on the states and others as "the supreme law of the land" (Article VI, Cl. 2).

C-2. *How did the U.S. begin its treaty-making policy with Indian tribes?*

> *A treaty is . . . to be read . . . in the light of that larger reason which constitutes the spirit of the law of nations.*
>
> U.S. Department of the Interior 1894, p. 665

The U.S. adopted the practice of negotiating formal treaties with Indian tribes directly from customs that were established by Great Britain and its colonial governments. At least 175 treaties had been concluded by these governments between 1607 and 1776. When the first colonists arrived in Virginia and Massachusetts, they were "shaking on the beach," as one Indian aptly described the situation to this author. They were in desperate need of four things in order to survive even their initial few months on the continent—land, food, shelter, and protection from attack. To secure these necessities the colonists began to negotiate formal agreements, both oral and written, with the powerful Indian tribes in their vicinities. This early treaty-making—which was acknowledged, encouraged, and later expanded by the British government—technically served to recognize tribal entities as members of the international community with sovereign powers to "treat" with, or contract with, European governments and their agents.

For the next 200 years, through the period of the American Revolution and on into the War of 1812, major Indian tribes, or alliances of tribes, were considered to hold the balance of power in their part of the world. These tribes, such as the great Iroquois confederacy in the north and the Creek federation in the south, had survived disease, conquest, and assimilation. The British, French, and, later, the U.S. then competed to secure treaties with the strategic tribes.

The first written treaty between the United States and an Indian tribe was the treaty with the Delaware Nation, dated September 17, 1778. A comparatively short document, it is reproduced in Appendix 4. This interesting agreement, which pre-dates the Constitution, even contains a provision that would allow other tribes to join the Delawares "and to form a state whereof the Delaware nation shall be the head, and have a representation in Congress"—but only with the approval of Congress.

There were a number of unwritten treaties that the U.S. entered into with tribes before the first written treaty with the Delaware Nation (Deloria and DeMallie 1999; Pruch 1994). These were negotiated and concluded in a no less solemn manner than the later written treaties. In fact, Deloria and DeMallie (1999, p. 8) make note of the unwritten treaties, which were negotiated according to traditional Indian treaty making customs. They say that when the Indian procedures for making peace (and the moral pledges that Indian diplomacy involved) are compared with the legalese of a European document, the European treaty pales and appears for what it truly is—a business transaction, rather than a diplomatic act.

Before 1815, the Delawares and other tribes negotiated their U.S. treaties from a position of some power. This was because they still exercised a good deal of control over the frontier and had the choice of allying with the British. When the War of 1812 ended and the British withdrew from U.S. territory, the tribes' bargaining power was reduced and U.S. policy began to reflect it. The Spanish withdrawal from Florida in 1819 further weakened the tribes' position and the U.S. took on the complete sense of superiority that continues today.

The format for Indian-U.S. treaties and the procedures for putting them into effect were the same as for U.S. treaties with foreign nations. After the U.S. Constitution was ratified in 1789, all treaties ratified with Indian tribes were "Article II treaties." (See C-1, "What Is A Treaty?") They were legally considered to have the same status, force, and dignity as the highest level of agreements with sovereign nations. As a result, the originals of Indian treaties were maintained by the Department of State after the Senate approved them. Each treaty file contained an original signed copy of the treaty (including the sometimes intriguing totem marks of the Indian signers), the presidential proclamation of it, the Senate resolution ratifying the treaty, and a printed copy of the treaty (Hill 1981). The original Indian treaties are now housed in the National Archives in Washington, D.C.

C-3. *Does the U.S. still make treaties with Indian tribes?*

No. The last official treaty with an Indian tribe, which the U.S. Senate ratified, was the Nez Perce treaty of August 13, 1868. In an obscure rider to an Indian appropriations bill, Congress abolished constitutional treaty-making with Indian tribes in 1871 (16 Stat. 566). The abrupt language of the statute reads:

> Hereafter, no Indian nation or tribe within the territory of the United States shall be acknowledged or recognized as an independent nation, tribe, or power with whom the United States may contract by treaty: **Provided, further,** That nothing herein contained shall be construed to invalidate or impair the obligation of any treaty heretofore lawfully made and ratified with any such Indian nation or tribe.

Several political forces were behind this action. In the early 1860s, for example, there were Union reactions to alliances made with the Confederacy by some of the southern Indian tribes. Colonel Ely S. Parker, Commissioner of Indian Affairs in 1869, believed that treaty-making by the Indians was a "farce" because he perceived a lack of sovereignty on their part. (Ironically, Parker was a Seneca Indian. He had served as General Grant's aide during the Civil War.) A third force included influential representatives of Protestant churches who felt treaty-making only served to perpetuate the "savage life" of the tribes. These people believed they were "called" to eliminate the Indians' culture. A fourth, and perhaps most important, force behind terminating the formal treaty process with Indian tribes was the U.S. House of Representatives. That body was tired of having no role in treaty-making; yet it had to appropriate funds to meet treaty obligations. The House wanted—and got—an equal voice in Indian affairs. As stated in the quotation above, the 1871 law did not in any way repeal or modify treaties that had been ratified prior to that date. If the 1871 legislation were to be fully repealed by Congress, formal treaties between the U.S. and Indian tribes would not seem to be barred by law. Some government officials have said that Indians' U.S. citizenship (since 1924) would legally preclude entering into new treaties (Deloria 1974a), but this is highly debatable.

The Treaty of Fort Laramie, negotiated in 1868 with the Sioux and Arapaho, was one of the last five Indian-U.S. treaties. The Indians (left to right) are Packs-His-Drum, Old-Man-Afraid-Of-His-Horses, and Red Bear.

C-4. *How have Indian tribes viewed the treaties they entered into with the U.S.?*

Historically, tribes viewed treaties as ways of preserving themselves as a people (Deloria and Lytle 1984). They sought two specific things from the federal government. One was a recognition of their rights to their specific homelands. The other was a commitment from the government to protect and defend their rights within those homelands from encroachment by non-Indians.

With the end of official treaty-making, most tribes came to view their treaties as sacred pledges on the part of the U.S. Later generations regarded the treaties as having the symbolic and moral significance associated with the Declaration of Independence and the Constitution. The federal government's unremitting antiseptic attitude toward the treaties (i.e., considering them to be routine legal documents that are subject to easy change and abrogation) is a continuing point of great concern among the tribes which have treaties with the U.S. (Kvasnicka 1988).

C-5. *Are Indian-U.S. treaties real treaties?*

Yes, although history shows that the terms of many treaties were not taken seriously. Many were violated by non-Indian civilians and government representatives even before the ink of the signatures was dry. Some were violated by the tribes. Furthermore, it is apparent that some treaties were unilaterally changed by members of the executive branch and the Senate, after the Indians had agreed to them, but before ratification. Nonetheless, it is abundantly clear—from numerous Supreme Court cases, historical actions of the President, and numerous acts of Congress—that Indian-U.S. treaties are solemn treaties according to international law. They are also unquestionably treaties according to the more restrictive standards of the United States Constitution. (See the quote from Chief Justice Marshall on page 79.)

A well-known international law publication, containing more than 230 volumes (Parry 1969), indexes all the treaties available from throughout the world that have been negotiated in the past several centuries. Listed, in chronological order with the rest of the world's treaties, are the treaties the United States has made with the Indian tribes. British and French publications which reprint international state papers also contain copies of Indian-U.S. treaties (Meyer 1984). (See Kappler 1904 for the texts of Indian-U.S. treaties.)

Millions of non-Indian Americans who own lands once ceded to the U.S. by Indian tribes, through treaties and "agreements" (as discussed in subsequent questions), ultimately hold valid title to their lands based on the validity of the treaties and agreements.

C-6. *What rights to land and related resources did treaties give to Indian tribes that the tribes did not already have?*

None. It was the Indian tribes which granted the U.S. rights to lands—generally in exchange for peace, protection, less desirable lands, annuities, rations, manufactured goods, and services. This is sometimes a confusing concept for non-Indians to understand at first, but it is straightforward.

Indian tribes with which the U.S. made treaties were considered to have specific prior rights of ownership in their lands, which they had held long before the U.S. became a nation. Non-Indians often call these Native land rights "Indian title," "rights of occupancy," or "aboriginal rights." The U.S. government wanted to acquire most, if not all, of the tribes' lands for various reasons, e.g., to re-sell or grant to settlers, commercial interests, or others some time in the future. Through 1871, the treaty process was the main legal way to do this.

When a treaty involved some sort of land transfer (many, but not all, did), it typically stated in one section that the tribe or tribes concerned would "cede, relinquish, and convey to the United States all their right, title, and interest" in a large tract of specified land, often exceeding millions of acres. (Quote is from Yakima Nation Treaty 1855). Often, a subsequent section of the treaty would "reserve" a smaller area of the Indians' lands which they would keep for the use and occupancy of the tribe(s). Thus a "reservation" was created out of what was left. The Indian tribes, as recognized governments, retained or "reserved" the land and sovereign rights they had not granted to the U.S.

A brief quote from the milestone Supreme Court case of *United States v. Winans* (1905) summarizes the overall point: "[T]he treaty was not a grant of rights to the Indians, but a grant of rights from them." The frequently heard term "treaty rights" thus refers to rights explicitly and implicitly retained by the tribe and not to rights granted by the U.S. government. It also refers to those obligations which the government owed the tribe in exchange for its lands as well as other consideration received from the federal government.

> *Treaty rights . . . have so many twists and turns as to make any statement on treaties appear to be an over-simplification.*
>
> Deloria 1974b, p. 59

C-7. *Do all the federally recognized tribes have treaties with the U.S.?*

No. Only a minority of the more than 550 federally recognized tribes have treaties with the U.S. While most tribes have no treaties, some have one or two, and others have half a dozen or more. The various bands of the Potawatomis, in over 90 years of treaty making with the U.S., entered into approximately 40 treaties. A few they signed alone, but most they signed with several other tribes.

C-8. *How many official treaties did the U.S. make with Indian tribes?*

From the first written Indian-U.S. treaty in 1778 to the end of official treaty-making in 1871, the U.S. Senate ratified about 370 Indian treaties (some sources report a few more or a few less). At least another 45 were negotiated with tribes during the same period but were never ratified by the Senate (Bureau of Indian Affairs 1903; Institute for the Development of Indian Law 1973). Even so, some of the unratified treaties took legal effect, as determined by the U.S. Court of Claims (Kvasnicka 1988).

For interested readers, there are several superb references on Indian-U.S. treaties, including Deloria and DeMallie (1999); Kappler (1904); Kickingbird et al. (1980); and Prucha (1994).

C-9. *What is the present status of the Indian-U.S. treaties?*

Some were superceded by more recent treaties, some have been entirely abrogated (nullified) by acts of Congress, some have been partially abrogated, and all have been affected in one way or another by federal legislation and court decisions.

Whether abrogated or not, all of the treaties provide the foundation for the expanding body of United States law known as Federal

Indian Law. As Kickingbird et al. (1980, p. 45) have stated: "Treaties form the backdrop of the past, confirm rights of the present, and provide the basic definitions for the evolving future."

A recent confirmation of this statement was the multi-faceted role played by the 1854 "Treaty of Medicine Creek" in the "Puyallup Tribe of Indians Settlement Act" passed by the U.S. Congress in 1989. This legislation affirmed a negotiated settlement of conflicting Indian and non-Indian land claims. It also recognized several other important claims of the Puyallup Tribe of Washington state.

In 1999 the world media made us all aware of the continued validity of many Indian-U.S. treaties when the Makah Tribe of Washington state exercised some of the rights it reserved to itself in its 1855 treaty with the U.S. The Makah are the only tribe in the U.S. to have treaty rights to whaling. Article 4 of their treaty states "The right of taking fish and of whaling . . . is further secured to said Indians."

Treaties like that of Medicine Creek and the Makah treaty will obviously continue to influence Indian law. Those people who question their validity solely because of the treaties' age are also, indirectly, questioning the validity of our 200-year-old Constitution, which not only pre-dates them but authorizes their negotiation and ratification. [For additional information, see Kickingbird (1995).]

C-10. *After 1778, were there other notable American Indian treaties besides those made with the U.S. government?*

Yes. American Indians were involved in hundreds of other treaties with states, between tribes, with Great Britain, with Spain, with Mexico, with the Republic of Texas, and with the Confederate States of America (see the tremendously useful two-volume set of source material by Deloria and DeMallie, 1999). Texas, alone, was signatory to treaties with Cherokees, Tonkawas, Lipan Apaches, Comanches, Kitsais, Tawakonis, Wacos, Wichitas, Shawnees, Delawares, Hainais, Anadarkos, Caddos, Chickasaws, and Biloxis. But, the most famous non-U.S. treaties were those of the Civil War era.

In 1861, attorney Albert Pike was named Commissioner of the Confederate States to the Indian Nations west of Arkansas. Pike competently negotiated more than a half-dozen treaties of "Friendship and Alliance" with the Five Civilized Tribes and with other so-called eastern and western tribes in the old Indian Territory, e.g., Osage, Shawnee, Seneca, Quapaw, Comanche, Wichita, Caddo, and Delaware (Gibson 1977).

The Confederate treaties with tribes in the Indian Territory were all similar. Their effect was to establish, through the Confederacy, the same rights and obligations that had been secured under U.S. treaties. Tribes were required to furnish troops to help defend Indian Territory against invasion by Union forces or by Indian tribes which were Union sympathizers. In turn, the Confederacy promised to protect the tribes from invasion or internal disorder. Another provision of the treaties allowed for tribal delegates to be accepted into the Confederate Congress. Of course, with the dissolution of the Confederacy at the end of the Civil War, all of the treaties became moot (Harlow 1935).

> *There shall be perpetual peace and friendship, and an alliance offensive and defensive, between the Confederate States of America and all their States and people, and the Cherokee Nation and all the people thereof.*
>
> Article I of the Confederate
> "Treaty with the Cherokees"
> October 7, 1861

C-11. *Can and do Indian tribes make treaties with each other?*

Yes. The practice of making inter-tribal alliances and other agreements has been going on as long as there have been tribes. This governmental function is an inherent right, included in that part of the tribes' sovereignty which they have not surrendered to the United States, and of which they have not otherwise been deprived.

Among the most famous inter-tribal treaties of historic times was the Iroquois alliance, negotiated and ratified some 400 years ago. For the tribes involved, the Iroquois alliance served much the same function as the U.S. Constitution (Deloria and Lytle 1984).

Treaty-making between tribes had been all but dormant in this century. Since the termination days of several decades ago, however, new needs and renewed tribal confidence and vigor may bring about a resurrection of this time-honored and functional tool of government-to-government relations.

For example, on October 1, 1991, four Oklahoma Indian tribes announced an historic inter-tribal treaty to improve law enforcement services within each of their adjoining jurisdictional areas (Anquoe 1991b). The Sac and Fox, Iowa, Kickapoo, and Citizen Band Potawatomi agreed to cross-deputize their police officers and provide cooperative and coordinated police training and services. This treaty affects 1600 square miles of eastern Oklahoma, representing the four combined tribal territorial areas. As this book went to press, the Navajo Nation and the San Juan Paiute Tribe were negotiating a treaty regarding the transfer of some Navajo Nation land to the landless Paiutes for a new reservation.

C-12. *What is an Indian-U.S. "agreement" as opposed to a treaty?* After official treaty-making ended in 1871, the federal government continued negotiating with the various tribes in just the same manner as it had for treaties. The end products of these negotiations, which most often had the primary purpose of achieving further reductions in Indian lands, were officially referred to as "agreements." It was sometimes difficult, however, to tell how the agreements differed from many of the earlier treaties. These agreements were submitted to both the Senate *and* the House of Representatives for ratification, whereas "treaties" had been ratified only by the Senate, under Article II of the Constitution. Agreements were occasionally approved by Congress in separate laws for the single purpose of ratification. The majority, however, were attached as riders to appropriations bills.

C-13. *Are formal Indian-U.S. "agreements" still made?*

Yes and no. The agreement era, which began in 1871, ended just over 40 years later, in 1913. That year, Congress amended and "ratified" an agreement, the last of that particular kind, between the United States and the Wiminuche Band of Southern Ute Indians. There was no specific policy to put an end to these types of agreements. The U.S. halted the practice, apparently, because it had obtained all the land and other concessions it wanted for that period. Later agreements have been referred to and treated as regular legislation.

A new, and somewhat different, agreement era seems to have begun as a result of (1) self-determination policies initiated in the late-1960s and (2) associated efforts by tribes to reclaim lost rights. The Alaska Native Claims Settlement Act of 1971 was, in effect, the largest "Indian" agreement ever ratified by Congress. Also, as recently as 1989, Congress enacted legislation to ratify a major agreement "between the Puyallup Tribe of Indians, Local Governments in Pierce County [Washington], the State of Washington, the United States of America, and certain private property owners." Though it was designated a "Settlement Act," one major stated purpose of the legislation was to "ratify" an agreement to which the Puyallup Tribe and the federal government, among others, were parties.

The traditional agreements of the late 19th and early 20th centuries primarily addressed such things as Indian land cessions to the U.S. and government annuities to the tribes. The newer "settlement agreements," which are likely to be negotiated and ratified into the foreseeable future, are apparently concerned with tribal land claims, water rights, resolution of conflicts involving Indians and non-Indians, and certain other issues related to tribal self-determination. (The more recent "Seneca Nation Land Claims Settlement," which was passed by Congress in 1990, involved another agreement in New York state. In this one, however, the U.S. served primarily as mediator for the Seneca Nation, the City of Salamanca, and the State of New York.)

The water rights settlement agreements that have been entered into by western tribes, the U.S., and other involved parties during the 1980s and 1990s, and which have been "ratified" by Congressional water rights settlement acts, involve what might be called a modern form of treaty making. These agreements will continue to be used well into the new millennium (as one example, see the Yavapai-Prescott Water Rights Settlement Act of 1994).

C-14. *How many of the traditional Indian-U.S. agreements were made and what is their legal status?*

Between 1871 and 1913, at least 98 traditional agreements were negotiated and 96 of them were ratified by Congress. Unless abrogated later, each agreement remains law in its original form or as otherwise modified or amended by subsequent legislation.

In the 1975 U.S. Supreme Court case of *Antoine v. Washington,* the subject of the legal status of traditional Indian-U.S. agreements was addressed. The court found as follows: "Once ratified by Act of Congress the provisions of the agreements become law, and like treaties, the supreme law of the land." Further, some of the 1871–1913 agreements are indexed in the international treaty publications referred to in the answer to question C-5 (Hill 1981; Meyer 1984).

The Supreme Court added another twist to the question of the legal status of older Indian-U.S. agreements in the case of *Waldron v. United States* (1905). Interpreting the status of the Great Sioux Agreement of 1889 (25 Stat. 888), the Court stated flatly that, while the agreement "appears in form as an independent legislative act of the government, it was and is a treaty or contract made by the United States and Sioux Nation of Indians."

C-15. *Is it true that all of the hundreds of treaties between the United States and the Indian nations say they will be in effect "so long as grass shall grow and water run?"*

No. In fact, none of the ratified Indian-U.S. treaties has this kind of phraseology (Prucha 1994). However, terms such as "in perpetuity," or "perpetual," or "from this day forward," or "forever" were employed for certain provisions within different treaties, such as provisions dealing with peace between the signatory parties. Also, the treaties of removal that were signed by the Five Civilized Tribes before the Civil War stated that their tribal lands in the Indian territory would "never" be included within the boundaries of a state. Despite this, in 1906 their reservation lands were abolished and made part of the state of Oklahoma.

It was actually the Civil War treaties between the Confederate States of America and the Five Civilized Tribes (except for the "Treaty with the Cherokee") and many of the other tribes of Indian territory, that employed the wording "so long as grass shall grow and water run" (Deloria and DeMallie 1999). The following is an example of precisely how the language was used in the treaties (from Article VIII of the "Treaty with the Choctaw and Chickasaw" (Deloria and DeMallie 1999, p. 605):

> The Confederate States of America do hereby solemnly guarantee to the Choctaw and Chickasaw nations to be held by them to their own use and behoof in fee simple forever, the lands included within the boundaries defined in article IV of this treaty; to be held by the people of both the said nations in common, as they have heretofore been held, *so long as grass shall grow and water run, . . .* [Emphasis added.]

SECTION D: MYTH, MISINFORMATION, AND STEREOTYPE

> *To kill an error is as good a service as, and sometimes even better than, the establishing* [of] *a new truth or fact.*
>
> Charles Darwin

D-1. *How did the United States government acquire America?*

This question is answered best with a quote by Felix S. Cohen (1947, p. 34–35), an early expert in federal Indian law.

> Every American schoolboy is taught to believe that the lands of the United States were acquired by purchase or treaty from Britain, Spain, France, Mexico, and Russia, and that for all the continental lands so purchased we paid about 50 million dollars out of the federal treasury. Most of us believe this story as unquestioningly as we believe in electricity or corporations. We have seen little maps in our geography books showing the vast area that Napolean sold us in 1803 for 15 million dollars and the various cessions that make up the story of our national expansion. As for the original Indian owners of the continent, the common impression is that we took the land from them by force and proceeded to lock them up in concentration camps called "reservations."
>
> Notwithstanding this prevailing mythology, the historic fact is that practically all of the real estate acquired by the United States since 1776 was purchased not from Napoleon or any other emperor or czar but from its original Indian owners. What we acquired from Napolean in the Louisiana Purchase was not real estate, for practically all of the ceded territory that was not privately owned by the Spanish and French settlers was still owned by the Indians, and the property rights of all the inhabitants were safeguarded by the terms of the treaty of cession. What we did acquire from Napolean was not the land, which was not his to sell, but simply the power to govern and tax. . . .

Cohen concluded his discussion on this point by emphasizing the distinction between a *transfer of governmental power* and a *sale of land.* As for the lands comprising the Louisiana Territory, he contrasted the 15 million dollars paid to Napoleon with the 20-times-this-amount eventually paid to Indian tribes. The former payment was for a cession (transfer) of political authority over the territory; the latter was to extinguish Indian title to the lands they ceded from within the area. Figure 2 illustrates how people generally believe the U.S. obtained the nation's land from Europeans. Figure 3, however, shows how the U.S. actually acquired title to most of the country through Indian land cessions. But even this does not present the broader story. About 180 separate tribal land areas were judicially recognized through Indian land claims, thus further subdividing most of the 67 areas shown in Figure 3. This was done because more

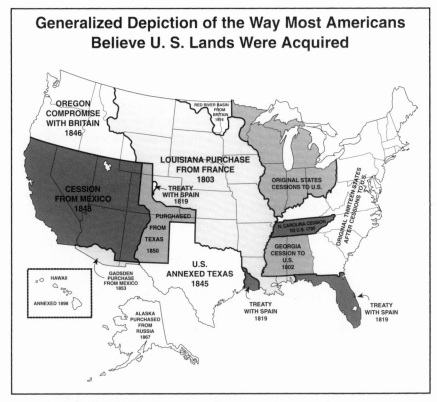

Figure 2. The United States obtained its lands in a number of ways. This map shows how the major blocks of land came under U.S. government control. It does not, however, show how most of the land was actually acquired through cessions from American Indians. (From Coggins and Wilkinson 1981.)

than just 67 tribal entities had claims against the government for taking their lands without compensation. (See Prucha 1990a.) For example, nine million acres in the western portion of unit 47 (on the map) were declared by the federal government to have been original homelands of the Yavapai people, not the Apaches.

D-2. *How did the term "Red Man" come into use?*

It did not originate from self-descriptions by American Indians. And, contrary to many beliefs, it did not begin with Columbus. He described the complexion of the Native people he encountered as "the color of the inhabitants of the Canaries [Canary Islands], neither black nor white . . ." (Wrone and Nelson 1973, p. 35).

The truth is that "red man" did not come into frequent use until the late-1700s. Further it was not until the early-1800s that "red" became a universally accepted color label for American Indians. Before this time, descriptions given of the color of Indians varied, and rightly so. In fact, Indians vary in color from a deep, rich brown to what would technically be considered a "white" complexion.

From the 1400s through the 1600s, colonists employed cultural (not color) descriptions to identify the indigenous people of America. The use of "Indians," "Natives," and "savages" was common. When color was referred to, it was most often "tawny," "olive," "copper," and "brown." Russet, yellow, and white were sometimes used, and occasionally black. The term "red" is conspicuously absent in the literature describing Indian complexions for the first 200 years or so of European presence on the continent.

Many prominent figures from Europe and colonial America of the 17th and 18th centuries commented on Indian color at one time or another. In 1643, for example, Roger Williams of Rhode Island, in common with a number of contemporaries, said the Indians in his area were white. William Penn, in the 1680s, inconsistently described Indians as black and as the color of "Italians." In the 1720s, the English naturalist, Richard Bradley, wrote of American Indians as "a sort of White Men. . . ." In the mid-1700s, Benjamin Franklin summed everything up

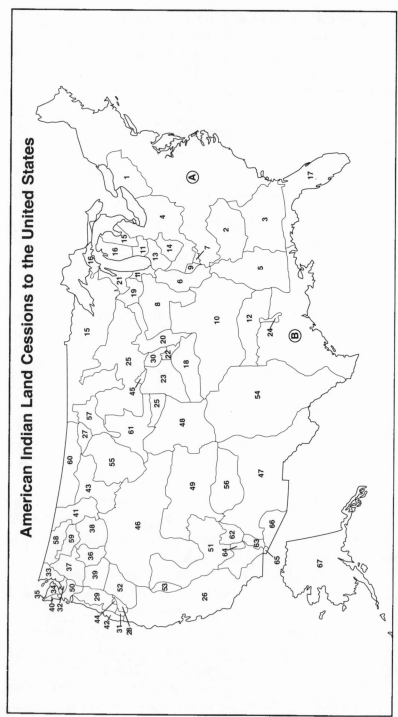

Figure 3. Title to the majority of lands acquired by the United States came through purchases from American Indian groups. Lands in the 67 areas shown on this map were ceded by the groups listed in the accompanying legend. (After Royce 1899.)

Legend for American Indian Land Cessions to the United States

Code numbers of map correspond with the tribes listed below, for land cessions in the United States after 1776.

1. Iroquois
2. Cherokee
3. Creek
4. Wyandot, Delaware, Chippewa, and allied tribes
5. Choctaw, Chickasaw
6. Kaskaskia
7. Delaware
8. Sauk, Fox
9. Piankashaw
10. Osage
11. Ottawa, Chippewa, Potawatomi
12. Quapaw
13. Potawatomi
14. Miami
15. Chippewa
16. Ottawa, Chippewa
17. Seminole
18. Kansas
19. Winnebago
20. Sauk, Fox, Sioux, Omaha, Iowa, Oto, Missouri
21. Menominee
22. Oto, Missouri

23. Pawnee
24. Caddo
25. Sioux
26. California Indians
27. Sioux, Cheyenne, Arapaho, Crow, Assiniboine, Gros Ventre, Mandan, Arikara
28. Rouge River
29. Umpqua, Kalapuya
30. Omaha
31. Chastacosta et al.
32. Nisqually, Puyallup et al.
33. Duwamish, Suquamish et al.
34. Challam
35. Makah
36. Walla Walla, Cayuse, Umatilla
37. Yakima
38. Nez Perce
39. Confederated Tribes of Middle Oregon
40. Quinault, Quileute
41. Flathead et al.
42. Coast Tribes of Oregon
43. Blackfoot, Flathead, Nez Perce

44. Molala
45. Ponca
46. Shoshoni
47. Apache
48. Arapaho and Cheyenne
49. Ute
50. Chehalis, Chinook et al.
51. Paiute
52. Klamath et al.
53. Washo
54. Comanche, Kiowa
55. Crow
56. Navajo
57. Arikara, Gros Ventre, Mandan
58. Methow, Okanagan et al.
59. Coeur d'Alene et al.
60. Gros Ventre, Blackfoot, River Crow
61. Sioux, Northern Cheyenne, Arapaho
62. Hualapai
63. Yuma
64. Mojave
65. Cocopa
66. Papago, Pima, Maricopa
67. Alaska Natives

NOTE: The area designated "A" on the map corresponds to lands already acquired by the British, through treaty, purchase, warfare, etc., prior to the American Revolution. The area designated "B" represents land which Spain and France had acquired earlier from Indians.

in his own way by saying "all" of the Indians were "tawny," which the dictionary describes as yellowish brown or tan, e.g., the color of a lion.

A clear turn toward "red" in descriptive terminology can be traced to Europe in the mid-1700s. European naturalists were rigorously working at classifying the world's known species of plants and animals. Charles Linnaeus, of Sweden, was perhaps the most notable of these naturalists. He used primary colors to label the four basic human groups he identified. Though he actually wrote little about his human classifications, what he did write on the subject gained wide acceptance. Linnaeus' four human groups were: *Europaeus albus* (white), *Americanus rubescens* (red), *Asiaticus fuscus* (yellow), and *Africanus niger* (black).

Beginning about 1750, the well-read people in Europe and America began to use the term "red man," or variations thereof, with more frequency. Usage of "red" began to proliferate by 1775, when average colonials, as well as some of the Indian people in contact with them, also picked up the term. This was perhaps due to overhearing it or from seeing Indians in what was referred to as red "war paint" during the many conflicts of the time. (Application of pigments to the skin for various reasons was common among American Indians. Historically, however, the term "war paint" has been too broadly applied to that use of pigments.)

At the time, three clearly identifiable "races" were found on the continent. One consisted of "white" colonists, and a second was "black" slaves. Describing Indians as "red" was a convenient outflow of pre-existing and very strong social, cultural, and racial distinctions. Thomas Jefferson, who wrote of the "white, red, and black" races may have been the first public spokesman to use the tri-color metaphor for the races of early America.

Vaughn (1982, p. 948), the main source for this information, summarizes his research on the "red" question as follows:

> The precise reason for the gradual adoption of red, instead of tawny or some other hue, can only be surmised. . . . Not until the second half of the eighteenth century did "red" emerge as a fairly common label. By 1765 some Indians may have adopted the primary color label for themselves. . . . By the 1760s the continuing association of red bodypaint and an almost perpetual enmity—later heightened by the War for Independence—made

"redskin" the most plausible epithet. Linnaeus' use of red gave additional impetus. Although the reasons for his choice remain obscure, most likely he sought a primary color to parallel the other races' black, white, and yellow. Red was the obvious candidate because Indians used red stains so widely and because it avoided the confusion that might have come from such colors as brown, olive, and tawny, which were sometimes applied to racial subgroups. . . . In any event [Thomas] Jefferson and some of his contemporaries used "red" as a racial category in the 1770s and 1780s, a trend that spread rapidly. . . . In the middle of the nineteenth century, James Fenimore Cooper's *The Redskins* (1846) and anthropologist Henry Rowe Schoolcraft's *The Red Race in America* (1847) symbolically marked Caucasian America's full recognition, in both fiction and science, of Indians as innately red and racially distinct.

D-3. *Was scalping first introduced by Europeans?*

No, but they helped spread the practice. This controversial issue was actively debated in the 1960s and 1970s, and it resurfaced in the 1990s (Associated Press 1991g; Jaimes 1992). In a research paper published in 1986, James Axtell and William C. Sturtevant, two highly respected scholars, also said the answer is no. Many of the tribes in North and South America engaged in the practice of taking scalps or heads, as trophies, long before the arrival of Europeans in the Western Hemisphere (Calloway 1997). This is not to say the practice of scalping victims or adversaries wasn't encouraged and promoted by Europeans. It was. Bounties were offered for Indian heads or scalps by Euro-Americans in various parts of North America from the 1600s to the 1800s (Churchill 1997). Frontiersmen and soldiers were also know to take heads or scalps without financial inducement. Even a few Indians were known to scalp other Indians for the bounty money offered by non-Indians (Wrone and Nelson 1973). It should be pointed out, however, that scalping was not practiced by all tribes.

In one widely cited book, Indian author Vine Deloria, Jr. (1969, p. 6) stated that scalping was "introduced prior to the French and

Indian War by the English." In support, he cited a scalp bounty offered in 1755 by Massachusetts. However, 220 years before this particular bounty was offered and 85 years before the English pilgrims landed, Jacques Cartier was shown "the skins of five men's heads, stretched on hoops, like parchment." In 1535, Cartier was making his second voyage up the St. Lawrence River when his Iroquois hosts in Quebec presented the five scalps taken from their enemies, the Micmacs. This and other convincing data regarding the widespread existence of scalping prior to European influence are cited by Axtell and Sturtevant (1986). Nonetheless, the myth that scalping was originally introduced to the continents by Europeans continues to be perpetuated in books and other media, for example, *Parade Magazine* (Winik 1999). (For a description of the traditional practices of trophy-taking and counting coup among the plains tribes, see Grinnell 1910).

D-4. *Is it true that Indians are generally more susceptible to the intoxicating effects of alcohol than are non-Indians?*

No. As far back as the 1950s this myth was being refuted by research (Warton 1974; May 1994). More recently, what people have stereotypically attributed to racial susceptibility has been tied directly to a particular consumption pattern that some Indians, like some non-Indians, tend to follow. Indian as well as non-Indian experts in the field of substance abuse refer to the pattern as binge drinking.

The binge pattern among Indians began to develop long ago in various groups whose members were encouraged by circumstances to drink hard and fast any liquor they acquired (Reynolds 1991). One function of this drinking style was to reduce the chances that authorities would discover and confiscate the alcoholic beverages. Depending on the circumstances, Indians could not legally acquire and consume alcohol in the same ways that non-Indians all around them could. This remains true for many reservation Indians.

Binge drinking seems to continue among some American Indian communities for two basic reasons. First, legal restrictions of the past encouraged it for so long that it may have become a consumption norm in some circles. Second, the pattern is still encouraged indirectly by the prohibitions against alcohol which tribes have in place on various reservations. On reservations where alcohol is not sold, Indians must go to border towns off the reservations to obtain it. Of those who do, some drink quickly in order to finish before returning to the reservations, where their purchases might be confiscated and they might be arrested or fined for mere possession. This scenario often leads to high profile problems in the border towns and on the roads back to the reservations. Media coverage reinforces the stereotype of the Indian.

The binge pattern does lead to one set of statistics that is much higher, per capita, for American Indians than it is for other population groups, i.e., the rates of alcohol-related problems such as arrest, accidents, death, and illness (Reynolds 1991; Rhoades, Hammond, Welty, Handler, and Ambler 1987). Some tribes have tried to address alcohol-related problems by legalizing the sale of alcohol on their reservations (Stago 2000). Advocates suggest that tribal control of alcohol sales will reduce the border-town syndrome, bootlegging, and perhaps other elements of the alcohol abuse equation (Associated Press 1991h).

There is a long history of alcohol use in Indian country. Several years ago, Peter C. Mancall (1995) wrote a book on "Indians and alcohol in early America." According to the prologue of this useful source, he felt there was a need to look at connections between the past and present in regard to Indian drinking. Recognizing that problem drinking knows no cultural or racial boundaries, Mancall reviews some of the contemporary literature on subjects such as a "genetic weakness" among Indians for alcohol (there is none that has been clinically identified). He focuses on history to provide a foundation for understanding present and future concerns about alcohol and Indians. (See also questions J-3 and J-4.)

D-5. *Are reservation Indians required to stay on their reservations?*
As surprising as it may seem, some people still believe that many, if
not most, Indians are somehow confined by the government to
reservations (O'Brien 1989; Bureau of Indian Affairs 1991a; Benally
2000a). This, of course, is not true. More than two-thirds of all Indians
do not live on reservations. But, whether they live on a reservation or
not, all American Indians can move about as freely as other Americans.
This was not always the case, however.

In the 19th century, especially during the 1860s through the
1890s, the government routinely issued orders that prevented individuals and entire tribes from leaving the boundaries of their reservations without special permission. In fact, such a decree was the
specific administrative action that led to the Battle of the Little
Bighorn in 1876 and the killing of Sitting Bull in 1890. Similar orders
played a part in other bloody conflicts, like the Wounded Knee
Massacre in 1890. In each instance, the government was worried
about Indian activities. It issued reservation confinement orders and
then followed up with force.

By the beginning of the 20th century, confinement of entire tribes
was no longer practiced. However, many individual Indians essentially became long-term prisoners of war. Two of the most notable
were Joseph (Nez Perce) and Geronimo (Chiricahua Apache). They
died in 1904 and 1909, respectively, after spending decades in forced
exile on reservations far from their homelands.

Joseph, who repeatedly tried to gain permission to return to his
native Idaho, once said, "I have asked some of the great white chiefs
where they get their authority to say to the Indian that he shall stay
in one place. They cannot tell me" (Capps 1975, p. 185). Perhaps the
misconception that may still exist about reservation confinement is
nothing more than a holdover from the reality of the late 19th and
early 20th centuries.

D-6. *What is the "politically correct" term to use in referring to American Indians?* **(See also questions A-2 and A-3.)**

> *Maybe the outside world will . . . call us by our tribal names.*
>
> Kevin Gover (Pawnee),
> Assistant Secretary of Indian Affairs (Winik 1999, p. 8)

The important social question as to how to refer courteously to the first Americans warrants some exploration. To reduce potential confusion, the eye-opening answer will be divided into three sections: Lower 48 states, Alaska, and Hawaii.

Lower 48 States

A lot of Anglo-American terminology has been used over the past 500 years to distinguish the Indian people of North America from non-Natives. It is instructive to review some of these appellations (those that are printable), especially the older ones appearing in numerous historic documents. They include:

Indians	West Indians	Savages
Heathens	Americans	Natives
Barbarians	Old People	Virginians
Wild People	Brutish People	Country People
Naturals	Inhabitants	Old Inhabitants
Red Devils	Indigenous People	Tawny Serpents
Redskins	Red Men	Aborigines

Obviously, nearly all of these terms fell into disuse long ago. Historically, however, "Indians" appears to have been most often employed. It is significant that, into the early and perhaps mid-18th century, the terms "Indians" and "Americans" were equivalent. Until then, "Americans" was not applied to those people of European heritage in North America (Vaughn 1982).

The more common of the acceptable modern terms that have been used to designate indigenous Americans (of the contiguous 48 states) include "Indians," "American Indians," "Native Americans," "Amerinds," and "Amerindians." Axtell (1988) says that Canadian social scientists are fond of the last two terms, but he and many others consider them to be awkward jargon. He also reports that reservation and rural Indians generally prefer "Indian" over "Native American." Axtell further suggests that urban Indians and non-Indian urban dwellers, along with federal grant and college application writers, frequently prefer "Native American." Urban academics also obviously prefer this term.

Deloria (1974b, p. 6) states that "Indian Americans," as opposed to "American Indians," is not a welcome term in Indian circles because it was derived from the "melting pot" social theory—a concept injurious to tribalism. Deloria's further comments, largely in agreement with Axtell's, are as follows:

> Just what "Indians" are to be called today remains a subject of great debate. Anthropologists have attempted to call us "Amerindians" or "Amerinds," but the phrase has not caught on. A great many younger Indian people have tried to popularize the phrase "Native Americans," but the older generation feels ill at ease with this name. In all probability no name other than "Indians" will ever satisfy most of the people known popularly as "Indians."

Since Deloria wrote those remarks, use of the name "Native Americans" has grown widely among Indians and non-Indians, but especially among the latter. Many non-Indians (e.g., Wills 1991) now mistakenly believe that it is the only correct term to use when referring to American Indians.

Tim Giago (1991b), former publisher of the largest Indian advocacy newspaper in the country, stated that the editorial policy of *Indian Country Today* included use of the terms "American Indian," "Indian," and "Native American." His preference was to use individual tribal affiliations whenever possible, e.g., Lakota, Onondaga, Pomo, etc. This is a good rule to follow in all situations where applicable. Several of Mr. Giago's comments on the nomenclature issue are worth quoting:

> We are, more and more, pulling away from using Native American, because, as so many phone calls and letters have pointed out to us, and correctly so, anyone born in America can refer to themselves [sic] as Native American.

> We realize the word "Indian" is a misnomer, but for generic purposes, we are forced to use it when speaking of many different tribes. American Indian is also acceptable in Indian country.

Any politically correct thinker who believes Native American is the preferred identification tag for the Lakota or any other tribe is wrong. Most of us do not object to the use of Indian or American Indian. And as I have said, Native American can be used by any American native to this land.

The terms American Indians *and* indigenous Americans *are interchangeably used in preference to* Native American *in this presentation. Some advocates of Indian rights self-identify with pride as American Indians; it is a term of choice among many indigenous peoples. The term also differentiates the tribes in the lower 48 contiguous states* [who generally are treated differently under federal law] *from Eskimos, Aleuts, and Hawaiians, who are also indigenous to what is now American soil. Finally, in conducting this research I have found the term "Native American" rubs salt in old wounds of Indian/Anglo relations in many parts of the West. It is a pointed reminder of whose ancestors got here first and what happened to them when the next group arrived. . . .*

In the broader sense of the term, anyone born in the Americas is a native, including the light-skinned descendants of northern Europeans. The irony is that although "American Indian" communicates meaning more precisely, it is also a continuing reminder of the geographic ignorance of the early, land-hungry European immigrants and of their persisting ethnocentric need to regard this continent's darker-skinned original inhabitants as somehow foreign to American soil.

Lloyd Burton,
American Indian Water Rights and the Limits of Law (1991, p. 4)

Alaska

In Alaska, "Natives" and "Alaska Natives" are the widely accepted terms for the three ethnologic groups of indigenous people—Eskimos, Aleuts, and Indians (Price 1978; Alaska Native Claims Settlement Act of 1971; Case 1984).

The Alaskan people who are still commonly referred to by Natives and non-Natives as "Eskimos" are now also called "Inuit." In 1977, at the Inuit Circumpolar Conference held in Barrow, Alaska, the term Inuit ("the people") was officially adopted as a preferred designation when collectively referring to Eskimos (Damas 1984). "Eskimo" has long been considered to have come from an eastern Canadian Algonquian term which means "raw meat eaters." Some, but not all, Inuit would rather it not be used. Major subgroups of Alaska's Eskimos are the North Slope Inuit (Inupiat), the Central Alaskan Inuit (Yup'ik), and the southern or Pacific Inuit (Sugpiaq). A number of Sugpiaq (e.g., on the Kenai Peninsula and Kodiak island) have come to accept and prefer the "Aleut" designation mistakenly applied to them by the Russians in the late-18th and early-19th centuries (Lantis 1984).

"Aleut" is the acceptable designation for the people of the western Alaska Peninsula, the Pribilof Islands, and the Aleutian Island chain. The name is of Russian origin and was probably borrowed from the Native village of Alut, located on the Kamchatka Peninsula of the Russian far east. Russian fur traders used "Aleut" to identify the people of the Aleutian Islands. The two major linguistic divisions of Aleuts are the Atkan (western) and Unalaska (eastern) branches (Lantis 1984).

"Indians" native to the Cook Inlet and interior regions of Alaska commonly refer to themselves as "Athapaskans," a broad ethnologic term. There are, however, a number of major Athapaskan groups, e.g., Kutchin, Koyukon, Nabesna, Han, Tanana, Holikachuk, Kolchan, Ingalik, Tanaina, and Ahtna (Prucha 1990a; Waldman 1985). Indian people of southeast coastal Alaska are often referred to as "Southeast Villagers" or "Southeast Natives," but their preferred tribal names, in north-to-south order, are Eyak, Tlingit, Haida, and Tsimshian.

Hawaii

The indigenous people of Hawaii prefer the terms "Hawaiians," "Hawaiian Natives," or "Native Hawaiians" over "Native Americans." In fact, some Hawaiians take such offense at being called "Native Americans" that the term is almost considered to be "fighting words" (Trask 1991). The reason is simple. Many Native Hawaiians harbor great resentment over the 1893 coup, orchestrated by American businessmen, which overthrew the government of the independent nation of Hawaii and led to annexation of Hawaii to the United States five years later. Annexation also led to great misery, hardship, and economic loss for the dispossessed Native Hawaiians and many of their descendants. (See Appendix 1.)

D-7. *Do Indians serve in the military?*

Yes. Indian men and women have the same obligations and opportunities for military service as other U.S. citizens. Indeed, they have a long history of serving with the nation's armed forces, dating back to the Revolution.

After the recent War with Iraq, the Bureau of Indian Affairs (1991a) updated its still incomplete information on Indian veteran history. It reported that about 3,000 Indian military personnel served in the Persian Gulf theatre of operations. Three Indian men were among those killed in action. A total of 24,000 Indian men and women were in the military in 1990 just prior to Operation Desert Storm.

During the Viet Nam War, 41,500 Indians served in the armed forces. Many of these people have helped organize important Indian veterans' groups, like the Navajo Nation Viet Nam Veterans. Also, thousands of Indians served in Korea, where one Indian soldier was awarded the Congressional Medal of Honor.

The Navajo Nation Veterans Cemetery at Fort Defiance, on the Arizona portion of the reservation. American Indians have the highest rate of military service of any ethnic group in the United States.

During World War II, about 25,000 Indian men and women were in the military, mostly the Army. They served on all fronts in Europe and Asia and were awarded at least 215 medals for valor, including two Congressional Medals of Honor. The most famous Indian exploit of World War II involved the Navy Department's use of Navajo Marines as "code talkers." Trained as battlefield radiomen, these Navajos converted military radio traffic to a special classified version of their own language and conversed without fear that the Japanese could break their "code." Stallings (1963) reported instances of Indian language being employed as "code" for battlefield phone use in World War I, but this was done mostly on the initiative of soldiers in the field and apparently had little official military sanction.

Approximately 8,000 Indians were in the military during World War I. Their valor and demonstrated patriotism helped move Congress to pass the Indian Citizenship Act of 1924.

Indian soldiers were also active in the Civil War, on both sides. For example, Colonel Eli Parker, a Seneca, was an aide to General Grant. Parker attended General Lee's surrender at Appamattox on April 9, 1865, and served as secretary, recording the conditions of surrender. Stand Watie, a Cherokee, was the last Confederate general to surrender, on June 23, 1865. One more Confederate Indian unit, in what was probably the final act of the war, surrendered in mid-July (Harlow 1935).

Today, about 200,000 Indians are veterans. Approximately one in four adult Indian men is a veteran, and just over 45 percent of current and recent tribal leaders are veterans.

D-8. *Where can one get information on the true story of the famous Navajo Code Talkers, and were there other tribes that had code talkers?*

> *When I visited the Vietnam Memorial, the "Wall," in Washington, D.C., I saw a bronze sculpture of soldiers: a white man, a black man, and a Hispanic man. I couldn't find a representation of an American*

Indian. Were the American Indians the forgotten Americans? Were they American citizens? These questions struck me.

They stayed with me until I met the Navajo code talkers one winter day in Window Rock, Arizona, two years after I had come to the Navajo Indian Reservation. They had been part of the United States Marine Corps, and they were impressive. They had used their own language, Navajo, as a secret code during World War II, in the South Pacific, where four hundred of them were on active duty. They were responsible for many victories during the war, as Japanese cryptographers could not break their "code."

Kenji Kawano
in *Warriors: Navajo Code Talkers* (1990, p. xxiii–xxiv)

When I was going to boarding school, the U.S. government told us not to speak Navajo, but during the war, they wanted us to speak it!

Code Talker Teddy Draper, Sr.
(Kawano 1990, p. xvi)

I supported my family by weaving rugs when my husband went to war. He was a very warm, caring person.

Mrs. Harry Belone, Sr.
(Kawano 1990, p. 31)

At one point during [the campaign], *I was captured by U.S. Army soldiers who thought I was Japanese.*

Code Talker Eugene R. Crawford
(Kawano 1990, p. 42)

The Japanese were preparing to attack an American installation on Guam. Our Marine reconnaissance found their location and the Code talkers sent a message to a battleship and two artillery units to tell them where the target was. The Japanese were wiped out and our commander, Major General Erikine, was saved by our language.

Code Talker George Kirk, Sr.
(Kawano 1990, P. 61)

Because I currently live on the Navajo Reservation and work for the Navajo Nation, I am periodically asked the code talker question, or ones like it, by a diverse group of people that I meet when I travel who are interested in the compelling story of code talkers in the U.S. military.

In order to find a better answer to the question about Navajo Code Talkers, I recently spoke with several code talkers and friends who are family members of one of the Navajo Code Talkers who had recently passed away. (He was in his 80s. All of these veterans are now in their late 70s and 80s.) I knew my friends had collected a list of books and videos to learn more about their uncle's participation in World War II. These sources are listed below.

Several books on the Navajo Code Talkers are currently available, though locating some of them may require an intensive search:

Nathan Aaseng, *Navajo Code Talkers* (1992)
Chuck Bianchi, *The Code Talkers* (n.d.)
Margaret Bixler, *Winds of Freedom: The Story of the Navajo Code Talkers of WW II* (1992)
Robert Daily, *The Code Talkers: American Indians in World War II* (1997)
Deanne Durrett, *Unsung Heroes of WW II: The Story of the Navajo Code Talkers* (1998)
Catherine Jones, *Navajo Code Talkers: Native American Heroes* (1999)
Kenji Kawano, *Warriors: Navajo Code Talkers* (1990)
Syble Lagerquist, *Philip Johnston and the Navajo Code Talkers* (1996)
S. McClain, *Navajo Weapon* (1994)
Doris A. Paul, *The Navajo Code Talkers* (1973)

There are also at least two good videos available on the Navajo Code Talkers. *Navajo Code Talkers* (1998) can be purchased from The History Channel at www.historychannel.com. The second video, *Navajo Code Talkers: The Epic Story* (1994), is available from Tully Entertainment, phone: 1 (800) 247-6553, or www.tullyent.com. There are reports in the media that at least one Hollywood motion picture on the Code Talkers is in the making.

With regard to the second part of the question—about code talkers from other tribes—during World War I the U.S. Army made limited use of code talkers from several different tribes. Britten (1997) reports that this code talker activity was initiated in October 1918, by the 142nd Infantry Regiment, when the regimental commander had two Choctaws serve as field telephone operators to foil German eavesdropping. During the last two months of the war a number of units employed the code talker tactic, and used Comanche, Osage, Cheyenne, and Sioux soldiers, in addition to Choctaw troops.

There were also code talkers other than Navajos (including Hopi soldiers) during World War II, though the Navajos were by far the largest code talker unit. On November 30, 1999, the last Comanche Code Talker from the second world war was honored at the Pentagon for his military service (Associated Press 1999). Charles Chibitty, age 78, from Oklahoma, is the last surviving member of the 17 Comanches who were recruited to serve in the Army's 4th Signal Brigade. They served in the European theater of the war in much the same way the Navajo Code Talkers served in the Pacific. When reporting on the ceremony honoring Chibitty, Rolo (1999) mentioned in passing that there had been Choctaw code talkers in the Pacific as well. Carroll (1998) mentions that there were code talkers from 17 tribes that served in the military during World Wars I and II, but she names only three—Navajos, Comanche, and Choctaw.

For additional information, the Navajo Code Talkers Association can usually be reached through the Navajo Nation Office of Veterans Affairs in Window Rock Arizona, phone: (520) 871-6413. Also, as of early 2001, Code Talker Thomas Begay and his wife, Nina, continue to travel and make presentations on the Code Talkers' Marine Corps legacy. The Begays can be reached at: P.O. Box 2338, Window Rock, Arizona 86515-2338, phone: (520) 871-4411.

D-9. *What offends many Indians about sports mascots such as the Washington "Redskins?"*

Not all Indians are offended. Some Eastern Cherokees, for example, have come out publicly in support of the Redskins, Kansas City Chiefs, Cleveland Indians, and Atlanta Braves. The tribe's principal chief in the early 1990s, Jonathon Taylor, unabashedly stated that the sports teams were good for the tribe's crafts business which had recently sold 300,000 mass-produced headdresses.

Nonetheless, tens of thousands of American Indians are clearly offended by the use of Indian mascots, though not in every

The Kansas City Chiefs professional football team is called "The Tribe." This is an example of what many—but not all—Indians consider to be inappropriate use of the Indian image. Photo © Costacos Bros. Sports.

instance—such as at some Indian schools. A major concern is racism, blatant or not. And, there is offense taken at what are seen as stereotypical and disrespectful antics by fans and players. Charlene Teters (1991), a Spokane with the National Congress of American Indians, made a point when she argued: "These symbols must be seen for what they are: relics from a time period when racism and manifest destiny were the common basis for decisions affecting Indian people. [They] honor neither Indian or non-Indian [and] should have gone by the wayside with Little Black Sambo and the Frito Bandito."

A third point of contention is the inappropriate use of items like pipes, body paint designs, and feathers, all of which are considered sacred in traditional American Indian cultures.

Non-Indians are responding with "Why haven't you complained before?" Some American Indians have, but nobody would listen. People need to understand the heavy cloud of repression that has hung over Indian country for so long, just as slavery and racism bottled up the voice of Black America. It was only 25 years ago that the cloud over Indian country began to lift in any significant way.

Growth of the mascot controversy indicates that more American Indians are feeling free to express their concerns publicly about things that have bothered them for a long time. Media interest, stirred in the 1990s by the Columbus Quincentennial, has also stimulated the exercising of American Indians' long-dormant right to freedom of expression.

One of those speaking out on Indian issues is Tim Giago, Oglala Lakota (Sioux) and former publisher of *Indian Country Today*, a national weekly newspaper. Printed below, with permission, is a pertinent editorial from Mr. Giago's "Notes from Indian Country" (1991c). It exemplifies the Indian point of view about some of the things they find offensive in the highly charged and symbolic issue of Indian sports mascots. Mr. Giago affirms a concern for racism but moves on to address religious aspects of the mascot issue that are sometimes overlooked.

MASCOTS, SPIRITUALITY, AND INSENSITIVITY

Indians as mascots has been a point of contention for many years among Native Americans.

Most of our ranting and raving has fallen on deaf ears lo these many years.

Suddenly, as the Atlanta Braves fought their way to the World Series, other voices picked up our indignant shouts and the issue has taken on national stature.

As a columnist and newspaper editor, these are the things we have struggled to get on the front pages of the national media for years and we are pleased to see it become a national issue.

As an American Indian writer who has spent much of his life "covering the coverage," it does my heart good to get this kind of support, support vitally needed by the Indian people if we are to see change.

The media has centered its attention on whether the sham rituals and painted faces in the stands at Braves' baseball games border on racism. In our minds (Indians) it does, but there is another side of this coin I have written about that needs to be expanded at this time.

The sham rituals, such as the wearing of feathers, smoking of so-called peace pipes, beating of tom-toms, fake dances, horrendous attempts at singing Indian songs, the so-called war whoops, and the painted faces, address more than the issue of racism. They are direct attacks upon the spirituality (religion) of the Indian people.

Suppose a team like the New Orleans Saints decided to include religious rituals in their halftime shows in keeping with their name. Would different religious groups feel insulted to see these rituals on national television?

For instance: suppose Saints' fans decided to emulate Catholicism as part of their routine. What if they carried crosses, had a mascot dressed up like the Pope, spread ashes on their foreheads, and displayed enlarged replicas of the sacramental bread of Holy Communion while drinking from chalices filled with wine?

Would Catholics consider these routines anti-Catholic?

Eagle feathers play an important role in the spirituality of Native Americans. Faces are painted in a sacred way.

The Pipes that became known to the white man as "peace pipes" are known to most Indians who use them as part of their spirituality as Sacred Pipes. . . . To most tribes of the Great Plains, the Pipe was, and is, their Bible.

Because the treaties signed between the sovereign Indian nations and the U.S. government were so sacred and so important to the Indian nations, the signing was usually attended by the smoking of a Sacred Pipe.

This spiritual gesture was intended to show the white man that the document just signed was a sacred one and would be treated as such by the Indian people.

Since most of the treaties were intended to bring about peace between white man and Indian, the *wasicu* (white man) called the Sacred Pipe a peace pipe.

The point I hope to make here is that there is a national insensitivity when it comes to the religious beliefs, traditional values and the culture of the American Indian.

It is bad enough that American sees nothing wrong in naming football teams after the color of a people's skin. Jack Kent Cooke [owner of the Redskins] considers the name Washington Redskins complimentary to the Indian people.

Would he consider a team called the Minnesota White-skins complimentary to the white race?

The Christian Bible says, "Do unto others as you would have them do unto you." Would God-fearing Christians use sports mascots that would insult the Jewish people, Muslims, Buddhists, Shintoists, Hindus or any other minority religious group?

If not, then why in the world would they do this to the indigenous people of the Western Hemisphere, the American Indian?

As we approach the Quincentennial of Columbus, it is important that America take a long, hard look at itself and its dealings with Native Americans over the past 500 years.

Most foreigners, particularly those from countries that have been colonized by others (African nations), look upon America as a nation with two faces.

One face shows it to the world as a land of democracy and freedom, the other it shows to its indigenous peoples as uncaring, greedy, dictatorial and often-times racist.

By the time December 31, 1992, rolls around, most of us will be sick of Christopher Columbus, revisionists, and politically correct thinkers, but that doesn't mean there is not a whole lot of truth in the things Native Americans are complaining about.

Stop insulting the spirituality and the traditional beliefs of the Indian people by making us mascots for athletic teams. Is that asking so much of America?

Tim Giago,
© 1991 *Lakota Times*

The Washington Redskins football team is thinking of changing its name. They're thinking of dropping the part about being a football team.

A 1998 monologue by Jay Leno on the Tonight Show
about the team's losing season
(Quoted in *American Indian Report* 1998, p. 3)

On April 2, 1999, three federal administrative trademark judges rendered a decision in the trademark case of *Harjo, et al. v. Pro-Football, Inc.* The tribal-member petitioners in that case, which was originally filed in 1992, were Suzan Shown Harjo, Raymond D. Apodaca, Vine Deloria, Jr., Norbert S. Hill, Jr., Mateo Romero, William A. Means, and Manley Begay. These individuals had filed a petition with the U.S. Trademark Office to cancel the registrations of the marks familiarly known as "THE WASHINGTON REDSKINS," "REDSKINS," and "REDSKINETTES"—trademarks which are owned by Pro-Football, Inc., the corporate owner of the Washington Redskins football team. The formal "pleadings" (or complaints) of these petitioners, as described in the decision, were as follows:

> Petitioners allege that they are Native American persons and enrolled members of federally recognized Indian tribes. As grounds for cancellation, petitioners assert that the word "redskin(s)" or

a form of that word appears in the mark in each of the registrations sought to be canceled; that the word "redskin(s)" "was and is a perjorative, derogatory, denigrating, offensive, scandalous, contemptuous, disreputable, disparaging and racist designation for a Native American person"; that the marks "also include additional matter that, in the context used by registrant, is offensive, disparaging and scandalous"; and that registrant's use of the marks in the identified registrations "offends" petitioners and other Native Americans. Petitioners assert, further, that the marks in the identified registrations "consist of or comprise matter which disparages Native American persons, and brings them into contempt, ridicule, and disrepute" and "consist of or comprise scandalous matter"; and that, therefore, under Section 2(a) of the Trademark Act, 15 U.S.C. 1052(a), the identified registrations should be canceled.

The Indian petitioners were relying on the judges to cancel the Washington Redskins' trademarks based on the following language in the Trademark Act (15 U.S.C. 1052(a):

No trademark by which the goods of the applicant may be distinguished from the goods of others shall be refused registration on the principal register[,] on account of its nature[,] unless it—

(a) Consists of or comprises immoral, deceptive, or scandalous matter; or matter which may disparage or falsely suggest a connection with persons, living or dead, institutions, beliefs, or national symbols, or bring them into contempt, or disrepute.

The Redskins' owner corporation denied all the allegations and declared that its trademarks "cannot be interpreted as disparaging any of the Petitioners or as bringing them into contempt or disrepute."

After a multipage discussion of the facts and the merits of the case, the judges decided in favor of the tribal-member petitioners on one of their points: "that the subject remarks may disparage Native Americans and may bring them into contempt or disrepute." They then denied the claim that the trademarks "consist of or comprise scandalous matter." But the denial on the second point did not really matter. The petitioners had already won. The judges ended the opinion with the statement: "The registrations will be canceled in due course."

This was an obvious setback for the Redskins, and something of a wakeup call for other teams like the Atlanta Braves, the Cleveland Indians, and the Kansas City Chiefs. The Redskins filed an appeal in June 1999 in U.S. district court, despite the fact that 24 religious leaders had written a letter in May asking that the ruling be allowed to stand (Begay 2000).

Four days before I sat down to write the above information on *Harjo, et al. v. Pro-Football, Inc.,* I was on a road trip, going north to the portion of the Navajo Reservation in Utah to meet with a BIA representative and do some "responsibility evaluations" for several abandoned oil and gas wells on Reservation land. I had caught a ride with a Navajo friend, also a tribal employee, who was headed to the same area. My friend is older than I am and is considered by several of my Navajo colleagues and me to be an "elder" from whom we can sometimes seek advice.

On our first day out, we were driving past Red Mesa High School, a state high school within the Arizona part of the Reservation. I had never been to the small community of Red Mesa before. As we passed the school's events sign along the highway, which announced a Valentine's Day dance, my jaw dropped open and my eyes got wider when I noticed the name of the school's team—the "Red Mesa Redskins." My friend saw the sign, too, but he showed no surprise—it was obviously not new to him.

Because the Washington Redskins trademark case was on my mind, I asked my friend what he thought about the "Redskins" names used back east and at Red Mesa. He said that neither one really bothered him. He thought that the football "Redskins" had chosen their name because it was something they could be motivated by. He felt the high school "Redskins" had a right to use the same name; especially because the student body had chosen the name themselves and the student population at Red Mesa was probably about 99 percent Navajo. He then asked me if any of my Indian students at Northern Arizona University ever wore hats, shirts, or coats—like some of the high school kids on the Reservation do—with logos on them "from the professional baseball and football teams like the Redskins, Indians, Braves, or Chiefs." I answered yes, because a small number of my students had indeed worn these things, and he nodded.

Sign at the Red Mesa High School on the Navajo Reservation. About 99 percent of the students at Red Mesa are Navajo, and they chose the name of their school mascot.

My friend was born in the 1940s but grew up in a 19th century lifestyle, in a hogan made of logs and dirt and with no vehicles, electricity, running water, or nearby stores from which to buy food, clothing, and other material "luxuries." Once in a while his family took a wagon to a trading post to get "essentials" like flour, sugar, coffee, lard, cloth, gardening implements, and other goods. His parents, who never went to school and never spoke any English, were very traditional and raised their 10 children that way. My friend did not begin to learn to speak English until he was about 12 years old. In light of all this, it is easy to understand his traditional perspective on the world.

After our initial brief discussion about the Redskins, we went north to Utah—talking only about the countryside and where the wells might be. On the return trip, however, he brought up the Redskins issue again when we neared Red Mesa. My friend said, "The team mascot that really bothered me when I first saw it, and that still bothers me today, is the "Sun Devils" of ASU [Arizona State University]. My parents taught us to pray to the sun and thank it for all the life and warmth it brings to us and the earth. When I saw that devil put with the sun there, all I could think was how could they put that ch'įįdii [evil] with something so good?"

We stayed overnight at a second work site 40 miles west of Red Mesa. The next day, on our way home, we decided to stop by another small Reservation community that I had never been to and he had not visited in many years. When we went by the high school, my friend and I looked at the school's announcement sign by the road. This time *his* mouth fell open and his eyes got wider. The school's mascot was the "Sun Devils," borrowed from ASU! My friend and I both shook our heads. He then turned the truck around and quietly drove us the rest of the 90 miles home.

The still-confusing lesson I've learned is that, depending on the circumstances, words that reflect one person's prejudice can sometimes reflect another person's pride.

D-10. *What stereotypical images are associated with Indians, and are some American Indians also guilty of stereotyping?*

> *Ugh. Me Gettum, Kemo Sabe?*
>
> Tonto, *The Lone Ranger*, 1933
>
> *Sometimes it was hard to believe that this strange bloody-minded red race was human at all. It was as if giant lizards had come on horses, mouthing and grunting their unearthly language that so few white men had ever understood.*
>
> From the 1957 "western" novel *The Unforgiven*
> Stedman 1982, p. 118

> *The Savages are utter Strangers to distinctions of Property, for what belongs to one is equally others! . . . Money is in use with none of them. . . . They'll tell you that amongst us [Whites] the People Murder, Plunder, Defame, and betray one another. . . . They think it unaccountable that one Man should have more than another. . . . 'Tis vain to remonstrate to them how useful the Distinction of Property is for the support of a Society. . . . In fine, they neither quarrel, Nor Fight, Nor Slander one another.*
>
> Quoting Baron de Lahontan, who helped invent the European vision of "The Noble Savage" for the 18th century era of European Enlightenment
> Leland 1990, p. 145

A stereotype may be defined loosely as a somewhat fixed or unvarying image which people have about something—be it an object, a set of beliefs or actions, or a group of people. The image can be uncomplimentary because it is frequently applied to all members of the same category, regardless of how true it is. Thus, stereotyping is often associated with prejudice. Most stereotyping overemphasizes one or more characteristics which may be partly true, and this often results in distortions about those characteristics.

In the Indian world, for example, everyone would agree that there were Plains tribes with horse-riding, feather-bonnetted warriors and that some of these tribes were viewed as a threat to White expansion. That, in itself, is not a distortion. It became a stereotype in motion pictures and television by endless repetition. It also occurred through the ignoring of hundreds of other Native societies, the other kinds of Indian-White relationships, Indian societies in their own terms, and the crucial roles of women among American Indian peoples (Price 1978).

Indian stereotypes are so numerous that hundreds of works address the issue, and entire volumes have been written on the subject. Books with titles like *Shadows of the Indian* (Stedman 1982), *The White Man's Indian* (Berkhofer 1979), *Killing the White Man's Indian* (Bordewich 1996), *The Invented Indian* (Clifton 1990), *Playing Indian* (Deloria 1998), *American Indians: Stereotypes and Realities* (Mihesuah

Stereotypical images are used to attract the attention of tourists where so-called "trading posts" and other curio shops are found. Some of these establishments do not even carry genuine Indian items. While not ill-intentioned, these totems are not always well received by American Indians.

1996), *Wild West Shows and the Images of American Indians* (Moses 1996), *Hollywood's Indian* (Rollins and O'Connor 1998), *Tonto's Revenge* (Strickland 1997), and *Native American Identities from Stereotype to Archetype in Art and Literature* (Vickers 1998) make informative and provocative reading.

Stereotypes applied to American Indians over the past 500 years show that Native people have been variously defined as innocent children of nature, subhuman demons, untrustworthy thieves, noble savages, bloodthirsty murderers, royal princesses, human curiosities, unfeeling stoics, natural-born warriors, innately inferior humans, shiftless wanderers, vanishing vestiges of the stone age, wild animals, oppressed and promiscuous "squaws," lazy parasites, incompetents, devil worshippers, completely democratic egalitarians, loyal "Men Friday," born bearers of wisdom, magical healers, depraved drunkards, born mystics, automatic knowers of nature, threats to female virtue, supernaturals, favored "pets" of the government, the enemy, racist "white-bashers," the antithesis to "civilization," and the bearers of a holy message to mankind. Throughout history, it seems

American Indians have been routinely regarded as almost anything but true-to-life men, women, and children who are as individualistic and human as any other people on earth (Josephy 1982).

Another stereotypical theme about Indians in the late 20th century is that of the "true Indian" archetype. This idea was nurtured by the attractively done motion picture "Dances With Wolves."

> "Spontaneous, Natural, Timeless, Original" have been the most common ways of characterizing the True Indian[s] as human beings, identifying what is specific to them with the additional provisos that True Indians live close to and in harmony with nature, and are just as agreeably fused with one another socially in conflict-free consensual communities.
>
> Simard 1990, p. 354–355

Viewing today's American Indians through impossible, non-Indian expectations is grossly unfair. Indians today simply do not fit the images portrayed in the "true Indian" stereotype. As Schickel (1975) wrote, "Total goodness is also less than human."

With the exception of certain Alaska Natives, few American Indians today live mostly "off the land." In fact, some non-Indians live "closer to nature" than do most Indians. Because of 500 years of uninvited change, most Indians reside in or near urban settings. All use one form or another of modern transportation and buy modern groceries. And, all have varying degrees of personal, interpersonal, and social conflict affecting their lives. Indians, Inuit, and Aleuts are human beings who possess the same general strengths and frailties as everyone else. They also have the same aspirations to take their self-defined and deserved place in the world without undesired interference or involvement by the larger society.

As to the matter of stereotyping by Indians, it obviously occurs among many. In the "them-and-us" scenario necessary for stereotyping to take place, the "them" is the "White Man." Naturally, this omits the millions of Hispanics, African Americans, and Oriental Americans who will jointly constitute the majority of American society in the 21st century. The stereotypical view which many Indians have of White society is that it always has the flaws. It is guilty of racism, historical injustices, continuing legal injustices, environmental pollution, introduction of alcohol and the death penalty, culture-crushing genocide, the killing off of Native religions, etc. Typical of stereotyping, there is frequently little room for someone defined as a "White Man" to have an individuality separate from the massed wrongs of the past and present. Whatever is wrong with "White" society is perceived as not being part of Native culture. This allows Indians to maintain claims of moral superiority over the majority race.

One has to admit to an overwhelming amount of historical and often continuing motivation for Indian stereotyping of the "White Man." The Lakota scholar, Vine Deloria (1970, p. 44), however, has thoughtfully criticized stereotyping by Indians and other minorities. "They must not fall into the same trap by simply reversing the process that has stereotyped them. Minority groups must thrust through the rhetorical blockade by creating within themselves a sense of 'peoplehood'." These are words of wisdom for everyone.

D-11. *Is it true that the famous environmental speech by Chief Seattle was actually written in the 1970s by a white man?*

Yes and no. Chief Seattle did indeed make a speech to Governor Stevens in the Puget Sound area of Washington Territory in 1854. It was said to have been translated for a white man, Dr. Henry Smith, who claimed to have been a witness to the original speech. Evidence in relevant literature suggests that Dr. Smith did not write down his memory of the speech attributed to Chief Seattle until 1887 (Clifton 1990; Bordewich 1996).

Seattle was a respected Suquamish leader (whose mother was Duwamish), an eloquent speaker, and a negotiator to the whites for his people. Much, but not all, of "the rest of the story" about the speech is found in a portion of an article from *The Denver Post* (1992), in which an anglo writer, who had written a version in 1971 that greatly exaggerated Seattle's original speech, is speaking to a reporter—who then adds commentary.

> "I never tried to pretend that Chief Seattle said the things I wrote," said Ted Perry, 54, a film writer and professor at Middlebury [Vermont] College. "I'm partly to blame in the fact that I

was presumptuous enough to try to write what Chief Seattle might have said." ...

Perry said he took a speech by the chief ... and strengthened its environmental theme while writing for an environmental film called "Home," produced by the Southern Baptist Radio and Television Commission in 1971.

"I was inspired by Chief Seattle and I told the producers to identify me as the author of the words," he said. "But they said it would be more authentic if Chief Seattle has said it." ...

The embellished version is revered by many as a piece of great significance to the environmental movement.

In Mr. Perry's version of the speech, Chief Seattle talks about things like "railroads," which did not exist in Washington Territory in 1854. This version also talks about the slaughter of the buffalo, but there were no buffalo in Washington Territory and Seattle probably never saw one. Further, the real buffalo slaughter by white hunters did not begin until after the Chief had died. Also, Chief Seattle and his people obviously did not live off buffalo meat, but off salmon and other foods provided by the marine, riverine, and coastal environments of their homeland.

Perry's version further described how the "dogs of appetite will devour the rich Earth and leave only a desert." Thus, any version of the Seattle speech that refers to railroads, buffalo, and "dogs of appetite" is not an original from the Suquamish chief.

In the early 1990s, in response to the public confusion and controversy over the Chief Seattle speech, the Book Publishing Company (1992) produced a small but informative publication on the speech that presents three versions. One is the version written by Dr. Smith in 1887, the second is Perry's version, and the third is another widely distributed 1970s adaptation that is attributed to a man named William Arrowsmith. If we rightfully include Seattle's original speech in his own language, there have been at least four versions of the speech.

D-12. *Where did the term "Manifest Destiny" come from and what does it mean?*

> *The settler and pioneer have had . . . justice on their side; this great continent could not have been kept as nothing but a game preserve for squalid savages.*
>
> Teddy Roosevelt, circa 1880s

The term "Manifest Destiny" was coined by newspaper editor John L. O'Sullivan in 1845 (George Philip Limited 1998). It was promptly made famous when President James K. Polk used it in his aggressive politics to justify the annexation of Texas in 1845, Oregon Territory in 1846, and lands taken from Mexico after the war with that country in 1846–1848. U.S. officials continued to use the theory of Manifest Destiny to justify the displacement of Indian tribes and the taking of their lands. The theory was further employed in the purchase of Alaska, the taking of Hawaii, and the taking of Spanish colonial lands in the Caribbean and the Pacific at the end of the Spanish-American War of 1898.

President Teddy Roosevelt also relied on Manifest Destiny for his policies of gun-goat diplomacy in the first decade of the 1900s. The theory provided much of the political foundation underlying U.S. duplicity in the Panamanian revolt against its parent country, Colombia, in 1903. And, it was at the root of U.S. policies that established and held the Panama Canal Zone until January 1, 2000.

With regard to the actual meaning of *Manifest Destiny*, many people mistakenly take the view that it is a two-word noun. In fact, the "manifest" part of the term is merely an adjective (meaning "self-evident") for the noun *destiny*. The term came from a growing sense of nationalism in the early and mid-1840s when many U.S. politicians were saber rattling to go to war with Mexico and perhaps Great Britain, and to claim all the land between the Mississippi and the Pacific—which they felt it was America's divinely ordained destiny to have. As they saw it, the natural providence of the U.S. was to expand westward to the Pacific. Thus, when land was taken from the Indians or others who were in the way, it was merely a manifestation, or self-evident fulfillment, of American destiny.

Dee Brown (1970, p. 31) discussed General James Carleton (circa 1865), who is most famous for his destructive roundup and removal of the Navajos to Bosque Redondo, New Mexico Territory, in the 1860s. The general was eventually disgraced by the failure of his grand experiment to assimilate the Navajos at Bosque Redondo, and was relieved of his command. (After signing a treaty with the U.S. in 1868, the Navajos were permitted to return to a portion of their original territory.)

About Carleton, Brown begins: ". . . no advocate of Manifest Destiny ever phrased his support of that philosophy more unctuously [in a more slippery-tongued way] than he":

> The exodus of this people from the land of their fathers is not only an interesting but a touching sight. They have fought us gallantly for years on years; they have defended their mountains and their stupendous canyons with a heroism which any people might be proud to emulate; but when, at length, they found it was their destiny, too, as it had been for their brethren, tribe after tribe, away back toward the rising sun, to give way to that insatiable progress of our race, they threw down their arms, and, as brave men entitled to our admiration and respect, have come to us with confidence in our magnanimity, and feeling that we are too powerful and too just a people to repay that trust with meanness and neglect—feeling that having sacrificed to us their beautiful country, their homes, the associations of their lives, the scenes rendered classic in their traditions, we will not dole out to them a miser's pittance in return for what they know to be and what we know to be a princely realm.

Besides, as Carleton had already bluntly reported to his superiors in Washington, "At all events, . . . we can feed them cheaper than we can fight them" (Brown, p. 30).

The newspapers in America were the great literary agents of change during the 19th century, and they exercised an enormous amount of influence over the development and implementation of ideas like those associated with Manifest Destiny.

A quote from the important work by John Coward (1999, p. 38), *The Newspaper Indian*, illustrates the national mindset of Americans of the 18th and 19th centuries, as directly influenced by print and other media, and the profound grip it had on the fate of the Indian people.

By promoting Indian "otherness," eighteenth- and nineteenth-century journalists, writers, and artists created Native American representations that undermined native status and provided support for a language and culture of domination. . . . The outsider status [assigned to Indians] had important and continuing consequences for Indian-white relations. For one thing, it positioned Indians as impediments to American ideas of progress, expansion, and national destiny. In the march across the continent, the Indian was something to be removed, exterminated, or otherwise subdued. Thus the American belief in Manifest Destiny was openly hostile to Indians and unsympathetic to their culture and their interests. [Historian Reginald Horsman reports that by the mid-19th century] . . . "the American public and American politicians had for the most part abandoned any belief in potential Indian equality. They now believed that American Indians were doomed because of their own inferiority and that their extinction would further progress."

> *Self preservation demands decisive action, and the only way to secure it is to fight them their own way. A few months of active extermination against the red devils will bring quiet, and nothing else will.*
>
> William N. Byers, editor of Denver's
> *Daily Rocky Mountain News*, in 1864. Byers's agitating
> words helped lead to the Sand Creek Massacre of
> Cheyenne Chief Black Kettle and his people by
> Col. Chivington's command on November 28.

D-13. *Have American Indian women generally been excluded from the literature on Indian country?*

Essentially, yes. A few of the hundreds of still very good books that are representative examples of the overwhelmingly male-dominated literature are: *The Great Chiefs* (Capps 1975), *The Patriot Chiefs* (Josephy 1989), *The Mighty Chieftains* (Woodhead 1993a), *The Way of the Warrior* (Woodhead 1993b), and *American Indian Leaders* (Edmunds 1980). There have been some distinguished works by and about American Indian women in the past, and the quantity of work including women has notably improved since the 1980s. There is now a substantial but largely undiscovered body of literature available that is written by and about Indian women. An excellent source of material can be found in the essays of a book edited by law professor Jo Carillo (1998, chap. 5). With essay titles like "Native American Women: An Update," "Mankiller: A Chief and Her People," and "Gender or Ethnicity: What Makes a Difference? A Study of Women Tribal Leaders," Carillo offers some informative and interesting material. In addition, a large number of sources can be found in the bibliographies in Carillos' book.

Additional sources are: Bataille and Sands (1984), Harjo and Bird (1997), Klein and Ackerman (1995), LaDuke (1999), Niethammer (1977), Roessel (1981), and Woodhead (1995). Harjo and Bird's *Reinventing the Enemy's Language: Contemporary Native Women's Writings of North America* is especially interesting because it presents a wide array of writings by women from approximately 50 different Indian nations.

> *I really feel better when I hear the women speak because they hold life. I know how much they mean to us and to our process of governance and how much we depend on them. When you have women like we have, things always look a little better, a little brighter.*
>
> From a colloquium speech by Oren Lyons (1993, p. 209), a traditional chief of the Onondaga Nation, Iroquois Confederacy

D-14. *Have American Indian women's roles in tribal society been disrupted and misinterpreted as a result of cultural domination by the larger society?*

Yes. But, the male-dominated literature described earlier (see D-13) has often avoided the reality that has long been faced by Native women. Jo Carillo (1998), for example, notes that various Indian scholars have made the point in recent years that the dominant society continues to refuse to take seriously the role of Indian women in tribal societies.

> *American Indian women have not been spared the attitude that*
> *until recently assumed the inferiority of all women. The view*
> *that the responsibilities of Indian women were less significant*
> *than male roles permeates early writings about native societies*
> *and appears in contemporary accounts about the position of*
> *American Indian women as well.*
>
> *The popular view of American Indian women disseminated*
> *by historians, anthropologists, sociologists, and educators, as*
> *well as novelists, accords women a low status. . . .*
>
> *If the roles of American Indian women in their societies and*
> *society at large are to be analyzed with fairness and accuracy,*
> *we must take a closer look, not from an outsider's viewpoint, but*
> *through the modes of expression within tribal society.*
>
> From Bataille and Sands (1984, p. vi, vii)

This assertion by Carillo and others is supported by Williams (1990) in his law review article *Gendered Checks and Balances: Understanding the Legacy of White Patriarchy in an American Indian Cultural Context*. There is further clarification of the disruption of women's roles, and not just the misinterpretation of those roles, through cultural domination in Castañeda (1992), Devens (1992), Foster (1993), and Medicine (1993). Medicine's article, *North American Indigenous Women and Cultural Domination*, goes right to the heart of the issue with such statements as:

> The Christian ethic of patriarchy—a male god and a patri-
> lineal kinship model with the imposition of patrilineal
> family names—virtually eclipsed the autonomy of native
> women. [p. 122]
>
> [T]he description of male roles and the dimished valua-
> tion of Indian women had great demoralizing and long
> lasting effects on native populations. [p. 123]
>
> Gender disequilibrium and social anomie are . . . part of
> everyday life of indigenous peoples of North America. [p. 124]

In some of the literature mentioned above and in question D-13, as well as in everyday discussions among Native women (Benally 2000), it is noted that more than a few native women, who come from either matriarchal or patriarchal societies, complain that some of their male counterparts seem to behave as if the dominant society has granted them a kind of license to behave in inappropriate ways, when compared to traditional norms, in their relationships with spouses, children, extended family, and in-laws. This surrogate disruption, through the influence of the larger society, also affects the roles and status of Indian women. (See also *Women's Leadership in Indigenous America* by Gonzales [2000].)

D-15. *With the enormous popularity of Indian heritage in the United States, is there really any continuing racism against Indian people?*

Because of the local ill feeling, the people of the States where they are found are often their deadliest enemies.

U.S. Supreme Court,
in *United States v. Kagama* (1886)

I am anxious to know where I may apply for a license to kill Indians. My forefathers helped settle the west and it was their tradition to kill every Redskin they saw. "The only good Indian is a dead Indian," they believed. I also want to keep faith with my ancestors.

Phillips Wylly, responding to the Makah
whale hunt (*Seattle Times*, May 23, 1999)

These people need to do something productive besides getting drunk and spending federal funds to live on.

Steve Grimwood (*Seattle Times*, May 23, 1999)

Racism is built into the foundation of this country and it has never gone away. It simply doesn't get articulated during periods of quiet when there is no conflict. It's moments like this when racism comes out into the open. But it was always there.

Dave Wellman, sociologist (*Seattle Times*, May 23, 1999)

Racism against Indians is alive and well in the United States and elsewhere. Although Wellman's quote (above) is correct in many situations, he is a professor at the University of California at Berkeley, in the San Francisco Bay area, and is not exposed to everyday reservation "border town" racism, or the racism of "local ill feeling" that is so pointedly mentioned in the Supreme Court's 1886 ruling.

People in urban areas, or quiet suburban and rural areas that are away from Indian country, often get their sense of what is happening from media coverage of certain "feel-good" issues—like the Sacajawea dollar, museum exhibit openings, popular movies (*Pocahontas* or *Dances With Wolves*), and so on. But, the truth is that for certain Indian people, especially reservation and border-town residents who are far from the bastions of "political correctness," racism is frequently all too real.

SECTION E: CULTURE AND RELIGION

> *So what is it you guys want . . . ? Secrets? Mystery? . . . I can tell you right now there are no secrets. There's no mystery. There's only common sense.*
>
> Oren Lyons, Onondaga elder
> comments to two non-Indian "seekers"
> in Wall and Arden (1990, p. 64)

E-1. *Do American Indians have a common cultural heritage?*

From a nationwide perspective, the general answer would have to be "no." The stereotypical image of horse-mounted warriors, wearing "war bonnets" and hunting bison, is far from being representative of the diverse cultural heritage of all American Indians.

At the time of first European contact, in the 15th century, hundreds of Native cultures existed in what is now the U.S. The fact is, there were as many individual cultures as there were tribes and smaller, self-sufficient living groups.

Anthropologists, archaeologists, and ethnologists have developed a broad system of 10 culture areas to classify the many Native cultures of America's past. (See Figure 4.) These areas were identified on the basis of such things as geographical influence, family and kinship systems, seasonal life, economic structure, and other factors (O'Brien 1989). Information relevant to these culture areas and the people who lived within them may be found in many thousands of books and articles published during the past century. Perhaps the best all-around source is the Smithsonian Institution's multi-volume work that is being published under the title "Handbook of North American Indians." Nearing completion, this 20-volume encyclopedic series summarizes what is known about the prehistory, history, and cultures of the indigenous peoples of North America. Most of the 11 volumes on the culture areas are now available through many libraries and book stores. (An easily accessible overview of early Native cultures is provided in the October 1991 issue of *National Geographic*. Other good starting places are: Champagne 1994; Dutton 1983;

Encyclopaedia Britannica 1990; Owen, Deetz, and Fisher 1967; Josephy 1994; Spicer 1982; Swanton 1969; Johnson 1999; Waldman 1985; and Woodhead 1992. A more extensive work is Trigger and Washburn 1996.)

Though the identified culture areas help in modern understanding of old cultures, it should be noted that they would have had no useful meaning for Native peoples of the past. Tribal territories were sometimes vague or changing. There was often much regional movement of tribes and transfer of cultural traits from one area to another. Interestingly, people of the same language family commonly lived in different cultures or even inhabited separate ends of the continent. The Athapaskan-speaking groups of the Subarctic and the Southwest are good examples.

Despite the diversity of traditional cultures, there are two broad phenomena which show a similarity in today's American Indians across the continent. These are: (1) nature-based, traditional lifeways and (2) a shared response to Euro-American society (Owen, Deetz,

Figure 4. The ten broad culture areas recognized for pre-Columbian American Indians on the basis of geography, kinship systems, seasonal life, economy, etc. (After Prucha 1990a.)

and Fisher 1967; Deloria 1973). With increased travel, communication, and inter-tribal marriage in the 21st century, the amount of
cross-cultural sharing and blending is also on the increase.

E-2. *What is the general relationship today between Indian tribes
and the anthropology profession?*

It is definitely strained. Some anthropologists (a term that includes
cultural, social, political, and economic anthropologists, and archaeologists as well) have good relations with tribes and some do not. A
number of tribes now have tribal anthropologists, some of whom are
tribal members. Generally speaking, however, most American
Indians greatly resent the fact that over many decades anthropologists have treated them and their ancestors not as fellow human
beings but merely as artifacts and subjects for research papers used
to advance their careers. In many cases, anthropologists are considered to have "stolen" cultural information and physical material
belonging to the tribes and their ancestors. And there is great resentment among tribes over the remains of their ancestors that have been
dug up and placed on public display in museum collections. The
federal government's Native American Graves Protection and
Repatriation Act of 1990 rose directly from that resentment.

In the past, anthropologists—through either arrogance, ignorance, insensitivity, or a combination thereof, and through a kind of
carte blanche afforded them by the federal government—called the
shots when it came to when, where, and how they would do their
archaeological and cultural studies. But this situation has been
almost completely reversed because of tribal activism.

The beginning of the modern movement against control by the
anthropology profession of American Indian artifacts and remains
can be traced to the publication of Vine Deloria, Jr.'s famous book
Custer Died for Your Sins in 1969. In a pointed tongue-in-cheek way,
Deloria begins his chapter "Anthropologists and other Friends" with:

> Into each life, it is said, some rain must fall. . . . Indians have
> anthropologists. . . . Over the years anthropologists have

succeeded in burying Indian communities so completely beneath the mass of irrelevant information that the total impact of the scholarly community on Indian people has become one of simple authority. Many Indians have come to parrot the ideas of anthropologists because it appears that the anthropologists know everything about Indian communities. Thus, many ideas that pass for Indian thinking are in reality theories originally advanced by anthropologists and echoed by Indian people in an attempt to communicate the real situation. (p. 78, 82).

But things have changed since Deloria fired his opening broadside. They have changed so much that in 1997, anthropologists Thomas Biolsi and Larry Zimmerman edited and published *Indians and Anthropologists: Vine Deloria, Jr., and the Critique of Anthropology.* It contains a series of ten insightful essays by noted anthropologists—the first by the editors themselves on "What's Changed, What Hasn't."

Perhaps a little ironically, the book's conclusion is written by Vine Deloria, Jr. After acknowledging changes he has noticed among anthropologists, Deloria points out areas that require additional attention. He then appeals to anthropologists to exercise a greater measure of humanity and intellectual and moral leadership in the profession. Deloria closes with:

It seems to me that after two decades of reasonably constructive reforms in the relationship between anthropologists and Indians, and with the passing of the elder generation of anthros who were victims of what Alfred North Whitehead described as "misplaced correctness," we have an opportunity to leave the colonial mentality behind us and bring the accumulated knowledge and insights of anthropology to bear on the larger arena of human activities. And we have the responsibility to do so. (p. 221)

Other useful works that explore the general issue of conflict between the archaeology profession and indigenous Americans include Swidler et al. (1997) and Watkins (2001).

E-3. *What is the basic philosophical difference between American culture at large and traditional American Indian culture?*

Recognizing that the two "cultures" are actually collections of numerous smaller cultures, a broad and contrasting comparison can nonetheless be made. Simply stated, *traditional* Native cultures (beyond the basic issues of survival) generally have had the acquisition of wisdom, the support of community, and the development of spiritual awareness as their philosophical goals. On the other hand, the larger American society is philosophically inclined toward acquisition of information and the development of profit—in financial or material form.

One caveat to remember is that there are no completely traditional Native cultures left in the United States. Many tribal groups, however, are philosophically close to their traditional past. The Hopi of Arizona and the traditional Kickapoo of south Texas are two examples. In addition, many Native groups that have not clung to their pasts still consider wisdom, community, and spiritualism their guiding ideals.

One further point is that western culture generally tends to measure its advancement by the distance it places between itself and nature. In contrast, traditional Native cultures tend to view greater closeness to the natural world and its cycles as a measure of significant achievement. [For a general comparison of traditional American Indian and traditional western European attitudes toward nature, see Callicott (1983).]

E-4. *Why are so many non-Indians especially interested in traditional Indian cultures, arts, and crafts?*

One can only surmise an answer, but this question addresses a truly ironic phenomenon. This country oppressed the Native people for so long through military, social, legal, educational, and economic measures. Yet, there is a surprisingly large segment of the population which, indeed, greatly admires the cultures of the first Americans.

In part, this admiration may stem from the romanticism which Americans associate with the larger nation's origins. The great human drama which unfolded as colonial America clashed with hundreds of smaller Native nations has always been a captivating theme. Many also recognize an inherent quality in the traditional social and material culture of American Indians that is generally lacking in our modern society. But, there is probably something much deeper.

Dr. Carl Sagan has said that humankind has always had a desire to feel connected with the cosmos. It is only in the last millennium that western society began to abandon the truly elemental life—a life that continued to be lived by a few Inuit in Alaska and Canada as recently as the early 1950s. Also, it was only in the 20th century—a mere snippet of the total period of human existence—that the television, radio, telephone, airplane, automobile, and other machines came to dominate the world. Could it be that, just below the surface of the popularity of Native culture, lies a faint human memory of an earlier era—when the "connectedness" Carl Sagan talks about was strongly felt by *all* people?

To explain this by example, in the early 1970s, T.C. McLuhan published what became an immensely popular book, *Touch the Earth* (1971). It consists, primarily, of beautiful photographs of American Indians taken at the turn of the century by renowned photographer Edward S. Curtis. The photographs are accompanied by selected quotations which describe a kinship with nature and unity with the elements. One could reasonably submit that many who acquire and read *Touch the Earth*, like the non-Indians who are actively interested in Native cultures, are vicariously trying to do as the title states.

Anthropology professor Alice Kehoe (1990) takes the explanation of the Indian popularity phenomenon one step farther. She ascribes much of it—as many others have—to "cultural primitivism," or the discontent of the civilized with civilization. "[H]undreds of thousands of Europeans and Americans, alienated by our culture . . . look to representations of non-Western cultures for 'authentic' experiences. To gain 'genuine' culture, they seek . . . Asian or American Indian" (Kehoe 1990, p. 194–195). This has also led to the relatively recent "Wanabe" syndrome. It is exemplified by thousands of "new age" non-Indians who want to be Indians in a spiritual sense. Unfortunately, in at least some instances, they interfere with the very cultures they so admire. (See, for example, Camp 1992, Little Eagle 1992, and Question E-5. See also the interesting book by Philip Deloria [1998], *Playing Indian.*)

E-5. *What do Indians think of the "New Age" non-Indians who take and teach from tribal cultures?*

> *We call them "poodle people," you know, "Dances With Poodles."*
> Two Navajo women and one White Mountain Apache, in response to the "New Age" question (February 2000)

This question was submitted to me by an acquaintance who is a member of a federally recognized tribe and has had what she calls "some offensive experiences with several newagers" coming to her reservation and interfering with her community.

Obviously, some Indian people (most that I've spoken with) view the "New Agers" as just silly. However, if a non-Indian's appropriation of culture and religion is more than minimal, many Indian people are greatly offended. On the other hand, there are some Indians who have taken economic and social advantage of the New Age phenomenon by becoming participants or even leaders of New Age groups.

Normally organizations like "The Rainbow Tribe" are viewed with disdain in much of Indian country. And publications of New Agers, such as Ed "Eagle Man" McGaa's *Rainbow Tribe: Ordinary People Journeying on the Red Road* or Winfried Noe's *Native American Astrology* (translated from German), are frequently scoffed at.

On the lighter side, reproduced below is selected material from an anonymous e-mail that recently circulated through Indian country in the U.S. and Canada. There is a message mixed with the humor.

> If you spend too much time around American Indians, you will discover that we have a deep dislike of "New Age Crystal Waving Twinkies" who shamelessly appropriate, distort, misuse and disrespect our cultures. Accordingly, if you want to get along with Indians, it is wise to avoid being a twinkie.
>
> The following test will help you determine if you're a twinkie. You might be a twinkie if [in the original e-mail version, this is followed by 125 statements, including the following]—
>
> 1. Your Indian spirit guide only speaks English.
> 2. You gave your dog an "authentic" Indian name.

3. Your great grandmother was a Cherokee princess.
4. YOU were a Cherokee princess—in a former life.
5. You don't know what a CDIB is, and wouldn't qualify for one if you did.
6. You mistook an Italian man (Iron Eyes Cody) for an Indian chief.
7. You are "part Cherokee" but you don't quite know how or how much.
8. You think Indians should put up with your New Age nonsense because, after all, "We are all related."
9. You just love what "Buffalo Spirit Woman" has to say on her website.
10. You had a dream in which you discovered your true name is "Spirit of the Red Wolf Who Runs with Crystals."

E-6. *What are the principal elements of the Indian Arts and Crafts Act of 1990?*

The Indian Arts and Crafts Act (IACA) is a remarkable piece of legislation, particularly concerning the no-nonsense penalties associated with it. The Act, which was amended in November 2000, is intended to promote the American Indian artwork and handcraft business, reduce foreign and counterfeit product competition, and halt deceptive marketing practices (Indian Arts and Crafts Board 1991a). Specifically, the act declares that, "It is unlawful to offer or display for sale or sell any good . . . in a manner that falsely suggests it is Indian produced, an Indian product, or the product of a particular Indian or Indian tribe or Indian arts and crafts organization, resident within the United States." Whoever knowingly violates the prohibition, if an individual, is subject to criminal prosecution and may be fined up to $250,000 for a first offense and jailed for up to five years. For a subsequent offense, the penalties can be up to $1,000,000 and 15 years of incarceration. If a violator is a corporation, the fines may be up to $1,000,000 on the first offense and up to $5,000,000 each time thereafter. The Indian Arts and Crafts Board of the Department of the Interior is authorized to receive relevant complaints and refer them to

Since passage of the sometimes controversial Indian Arts and Crafts Act of 1990, the work of American Indian artisans has enjoyed a greater degree of protection from counterfeit competition. Here, Evalena Henry, Master Basket Weaver, is shown demonstrating the process of making a basket in Tucson, Arizona. She is a San Carlos Apache.

the FBI for investigation. The Board may also recommend prosecution by the U.S. Department of Justice.

Civil suits may be brought under the Act by the U.S. Attorney General or an Indian tribe on behalf of itself, an individual Indian, or an Indian arts and crafts organization. Civil penalties can include an injunction, or other equitable relief, and the greater of (1) treble damages or (2) $1,000 for each day the violation continues for each aggrieved Indian, tribe, or Native arts and crafts association. Punitive damages and legal costs may also be awarded.

The IACA defines an Indian as an individual who is a member of an Indian tribe or who, if not a member, is certified as an Indian artisan by a tribe. Tribes cannot charge a fee for certification, and they are not required to have an artist certification program. "Tribe" is defined as (1) any tribe, band, nation, Alaska Native village, or other organized group or community which is federally recognized or (2) any Indian group which is formally (legally) recognized by a state.

Regarding the sale of Indian products from Canadian, Mexican, Central American, or South American Native groups, the Indian Arts and Crafts Board now recommends that sellers clearly state that the products are not made by U.S. Indians. The Board also recommends to Indian artists, tribes, museums, and retailers that, before an art work or hand craft is offered or displayed for sale, verification of the maker's tribal membership be furnished or obtained. Copies of tribal documents showing membership (such as CDIBs), artist enrollment numbers, or written guarantees of intermediate sellers would probably be sufficient to show compliance with the Act in most cases (Indian Arts and Crafts Board 1991b). The Board has promulgated specific regulations for implementation of the IACA. The regulations, which were adopted in 1996, are intended to clarify ambiguities in the act and specify compliance procedures. They are published in Part 309 of Title 25 of the Code of Federal Regulations.

E-7. *How many Indian languages are there?*

> *Language defines our lives. It heralds our existence, it formulates our thoughts, it enables all we are and have.*
>
> Steven Fischer (2000, p. 100), from
> *A History of Language.*

It is believed that about 300 languages were spoken by the Native residents of North America in 1492 when Columbus arrived in the Western Hemisphere (Campbell and Mithun 1979). These ancestral languages have been classified into several major linguistic groups. Though not all experts agree on the classifications, eight language group names have been commonly employed: Algonquian, Athapaskan, Caddoean, Iroquoian, Muskhogean, Penutian, Siouan, and Uto-Aztecan (Bureau of Indian Affairs 1974).

About 250 Native languages are identified with what is now the United States. Many are no longer viable because they are rarely, if ever, spoken. Even so, more than 100 languages are spoken by contemporary American Indians. In some tribes, however, only a handful of speakers remain. It is estimated that approximately one-third of all American Indians still speak their languages (Parsons Yazzie 2000). Navajo, Iroquois, Inuit (Eskimo), Tohono O'odham, Pima, Apache, and Sioux peoples show the highest percentages of Native speakers (Waldman 1985).

On October 26, 1992, President Bush signed into law a legislative measure that helps counter the loss of Native languages. It authorizes the Administration for Native Americans to make grants to tribal governments and other groups to teach children, train educators and interpreters, compile histories, develop teaching materials, and acquire equipment for language lessons (Indian Country Today, November 5, 1992).

E-8. *Was the speaking of Native languages prohibited historically?*

> *For the first half of this century, my agency, the BIA, tried to destroy Native languages.*
>
> Kevin Grover, USDI Assistant Secretary of
> Indian Affairs (*In* Rolo 1999, p. 1).

Yes, but the prohibition was not a legislative or wholesale one. It was generally limited to the religious and government schools attended by Indian children (Deloria 1973). The effects of enforced limitations on language in schools throughout the country, from the 1870s through the 1950s, have been marked. Because so many Indian children attended boarding schools during this era, their young-life experiences provided little opportunity for learning their own languages. They, in turn, often raised children who learned only English.

Religious schools established for Aleut people in Alaska, in the 19th century, taught written and spoken Aleut until the last school, at Unalaska, was forcibly closed in 1912 by education officials who opposed the use of Native languages (Lantis 1984).

E-9. *What is the "Native American Languages Act?"*

General enlightenment, increased emphasis on the importance of culture, and increased tribal control over education have brought an end to the language prohibition policies described in question E-8. A highlight of this evolution occurred on October 30, 1990, when Title I of Public Law 101-477 was signed into law as the Native American Languages Act. It declares a United States policy "to preserve, protect, and promote the rights and freedoms of Native Americans to use, practice, and develop Native American languages." This act officially reversed the scattered policies of the 19th and 20th centuries that so devastated Native languages.

The act covers the Native languages of all Native Americans, be they Indian, Inuit, Aleut, Chamorro, Native Hawaiian, Samoan, or Northern Marianan (25 U.S.C. sec. 2901).

E-10. *How do tribal members feel about their languages, language loss, and how their languages should be maintained and preserved?*

It is healing to totally embrace your spirit and who you are by speaking your language. It's like coming home.

Lee Staples, Ojibwe elder
(Associated Press 2000a, p. C-6)

The language is alive. When we translate it to English, we lose that life.

Dr. Betty Bastien, Blackfeet educator
(Mistaken Chief 2000, p. 27)

The ceremonies are supposed to be done in the language given to us, and that's not happening any more.

Larry Smallwood, Ojibwe language teacher
(Associated Press 2000a, p. C-6)

> *To save our languages, we must change our teaching methods.*
>
> Dr. Richard Littlebear, Cheyenne educator
> (Littlebear 2000, p. 18)

Only about 20 of the 155 Native languages now spoken in the U.S. are expected to survive through the next century (Associated Press 2000b), therefore tribal languages are of special concern. When we also realize that only about 35 of the remaining Native languages in the U.S. and Canada are currently being spoken by children, a very real sense of urgency develops, because when the children are no longer learning a language, the language is dying (Reyhner 2000; see also Crawford 1994).

The spring 2000 issue of *Tribal College,* the journal of American Indian higher education, was dedicated to Native languages, a subject that is much more complicated and charged with emotion than most of us are able to comprehend.

In that issue Jon Reyhner (2000) of Northern Arizona University assembled a remarkable collection of information sources in *A Resource Guide: Native American language renewal.* His sources on Native language materials are listed under the subheadings of: Programs and Organizations; Videos; Internet Indexes, Sites, and Discussion Groups; Books, Monographs, and Conference Proceedings; Special Issues of Journals; and Online Articles, Chapters, & Papers. No serious student of American Indian language issues can ignore this useful resource guide. (*Tribal College* has a website at www.tribalcollegejournal.org. The telephone number is (970) 533-9170.)

> *At the same time that R. C. Gorman* [the famous Navajo artist] *was being punished for speaking Navajo at school, his father, Carl Gorman, was serving as a Navajo code talker in the Marines* [in WWII].
>
> Marjane Ambler, Editor of
> *Tribal College* (2000, p. 8)

E-11. *What religious practices have Indian people generally observed, both before and after Euro-American influence?*

BEFORE

There were at least as many specific religions as independent tribes, bands, clans, villages, and living groups. Nonetheless, all religious activity evolved within a common framework of life processes affected by a familiar natural environment. Ruth Underhill (1957) developed a generalized overview of past Indian religion, based on her extensive research. That overview is summarized here and is supplemented with information from Lamphere (1983) and Lantis (1984). Underhill also gave an excellent, in-depth introduction to traditional Native religion in her 1965 book, *Red Man's Religion: Beliefs and Practices of the Indians North of Mexico*. And, Vecsey (1991) has compiled some useful essays in a book on traditional Indian religious issues that are often debated in the media and sometimes contested in court. Another classic work on Native religions is by Hultkrantz (1987).

American Indians' homelands and religions were closely intertwined. The land, the environment, and a strong sense of place all had great religious significance. Essentially everything was tied to the supernatural, which led to a proliferation of religious practices across the continent. Despite their great number, most of the practices come under one or more of six basic areas of supernatural concern.

Universal Force

Native religion was often imbued with the concept that an invisible force pervades the universe. This force could be focused on any special place, being, or object, endowing it with supernatural power. Such words as the Aleut *Agudar*, Lakota *Wakan*, Iroquois *Orenda*, and Algonquian *Manitou* were used to refer to this universal force.

Taboo

Certain taboos developed because the focus of power in a being or object could be dangerous to someone who was not in a sacred state. The most widespread taboos pertained to the three "life crises" of birth, puberty, and death. Rituals or techniques of avoidance were used to deal with these uncontrollable events, not because of uncleanliness,

These Piegan Blackfeet are taking part in a Medicine Lodge ceremony. They are Spotted Eagle, Chief Elk, and Bull Child. The whistles they are blowing are made from sacred eagle bones.

but because those in "crisis" were subject to supernatural power. They, or those nearby, needed to do things to keep themselves and others safe. Menstruating women and those giving birth were often secluded, especially among the hunter and gatherer groups. Some form of spiritual purification (e.g., a "sweat") or a period of withdrawal might also be observed by the bereaved, and even by hunters after killing a particular animal such as a whale. This was because the soul of the dead person or special animal might desire company or revenge.

Spirits

All groups believed in spirits and the need to deal with them, one way or another. Besides spirits of the dead—some of whom might end up as individual or group guardians—there were the spirits of plants, animals, places, and natural phenomena. Underhill (1957) wrote:

> To most Indians, there [was] no sharp dividing line between these and human beings. The Sioux spoke of all living things as the two-leggeds, the four-leggeds, and the wingeds. All these had life and must be treated as fellow beings. So must plants and Mother Earth who bore them.

Wild things were treated with consideration, and apologies were sometimes made to game after the kill. The hope was that the animal spirits would be appeased and go back to their own villages, later to return in tangible form to again feed the people.

Not all groups identified a high god or supreme spirit. Some who did were the Algonquian ("Great Spirit"), the Creek ("Master of Breath"), and the Lakota ("Creator").

Visions

These took many forms among Native groups. Some visions were sought at puberty, especially among boys, to guide their personal growth and success through life as hunters, warriors, cultivators, or group leaders. A vision quest might be done once, or it might be repeated through life. Seclusion and fasting often played roles, and, perhaps, ordeals of self-inflicted pain and suffering were experienced. Frequently, the vision included an animal guide who might teach a special song, give instructions, or describe a power-giving fetish.

The Shaman

A "medicine man," or shaman, was a top visionary. His, and sometimes her, power frequently came from direct contact with the supernatural. In addition, it might be enhanced by inheritance, or training as an apprentice. A shaman's baseline power could be obtained through quest, ordeal, or unsought dreams. It was the hunter-gatherer groups which had full shamanic belief systems. Their cultural and physical survival depended on a balance of various natural and supernatural forces, of which the shaman was guardian.

Acting as a mediator between the visible and invisible worlds, the shaman's jobs were many. They included foretelling the future, and helping to achieve good hunting, good fishing, a good harvest, success in battle, favorable weather, health, and safe childbirth. Often, the shaman's primary function was curing, frequently by "removal" of some maligning influence in a patient. This might be accomplished through rubbing, blowing, smoking, brushing, singing, art symbolism, the spreading of sacred pollen or meal, and sometimes herbology.

In some societies a distinction was made between a shaman, as a holy man, and as an herbal healer. A shaman, acting as a priest, could direct one or more sacred ceremonies, but someone with only herbal training would not have been qualified to direct these special events.

Communal Ceremony

Groups held ceremonies because they served as a communal appeal to the spirits, asking for their help in achieving some common goals. Typically, such goals included maintaining or increasing necessary plant and animal life, protecting warriors, restoring of health, giving thanks, and securing long life and well-being for individuals and the community. Hunters and food gatherers found it difficult or impossible to participate in large ceremonies during most of the year because there was not enough food available to sustain everyone. On the plains, for example, ceremonies might occur only during such times as an annual buffalo drive. Large ceremonies were most frequently observed by the agriculturists, like those of the Pueblo communities, whose food supplies and more sedentary circumstances would support the activity. Some of the practices observed in communal ceremonies included sacred dancing, singing, smoking, drumming, feasting, and making use of holy objects.

AFTER

By various means, Christianity has made enormous inroads into Native society over the last five hundred years. Among some groups, like the Aleut who were thoroughly converted to the Russian Orthodox Church in the 19th century, few if any traditionalists remain. Today, most (but certainly not all) religious Native people practice Christianity, or a combination of it and Native religion. During the past three decades, however, there has been a resurgence of Native interest in traditional religious practices. This has occurred throughout the country and includes groups which had been separated from their religious traditions for many years. Religious freedom is a premier concern among American Indians today.

Several useful sources on Indian religion are not cited in the above answer. They are: Basso, *Wisdom Sits in Places* (1996); Deloria's books *God is Red* (1973), *Red Earth White Lies* (1995), and *For this Land* (1999); Echo-Hawk, *Native American Religious Liberty* (1992); LaBarre, *The Ghost Dance* (1972); and the scattered materials on religion in volumes 5–15 of the Smithsonian Institution's *Handbook of North American Indians*.

Some additional introductory works, suitable for a wide age-range, include Woodhead (1992b), Hirschfelder and Molin (1992), and Champagne (1994).

You have got our country, but are not satisfied; you want to force your religion upon us. . . . Brother, you say there is but one way to worship and serve the Great Spirit; if there is but one religion, why do you white people differ so much about it? Why do you not all agree, as you can all read the book? . . .

We are told that your religion was given to your forefathers, and has been handed down from father to son. We also have a religion which was given to our forefathers, and has been handed down to us, their children. We worship that way. It teacheth us to be thankful for all the favors we receive; to love each other; and to be united. We never quarrel about religion.

Brother, the Great Spirit has made us all; but he made a great difference between his white and red children; he has given us a different complexion, and different customs. . . . Since he has made so great a difference between us in other things, why may we not conclude that he has given us a different religion? . . .

Brother! We do not wish to destroy your religion, or take it from you. We only want to enjoy our own.

> Seneca "Sagoyewatha" (He who Keeps Them Awake),
> or "Red Jacket," in the late 1700s, responding
> to a member of the Boston Missionary Society
> (Josephy 1994, p. 283)

Ancient traditional religions survive and remain strong among some native peoples while others practice Christianity exclusively. Some Indian people pray in church and attend Indian healing ceremonies, finding that both traditions offer spiritual comfort. Some people mix

> *Catholocism and ancient practices, and others follow the practices
> of the Native American Church, which attracts followers from many
> tribes.*
>
> Hirschfelder and Montaño (1993, p. 111)

E-12. Is it true that traditional Indian religious ceremonies were outlawed historically?

> *What destroyed our culture the most was the coming of the mission-
> aries. . . . They tried to destroy our beliefs. . . . The language has been
> almost completely lost. . . . [A]ll the Christian religions prohibited
> us from speaking our own language. . . . And by doing so, then they
> were entering into our lives very, very fast. So what was going on
> in the background was a big loss of identity. A loss of culture.*
>
> Danielle Sioui (Huron)
> *In* Josephy 1994, p. 283

Yes. Spanish prohibitions are well known. They began shortly after the arrival of Columbus and coincided with the Spanish Inquisition. Horrible punishments were meted out for "pagan" activities. Those charged were tortured in a number of ways, including slow roasting over a fire or being garroted. The latter was a common practice used by the Spaniards to achieve strangulation by progressively twisting a rope around the neck (Rosenstiel 1983).

Though generally much less severe than the Spanish policy, American colonial policy was also oppressive. As early as 1646, the Massachusetts Bay Colony, following requests by "Apostle" John Elliot, outlawed the practice of Native religion in the special "pray-ing towns" set aside for certain Indian groups. Some sources say violation of the religious practice rule was done "under pain of death" (Axtell 1988), though others suggest the death penalty was limited to murder, bestiality, and adultery (Spicer 1969).

In 1883, Secretary of the Interior Henry M. Teller (with backing from Christian religious organizations) established what came to be known on Indian reservations as "courts of Indian offenses." Teller's initial goal for the courts, which evolved to cover numerous minor offenses, was to eliminate "heathenish practices" among the Indians. The rules of the courts, published in the 1880s and 1890s, effectively forbade the practice of all public and private religious activities by traditional tribal members on their reservations (Prucha 1990b). Significantly, non-Indians were not subject to prosecution for participating in the same activities.

4. *Offenses.*—For the purpose of these regulations the following shall be deemed to constitute *offenses*, and the judges of the Indian court shall severally have jurisdiction to try and punish for the same when committed within their respective districts.

(a) Dances, etc.—Any Indian who shall engage in the sun dance, scalp dance, or war dance, or any similar feast, so called, shall be deemed guilty of an offense, and upon conviction thereof shall be punished for the offense by the withholding of his rations for not exceeding ten days or by imprisonment for not exceeding ten days; and for any subsequent offense under this clause he shall be punished by withholding his rations for not less than ten nor more than thirty days, or by imprisonment for not less than ten nor more than thirty days. . . .

(c) Practices of medicine men.—Any Indian who shall engage in the practices of so-called medicine men, or who shall resort to any artifice or device to keep the Indians of the reservation from adopting and following civilized habits and pursuits, or shall adopt any means to prevent the attendance of children at school, or shall use any arts of the conjurer to prevent Indians from abandoning their barbarous rights and customs, shall be deemed to be guilty of an offense, and upon conviction thereof, for the first offense shall be imprisoned for not less than ten nor more than thirty days: *Provided,* That for any subsequent conviction for such offense the maximum term of imprisonment shall not exceed six months.

Official antagonism toward Native religion by the federal government continued at least into the 1920s when Commissioner of Indian

Affairs Charles Burke sent his famous letter "To all Indians." He urged them to give up "dances" and "ceremonies" voluntarily or he might be forced to "issue an order against these useless and harmful performances" (Spicer 1969, p. 241). Unofficial antagonism continues today, both directly and indirectly, through adverse legislative, executive, and judicial decisions and actions. This is in spite of the fact that a Congressional resolution on American Indian Religious Freedom was passed in 1978 and amended in 1994. (See also the Religious Freedom Restoration Act of 1993.)

> *TRADITION IS THE ENEMY OF PROGRESS.*
>
> Message on a large sign at the entrance to a Christian mission on
> the Navajo Reservation, circa 1950s

E-13. *What is the Native American Church?*

> *The right to free religious expression embodies a precious heritage of our history.*
>
> California Supreme Court
> *People v. Woody* 1964, p. 821

The Native American Church (N.A.C.) is a greatly misunderstood religious organization of Indians. Its practices, which are threatened, have been at the forefront of the recent struggle for Indian religious freedom in the United States. The church is numerically important because it has the largest membership of any Indian organization in the country—approximately 250,000 members from more than 50 tribes in the U.S. and Canada. Official membership in the U.S. has been judicially recognized as being "limited to Native American members of federally recognized tribes who have at least 25 percent Native American ancestry" (*Peyote Way Church of God, Inc. v. Thornburgh* 1991). Non-members, both Indian and non-Indian, have sometimes been allowed to participate in peyote rituals by subgroups of the church.

The religion teaches an ethical doctrine very similar to those of the monotheistic religions, and is related to Christianity. However, it has avoided the specific "Christian" label, partly in reaction to the subordinate place so often given to Christian Indian converts in church organization (Underhill 1974). The most notable and controversial aspect of the N.A.C. is its use of the peyote cactus as a sacrament.

Peyote

Stewart (1987) describes peyote as a small, spineless cactus native to the Rio Grande region of south Texas and northeast Mexico. It grows several inches high from a long tap root, sprouting single or multiple fleshy "buttons" of one to two inches across. The buttons contain alkaloid compounds, the most significant of which is mescaline, an hallucinogen. They are extremely bitter. When ingested by chewing or in a tea, peyote frequently causes nausea and sometimes vomiting.

Peyote buttons are harvested by severing them from the tap root, which will continue to produce buttons. After removal, they are dried before consumption. Peyote buttons can produce sensations that include a warm and pleasant euphoria, an agreeable point of view, relaxation, colorful visual distortions, and a sense of timelessness. Non-religious consumption of peyote is considered by N.A.C. members to be a very serious sacrilege (Slotkin 1967). Drug experts, anthropologists, and courts have determined that peyote is not habit-forming and that the peyote religion does indeed have an observed positive moral effect on its Indian members. (See *Peyote Way Church of God v. Thornburgh* 1991; Stewart 1987; Farb 1968; *People v. Woody* 1964; *Toledo v. Nobel-Sysco, Inc.* 1986; Underhill 1965 and 1974.)

Church History

Some people believe the N.A.C. was an offshoot of the "hippie" era of the 1960s. This is completely untrue. However, that view probably arose with publicity surrounding a high degree of non-Indian use of peyote during the era (Brand 1988). The federal government's first prohibition of non-religious use of peyote occurred in 1966.

Peyote use in Mexico as a folk remedy and for religious purposes predates European arrival. References to peyote religion in Spanish records go back to 1560. Also, Spanish attempts to outlaw peyotism because of its competition with Catholicism began at least as early as 1620. Use of peyote by some members of Pueblo tribes in what is now New Mexico was recorded in the 1630s. Therefore, investigation into the origins of modern peyotism among American Indians discloses a history of centuries (Anderson 1996; La Barre 1989; Stewart 1991).

Tribes from the areas which became New Mexico and Texas, who were familiar with peyote from the early 1600s, include the Lipan Apache, Tonkawa, Mescalero Apache, Caddo, Carrizo, and Karankawa. Later, the Comanche, Kiowa, and Kiowa-Apache encountered peyotism as a result of extensive raids made in Mexico. In the mid- and late-1800s, all but the Mescalero were removed by the U.S. to Oklahoma. For 400 years, the various Oklahoma tribes had scattered experiences with the religion. Late in the 1800s, the Plains version of peyotism arose in Oklahoma. The "new" religion helped tribes cope with loss of their cultures and freedom, maintain a sense of spiritual independence from the ever-present missionaries, and deal with repressive control exercised over them by White society (Farb 1968).

Comanche Chief Quannah Parker and 10 other leading peyotists supported peyotism at the 1907 Oklahoma Constitutional Convention. The state legislature subsequently recognized peyotism as a bona-fide religion in 1908 (Stewart 1987 and 1991). In 1918, the N.A.C. was officially organized in Oklahoma as the corporate form of the peyotist religion. A need to broaden the church arose as the religion spread around the U.S. Another Oklahoman charter established the N.A.C. of the United States in 1950. The name was soon revised to the N.A.C. of North America to accommodate peyotists of Canada. It is now the official primary church of Native peyotists of the continent, many of whom have incorporated local N.A.C. chapters where permitted by law.

Theology

American Indian peyotists believe peyote is a sacred and powerful spiritual plant. Even its name, coming from the Aztec word *peyotl*, means "divine messenger." The several forms of the peyote religion combine Indian and Christian elements in varying degrees. In many tribes, the cactus is personified as Peyote Spirit—considered to be God's equivalent for the Indian to His Jesus for the non-Indian. Peyote is seen as a medicine, protector, and teacher. Consuming it in a ritual context allows an individual to commune with God and the spirits and to receive spiritual power, guidance, reproof, and healing. Peyotism teaches brotherly love, obedience to parents, fidelity to spouse, family care, charity, self-support through steady work, and avoidance of alcohol. This way of life is known as the Peyote Road. (See *Toledo v. Nobel-Sysco, Inc.* 1986; Encyclopaedia Britannica 1990; Stewart 1987.)

Ritual

Peyote ceremonies are held on the request of a church member. They may be conducted for healing, to honor a person, to acknowledge a death, to send someone away, to welcome someone home, and for general purposes of worship. The all-night ritual usually begins on a Saturday evening and usually takes place in a teepee around a crescent-shaped earthen altar and a sacred fire. Services are directed by a "Road Man" and include prayer, singing, sacramental eating of peyote, water rites, contemplation, and testimonials. At dawn on Sunday morning, a communion breakfast is eaten. Prayers are then offered, asking God's help for Indians, non-Indians, and all the world, thus ending the meeting (Stewart 1987; Underhill 1965 and 1974).

Legality

Federal legislation outlaws possession and distribution of peyote (21 U.S. Code, Secs. 812, 841, and 844). However, bona-fide religious use of the cactus by members of the N.A.C. is currently exempted from the law (See American Indian Religious Freedom Act Amendments of 1994; 21 Code of Federal Regulations, Sec. 1307.31; *Peyote Way Church of God, Inc. v. Thornburgh* 1991). The federal exemption is legally considered to be political and not racial, based on (1) the "quasi-sovereign" nation status of the tribes to which the church's members belong and (2) the government's objective and responsibility of preserving American Indian culture. In the *Peyote Way* case, the court said that each state had three legal options concerning peyote use. It could forbid anyone to use it, allow use only by members of the N.A.C., or allow all bona-fide religious use of the cactus. The states seemed willing to accept only one or the other of the first two options, but Congressional legislation is the controlling authority.

In 1987 the Pentagon issued rules that recognize and control the sacramental use of peyote by members of the U.S. military who are also bona fide members of the Native American Church (Native American Rights Fund 1997).

E-14. *Is there more tolerance for Native religions today?*

Though it is not universal, the general answer would have to be "yes." A moving example is the "Public Declaration of Apology" made in 1987 to Indian and Eskimo people of the Pacific Northwest by an ecumenical group of Christian religious leaders (See Appendix 5.) In addition, on October 30, 1991, clergy from Alaska's Roman Catholic, Lutheran, Russian Orthodox, and Presbyterian Churches made public apologies directed to all Alaska natives. They referred to their churches' actions for the past 200 years by saying:

> We have responded with fear, suspicion, arrogance, hostility, and a patronizing attitude that treats your people like children. . . . [We] pray for your forgiveness for our sins against your people.
>
> Associated Press 1991a

Officiating at the special service was Father John Hascall, a Catholic Priest and Ojibwe medicine man from Michigan. Father Hascall was quoted (Associated Press 1991a) as saying to the non-Indian participants, "I don't want you to feel sorry for us. I want you to look at us as Native people, as people of sovereign nations, which we are. As people of high morals. As people of high respect. As people who want to be equal."

Despite these statements and similar apologies, a major need remained to strengthen the American Indian Religious Freedom Act through legislative action. Primary purposes behind changing the act included protecting traditional Native religions, sacraments of the Native American Church, and sacred sites (see E-15). Sacred sites have not received the kind of federal legislative protection that many Indian people had hoped for, but some of them prevailed upon President Clinton to issue an executive order (1996) directing federal agencies to accommodate access to and ceremonial use of sacred sites by "Indian religious practitioners."

E-15. *What is the American Indian Religious Freedom Act?*

The original 1978 "Act" (reproduced on page 157–58) is actually a joint resolution by the U.S. Senate and House of Representatives. It expresses the general policy of the U.S. government toward traditional "Native American" religions (since Native Hawaiians were included) and their practice. The resolution's specific purpose, as stated in its legislative history, is "to insure that the policies and procedures of various Federal agencies, as they impact upon the exercise of traditional Indian Religious practices, are brought into compliance with the constitutional injunction that Congress shall make no laws abridging the free exercise of religion." The brief resolution had no enforcement provisions. This deficiency, as well as Supreme Court cases which all but made a mockery of the resolution (e.g., *Lyng v. Northwest Indian Cemetery Protective Association* 1988 and *Employment Division, Department of Human Resources of Oregon v. Smith* 1990), stimulated legislative proposals to strengthen protections for Native religious activity. The 1988 *Lyng* case dealt with sacred sites, and the 1990 *Smith* case dealt with sacramental use of peyote.

Public Law 95–341
95th Congress

Joint Resolution
American Indian Religious Freedom.

Whereas the freedom of religion for all people is an inherent right, fundamental to the democratic structure of the United States and is guaranteed by the First Amendment of the United States Constitution;

Whereas the United States has traditionally rejected the concept of a government denying individuals the right to practice their religion and, as a result, has benefited from a rich variety of religious heritages in this country;

Whereas the religious practices of the American Indian (as well as Native Alaskan and Hawaiian) are an integral part of their culture, tradition and heritage, such practices forming the basis of Indian identity and value systems;

Whereas the traditional American Indian religions, as an integral part of Indian life, are indispensable and irreplaceable;

Whereas the lack of a clear, comprehensive, and consistent Federal policy has often resulted in the abridgment of religious freedom for traditional American Indians;

Whereas such religious infringements result from the lack of knowledge of the insensitive and inflexible enforcement of Federal policies and regulations premised on a variety of laws;

Whereas such laws were designed for such worthwhile purposes as conservation and preservation of natural species and resources but were never intended to relate to Indian religious practices and, therefore, were passed without consideration of their effect on traditional American Indian religions;

Whereas such laws and policies often deny American Indians access to sacred sites required in their religions, including cemeteries;

Whereas such laws at times prohibit the use and possession of sacred objects necessary to the exercise of religious rites and ceremonies;

Whereas traditional American Indian ceremonies have been intruded upon, interfered with, and in a few instances banned; Now, therefore, be it

Resolved by the Senate and House of Representatives of the United States of America in Congress assembled, That henceforth it shall be the policy of the United States to protect and preserve for American Indians their inherent right of freedom to believe, express, and exercise the traditional religions of the American Indian, Eskimo, Aleut, and Native Hawaiians, including but not limited to access to sites, use and possession of sacred objects, and the freedom to worship through ceremonials and traditional rites.

SEC. 2. The President shall direct the various Federal departments, agencies, and other instrumentalities responsible for administering relevant laws to evaluate their policies and procedures in consultation with Native traditional religious leaders in order to determine appropriate changes necessary to protect and preserve Native American religious cultural rights and practices. Twelve months after approval of this resolution, the President shall report back to Congress the results of his evaluation, including any changes which were made in administrative policies and procedures, and any recommendations he may have for legislative action.

Approved August 11, 1978.

In response to the U.S. Supreme Court's damaging decisions in *Lyng* and *Smith* and other non-Indian cases, Congress passed the "Religious Freedom Restoration Act" in 1993 (it is sometimes *unofficially* referred to as one of the "American Indian Religious Freedom Act Amendments"). The act stated that, generally, the "Government shall not substantially burden a person's exercise of religion if the burden results from a rule of general applicability." It then gave the exceptions that (1) there can be a burden if a rule "is in the furtherance of a compelling governing interest," and (2) the rule is the "least restrictive means of furthering that compelling governmental interest."

The 1993 act (in conjunction with the 1996 Executive Order by President Clinton) provided help with "sacred sites" issues for American Indians, but significant difficulties remained for members of the Native American Church regarding their use of peyote as a sacrament. Therefore, Congress passed the American Indian Religious Freedom Act Amendments of 1994 specifically to overcome the impediment created by the *Smith* case and other legal problems existing in the laws of a number of states. The key declaration of the 1994 legislation is: "the use, possession, or transportation of peyote by an Indian for bona fide traditional ceremony purposes in connection with the practice of a traditional Indian religion is lawful, and shall not be prohibited by the United States or any state. No Indian shall be penalized or discriminated against on the basis of such use, possession or transportation." [Sec. 1996(b)(1)].

E-16. *What is the Native American Graves Protection and Repatriation Act?*

> *The act* [NAGPRA] *is important because it represents the new American consensus about sacred objects and cultural patrimony, a consensus not only of members of the Congress and of Native peoples, but also of very diverse groups of scientists, museum*

> *trustees, and art collectors. That consensus is: The sacred culture of Native American[s] and Native Hawaiians is a living heritage. This culture is a vital part of the ongoing lifeways of the United States and, as such, must be respected, protected, and treated as a living spiritual entity—not as a remnant museum specimen.*
>
> Rennard Strickland (1997, p. 85–86)

The Native American Graves Protection and Repatriation Act, or NAGPRA, became law in 1990. It is now the strongest federal legislation pertaining to aboriginal remains and artifacts. The act acknowledges the interests which Native communities, including Native Hawaiians, have in this aspect of their heritage (Price 1991). The act has several significant provisions. All agencies and private museums which receive funding from the federal government were given five years to inventory their collections of Native American human remains and related funerary objects. After they completed their inventories, the agencies and museums were required to notify the tribes where the materials originated, or which are culturally affiliated, or from whose land the materials came. If a tribe requests that remains and objects be returned, that request is to be honored.

The law establishes that American Indian tribal groups own or control human remains or cultural items which are discovered on tribal and federal lands. They also have the right to determine the disposition of such discovered remains and items. NAGPRA further prohibits trafficking in aboriginal human remains and cultural items when these materials are obtained in violation of the act's provisions (Price 1991; Sockbeson 1990).

The act does not apply to materials found on private or state land, and the Smithsonian Institution is also exempted from the law. An earlier and separate law, the National Museum of the American Indian Act (1989), specifically addresses the repatriation issue as it pertains to the Smithsonian.

An excellent early source on NAGPRA is the Spring 1992 issue of the *Arizona State Law Journal* (De Vallance 1992), which contains contributions by Sen. John McCain, Walter Echo-Hawk, Sen. Daniel Inouye, Rennard Strickland, and 21 other notable authors. A more recent book on NAGPRA and the repatriation of American Indian remains is by Mihesuah (2000).

In the summer of 1986, . . . a number of Northern Cheyenne Chiefs visited Washington, D.C. During the course of their visit they arranged to tour the Smithsonian Institution's Cheyenne collection at the National Museum of Natural History. "As we were walking out," a Northern Cheyenne woman who worked on Capitol Hill later recalled, "we saw [the] huge ceilings in the room, with row upon row of drawers. Someone remarked there must be a lot of Indian stuff in those drawers. Quite casually, a curator with us said, 'Oh, this is where we keep the skeletal remains,' and he told us how many— 18,500. Everyone was shocked." . . . This discovery . . . helped generate a national Indian movement that eventually resulted in . . . enactment [of] NAGPRA.

Sockbeson 1990, p. 1

In 1868, for example, the Surgeon General of the United States ordered Army personnel to procure as many Indian crania as possible for the Army Medical Museum. Under that order, the heads of more than 4,000 Indians were taken from battlefields, prisoner camps and hospitals, and from fresh graves or burial scaffolds across the country.

Sockbeson 1990, p. 2

The NAGPRA represents a major federal shift away from viewing Native American human remains as "archaeological resources" or "federal property" alone. Instead, the government is slowly beginning to view these remains as Native Americans do—as our ancestors.

Sockbeson 1990, p. 2

E-17. *What is the Indian Child Welfare Act?*

In 1978, Congress passed two major pieces of legislation to help protect the social and cultural integrity of American Indians. The first was the joint resolution on American Indian Religious Freedom. The second was the Indian Child Welfare Act. In this act, Congress addressed a major concern: that Indian children who had to be placed with foster or adoptive parents often ended up with non-Indian families and were raised outside their Native culture.

Congress declared that part of the federal trust responsibility of the United States is:

> to protect the best interests of Indian children and to promote the stability and security of Indian tribes and families by the establishment of minimum federal standards for the removal of Indian children from their families and placement of such children in foster homes . . . which will reflect the unique values of Indian culture, and by providing for assistance to Indian tribes in the operation of child and family service programs.

The heart of the act has four basic provisions. They include: (1) definitions of tribal and state jurisdictions over child placement, (2) authorization for tribes and states to enter into agreements for the care and custody of Indian children and jurisdiction over child custody proceedings, (3) a provision that full faith and credit be accorded by states to the laws and court decisions of Indian tribes in child placement cases, and (4) a requirement that preference be given to an Indian child's extended family or Indian homes and institutions if a foster home or adoptive placement is necessary (Cohen 1982).

The Indian Child Welfare Act does not cover custody proceedings between parents in connection with divorce. It was specifically designed to protect the integrity of tribes and the heritage of Indian children. The act does this by directly inhibiting the common practice of taking Indian children, who were in troubled homes, from their families and tribes and then raising them as non-Indians (Canby 1981).

E-18. *Are cultural and intellectual property rights important issues to Indian tribes?*

Very much so. Cultural property is often defined as historical, archaeological, and ethnographic objects, works of art, and architecture that represent a culture (Guest 1995). Hundreds of tribes demonstrated their desire to protect such properties when they supported passage of the Native American Graves Protection and Repatriation Act of 1990 (see E-16). The act was passed by Congress to protect not just graves, but the sensibilities and dignities of tribal peoples and aspects of tribal cultures that involve particular kinds of cultural property. Although NAGPRA obviously focused on protection of graves, remains, and funerary objects, its passage signaled a national turning point in: (1) the desire by tribes to be taken seriously regarding *their* claims to the many aspects of *their* cultures, and (2) the larger society's willingness to actually take Indian concerns seriously.

The title alone of an article on NAGPRA by Cherokee attorney Rennard Strickland (1998) speaks volumes: "Implementing the National Policy of Understanding, Preserving, and Safeguarding the Heritage of Indian Peoples and Native Hawaiians: Human Rights, Sacred Objects, and Cultural Patrimony." In this article, Strickland joins others who voice the belief that tribes have to be the ones who establish and maintain, from their own traditions, the standards of consideration for their cultural property that the larger society must use in implementing protective programs like those of NAGPRA.

Passage of NAGPRA unquestionably spurred a new national debate, which is reflected in current discussions about the ethics of collecting cultural property (see, for example, Messenger 1999) and in an increased willingness of tribes to stand up for and protect their heritage when it is threatened or misappropriated by outsiders. One widely publicized example is Zia Pueblo's assertion of a claim to the 800-year-old sacred sun symbol that adorns the New Mexico state flag, the governor's stationery, and the business cards and advertisements of hundreds of commercial enterprises in and around New Mexico (Lopez 1999; Patton 2000).

Partly as a result of the Zia claim, in 1998 Congress ordered the federal Patent and Trademark Office to begin an investigation of the legal status of American Indian tribal symbols. The news to date has not been good for the tribes. Although the symbols of municipalities, states, and nations are protected from unauthorized appropriation by others under U.S. law, apparently tribal symbols are not.

The "intellectual property" of Indian tribes, including some that has been referred to as "local knowledge" by anthropologists (Geertz 1983), is another subject of increased concern. While cultural property involves tangible things, "intellectual property" is not *property* in the normal sense; it involves rights to do or know certain things and prevent others from doing or knowing certain things. For tribes,

> examples of intellectual property would include the rights to the knowledge of medicinal qualities inherent in indigenous fauna and flora; the embodiment of oral traditions and religious cere-monies; the expression of native art and designs; the use of tribal names and symbols; and most importantly, the right to prohibit their use by others. (Guest 1995, p. 114)

Hershey and Guest (1994) further explain:

> In the United States, the most common forms of intellectual property are protected through patent, copyright, and trademark law. Generally, patent law is the protection of novel ideas or inventions; copyright law is the protection of original expres-sions; trademark law is the protection of a company's name and symbols. (p. 173)

Although existing patent, copyright, and trademark law in the U.S. provide significant protection and economic benefit for indi-viduals and companies, they fail to recognize and protect the unique nature of American Indian intellectual property (Guest 1995). To briefly explain how these three areas of law are relevant, a kind of tribal property that could be associated with patent law would be something like traditional seeds or certain traditional varieties of crops. Copyright law might involve things like tribal designs. And, as mentioned in relation to the Zia sun symbol, trademark law can involve questions relating to tribal symbols and also tribal names.

Existing laws, including the Indian Arts and Crafts Act, NAGPRA, and the National Historic Preservation Act, can provide limited assis-tance to tribes in their efforts to protect some cultural and intellec-tual properties. But tribes believe there is still a need for more specific protections, especially of intellectual property. This controversy has just begun, and it will no doubt continue in coming years because heritage, money, media and commerce are involved.

E-19. *Where does the word "pow wow" come from and what does it mean?*

"Pow wow" represents the modern spelling of a word derived from the Algonquin-speaking Narragansett tribe of the Rhode Island region. In its original usage, it meant a Native healer or priest. For example, in 1646, the Massachusetts Bay Colony defined "pawwows" as "witches or sorcerers that cure by the help of the devil" (Spicer 1969, p. 174). In 1674, another observer wrote, "Their physicians are Powaws or Indian Priests" (Oxford English Dictionary 1989). Early on, the meaning of pow wow was expanded by non-Indians to include ceremonies in which Indian healers or religious leaders

Modern pow wows, such as this inter-tribal gathering in Arizona, provide opportunities for Indians to share their cultural heritage. Visitors are usually welcome to attend such functions.

participated. The word was later widely applied and accepted by Indians and non-Indians as a generic term to cover nearly all Indian gatherings involving feasts, councils, or inter-tribal conferences. Today the term is still applied to healers and spiritual leaders, but that meaning is used mostly by some of the eastern tribes. In Indian country, "pow wow" currently means a tribal or inter-tribal dance, fair, rodeo, celebration, or other gathering. These may vary in size from small social functions to the very large "Gathering of Nations" pow wow, which annually draws people to Albuquerque, New Mexico, from throughout the U.S. and Canada. In addition to their recreational value, pow wows are socially significant for individual participants and are important to Indian solidarity, spirituality, cultural identify, and exchange of socio-political information.

E-20. *Why are feathers so important in American Indian cultures?*
From the Inuit of the Arctic to the Seminoles of the Everglades, feathers have always had highly significant practical and symbolic importance. On the practical side, Hodge (1907) reported many uses that were common in the past. Parkas, for instance, were made form feathered bird skins sewed together by Arctic peoples. Eastern tribes cut bird skins into strips and sewed them into blankets, just as certain western tribe did with rabbit skins. Fans and clothing accessories were made by the Iroquois and other tribes. Captain John Smith, for example, wrote of seeing beautiful cloaks of knotted feathers worn by the Indians of Virginia. For stabilizing the flight of arrows, Native hunters secured either flat or split feathers on the shafts. Among some California tribes, bird scalps were even treated as a form of money. And, the uses of feathers for everyday decoration have been myriad. Simple examples come from the Yupik Inuit, who sewed attractive sprays of down into the seams of garments, and many California tribes which decorated their woven basketry in a similar way. The most striking uses of feathers, however, continue to be in connection with social customs and religious symbolism.

Feathers are tangible symbols of the birds from which they come. And it is birds, unique within creation, which fly among or with supernatural powers or spirits. In the plains states, the Kingfisher often symbolizes the powers of quickness and agility (Capps 1973). In Alaska, the raven is considered a descendant of the creator or "Raven Father" (Royce 1899). In the Southwest, hummingbirds might be entreated to carry messages from human speakers to spirits, while owls may represent spirits of the dead (Ortiz 1983). And everywhere, the revered eagle has extensive spiritual, healing, and magisterial powers (Hodge 1907; O'Brien 1989). The eminence of eagles is not lost on non-Indian culture, either, as the symbol printed on the right rear of every American dollar testifies.

Feathers are often featured prominently in ceremonial clothing such as that worn by a young Indian boy at a pow wow in Arizona.

Indians can access the special powers and social symbols associated with birds by acquiring and using the right feathers from the right birds. Feathers, whether plain or specially notched and painted, may be used for different purposes. They may be worn in the hair or atop the head. In the past, wearing feathers in this manner was commonly practiced by many tribes to indicate rank or personal achievement. The headdress of the Plains Indians, with feathers representing deeds or exploits, is the dominant image the public has of the way Indians use feathers.

Feathers are very important in ceremonials. For curing ceremonies, bundles of feathers may be brushed over a patient to sweep away or pull out causes of illness. They may also be used to help a celebrant "see" more clearly with his or her own mind or spirit. Some tribes' ceremonials associate feathers with the clothing of supernaturals, or with rain and water. Power in feathers may also be invoked as a protection or to bring about a desired outcome of events.

For these reasons, and for other aesthetic, ceremonial, and sacred purposes, many American Indians routinely place feathers on themselves and on special possessions such as prayer sticks, dance wands, effigy figures, pipe stems, shields, spears, clubs, rifles, baskets, clothing, drums, and horses. Feathers are thus employed as bridges between the spirit world and ours. In summary, ceremonial and religious feathers can be described as antennae directed to the cosmos (Chasing Horse 1991).

Brief, non-technical overviews on the meanings or definitions of some of the more prominent cultural symbols, items, and terms of various tribes may be found in *Turtle Island Alphabet* by Hausman (1992). A much older, but excellent, encyclopedic reference on hundreds of similar topics is the two-volume set by Hodge (1909 and reprinted in 1975), titled *Handbook of North American Indians North of Mexico*. Another contemporary work on cultural topics is *Indian Givers*, by Weatherford (1988).

SECTION F: WARFARE

> *Gone to fight the Indians. Will be back when the war is over.*
>
> Note tacked on the Washington, D.C., office door of
> Archibald Henderson, Commandant of the Marine Corps,
> in relation to the Creek Indian War of 1836
> Heinl 1962, p. 41

> *The term "Indian Wars" means the campaigns, engagements, and*
> *expeditions of the United States military forces against Indian tribes*
> *or nations, service in which has been recognized heretofore as*
> *pensionable service.*
>
> From Title 38 U.S. Code (Veterans Benefits) Sec. 1501

> *I only know the names of three savages upon the plains, Colonel*
> *Baker, General Custer, and at the head of all, General Sheridan.*
>
> Wendell Phillips, human rights activist, 1870

Warfare has always been a gripping subject because of the human drama involved. It has also had a profound and continual effect on Indian country and on the transformation of North America from the time of first contact until the last decade of the 19th century.

There is much more information on the subject of warfare involving American Indians than can be even briefly mentioned in an introductory book of this nature. For example, there are hundreds of books on various military engagements: English warring on the Secatons, south of Chesapeake Bay in 1586; the Powhattan Confederacy war with the Virginians in 1622; the war against the Pequots in 1635; King Phillip's War of 1675 and 1676; the French and Indian War of the mid-1700s; Pontiac's Rebellion in 1763; the American Revolution of 1775–1783; Tecumseh's intertribal resistance movement of 1806–1813; the Blackhawk War in 1832; the so-called Navajo "wars," first with the Spaniards (1587–1823), then with the Mexicans (1823–1846), and finally with the Americans (1846–1868); the Sioux uprising in Minnesota in

1862; the wars for the Plains from 1850–1880; the Modoc War of 1872 and 1873; and the Apache Wars of the 1870s and 1880s, to name a few.

In addition to the references noted in this section, other good sources of information include: Abel (1992a, 1992b, and 1993); Calloway (1995 and 1997); Capps (1973); Drinnon (1997); McDermott (1998); McNitt (1972); Slotkin (1985); Spicer (1962); Stannard (1992); Starkey (1998); Sugden (1997); Utley (1981a, 1984a, 1984b, and 1994); Utley and Washburn (1985); Woodhead (1993 and 1994); and Wooster (1995).

F-1. *Over how many years did the U.S. military engage in armed conflict with Indians, and just how much fighting was there?*
Official U.S. military involvement in warfare against American Indians occurred over a 115-year period, from 1776 to 1891. However, the U.S. Army was involved in a dozen or more "police actions" relating to Indian tribes between 1891 and 1907, which would qualify under the "Veterans Benefits" definition of Indian Wars given above.

A review of military records, some of which are incomplete, shows at least 1,470 official incidents of Army action against Indians from 1776 to 1907 (Harlow 1935; Hill 1981; Old Army Press 1979; U.S. Department of the Interior 1894; Webb 1966; Washburn 1988). These actions varied from nonviolent pursuits or minor exchanges of gunfire to large scale battles.

The 1,470 federal incidents do not include independent actions against Indians by the U.S. Navy. This is because the Navy's records pertaining to Indian-related operations are so widely scattered that they are extremely difficult to locate and enumerate. The Navy's actions were not at all numerous when compared with the Army's. Nonetheless, the Navy and the Marine Corps played significant roles in the Creek War of 1836, in multi-year campaigns against the Seminoles in Florida, in efforts to subdue the Puget Sound tribes in Washington, and in making a show of force to coastal Natives in southern Alaska. In addition to supporting land operations involving the Army, the Navy engaged in some of its own such operations and is also know to have shelled Native villages on two, and probably more, occasions (Heinl 1962; Hill 1981; Wrone and Nelson 1973).

The vast majority of military-Indian fighting occurred between 1866 and 1891. Army records for this period show that the Army fought 1,065 combat engagements with Indians during that 25-year period. It was a time of relentless pursuit and conquest by a U.S. military establishment baptized in the Civil War. Federal casualties for~t during~ the period totaled 948 killed and 1,058 wounded. Indian casualties listed by the Army for the same 25 years are 4,371 killed and 1,279 wounded, with 10,318 captured. Experts caution that the Indian casualty figures may be somewhat exaggerated (Utley 1988). Over the many decades of conflict, far more Indians were killed by disease, despair, and starvation than by bullets.

Lt. Edward W. Casey, who commanded a troop of Cheyenne scouts recruited in Montana, is often referred to as the last combatant killed in an "Indian war." While on a scouting mission with two of his men in the final days of the so-called "Sioux Ghost Dance War," he was shot by Plenty Horses, a young Lakota warrior. Plenty Horses, a Brulé (Sicangu), had been educated at Carlisle Indian School in Pennsylvania. This incident occurred on January 7, 1891. (See also F-9.)

Referring to sources like the *New York Times* and *Nation* magazine, Matthiessen (1991) stated that the U.S. Army got directly involved in behind-the-scenes operations for "Wounded Knee II" in 1973. FBI agents, U.S. Marshals, and BIA police besieged lightly armed Indian protestors who had occupied the tiny community of Wounded Knee, South Dakota, on the Pine Ridge Reservation. Military intelligence and counsel, and perhaps weapons and equipment, were provided to the civilian authorities, with unofficial approval reportedly coming all the way from the White House. A lot of ineffective gunfire was exchanged during the 71-day stand-off, but two Indians died and one federal officer was crippled. It is reported that, at one point, the FBI requested the assistance of 2,000 soldiers to seize control of the entire reservation. This would have allowed the FBI to focus on making its desired arrests. The request was wisely refused.

The most recent pitched shootout between a semi-organized group of American Indians and U.S. federal law enforcement officers occurred in 1975 on the Pine Ridge Reservation. During the brief firefight, one Indian and two FBI agents were killed. As far as is known, the U.S. military had no involvement, even indirectly, with the 1975 incident. (See Matthiessen's detailed but controversial book.)

If all hostile actions involving non-Indians, on one side, and Indian people, on the other, could be counted, they might far exceed the U.S. military numbers given above. As an example of uncounted incidents, during the three decades after gold was discovered in California, mounted militia and private armies were periodically organized to hunt and exterminate entire tribes or bands of Indians. The participants in some of these genocidal expeditions were reimbursed for their expenses with federal funds. In 1894, the U.S. Department of the Interior reported, "It has been estimated that since 1775 more than 5,000 white men, women, and children have been killed in individual [non-military] affairs with Indians, and more than 8,500 Indians [killed]. History, in general, notes but few of these combats" (U.S. Department of the Interior 1894, p. 637).

One cavalry-like action, thought to be the last of its kind in the U.S., occurred in 1911. Mounted troopers of the Nevada State Police tracked down and killed a small band of "free" (i.e., non-reservation) Shoshone who had been accused of the death of a Basque shepherd in the far western part of the state. To this day, a controversy remains as to whether the Indians killed the shepherd, or whether it was done by some of the cattlemen who accused them.

The following quotations, attributed to various sources, are taken from "How to Fight Savage Tribes," a paper by Eldridge Colby, Captain, United States Army, which was published in *The American Journal of International Law* in 1927. It illustrates a distinctly different and even racist attitude about the conduct of warfare against "normatively divergent," or culturally different, peoples that was prevalent from the 16th through the early 20th centuries.

HOW TO FIGHT SAVAGE TRIBES

All who can bear arms [can be justifiably exterminated, at times], *but in a war with Christians this would not be allowable.*

Franciscus de Victoria, the famous Spanish
scholar of international law, 1532

Against peoples possessing a low civilization, war must be more brutal in type.

British Colonel J. F. C. Fuller

The real crux of the matter of warfare between civilized and uncivilized peoples almost invariably turns out to be a difference in fact as well as a difference in law. In fact, among savages, war includes everyone. There is no distinction between combatants and noncombatants.

Captain Eldridge Colby

Both men and women struggled to the last . . . without asking quarter [and] *not one would desert the field, but men, women, and children perished together.*

U.S. Army General John Coffee, upon defeating the Creek Indians of Mississippi, November 3, 1813

The long list of Indian wars in which the troopers of the United States have defended and pushed back the frontiers of America bear eloquent testimony . . . to the almost universal brutality of the red-skinned fighters [and other "savage" tribes around the world]. *With these* [people] *there can be little thought of international law.*

Captain Eldridge Colby

Respect no rights and know no wrong.

U.S. General Hull, in remarks about how to carry combat to the Indian allies of the British during the War of 1812

This species of warfare has been invariably pursued by every nation engaged in war with the Indians on the American continent.

James Monroe, U.S. Secretary of State, when he justified U.S. General Harrison's wholesale destruction of Indian villages during the War of 1812

It is good to be decent. It is good to use proper discretion. It is good to observe the decencies of international law. But it is a fact that against uncivilized people who do not know international law . . . there must be something else. The "something else" should not be a relaxation of all bonds of restraint. But it should be clear understanding that this is a different kind of war, this which is waged against native tribes. . . . If a few "non-combatants"—if there be any such in native folk of this character—are killed, the loss of life is probably far less than might have been sustained in prolonged operations of more polite character. The inhuman act thus becomes actually humane, for it shortens the conflict.

Hiroshima   from Captain Eldrige Colby's concluding remarks

F-2. Was the "Battle of the Little Bighorn" the greatest single military defeat for the United States in the so-called Indian Wars?

No. But it is next in line. As a result of action against a large gathering of Sioux (plus some Cheyenne and Arapaho allies) at the Little

PHOTO COURTESY OF THE SMITHSONIAN INSTITUTION

Red Horse, a Minneconjou Sioux who participated in the Little Bighorn battle, drew this picture sometime after the engagement.

Bighorn River in Montana Territory, on June 25, 1876, the U.S. 7th Cavalry lost 289 men killed and 51 wounded out of a total force of about 600 (Graham 1959; Time–Life books 1990). About 225 of the dead were in the five companies that were directly under the command of Lt. Colonel George Custer. The remainder of the killed, as well as all the wounded, were commanded by Major Reno and Captain Benteen. The latter were surrounded and besieged for a day, several miles from where Custer met his end. Indian dead in the Little Bighorn battle are estimated to have been about 100, by some historians. (See question F-3.)

On November 4, 1791, nearly 85 years before the Battle of the Little Bighorn, the greatest single military defeat of U.S. forces by American Indians took place. The encounter occurred near what is today the community of Fort Recovery, Ohio, on the upper Wabash River, in the western part of the state. President George Washington had appointed Arthur Saint Clair to command an army that grew to include 625 regulars, 1,675 citizen soldiers called "levies," and 470 militiamen. Their mission was to subdue Indian tribes in the Ohio region. Just before dawn on the 4th, the federal encampment of 2,770 men was attqacked by a force of up to 2,000 warriors. This was an intertribal army of Miamis, Wyandots, Delawares, Shawnees, Ottawas, Chippewas, Potawatomis, and Kickapoos. Only 1,400 of the disorganized U.S. forces were able to engage in the defensive action. Total federal casualties amounted to 632 killed and 264 wounded; much of the army ran off in a panic. Exact Indian casualties are unknown but are thought to have been much less than on the federal side. Little Turtle of the Miami and Tecumseh of the Shawnee were two of the better known Indian participants. The episode, called "Saint Clair's Defeat," stunned the nation and precipitated the very first Congressional inquiry into the conduct of the executive branch (Iacopi 1972; Mahon 1988; Webb 1966).

F-3. *What were the casualties for the Indians who fought the Seventh Cavalry at the Little Bighorn?*

> *You say that the parents of Lieutenant Crittendon loved him, that he was their only child, and that they were sorely grieved at his death. You can judge of the grief and anguish of the parents of the nine young [Indian] men found by the whites after the battle, lying in the [funeral] lodge. They were all brave and good, yes, fine young men, and the grief of the parents is great.*
>
> Statement by Little Buck Elk,
> Hunkpapa Sioux, at Fort Peck, Montana,
> three months after the Little Big Horn battle
> (from Hardorff 1993, p. iii)

The excerpt above from Little Buck Elk's statement, taken on September 26, 1876, shows an attempt to explain that the Indian dead were also worthy of recognition for their sacrifice. But, the attempt fell on deaf ears.

Again in 1926, during a reinternment ceremony for what was thought to have been one of Major Reno's soldiers, a veteran Minneconjou warrior was

> told by his interpreter that this dead man was considered a hero among the whites[;] the old man asked to be heard. He told the assembled crowd that the Indians, too, had suffered casualties— brave men who had fallen on the land on which the whites were now standing. After a short pause, he added reflectively that the families of these slain men had "cried" for the loss of their sons, brothers, and fathers, and that these slain Indians were also considered heros among the Lakotas and the Cheyennes. (Hardorff 1993, p. 14)

Richard Hardorff's research into the Indian casualties at the Little Big Horn focuses on numerous records of interviews with Indian survivors that were conducted from 1876 up to 1938. After much analysis, checking, cross-checking, and informed speculation, his best conclusion is that 31 men, 6 women, and 4 very young children were killed. Perhaps as many as 80 to 100 additional people were wounded, some number of whom, no doubt, died.

Hardorff also discloses that the first person killed at the Little Bighorn seems to have been a ten-year-old Sans Arc boy, known in various sources as Deeds (or something akin to "Wicohan," in Lakota), Noisy Walking, Thunder Earth, and perhaps at least one more name. Although the accounts are confusing and sometimes conflicting, it appears that sometime before the battle Deeds and an adult companion, probably his father, were discovered by a group of Custer's Crow scouts while the two were gathering up a couple of horses a few miles away from the large Indian encampment on the Little Bighorn. Deeds and his father started off to warn the camp, but gunfire from the scouts killed the boy. His father rode on to raise an alarm at camp.

F-4. *Was Crazy Horse's greatest military achievement the defeat of Custer's command at the Battle of the Little Bighorn?*

No. Although Crazy Horse's military ability in the Little Bighorn battle has been given the most historical attention, that engagement was actually won by the rapid response of overwhelmingly superior numbers. The most convincing demonstration of strategic and tactical supremacy by Crazy Horse and his comrades in arms took place a week earlier on June 17th, at the Battle of Rosebud Creek in Montana Territory, less than a full day's ride south and east of the Little Bighorn site (Vaughn 1956; Utley 1993).

In the latter half of 1875, a federal policy was established declaring that all members of upper plains tribes had to be living on their reservations by January 1876, or they would be declared "hostiles" and would be subject to military action to force their compliance. Various bands of Lakotas and Cheyennes either did not acknowledge or simply refused to heed the new policy and, instead, headed for the buffalo country of the Powder and Tongue Rivers of northeast Wyoming and southeast Montana Territories.

In May 1876, Brigadier General George Crook organized a command of 1,325 men, including 176 Crow scouts and 86 Shoshone scouts, in the area of today's Douglas, Wyoming; roughly 250 miles south-southeast of what would soon become the Rosebud and Little

Bighorn battle sites. Interestingly, there were also five newspaper correspondents along for the ride, as well as the soon-to-be notorious Calamity Jane, who was dressed as a man and driving a team in the wagon train. She was discovered several days before the battle took place and forced to remain behind at the base camp with the supply wagons and the 100 troops left to protect the wagons.

General Crook and his command formed one of three forces that were to cooperate in a punitive expedition against the large camps of Cheyennes and Lakotas in the region, including those with Crazy Horse and Sitting Bull.

Crook was to move his command north, while Colonel Gibbon moved east from Fort Ellis (near present-day Bozeman, Montana), and General Terry pushed west from Fort Lincoln (near today's Bismark, North Dakota). Custer's 7th Cavalry was assigned to General Terry's force. The objective was to trap and punish the uncooperative camps of "hostiles."

General Crook started his northward march on May 29th. He reached the headwaters of Rosebud Creek on June 16th, having already crossed the Tongue River. Crazy Horse had previously warned the Army not to cross the Tongue River, or they would be attacked.

The next morning the column was on the move by 6:00 A.M. With as many as 2,000 horses and mules, it stretched out for more than two miles. By 8:00 General Crook called for a halt to rest and had the men unsaddle their animals to let them graze. Suddenly, the Crow scouts warned there were signs that Sioux had recently camped in the area. The Crows were uneasy and cautioned the general to keep his men prepared for a change in circumstances, but 30 minutes passed and nothing happened. So the men relaxed, and even General Crook sat down to play a game of cards with several officers. They were waiting for the rear of the column, which was still on the march, to catch up and join the rest of the men and their mounts at the sprawling bivouac area.

At about 8:30, shots were heard to the northeast. Then Shoshone and Crow scouts dashed toward the command at a dead run, shouting "Lakota! Lakota!" They had encountered Crazy Horse's outriders about ten miles away, and had engaged in a running skirmish on the way back. Even as the scouts were making their report, Crazy Horse's advance warriors of Lakotas and Cheyennes were attacking Crook's pickets in small groups. Crazy Horse then launched a full attack against the rear of Crook's command. Sitting Bull was also on the battle field, but he did not actually fight (Utley 1993, p. 141). His arms were still swollen and recovering from the flesh-giving sun dance he had participated in the week before, so he was limited to riding the lines and encouraging his fellow warriors.

Meanwhile, Crook and the officers he had been playing cards with could not see what was going on; the terrain was too broken and obscured, and his command too large and spread out. Crook knew he needed to get organized immediately, but in order to do so he had to find some high ground and see what was happening.

Realizing that time was of the essence, the Chief of Scouts, Major Randall, called together his scouts, who were instantly ready to go into battle, and rode off with them to the north. They inserted themselves between the attacking warriors and the main command, fiercely repelling attack after attack for 20 minutes. This action by the scouts helped avoid a disaster and allowed General Crook and his senior officers the critical time they needed to get their troops organized, remounted, and deployed for battle.

What happened during the next six hours was like a confusing military chess game. Crook's command could not get fully joined up to take advantage of their superior numbers and their great potential to maneuver. On the other hand, Crazy Horse took full advantage of the terrain and seemed to counter nearly every move of Crook's separated units with moves of his own warriors, who probably numbered around 500 men—about half of Crook's fighting force.

Time and again the Army troops, in units up to battalion size, would charge or countercharge, clear an area of combatants, and take control of some new ground, only to find that the Lakotas had taken over the ground that the soldiers had just left behind. The soldiers might then be cut off from supporting units and have to fight their way back to where they had been.

Because the Lakotas were always mounted when fighting, they were highly mobile. They would fiercely charge an exposed unit, prevent it from achieving strategic success, and then retreat just as quickly, before the inevitable counterattack could do any measurable damage. This mobility kept the Lakotas' casualties to a minimum, though it also reduced their ability to inflict casualties on an almost equally mobile force of cavalry, mounted infantry, and mounted scouts.

At one point, a substantial body of warriors completely circumnavigated Crook's entire command—a maneuver that required a difficult ride of perhaps six or more miles. This was unnerving to the soldiers who, along with their general, had believed up until that time that their large force was unbeatable by ill-trained and poorly equipped "savages."

This entire engagement was a very sobering experience for the military participants. Even General Crook, at one point, came close to severe injury or death when his mount was shot out from under him and he went crashing to the ground over the head of the unfortunate animal.

It was only the skill and bravery of Crook and his officers, troops, and scouts that prevented serious losses or a possible rout. There were a number of Civil War veterans among the soldiers, and tribal war veterans among the scouts, who set good examples for the rest of the command while under intense pressure.

By 2:30 P.M., the Lakotas had grown weary and hungry. They decided to call it a day and rode off to gather up their people and move west to the Greasy Grass, or Little Bighorn, where more history was waiting.

Crook was left in charge of the field, so he would later claim victory. But during the fighting, the warriors were free to maneuver at will throughout most of the day; the Army units were not. Nearly every move by the Army units to gain the upper hand was strategically and tactically frustrated. And the main military goal of the campaign—to locate and destroy Crazy Horse's village—became completely impossible to accomplish. When it was all over, Crook did not follow up his "win," but returned to his base camp and did not venture out until he was heavily reinforced weeks later (Utley 1993).

As with so many encounters of this type in the West, the number of casualties, even for the military, remains unclear. The army apparently suffered around 15 to 20 killed and about twice that many wounded. The Lakota and Cheyenne reports on casualties vary widely, but Vaughn (1956) believes the numbers later reported by Crazy Horse are the most reliable. He said there were 36 killed and 63 wounded.

It is historically important to note that if Crook had actually "won" by achieving the orders he had been given, then the Little Big Horn battle, which the world is now so familiar with, would never have occurred.

It is also fair to say that through surprise, mobility, maneuver, use of terrain, and rapid redeployment in the face of changing circumstances, Crazy Horse and his fellow warriors (though probably outnumbered 2-to-1) bested one of the finest United States Army field commanders in the last quarter of the 19th century.

F-5. Which American army general said, "The only good Indian is a dead Indian?"

It was General Philip Sheridan, of American Civil War fame. But what he said is not exactly like the quote. In December 1867, at Fort Cobb in Indian Territory, General Sheridan was overseeing the surrender of a number of bands of Arapahos, Cheyennes, and Comanches. Tosawi, a chief of the Comanches, had just brought in his people to surrender. As Brown (1970, p. 170) describes it, when Tosawi was introduced to Sheridan, he said to the General, "Tosawi, good Indian." General Sheridan then replied, "The only good Indians I ever saw were dead."

General Sherman, Sheridan's commander after the Civil War, was known to be sympathetic to tribes that were passive and not engaged in armed resistance. But, regarding those that resisted, he was known to say things such as, "The more we can kill this year the less will have to be killed the next war, . . . they all have to be killed or be maintained as as species of paupers" (Capps 1973, p. 192).

For readers interested in what some historians refer to as a "more balanced" view of the character of the army in the war for the Plains, see Utley's 1981 essay "The Frontier Army: John Ford or Arthur Penn?"

F-6. What were the root causes of "The Great Pueblo Revolt"?

This question and question F-7 were presented to me by two Pueblo acquaintances who enjoyed the first edition of the book, but were concerned that (1) I had overlooked the most important warfare achievement of the numerous Pueblo nations since non-Indians first came to their homelands over 450 years ago, and (2) I had not acknowledged what various historians have said was the most significant military reversal of European colonization by Indian people in all of North America. They asked me to develop an answer to their question that could be appreciated not only by general readers, but also by interested and informed Pueblos. I agreed to give it a try.

Although the Pueblo Revolt occurred more than 150 years before the U.S. conquest of upper Mexico (which included all of the current American Southwest, as well as California, Nevada, Utah, and western Colorado) in 1846–1848, it remains fresh in the cultural memories of many of the New Mexico Pueblo people and, to some degree, still affects their view of and relationship with the non-Indian society around them.

The story of the Revolt, and how it came about, is an important part of southwestern history that is unknown to most Americans. It deserves to be told more often and to be put into context. Dozier (1970), Folsom (1973), Fontana (1994), Knaut (1995), Schroeder (1998), Spicer (1962), and Weber (1992) present the story well, and much of this answer is summarized from these six books, with particular reliance on Folsom (1973) and Knaut (1995).

Beginning when the Spanish explorers (or "invaders," from a logical Pueblo point of view) first entered the region of today's New Mexico and Arizona in 1540, they established a pattern of alternating cruelty and friendliness in their relations with the Pueblo communities. Coronado's expedition was the earliest, and he and his men set the precedent for cruelty, often through deadly oppression. During the two years they were in the region, they destroyed at least a dozen pueblos and attacked a number of others in a quest for food, clothing, and material wealth. When the Pueblo people of Arenal defied Coronado's demands for food and other provisions, he set fire to the village and burned 30 of its residents at the stake. Similar atrocities were committed against Pueblo communities by Spanish expeditionary groups in 1581, 1582, and 1590.

In 1598 the first Spanish settlers entered the region under the leadership of the newly appointed governor, don Juan de Oñate. He planned to use the approximately 130 men accompanying him, and his strong sense of military and cultural superiority, to dominate the thousands of Pueblos in their scattered villages. His ultimate aim was to establish a permanent pioneer community for the Spanish empire. Oñate succeeded, eventually establishing his headquarters at Santa Fe. And, though he was under orders to pacify the people and entice them to the church and the Spanish way of life through a good example of Christian behavior, Oñate readily resorted to violence if he felt the need.

Perhaps the most famous incident that caused the "need" to arise took place in December 1598. It was the rebellion of the people of Acoma against the demands of Oñate's nephew, and a company of 31 soldiers, for food and supplies from the village. The Spaniards had established a pattern of moving into an area and demanding provisions, and it was a habit that would continue for more than a century. None of the Pueblos appreciated it. But the people of Acoma were especially angry, because Oñate's nephew briefly took eight Acoma hostages in order to force the pueblo to give up the provisions for his troops.

The hostages were soon released, but it was too late—Acoma had had enough. Not long after half the company of soldiers ascended Acoma's isolated mesa and reentered the pueblo to collect the sought-after provisions, they were attacked. Most were killed, including Oñate's nephew. The few who escaped returned to Santa Fe with the remainder of the company to report what had happened.

It didn't take long for a reprisal to be planned. Oñate and his advisors decided they had to do something fierce to keep Acoma and all the other pueblos in check. Terror, they determined, was their best initial weapon (they could later balance it with offers of friendship from the priests). How else could only a few hundred Spaniards maintain control over thousands of Native people scattered in villages that were spread over thousands of square miles?

In late January 1599, Oñate sent a small but very well-armed force of 70 men to Acoma under the command of Vincente de Zaldivar, the brother of Oñate's slain nephew. From below the mesa, Zaldivar demanded the Acoma surrender. The Pueblos refused with a shower of arrows. Zaldivar began his attack that afternoon.

When darkness fell, Zaldivar had part of his small force maintain a steady by limited attack on the north side of the bluffs, while he and the main body of soldiers secretly scaled the southern cliffs up to an uninhabited portion of the Acoma mesa. They also hauled up two small cannons, with plenty of powder and grapeshot.

When morning broke, Zaldivar and his men set fire to the village and raked the defenders with the shotgun-like fire of their cannons. The assault continued for hours. Ultimately, hundreds of Acoma people were killed. The Spaniards suffered only one wounded. Several hundred Acomas were taken prisoner, including 80 "men," meaning males over the age of 12.

The Acoma prisoners were taken to San Juan in February and tried and convicted for the deaths of 11 Spaniards and two servants. The 24 Acoma men over the age of 25 had their right feet cut off, and they were further sentenced to 20 years of slavery with individual officers and soldiers of Oñate. The men aged 12 to 25 were likewise sentenced to 20 years of slavery, as were the women over 12. Sixty young girls were assigned to a priest and were eventually sent to Mexico, never to return. The young boys were assigned to Zaldivar. In addition, two Hopis who had been visiting Acoma when the attack took place had their right hands cut off as warnings to the western Pueblos (Diaz 1998a; Knaut 1995).

Oñate's plan worked. News of the horrific results of Acoma's defiance quickly traveled to all the other pueblos, and there was no more organized resistance to Spanish authority for decades, even though until the year 1692 there were never more than 200 Spanish fighting men in the entire province of New Mexico and only 35 or so were real professional soldiers. The Spanish relied on Indians converted to Christianity to make up the hundreds of men in their "armies" that periodically went out on punitive and slaving expeditions against the Apaches, Navajos, Utes, and other non-Pueblo people, such as the plains tribes in the region. On occasion, Christianized males from one or more of the pueblos were formed into Spanish-controlled armies to intimidate the members of other rival pueblos that were not in full compliance with Spanish rules. But after the events at Acoma, the Spaniards were able to go about the business of controlling and assimilating the Pueblos with much less difficulty than they had in 1598 and early 1599.

Still, there were serious Pueblo complaints and related difficulties for the Spaniards form time to time, including a threatened but failed revolt of the Tiwas in the 1650s, and another by the southern Pueblos in 1668. There was also a resurgence of the open exhibition of some Pueblo religious practices in the 1660s, but this, too, was repressed. Then, in 1675, the government and church authorities established their strictest policy regarding the practice of Pueblo traditions. All traditional Pueblo religious practices were expressly forbidden. The non-Christian Pueblos, who were still in the majority among their people, now suffered their greatest generalized religious persecution since the Spanish arrival. This was a turning point.

F-7. *What actually occurred during the Pueblo Revolt?*

The New Mexico governor from 1675 to 1677 was Juan Francisco Trevino. At one point in his first year he ordered the arrest of 47 medicine men from various pueblos and had them publicly flogged in Santa Fe for practicing witchcraft. He then ordered four of them hanged and the rest imprisoned. All of this was done in order to bring a halt to traditional Pueblo religious practices.

So enraged were the Pueblos that a group of 70 San Juan warriors made their way into the governor's home one night, while additional warriors waited in the countryside around Santa Fe. Trevino was forced to order the release of the medicine men, or else he and his family would have been killed. One of the medicine men who had been arrested, whipped, imprisoned, and released was Popé, a Tewa from the northern pueblo of San Juan.

Popé was a respected healer and practitioner of traditional ways. One of his more frequent declarations translates as, "Indians must once again be Indians." After his release, he returned to San Juan and continued to preach what the Spaniards considered to be insurrection.

From Popé's viewpoint, for four generations the Spanish had taken the Pueblos' best fields, had taken their food, had forced them to tend Spanish crops and Spanish livestock, and had taken tribute from the Pueblos in the form of woven blankets and tanned animal hides, which the Pueblos needed themselves. The priests had also destroyed many of the Pueblos' holy items and had forced them to pray, instead, to the white god and to the cross. In addition, many kivas (the subterranean "churches" of the Pueblos) had been destroyed by the Spanish. All in all, the economic, cultural, intellectual, and spiritual lives of the Pueblos had been invaded and largely stolen by the colonizing Spaniards

For Popé, enough was enough. The time had come to take back Pueblo freedom.

Although the different groups of Pueblos seemed to lead similar lives, each had a strong sense of independence from the others. And, there were no fewer than 10 different language groups among them. This sense of separateness was one thing the Spanish had always taken advantage of to control the Pueblo people. Getting all of the disparate groups to work together for one cause would be difficult.

Over several years, through unending encouragement from Popé and his growing numbers of adherents, various Pueblo groups began to take seriously the idea of a possible revolution. Bilingual and multilingual Pueblo traders and medicine men were used to spread the word. But not all people could be trusted.

After 80 years of subjugation, many Pueblo people had become converts to Spanish ways and saw themselves as loyal subjects. Still others had some or even a majority of Spanish blood and felt loyalty to that part of their heritage. These dangerous facts caused Popé and his co-conspirators to observe tight and sometimes even extreme security precautions. In one incident, Popé had his pro-Spanish son-in-law, Bua, killed. Although Bua was an Indian, he was also an appointed official of the Spanish and he had discovered details of the plans for revolt.

Many secret meetings between Pueblo leaders took place during the Catholic saint's day celebrations for each of the pueblos. This reduced the suspicions the Spaniards would have had if numerous Pueblo leaders had randomly shown up for a meeting at a single pueblo. Still, troubling rumors reached the authorities, and one of the senior military leaders warned Popé to stop any troublemaking he might be involved in or he would be prosecuted. Popé moved out of San Juan and up to Taos, but he kept up his organizing with co-conspirators like Saca of Taos, Little Pot of San Ildelfonso, Tupatú of Picuris, the Keresan leader known as Malacate, Catití of Santo Domingo, Romero of Tesuque, Naranja of Santa Clara, and numerous others from Pecos, San Lorenzo, and Jemez. By August 1680 the plan was in place, and messengers carried the plan to each of the pueblos in the from of a picture code painted on deer hides. The messengers related what the pictures meant as they met with the Revolt organizers at each pueblo.

The core of the plan was to kill all the Spaniards, or "Metal People" as they were referred to, who were in the Santa Fe area and the five pueblos to the north. In addition, they all had to be attacked at the same time so they could not come to each other's defense. The governor had to be convinced that all the Spaniards in New Mexico were going to die if they didn't run for their lives. The Pueblos hoped he would then order all of the remaining Spaniards in New Mexico to head south for old Mexico.

Popé and the Revolt planners originally chose August 12 as the first day for fighting. But they had to develop some means to spread the word and coordinate the action so everything would happen on time and according to plan. This was an extremely difficult problem because some of the pueblos were more than 150 miles apart, and communication was made by word of mouth and carried by runners—Pueblo people were generally not permitted to have horses.

It was decided that the runners would carry knotted cords to all the Pueblos, untying a knot each day they traveled and each remaining knot signifying a day until the day of the Revolt. The five Piro Pueblos south of Isleta were left out of the Revolt because it was feared they might report it to the Spanish authorities.

There was one final precaution about timing and betrayal. The planners decided to send out a false starting date for the Revolt—one that was several days past the real date. This would allow Popé and his close confederates to see if they were being betrayed by some of their own people, and it would also cause the Spanish to think they had more time to prepare for trouble than they actually did.

As it turned out two Tewa boys from Tesuque, Omtua and Catua, were chosen to be among the runners who would carry the false message that the Revolt would begin on August 13th. They were betrayed by an Indian official of the Spaniards when they made their journey to San Cristobal, which was about 15 or 20 miles south and east of Pecos. However, before they could be captured they were able to make the return run to Tesuque and warn the village elders.

The boys were subsequently taken into custody by Spanish soldiers who came to Tesuque, and they were delivered to governor Antonia de Otermín in Santa Fe. Omtua and Catua were carefully interrogated by the governor. They mostly told the truth, because they had not been informed of everything by the leaders of the Revolt, which was a protective measure for both the runners and the Revolt. Feeling he had learned everything he could from the two, and primarily that the Revolt would begin on the 13th, which was several days hence, Otermín ordered the boys hanged. Reportedly, they were hanged from the beams of the government building on the north end of the plaza. He also sent out word to the seven government districts in the province to be prepared for a rebellion to begin on the 13th, or soon thereafter.

When the two boys were arrested, the leaders of the Revolt sent out an updated message with new runners and new knotted cords. All participating pueblos sent up columns of smoke from special fires of acknowledgment, and the Revolt was on for the morning of August 10, 1680.

With the sunrise the fighting started. The Pueblo military leaders of each village in the northern reaches of the province had wisely separated their warriors into independent fighting groups. Each group had been assigned to attack and destroy the Spanish people and property in their villages and in the surrounding area. This was done with great efficiency. All men (including priests), women, and children in every Spanish home, hacienda, or government location north of Santa Fe were killed, with the exception of five Spaniards who escaped to Santa Fe. A total of 70 people were killed in and around Taos alone.

Because all the attacks were made simultaneously, no Spanish group could come to the aid of another, which was pivotal in the Revolt's success. As warriors achieved their objectives, they began to concentrate and move southward to Santa Fe. They took with them the horses, weapons, and food they had collected from the vanquished Spaniards.

By the end of the day on August 10th, a thousand Spanish and Pueblo refugees, who remained loyal to the Spanish, had crowded into the plaza area of Santa Fe. Among them were some revolutionaries who pretended to be frightened loyalists, but who were actually there to serve as spies and to spread lies about what was really happening at the northern pueblos—such as the story that all the Spaniards in the Isleta Pueblo area, which was considered to be a Spanish stronghold, had been killed.

Although the governor believed that his people at Isleta had been destroyed, the opposite was the case. Because of some late communications from the Revolt leaders, the Pueblos' objectives were not being met as well in the southern villages as they had been in the north. Word arrived a little late in the day for the Zunis and Hopis to the west, but they too took up arms and avenged past Spanish misdeeds with violence against the few to be found in their part of the province. Even in Pecos, the easternmost Pueblo, where as many as half the villagers had taken up Christianity, the revolution took hold. By nightfall the first day, the Pueblo people were in charge of more of their country than they had been for 80 years.

On Tuesday August 13, a 500-man army of Pueblo warriors from south of Santa Fe showed up on the southern edge of the town. On Wednesday the 14th, an equally large army of northern Pueblo warriors showed up near the northern edge of the town. Also on the 14th, the Spanish soldiers and refugees at Isleta, thinking the governor and all who were with him in Santa Fe had been killed, made a decision to go south toward Mexico. As these Spaniards fled, they convinced the frightened and uninformed Piro Pueblo people to go with them, saying that the revolutionaries were going to kill them too.

Meanwhile at Santa Fe, because the governor refused to surrender, the warrior armies laid siege to the town, cutting it off from water and additional food supplies. After two days, some of the livestock began to die. The situation was getting desperate, especially in light of the fact that the governor and all of his military men had been wounded in some way by the arrows and gunfire that periodically rained down on the government buildings around the plaza where the Spaniards had taken cover. The governor himself had sustained two arrow wounds to the face and a gunshot wound to the chest.

Out of his sense of desperation, the governor decided to form a small command of soldiers and slaves to break out of the plaza and attack. They did this and caught the warriors completely by surprise. The governor and his tiny army succeeded in setting fire to the buildings on the south side of town that the Pueblo warriors had fortified. Many Pueblos were killed in the fire, and scores of others were also killed out in the open near the plaza and elsewhere. On the way back to the safety of the government buildings, the governor and his men captured over 40 hostages and also were able to get water for themselves and their fellow refugees. After questioning the hostages, the governor had them shot.

Worrying for awhile about what to do next, the governor and his advisors finally determined it was time to leave. They decided they would gather everyone together in a large cavalcade of a thousand people and walk out of the plaza to the south.

When this actually happened, on August 21, the Pueblo warriors did nothing. It was what they had wanted all along. They merely traveled along at a safe distance to assure that the Spaniards would not double back.

The 1,500 refugees who had gone south from Isleta and the 1,000 who left Santa Fe, eventually combined their groups on the Rio Grande, far south of the Pueblo country, near present-day Juarez, Mexico, and El Paso, Texas. Here they waited, for a dozen years, before the Spanish could mount sufficient forces with sufficient supplies for the reconquest of the New Mexico Pueblos.

For a brief time the Pueblos experienced a general peace and a return to their old traditions, but that tranquility was short-lived.

Discord between the Pueblos began to grow. It was fueled by actions such as Popé's declaring that he was now the grand ruler of all the Pueblos. He even went so far as to demand tribute from villagers on his own personal inspection tours.

Other inter- and intra-pueblo strife developed until, in 1693, when the Spanish reentered the Pueblo country for their long-awaited reconquest, they were able to permanently reestablish themselves. This they did with auxiliary military help from the warriors of several pueblos, despite another attempt at a general Pueblo revolt.

Thus ended the one brief period in the last four centuries when all the Pueblos regained their original self-governing powers and were not subject to the domination of the governments and cultures of Euro-Americans.

After 1693, during the remainder of the colonial period, only the Hopis, far to the west of the main Spanish settlements, were left free of Spanish control.

F-8. *Were Oklahoma (Indian Territory) tribes involved in the Civil War?*

Yes. More than a dozen tribes formally allied themselves, through treaty, with the Confederate States of America. In addition, large and small factions of some of these tribes maintained less formal allegiances to the Union. In fact, there were enough "loyal" Indians from Indian Territory and the neighboring states of Kansas, Missouri, and Arkansas, for the federals to raise an "Indian Brigade" for service in the region. It consisted of perhaps several thousand men.

Indian Territory was mostly a Confederate stronghold and was made part of the Confederate Army's Department of the Trans-Mississippi. Four Indian regiments were raised, with total forces exceeding 5,000 men. In the Indian Territory, these troops engaged in some significant battles against organized federal forces during the early part of the Civil War. Subsequently, most fighting involved inter- and intra-tribal conflict between opposing factions allied with the Union or Confederate causes.

General Robert Edward Lee surrendered his Army of Northern Virginia at Appamattox Courthouse on April 9, 1865. Confederate General Edmund Kirby-Smith surrendered his Trans-Mississippi forces on May 26. However, because of their independent nation status, the Confederate Indian regiment of the Trans-Mississippi held out. The last Confederate general to surrender was Cherokee Brigadier General Stand Watie, who capitulated on June 23. It seems, however, that the distinction of being the last organized regiment of Confederate troops to surrender to Union forces goes to the Chickasaws, who had been under the command of Colonel Tandy Walker (Choctaw) and who formally laid down their arms on July 14, 1865—three full months after Appamattox (Harlow 1935).

F-9. *When was the last official surrender of an Indian tribe, and who was involved?*

The final surrender which closed out what the federal government officially termed the "Indian wars," took place on January 15, 1891.

The surrender specifically ended the two-month-long "Sioux Ghost Dance War," which had become the largest military operation in the U.S. after the end of the Civil War. It was during the Ghost Dance campaign that the Wounded Knee massacre occurred, on December 29, 1890. Historians report that 200 to 300 Indian men, women, and children were killed by federal troops at Wounded Knee (Utter 1991).

At the start of the campaign, thousands of Lakota Sioux had been frightened, confused, intimidated, and angered by the deployment of 3,500 federal troops in and around their South Dakota reservations late in November 1890. Government officials had sent troops to suppress the Ghost Dance religion, a theology that swept through the tribes of the West in 1890 and which Indian practitioners had hoped would restore the old life. (See Utley 1963 for an excellent presentation of the story.)

On a hill overlooking Wounded Knee Creek, on the Pine Ridge Indian Reservation in South Dakota, lies a mass grave. It is where the bodies of many Indian men, women, and children were buried by the U.S. military after the infamous "Massacre at Wounded Knee" on December 29, 1890. The site now serves as an Indian cemetery as well as a memorial to those who died in 1890. Photo by Jack Schultz.

The surrender procession of the Lakota, which included about 4,000 men, women, and children, was described in a publication by Captain W. E. Dougherty, U.S. Army, shortly after the event:

> It was a spectacle worth beholding. They moved in two columns up White Clay Creek, one on each side, about 5,500 [sic] people in all, with 7,000 horses, 500 wagons, and about 250 travois, and in such good order that there was not at any point a detention on any account. . . . The rear and right flank of this mass was covered during the movement by a force of infantry and cavalry deployed in skirmish order, and moved with a precision that was a surprise to all who witnessed it.

Utley 1963, p. 260

Also present and surrounding the Lakota were the Sixth, Seventh, and Ninth Cavalries; the First, Second, and Seventeenth Infantries; and a contingent of cavalry from Fort Leavenworth. Major General

Kicking Bear, who fought vigorously at the Little Bighorn in 1876, was a Lakota Ghost Dance apostle. He was the last Indian leader to officially surrender to the U.S. Army, on January 15, 1891.

Nelson A. Miles was the senior commander of all troops in the region and had been in charge of the Army's Ghost Dance campaign from the beginning. The single formality observed during the surrender took place when Kicking Bear, first cousin to Crazy Horse and a Ghost Dance apostle, laid his rifle at the feet of General Miles.

F-10. *Were there any deadly U.S. Cavalry actions in the 20th century?*

Yes. In 1907, the United States Army was asked by the Secretary of the Interior to supply cavalry troops to make an arrest of a defiant medicine man and his followers, who refused to comply with the orders of the local Indian agent. Two Indian deaths by gunfire resulted from this action (Correll 1970; Parman 1978). As far as can be determined, this was the last deadly U.S. Cavalry action against Indian people in the United States.

In 1903 the Bureau of Indian Affairs (BIA) of the U.S. Department of the Interior assigned William T. Shelton as the agent of the newly established San Juan Indian Agency at Shiprock, New Mexico. Shelton was a tall man and had a forceful personality. He has been described as puritanical, arbitrary, and autocratic, as well as intolerant of opposition to his methods. Shelton demanded adherence to his white middle-class views of morality. He also demanded that Navajo children in his agency area—which covered tens of thousands of acres in northwest New Mexico and northeast Arizona Territories, and southeast Utah—attend the boarding school in Shiprock.

Shelton and his orders were strongly opposed by a medicine man named *Bai-a-lil-le* (in the English spelling of the day), who some Navajos say had a checkered past. It has been reported that as a young man, Bai-a-lil-le admitted to using his special powers to bring about the death of another Navajo. Certain Navajos saw him as contentious and quarrelsome; he even frightened some of them with his claim of great power and his belligerent behavior.

Bai-a-lil-le was born around 1859, near present-day Chinle, Arizona. He and his family, and many other Navajos living in the

Bai-a-lil-le, Navajo medicine man, whose imprisonment stirred a legal furor and a public outcry against the Army and the BIA.

PHOTO COURTESY OF NATIONAL ARCHIVES

Aneth, Utah, region at the turn of the century, had escaped the incarceration of up to 11,000 Navajos at Bosque Redondo, New Mexico, in the 1860s. This mass removal had been orchestrated by Gen. James Carleton, and carried out by Lt. Col. Kit Carson. BIA authorities in the early 1900s thought that the lack of military subjugation and oppression in the history of the Aneth area Navajos was part of the root cause of their resistance to white authority. In addition, because of their remoteness from federal authorities, the Aneth Navajos had rather easily resisted the forced removal of their children to the BIA boarding school in Fort Defiance, A.T. (Arizona Territory), from the late 1800s up to the 1903 arrival of Agent Shelton at the new, and closer, Shiprock Agency some 40 miles away. Then things got much tougher.

On various occasions Shelton attempted, among other things, to get Bai-a-lil-le and his 40 or so adult followers to send their children to school. Time after time they refused. Bai-a-lil-le even declared that he and his people would fight to stop the government from taking their children away, and, saying that he "was not afraid to die," he challenged Shelton to try.

Fed up and perhaps a little embarrassed that he could not control the Aneth Navajos who followed Bai-a-lil-le, Shelton contacted Commissioner of Indian Affairs Francis L. Leupp for assistance. Parman (1978) and Correll (1970) described what was relayed to Commissioner Leupp:

> In September Shelton reported that Bai-a-lil-le's group contin-
> ued to resist his authority. The headman, he charged, had again
> rejected intermediaries, threatened pro-government Indians
> with witchcraft, and refused to dip his sheep as ordered. Shelton
> added that his Navajo police were too afraid of Bai-a-lil-le's
> medicine to arrest him. He asked that two troops of cavalry be
> sent to Aneth to hold Bai-a-lil-le until he became amenable to
> regulations or until the Indian policemen regained their courage.
> (Parman, p. 346)

Correll (1970) included Agent Shelton's statements:

> This man Bai-a-lil-le is a medicine man . . . ; the Indians believe
> he . . . is keeping the rain from coming because so many of them
> are listening to the Government's advice and trying to pattern
> after the white people. . . . He threatens to kill those who oppose
> him and his followers. . . .
>
> Bai-a-lil-le has, with a heavily armed band of over 30 bucks, gone
> to the Indians in the outlying districts and threatened to exter-
> minate them if they sent any children to school or took up the
> white man's ways; the more ignorant he has threatened with his
> power as a medicine man to bring all kinds of disaster upon
> them. (Correll 1970, p. 13–14)

Leupp had a recent history of using troops to control Indians, and he had employed them at Fort Defiance in 1905 to help arrest seven Navajo men. These dissidents were sent to the military prison at Alca-traz Island without trial. In 1906, Leupp again used the Army to arrest and imprison, at Alcatraz and elsewhere, a sizable number of Hopi men who were resisting BIA orders they felt were a threat to their culture.

Leupp now decided to travel to Shiprock to size things up on his own. It didn't take him long to ask the Interior Secretary, James

Navajo prisoners captured near Aneth, Utah, on October 28, 1907. *(standing, left to right)* Superintendent William Shelton (with badge), Captain Harry O. Williard (holding rifle with bayonet), James M. Holley (with mustache). *(seated, center to right)* Polly (light shirt) and Bai-a-lil-le (with dark headband).

PHOTO COURTESY OF NATIONAL ARCHIVES

Garfield, to request the Army's involvement. Garfield did so on October 12, 1907. On October 22, Troops I and K of the U.S. Fifth Cavalry left Fort Wingate, New Mexico, under the command of Captain Harry O. Williard. They arrived in Shiprock four days later. There, it was decided that the 85 federal troops (including "three Indian scouts") would try to effect a surprise arrest of Bai-a-lil-le and his main male followers. Parman (1978, p. 346–347) briefly describes what occurred after the cavalry moved on to the Aneth area.

> Williard's efforts to achieve surprise were successful. At 2:30 on the morning of October 28, he led his troops and accompanying Indian police down the San Juan Valley and surrounded the camp where Bai-a-lil-le had been conducting a curing ceremony. At dawn, the soldiers rushed into the hogan where Bai-a-lil-le, Polly, and others were sleeping and quickly subdued and handcuffed

them. Indians who came out of nearby hogans were similarly seized. Firing, however, broke out when Williard's men attempted to arrest all the Indians found in the neighborhood. Two young Navajos were killed and one wounded during the brief [15 to 20 minute] skirmish.

"Little Warrior," who was shot through the stomach, and "Little Wet," who was shot through the head, appear to have been the final two fatalities caused by U.S. military combat action against American Indians—actions stretching back 129 years to 1775. "Fuzzy Hat," who was wounded in the leg, escaped.

Captain Williard, who would soon receive great praise for his unit's action—including a commendation from President Teddy Roosevelt—described Bai-a-lil-le and his most ardent supporter, Polly, as a truly "villainous" pair. He and Shelton recommended ten years imprisonment for these two, and two years for the other eight prisoners. Commissioner Leupp ordered all ten to be sent to Fort Huachuca in southeast Arizona and placed at hard labor for an indefinite period. But, first, they were paraded before a large group of Navajos gathered in Shiprock, where the prisoners told the other Navajos they had been "bad Indians" and would now have to pay for it. They would learn their lesson in prison and would later return to be good Indians and do what Washington told them to through their white Indian agent. They urged their fellow tribesmen to do the same.

Sympathizers to the Navajo prisoners brought national media attention to the Navajos' circumstances. This caused President Roosevelt to launch a military investigation, with hearings at Aneth, Utah, to determine if any laws had been broken and rights violated. The military conclusion was no. This was, however, a "whitewash," according to Parman (p. 348).

Commissioner Leupp came under fire about the probable illegality of his actions and those of the Army. He retaliated with grandiose statements about how certain circumstances demand certain actions in Indian administration, whatever the law may be. Parman (1978) reports:

> Leupp heatedly proclaimed that "there comes a time in the experience of every man who has authority when he has got to make his own laws." Having no alternative in dealing with the vicious

> Navajos, he had done what seemed best, and he would "stand on that record, law or no law." He added that "it seemed more important to me that these people—the bad element—should know that there is a government in Washington that was going to protect the good element," than observing the Constitution or a statute. (p. 353)

Eventually, a writ of habeas corpus was sought in the district court in Tombstone, A.T., by the local lawyer, O. Gibson, who was hired by the Indian Rights Association on behalf of the Navajo prisoners. The writ was denied, partly because the government attorney said the Navajos were prisoners of war. Plus, the federal territorial judge obviously did not want to get involved in issuing an order against the federal War Department or the federal Interior Department— although it was becoming more and more obvious that a number of state and federal laws, and the Navajo-U.S. Treaty of 1868, had been violated. Despite the defeat of the Indian Rights Association's first habeas corpus attempt, the BIA had everyone but Bai-a-lil-le and Polly released by the Army anyway.

An appeal was made by lawyer Gibson to the Supreme Court of Arizona Territory. He cited two important precedents, the cases of *Wiley v. Keokuk* (1870) and *Standing Bear v. Crook* (1879), in which writs of habeas corpus were granted to Indians who were being unlawfully held by civil and military authorities, respectively. In his brief to the court (Parnam 1978, p. 357) Gibson noted, about Bai-a-lil-le and his small group of followers, that "at worst they were a band of ruffians, who needed to be [legally] arrested and dealt with in the civil courts [under the laws of due process]." The Navajos' lawyer also declared that he found the entire record of the case and the violation of his clients' rights to be "sickening."

In this appeal action, the government lawyer argued that the imprisonment was a criminal confinement based on prisoner of war status, or, alternately, that it was not criminal punishment but was "merely a disciplinary and educational action normal in the guardian-ward relationship" (Parman 1978, p. 358). To support his prisoner-of-war theory of authority, the government lawyer pointed out that Geronimo and his people were still being held under that technical status in Fort Sill, Oklahoma. (Geronimo died at Fort Sill on February 17, 1909, while the Bai-a-lil-le habeas corpus case was still being argued.)

On March 20, 1909, a unanimous Arizona Territorial Supreme Court ordered the release of the last two Navajo prisoners, Bai-a-lil-le and Polly. They concluded that imprisonment or other confinement was improper unless authorized by law. Every argument the government lawyer had put forward was invalidated by the court's ruling.

Bai-a-lil-le and Polly went back to Aneth, Utah, and began to live much less controversial lives. At one point, in response Agent Shelton's personal invitation, Bai-a-lil-le addressed the Navajo children at the Shiprock boarding school on the merits of their educational opportunity at the hands of the BIA. In May 1911, Bai-a-lil-le drowned while attempting to boat across the rain-swollen San Juan River.

In sharp contrast to Indian Agent William Shelton's self-righteous moralizing about Bai-a-lil-le's alleged degenerate and nonconformist behavior, the National Archives' records on the San Juan Indian Agency indicate that Shelton was later dismissed from his job for impregnating some Navajo school girls (Parman 2000).

F-11. *What were the "Indian Depredation Acts?"*

The Indian Depredation Act of 1891 is the primary piece of congressional legislation that is considered when the issue of "Indian depredation" is discussed. In 1891, Congress gave the U.S. Court of Claims jurisdiction over: "All claims [that had accrued before the act was passed] for property of citizens of the United States taken or destroyed by Indians belonging to any band, tribe, or nation, in *amity* [i.e., at peace] with the United States, without just cause or provocation on the part of the owner or agent in charge [of the property], and not [already] returned or paid for" (Cohen 1982, p. 10, emphasis added).

What this meant was that the Court could hear and decide cases wherein a claim was filed by a citizen of the U.S. for property that a member or members of an Indian tribe took, damaged, or destroyed, during times of peace. For example, there were more than a few cases involving herds of horses that were taken from private citizens. The citizens would then file a claim against the U.S. and/or the tribe involved. Depending upon the circumstances, the U.S. could be found jointly liable with the tribe, or separately liable, because the federal government had, and still has, responsibility for Indian tribes. If, however, a private citizen filed a claim for property lost during a period of officially recognized *enmity* (i.e., war or hostilities), between the involved tribe, band, or nation and the U.S., neither the tribe, band, or nation nor the U.S. would be held liable for the loss. This government policy from 1891 is similar to an insurance policy which declares that the insurance company issuing the policy is not liable for damages suffered by its policy holder from "acts of war."

In the U.S. Supreme Court case of *Montoya v. United States* (1901), the court considered the validity of a claim brought by E. Montoya & Sons against the Mescalero Apache Tribe and the United States for loss of mules and horses, in March 1880, to Victorio's mixed band of Chiricahua and Mescalero Apaches. Victorio, a Chiricahua, had persuaded up to 250 Mescaleros to depart from their southern New Mexico reservation to join him, leaving the majority of their tribe behind.

In analyzing whether or not the depredation act applied to this case, the Supreme Court said:

> The object of the act is evidently to compensate settlers for depredations committed by individual marauders belonging to a body which is then at peace with the government. If the depredation be committed by an organized company of men constituting a *band* in itself, acting independently of any other band or tribe, and carrying on hostilities against the United States, such acts may amount to a war for the consequences of which the government is not responsible under this act, or upon general principles of law.

The Court dismissed the claim of the Montoyas because it concluded that Victorio's band was independent from the main Mescalero tribe and was independently engaged in hostilities against the United States.

There is an interesting section in today's United States Code that deals with the subject of Indian depredations and tribal liability, and which was originally passed by Congress in the years 1834 and 1859. It is found in Title 25 U.S.C. Sec. 229, and reads as follows:

If any Indian, belonging to any tribe in amity with the United States, shall, within the Indian country, take or destroy the property of any person lawfully within such country, or shall pass from Indian country into any State or Territory inhabited by citizens of the United States, and there take, steal, or destroy any horse, or other property belonging to any citizen or inhabitant of the United States, such citizen or inhabitant, his representative, attorney, or agent, may make application to the proper superintendent, agent, or subagent, who, upon being furnished with necessary documents and proofs, shall, under the direction of the President, make application to the nation or tribe to which such Indian shall belong, for satisfaction, and if such nation or tribe shall neglect or refuse to make satisfaction, in a reasonable time not exceeding twelve months, such superintendent, agent, or subagent shall make return of his doings to the Commissioner of Indian Affairs, that such further steps may be taken as shall be proper, in the opinion of the President, to obtain satisfaction of the injury.

One of the most famous and instructive depredation cases to reach the U.S. Supreme Court involved a claim for property damages resulting from the 1878 flight of Dull Knife's band of Northern Cheyennes from the Indian territory back to their original homeland in northwest Nebraska. (See *Conners v. United States* 1901.) Additional information and references relevant to the general subject of depredation legislation and related cases can be found in Cohen (1982, pp. 10–11, 244) and Skogen (1996).

F-12. *Can an Indian tribe still have a legally recognized war with the United States?*

This question comes up every time I teach a course on the history of federal Indian law. Readers should first be aware that no formal declaration of war was ever made by the Congress against an Indian nation during the "Indian wars" of the 18th and 19th centuries. The Supreme Court has nonetheless ruled that states of war, which the Court and the Congress sometimes officially referred to as "hostilities" and "enmity," did indeed exist between Indian nations and the United

States. The Congress has also acknowledged, in legislation surviving from the 1870s, that Indians can be "at war" with the United States. This variable terminology for Indian wars—"hostility," "enmity," and "war"—is roughly similar to the variable language applied to the Korean "police action" and the Viet Nam "conflict." The U.S. Congress never declared war against the North Koreans or the North Vietnamese (or the Viet Cong) pursuant to the war declaration provision of the Constitution (Article I, Sec. 8, Cl. 11). These military conflicts were still considered "wars" for a number of legal purposes.

In the 18th and 19th centuries, when an officially recognized "war," or "hostilities," existed between the United States and a tribe, band, or nation of American Indians, the Indians involved were usually considered by the U.S. to be combatants, and not perpetrators of actual crimes. When captured, or after surrender, these combatants were almost always treated as prisoners of war by the U.S. and, in most cases, were not prosecuted for crimes and were eventually released after formally agreeing to live peaceably.

The largest single exception to this general principle was the aftermath of the Santee Sioux uprising of 1862 in Minnesota, during which 800 settlers were killed, many of them brutally (Utley 1988). It was not unlike what had happened to many tribal people at the hands of non-Indians (Brown 1970). (The number of Santees killed remains unclear.) A military commission, which considered many of the uprising actions of the Santees to have exceeded the bounds of warfare, sentenced 303 Indians to death, but President Lincoln reduced the death sentences to 38. All were hanged, en mass, on December 26, 1863 (Utley 1988).

There is not a clearcut answer to the question on warfare. Legislation, like the depredation acts (see question F-9) and the late 19th and early 20th century court cases that have addressed the issue of when bona fide "hostilities" exist between an Indian tribe, band, or nation and the U.S., suggest that the answer is "yes." However, because the Indian citizenship act was passed in 1924 (after the other laws and cases referred to were passed or decided), a few historians and lawyers have suggested that the answer should be "no." They feel that an official "state of war" or hostilities, such as can exist between separate sovereign nations, cannot exist between citizens of the U.S. and its government. They say any modern-day attempt at tribal warfare or hostilities with the U.S. would either have to be defined as a treason-ous revolt or insurrection, or as a civil disturbance of some kind.

However, the well-known encyclopedic reference on federal Indian law by Cohen (1982, p. 244, note 25) has this to say: "The power of tribes to make war . . . has been recognized by the courts. E.g., *Montoya v. United States,* 180 U.S. 261 (1901). Several statutes which are still effective contemplate the unlikely possibility of hostil-ities by an Indian tribe. *E.g.,* 25 U.S.C. Secs. 72, 127–129."

The following quotations are taken directly from the U.S. Code sections just cited, which are legally in effect today.

[Sec.] 72. Abrogation of Treaties

Whenever the tribal organization of any Indian tribe is in actual hostility to the United States, the President is authorized, by proclamation, to declare all treaties with such tribe abrogated [cancelled] by such tribe if in his opinion the same can be done consistently with good faith and legal and national obligations.

[Sec.] 127. Moneys or annuities of hostile Indians

No moneys or annuities stipulated by any treaty with an Indian tribe for which appropriations are made shall be expended for, or paid, or delivered to any tribe which, since the next preceding payment under such treaty, has engaged in hostilities against the United States, or against its citizens peace-fully or lawfully sojourning or traveling within its jurisdiction at the time of such hostilities; nor in such case shall such stipu-lated payments or deliveries be resumed until new appropria-tions shall have been made therefore by Congress.

[Sec.] 128. Appropriations not paid to Indians at war with the United States

None of the appropriations made for the Indian Service shall be paid to any band of Indians or any portion of any band while at war with the United States or with the white citizens of any of the States or Territories.

[Sec.] 129. Moneys due Indians holding captives other than Indians withheld

The Secretary of the Interior is authorized to withhold, from any tribe of Indians who may hold captives other than Indians, any moneys due them from the United States until said captives shall be surrendered to the lawful authorities of the United States.

Those people who today answer "yes" to the question of modern warfare are therefore saying that if the type of legislation quoted above is still on the books, it has a legal reason for being there. In other words, the fact that the legislation is there acknowledges there may still be legally recognized warfare between an Indian tribe, band, or nation and the U.S. (Note: The legislation granting the president authority to proclaim that a treaty has been abrogated by the hostilities of a treaty tribe does not suggest that *only* treaty tribes can legitimately go to war with the U.S. It merely states that if a tribe that is engaged in hostilities with the U.S. has a treaty, that treaty can be quickly proclaimed as canceled by the president.)

In order for the question of "warfare" to arise, an entity that is an independently acting Indian *tribe, band,* or *nation* must be in *enmity,* or hostilities, with the U.S. For example, if a few tribal dissidents got angry and went on a rampage against federal officers, this would not be a hostile act of an Indian tribe, band, or nation. If the dissidents survived and were captured, they would not be held as prisoners of war, but probably as criminals or as traitors.

But the other side of the warfare question remains: If the U.S. initiates hostilities against an Indian nation, would that be legally recognized as a state of war? A reasonable reply would be that if the answer to the question of whether or not a tribe can initiate a war under present-day circumstances is "yes," then the U.S. is probably equally empowered to do the same.

We did not think of the great open plains, the beautiful rolling hills, and the winding streams with tangled growth, as "wild." Only to the white man was nature a "wilderness" and only to him was the land "infested" with wild animals and "savage" people. To us it was tame. Earth was bountiful and we were surrounded with the blessings of the Great Mystery. Not until the hairy man from the east came and with brutal frenzy heaped injustices upon us and the families we loved was it "wild" for us. When the very animals of the forest began fleeing from his approach, then it was for us the "Wild West" began.

Luther Standing Bear, 1933

SECTION G: LAND, RESOURCES, AND NON-GAMING ECONOMICS

When the first edition of this book was written, Indian gaming was only beginning to gain momentum and had not reached the great proportions it has today. Because gaming is such a unique economic activity, and because of its primacy in the economic outlook for so many tribes, a new section of the book, Section O, has been added in this edition to answer key questions on Indian gaming.

G-1. *What is an Indian Reservation?*

A reservation is an area of land "reserved" for an Indian band, village, nation, or tribe (or tribes) to live on and use. Title to the Indian-owned reservation land is held in trust by the United States for the benefit of said Indians (Bureau of Indians Affairs 1968; Cohen 1982). The name "reservation" is taken from the early practice whereby Indian tribes were coerced, enticed, or otherwise persuaded to relinquish, or "cede," the majority of their homelands by treaty to the federal government, while holding back or "reserving" a portion of their original lands for their own use. The practice goes back to at least 1640, when the Mohican chief, Uncas, ceded a large part of the colony of Connecticut and retained a reservation for his tribe (Cohen 1947).

Not all reservations have been created by treaty, however, nor have all been established on tribal homelands. Acts of Congress, executive orders of the President (until prohibited in 1919), and congressionally authorized actions of the Secretary of the Interior have been used in the establishment, expansion, and restoration of Indian reservations (Canby 1981). It was also common for tribes to be removed from ancestral lands and to be placed on reservations entirely outside those lands. That practice began as early as the 1820s. The most well known examples involve the many former reservations of Oklahoma, established for about 40 tribes who were moved there from various parts of the U.S. during the 1800s.

Depending on the federal policies that have affected a particular reservation, some or even most of the land may now be owned *not* by the tribe but by individual Indians or even non-Indians. Lands owned by non-Indians are no longer held in trust by the U.S. They passed out of Indian ownership as a result of the land allotment system established by Congress in 1887 and continued until repeal of the system by the Indian Reorganization Act (1934). (See Part III for more on the history of federal Indian policy.)

G-2. *What are the largest and smallest federal Indian reservations?*
By far, the largest is the Navajo Reservation which covers roughly 15 million acres of trust lands in Arizona, Utah, and New Mexico, about 95 percent of which is tribally owned (Bureau of Indian Affairs 1987b). The rest is held under individual Indian allotments. Only

about 45 percent of all federal reservations contain land that is wholly owned by the tribes.

Each of 11 additional reservations has more than a million acres of Indian trust lands (Russell 1991). They are listed on the following page, with acreage figures rounded to the nearest 1,000 acres (Bureau of Indian Affairs 1985a).

Many small reservations are found in a number of states, like the rancherias in California. The smallest reservation is probably Sheep Ranch Rancheria, east of Sacramento, which contains slightly more than nine-tenths of one acre, or around 80 yards of a football field. Blue Lake Rancheria, in far northwestern California, comes in a close second and is also less than one acre.

State	Reservation	Acreage
Arizona	Fort Apache	1,665,000
	Hopi	1,561,000
	San Carlos Apache	1,827,000
	Tohono O'odham	
	(Sells Unit)	2,774,000
Montana	Crow	1,516,000
South Dakota	Cheyenne River	1,396,000
	Pine Ridge	1,779,000
Utah	Uintah & Ouray	1,096,000
Washington	Colville	1,063,000
	Yakima	1,130,000
Wyoming	Wind River	1,888,000

G-3. *How many federal and state Indian reservations are there, and where are they located?*

Federal

The number of federal Indian reservations totals about 310 (Russell 1994), and they are located in 33 states. These reservations include not only areas referred to as "reservations," but also Indian pueblos, rancherias, communities, and colonies where a land base of some size is held in trust by the U.S. or is otherwise protected by the government. Obviously, there are more tribal entities (greater than 550) than reservations. Thus, to be federally recognized does not necessarily mean that a tribe has been able to retain or acquire lands which can be designated as a reservation. Twenty-one of the 24 states west of the Mississippi River have at least one Indian reservation within their borders. The exceptions are: Missouri, Arkansas, and Hawaii. Only 11 of the 26 states east of the Mississippi have one or more federal Indian reservations (Bureau of Indian Affairs 1989a).

California has the highest number of federal reservations—approximately 100—but about half of these are small rancherias which range in size from less than one to several hundred acres. In fact, the total acreage of reservation land in the state is just under 450,000 acres—much less than is included in many single reservations in the western states. The highest concentration of Indian reservation trust land is in Arizona, where approximately 27 percent (about 20 million acres) of the state's 73 million acres lies within the boundaries of some 20 reservations (Bureau of Indian Affairs 1985a).

State

According to the Bureau of Indian Affairs (1989a, and 2000), there are currently 10 small Indian reservations, located in six eastern states, which have been established and administered by agreement between the states and tribes affected. The states and their associated reservations are:

Connecticut	Shagticoke, Paugusett (2), and Paucatuck Pequot
Massachusetts	Nipmuc-Hassanamisco
Michigan	Potawatomi
New York	Poosepatuck and Shinnecock
Virginia	Pamunkey and Mattaponi

Federal and state Indian reservation lands are shown in Figure 5. Indian groups which do not have reservations are shown in Figure 6.

Federal and State Indian Reservation Lands

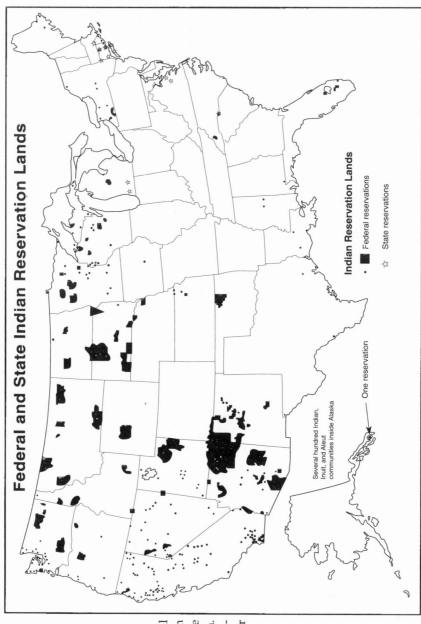

Indian Reservation Lands

■ Federal reservations
☆ State reservations

Several hundred Indian, Inuit, and Aleut communities inside Alaska

One reservation

Figure 5. Federal and state Indian reservations are located as shown. Very small reservations appear as black dots.

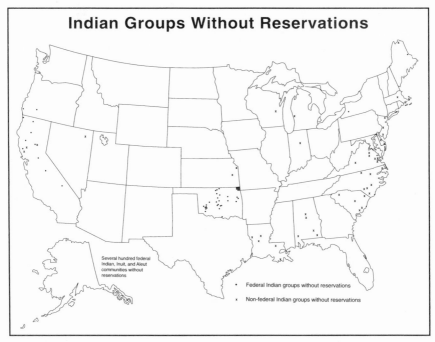

Figure 6. Indian groups which do not have reservations are shown on this map. Some are federally recognized, others are not.

G-4. *What is (or was) Indian Territory?*

In the early 1830s, during the administration of President Andrew Jackson, a policy proposal arose to establish an Indian territory in the West (Cohen 1982). The territory was to be formally organized by the U.S. and governed by a confederation of tribes. Several bills, including the "Western Territory" bill of 1834, were introduced in Congress to officially establish this Indian territory. It was to include the land area in all of present-day Kansas, most of Oklahoma, and parts of what became Nebraska, Colorado, and Wyoming. Although no such legislation was ever enacted, and no territorial Indian government was ever established, the name "Indian Territory" came into common use by Congress and others.

Indian Territory steadily diminished in size as new official territorial governments were established and states were carved out of it. By the 1870s, Indian Territory was reduced to the size of today's Oklahoma, excluding the panhandle. Many plains tribes were "removed" to western Indian Territory on lands yielded in 1866 by the Five Civilized Tribes, after the Civil War. Congress was pressed by thousands of non-Indians, the railroad interests, and land speculators to open up more of the Indian land to use by non-Indians. They got their way.

In 1890, the Oklahoma Organic Act created Oklahoma Territory out of the western portion of Indian Territory. All that remained of the original Indian Territory was the combined lands of the Five Tribes and the Quapaw Agency tribes. It was an area which included roughly all the land in Oklahoma located south and east of a line running from Bartlesville (in the northeast) to Lawton (in the southwest).

During the succeeding years, Congress passed several laws to make allotments of tribal lands to individual Indians and then sell off the "excess." One such law was the Curtis Act of 1898.

In 1906, the Oklahoma Enabling Act provided for combining Oklahoma Territory and Indian Territory and admitting them as the state of Oklahoma. Statehood was proclaimed in 1907, and Indian Territory ceased to exist.

(Note: Indian Territory differs from "Indian country." See the answer to question H-12 for information about Indian country.

G-5. Did the Indians of North America have clear conceptions of land ownership before European contact?

> One does not sell the land upon which the people walk.
>
> Crazy Horse
> Oglala Lakota

Yes, though theirs differed from the European concept. For example, buying and selling land and establishing arbitrary, straight-line, and razor-sharp boundaries were alien ideas.

Land was of primary value in American Indian societies. Without a politically defined and controlled land and resource base, survival of tribes or bands was greatly impaired or impossible. That is the reason so many serious conflicts about land and resources occurred, both before and after Europeans arrived in the Western Hemisphere (Arnold 1976).

Considerable variation existed among tribes with respect to their concepts about ownership, but a few general statements can be made. In addition, the resources of a particular land area might often be given higher value than the land itself. First, most land was not individually owned. There were, in some instances, cultivated tracts, fishing sites, and wild seed, fruit, or vegetable patches held by individual families (Ceram 1971). These were, however, often scattered within much larger areas under the communal control or "ownership" of all tribal members.

Another significant aspect of band or tribal ownership was its sometimes exclusive nature. Some tribes held their land for tribal use only—not making it available to other groups for any purpose, including settlement, hunting, gathering, or travel. Bands or tribes usually had clearly identified boundaries that were associated with land features and were known to all groups in the region. To trespass on another tribe's property, in some settings, could be a very risky undertaking, similar to a serious breach of international etiquette. Depending on the attitudes and relative power of the groups involved, and the severity of the trespass, an encroachment might lead to the capture, punishment, or even death of the violators. Further, it might be considered an outright foreign invasion, whether intended or not, and precipitate a war.

Finally, individual tribes' concepts of their land ownership and boundaries were often specific enough that they were used to describe land cessions in treaties and agreements. These boundaries, of course, were subsequently defined by federal surveys that would locate precise land lines. Later, the pre-survey descriptions were sometimes used in establishing judicially recognized Indian land claims for which the U.S. government, and occasionally other interests, owed compensation to various tribes (U.S. Indian Claims commission 1978). Land and resource issues remain extremely important to Indian people.

G-6. *What is the specific meaning of "aboriginal title," and is it relevant today?*

> *All . . . claims of aboriginal title in Alaska . . . are hereby extinguished.*
> Alaska Native Claims Settlement Act 1971

"Aboriginal title," "original Indian title," or just "Indian title" are three terms applied to a land ownership concept that was attributed to the Native people of the Western hemisphere by Euro-American governments.

From the beginning, Europeans wanted to determine what kind of Native land rights should be recognized legally. Two very different sides of the debate emerged. One put forth by many was that Indians had no rights after "discovery." They were infidels who stood in the way of much superior civilizations and should be swept away. On top of that, they had no deeds with notary seals and ribbons attesting to their ownership, as the Europeans had.

The preeminent Spanish theologian, Francis de Vitoria, developed an opposite and quite liberal view as early as 1532. He dismissed the hallowed discovery doctrine (see Part I), declaring it applied only to lands not already possessed by other peoples. Furthermore, in his analysis, the Indians "were true owners, both from the public and the private standpoint" (Cohen 1947, p. 45). So powerful were Vitoria's arguments that Pope Paul III incorporated them into a 1537 proclamation addressing Indians' rights to property and freedom from slavery. In response, and for several centuries thereafter, colonial governments vacillated somewhere between Vitoria's precept and the "no rights" contention. Of course, Indian views were never solicited.

For the United States, the issue was settled by the Supreme Court in *Johnson v. McIntosh* (1823). Chief Justice Marshall, writing for the court, chose a compromise position. He embraced the European doctrine of title by discovery, but said it did not completely extinguish all Indian rights. The government held a superior sovereign title to the land, but the Indians retained a right to occupy and use it as they always had, until their right was extinguished through conquest or purchase by the federal government. Therefore, *aboriginal title is an exclusive right of occupancy and use.* It is superior to any claimed right of a state or individual, but it is not an outright and full ownership of the land exclusive of a *federal* interest.

When Indian groups ceded land to the government—which had to be done before their land could legally be taken into possession by the government or anyone else—Indian title to the land was said to be "extinguished." It then became part of the public domain, available for sale or other disposition under the federal land laws. Again, only the federal government could extinguish aboriginal title, and it did so to roughly 2,500,000 square miles of land (Cohen 1947; Alaska Native Claims Settlement Act 1971). This was done through hundreds of treaties and agreements and the expenditure of millions of dollars, in often below-market compensation. (Reservation trust land is not held under the partial ownership doctrine of Indian title. Rather, it is held generally under a full title that is established, sanctioned, and held in trust by the U.S. government.)

The largest extinguishing of aboriginal or Indian title in the U.S. came in 1971 when Alaska Natives ceded their rights to more than 300,000,000 acres of the state to the federal government. This relatively recent action, however, was not the last involving Indian title. Other famous but much smaller claims by several eastern tribes have followed, e.g., Maine Indian Claims Settlement Act (1980) and Mashantucket Pequot Indian Claims Settlement Act (1983). There is also a current land claim dispute involving 100 square miles of Cayuga land that was illegally taken by the state of New York in 1795 and 1807 (Associated Press 2000c). Thus the issue is not yet irrelevant in the U.S. It continues to arise periodically in relation to land claims wherein Indians discover and assert that former tribal lands were taken in ways inconsistent with established federal law. Some members of Congress, like Senator Helms of North Carolina, are trying to change federal law to bar such claims.

The general U.S. idea about aboriginal title has been borrowed by other countries in the Western Hemisphere, like Canada for instance. Recently the Canadian government negotiated an agreement with the Inuit (Eskimos) of the Northwest Territories. The land cession involved dwarfed even the Alaska claims. Under the agreement the approximately 20,000 Inuit involved gave up aboriginal claims to as much as a million square miles of land and sea area. In exchange, they received direct control over 135,000 square miles within a new government territory of 740,000 square miles, called "Nunavut." In addition, the Inuit retained a right to hunt, fish, and trap across all of Nunavut, which was carved out of the old Northwest Territories (Carroll 1999).

Agreement on the Nunavut issue, which took 20 years of negotiations, still left much to do in the settling of aboriginal land claims in Canada. More than 600 remain (Anquoe 1991a). In the coming decades, more will also be heard about aboriginal rights in Mexico and in Central and South America, especially as the Native people in those areas are able to organize and educate themselves to press their long-dormant claims.

G-7. What is Indian trust land, how much is there, and is the amount increasing or decreasing?

Beginning with a simple definition, Indian trust land is Indian-owned land, title to which is held in trust by the United States. What this essentially means is that the "ownership" is divided between the federal government, which holds "bare legal title," and the tribe (or, in some cases, individual Indian) which holds full equitable title (National Congress of American Indians 1976).

The great majority of trust land is reservation land, but not all reservation land is trust land. This is a result of the now defunct reservation allotment policies which functioned in earnest from 1887–1934. Great sell-offs of reservation land (within reservation boundaries) to non-Indians resulted. This led to the "checker board" land ownership patterns seen in many reservations. Not all reservations were affected, however. In addition to holding title to trust land, the U.S. government also exercises a significant measure of oversight authority regarding its use and management. During the 19th century, the federal government decided a major part of its government-to-government trust responsibility toward the tribes was to hold their lands in trust. The intended purpose was to prevent "unscrupulous" business and government interests from wrongfully acquiring Indian lands. Trust land had been established in five different ways: (1) by treaties with the U.S. government, (2) by legislative agreements negotiated with tribes, (3) by specific legislative designations, (4) by executive orders of the President, and (5) by administrative land "withdrawals" of the Secretary of the Interior, setting aside public domain lands as reservation lands (Hall 1981).

As already suggested, there are two types of trust land—that owned by individuals and that which is tribally owned. Presently available data indicate that the individual owned total is approximately 10,059,000 acres (Bureau of Indian Affairs 1997). The tribal total is about 46,000,000 acres, for a grand total of about 56,000,000 acres of trust land (Jones 1991, Bureau of Indian Affairs 1997). (The trust land figures change little. See the BIA website: www.doi.gov/bia/realty/consol/97.html.) In general, neither the government nor the Indian owner can sell or otherwise dispose of trust land without consent from the other. The major exception is that Congress can unilaterally take Indian lands for dams, irrigation projects, federal highways, or other "public purposes" under its controversial "plenary," or near absolute, power over Indian affairs.

Approximately 98 percent of the trust land is in the lower 48 states, but it represents only 2.8 percent of the total land area there. In Alaska, however, there is a very substantial amount of non-trust, privately held Indian land. Because of the different legal status of nearly all Native lands in that state, particulars about the Alaska situation are discussed in Section M of this book.

Nationwide, the total of Indian trust lands has increased by approximately 3,000,000 acres since 1985 (Bureau of Indians Affairs 1997). This growth has occurred only within the lower 48 states and was accomplished by congressional, Interior Department, or direct tribal acquisitions of lands that were converted to trust status. The "increase," however, has to be put into historical perspective.

In 1887, the year allotment began in earnest—and long after the reservation system had been well established—the total of Indian landholdings was 138,000,000 acres. This represented about seven percent of the area of the lower 48 states. By the end of the allotment period in 1934, however, the area of Indian landholdings had been reduced to 48,000,000 acres (Collier 1934). At the rate of increase that has taken place since 1934 (to the present 56,000,000 acres), it would take another 600 years for the tribes to regain the reservation lands they held in the late-1880s. This is not going to happen, of course, because most of their former reservation lands are covered with cities, towns, farms, ranches, military reservations, factories, national parks, national forests, and so on.

G-8. *What significant natural resources do American Indian tribal groups have?*

Land

First and foremost among the natural resources controlled by American Indians is land. Its value is often three-tiered: economic, social, and spiritual. These values can create strongly competing concerns when questions of land and resource development arise. Indian trust lands (56,000,000 acres) and Alaska Native corporation lands (44,000,000 acres) now cover 156,250 square miles of U.S. territory. This amounts to four percent of the nation's total land area of 3,615,210 square miles.

Minerals

Politicians of the 19th century, through their policies, deprived the Indian people of much of their good land and other subsistence resources. Unknowingly, however, they left a number of tribes with non-subsistence resources, such as coal, oil, gas, and uranium, that would become very valuable in the 20th century. For example, in 1996 (the most recent year for which figures are readily available), Indian trust lands produced $165 million from mineral leases, mostly for oil, gas, and coal. Roughly 10 percent of the nation's total coal reserves and a third of its low-sulfur coal lie beneath American Indian land. Oil is also found in substantial quantities on several reservations and under some Alaska Native corporation lands. And, nearly one-sixth of America's natural gas reserves may lie under Indian land.

In the 48 states, however, only 29 percent of Indians belong to tribes with notable amounts of mineral resources (O'Brien 1989).

During the 20th century, periodic mismanagement or corruption within the Bureau of Indian Affairs, as well as within certain state and tribal agencies, has resulted in the cumulative loss of hundreds of millions of dollars in tribal and individual royalty revenues from oil and gas leases (Hall 1981; Hill 1999; Howarth 2000; Melmer 1999; White 1990; White and Cronon 1988).

Besides the carbon-based minerals, more than half of America's uranium is on Indian land. Other mineral and related resources that are found in varying amounts within one or more Indian reservations or Native communities include gold, silver, copper, molybdenum, zeolite, phosphate, vanadium, sandstone, basalt, shale, sulfur, limestone, chat, lead, zinc, peat, iron, clay, gypsum, volcanic cinders, sand, gravel, and building stone (Washburn 1988).

Timber

About one-fourth of all Indian reservation lands, or nearly 13 million acres, have some kind of forest cover. Almost a third of the forest land is considered to be of "commercial" quality, which means it is theoretically capable of growing timber at a volume that can be harvested for a profit on a renewable basis (Bureau of Indian Affairs 1992a). In the pre-gaming years, nearly 60 tribes obtained 25 to 100 percent of their non-federal revenues from timber operations (Hall 1981), and as many as 130 tribes belong to the "Tribal Timber Consortium" (O'Brien 1989).

Timber mismanagement has plagued BIA-directed forestry programs, where "getting the cut out" has sometimes taken precedence over long-term protection of ecosystems. Similar problems affect the national forests. Many Indians and non-Indians, who now see that forests are more than mere sources of timber and other commodities, are pressing the issue of forest conservation with their leaders and government agencies.

Water

Water is the most critical resource in the western states, and that is where most Indian reservations are located. Therefore, intense competition and conflicts over water are found between tribes and non-Indian interests. The issue frequently centers on the fact that Indians legally "have" the water, or rights thereto, and some other individual, group, agency, corporation, or local government "wants" it.

In the West, as elsewhere, Indian rights to fisheries and water resources have been the focus of intense controversy over the years. Natives in the Northwest, for example, have fished the Columbia River system for centuries, but the development of hydroelectric power, along with fishing competition from non-Indians, created conflicts. Photo circa 1930s.

Reservation Indians and tribes have well established rights to large but not yet fully quantified amounts of water. These rights are based on the doctrine of reserved water rights, first acknowledged in the famous Supreme Court case of *Winters v. United States* (1908) and later affirmed and clarified in the equally important case of *Arizona v. California* (1963). The concept behind the doctrine is that the establishment of Indian reservations meant not only that the land was "reserved" but also that the right to sufficient water to fulfill the purposes of the reservation was also reserved. In other words, the government could not put Indians on reservations and leave them without rights to sufficient amounts of water to maintain and later develop their reservations and resources (Cohen 1982).

As tribes continue to hold and use their water rights, while population and development pressures in the West further strain the already over-extended water resources, conflict with competing interests will increase. Precisely how the problems will ultimately be resolved, if they ever are, is unclear. But what is clear is that the roles of the tribes in brokering and adjudicating western water rights will continue to grow in importance.

For more on the extremely important and complex issues of Indian water rights and water rights settlements, see Burton (1991); Getches, Wilkinson, and Williams (1998); McCool (1987, 1993a, 1993b, and in press); McGuire, Lord, and Wallace (1993); Shurts (2000); and Sly (1988).

G-9. *How did the Indian Claims Commission come into being, and what was its purpose?*

> *Indian claims are, by and large, the backwash of a great national experiment in dictatorship and racial extermination.*
> Felix Cohen, Indian law scholar and Interior Department lawyer, in a 1945 statement (from Hagan 1988, p. 17)

Felix Cohen was one of a number of government officials, including the influential John Collier, Commissioner of Indian Affairs from 1933 to 1945, who promoted establishment of a special federal forum to address tribes' longstanding legal and related claims against the United States. But the issue of formally addressing Indian claims, the majority of which involved land, began long before Cohen and Collier became policy makers.

The government has always had an official policy of purchasing tribal lands rather than taking them by conquest (see question D-1 and Part III.) But most of these purchases involved inherent and substantial injustices that were worked into the treaties and agreements through which the lands were acquired. In addition, the dollar amounts paid were often incredibly low, and the food, clothing, and manufactured goods that were sometimes promised as partial payment were often so poor in quality they were useless. There were also tribes who were completely overlooked and were never paid anything for the lands they lost. Therefore, tribes had many formal claims against the federal government.

As a sovereign power, the U.S. has sovereign immunity and cannot be sued in its courts without granting permission for this to occur. In the 18th century and up until the mid-nineteenth century, tribes (and everyone else) were cut off from bringing direct suit against the U.S. Until the mid-1850s, the remedy for aggrieved parties was to get a special compensation act passed by Congress for their own specific claim. This, of course, was a very difficult thing to do.

In 1855, Congress passed legislation that created the first U.S. Court of Claims, which allowed certain kinds of claims to be brought by aggrieved parties against the U.S. (Hagan 1988). Several tribes filed cases in the new court but, in 1863, before any of the cases was decided, Congress passed legislation that specifically excluded Indians from using the Court of Claims. The individual tribes were left with two options: to get specific legislations passed that would right particular wrongs, or to get legislation passed that would allow a tribe to file suit in the Court of Claims.

It was in 1881 that Congress first granted permission to a tribe to file suit in the Court of Claims. The average number of cases filed by tribes over the next 40 years was one a year. Only 17 of these cases resulted in awards to tribes.

The number of requests to Congress for access to the Court increased dramatically after the Indian Citizenship Act was passed in 1924. By 1946, another 200 claims had been approved by Congress for adjudication in the Court of Claims. However, a number of requests had been refused, and even if a tribe *did* make it to the Court, there was a good chance its case would be dismissed on a technicality. Congress and the tribes were burdened by and frustrated with this cumbersome process (Getches, Wilkinson, and Williams 1998; Hagan 1988).

In 1946, Congress passed the Indian Claims Commission Act. The Act was considered to be liberal in the breadth of claims that were permissible under its provisions (Canby 1998). However, the overall intent of Congress in passing the Indian Claims Commission Act was to settle for all time the claims arising from federal dealings with the Indians, and "as a result, payment of an award under the Act defeats any further tribal claim of an aboriginal right to occupy the lands for which compensation was paid" (Canby 1998, p. 355).

The Commission's scope of reviewable claims was defined in Section 2 of the Act:

> The Commission shall hear and determine the following claims against the United States on behalf of any Indian tribe, band or other identifiable group of American Indians residing within the territorial limits of the United States or Alaska: (1) claims in law or equity arising under the Constitution, laws, treaties of the United States, and Executive orders of the President; (2) all other claims in law or equity, including those sounding in tort, with respect to which claimant would have been entitled to sue in a court of the United States if the United States was subject to suit; (3) claims which would result if the treaties, contracts, and agreements between the claimant and the United States were revised on the ground of fraud, duress, unconscionable consideration, mutual or unilateral mistake, whether of law or fact, or any other ground cognizable by a court of equity; (4) claims arising from the taking by the United States, whether as a result of a treaty of cession or otherwise, of lands owned or occupied by the claimant without the payment for such lands of compensation agreed to by the claimant; and (5) claims based upon fair and honorable dealings that are not recognized by any existing rule of law or equity. No claim accruing after the date of the Act shall be considered by the Commission.

Although the Commission was originally to last only ten years, it was periodically extended by Congress until 1978, when it was terminated and all pending claims were transferred to the Court of Claims (Canby 1998; Prucha 1990b).

By the time the Commission was dissolved, on September 30, 1978, it had adjudicated over 500 claims—the vast majority of them dealt with land. The tribes had won favorable judgments in over 60 percent of the cases, and the total awards amounted to over $800 million dollars.

The tribes, including those that won awards, were generally disappointed with the outcome of the Commission's activities and the rules under which it operated. The biggest disappointment was that Congress limited awards to monetary payments only, no land was allowed to be returned to the tribes as compensation for their claims (Hagan 1988; Prucha 1986). Also, the amounts paid for the claims were determined on the value of the land in the nineteenth-century (which averaged out to less than one dollar per acre), and no interest was paid, except in a limited number of cases in which the land taking violated the Fifth Amendment of the Constitution. In addition, the Act allowed the government to deduct from monetary awards old payments that had been made to the claimant tribes. Thus, as Canby (1998, p. 356) concludes, "An award for land measured by nineteenth century values without interest falls many times short of restoring a tribe to the position it would have occupied had it retained the lost land." Hagan (1988, p. 24) thoughtfully adds to this assessment. "What the Commission did most successfully was to erase the collective conscience of the American people about injustices perpetrated countless times by their government since 1790."

Our land is worth more than your money.
> Blackfeet chief to U.S. treaty negotiators (circa 1850s)

Were we paid a thousand times the market value of our lost holdings, still the payment would not suffice. Money never mothered the Indian people, as the land has mothered them, nor have any people become more closely attached to the land, religiously and traditionally.
> Statement in an Indian Claims report from a
> conference of tribespeople at Chicago, 1961
> (from Hagan 1988, p. 21)

G-10. *How important are American Indian hunting and fishing rights, and what are some of the major controversies pertaining to those rights?*

When Europeans arrived in the southern and eastern part of the continent in the late 15th century, and in Alaska in the mid-18th century, hunting, fishing, and related activities were absolutely vital to tribal life. Understandably, preservation of the rights to continue pursuing such activities became central topics in peace negotiations and land cessions, and were directly or indirectly guaranteed through treaties, agreements, legislation, or executive actions. As the 21st century has begun, these very same rights continue to have critical importance to hundreds of Native communities—for both cultural and economic reasons.

In Alaska, where no official treaties were entered into by the U.S. and Native people, hunting and fishing rights are part of the overarching issue of "subsistence." The subsistence issue, because it relates specifically to Alaska, is discussed in Section M of this book.

To say that the controversies surrounding tribal hunting and fishing rights in the lower 48 states can be complicated and intense is putting it mildly. Some conflicts in the Northwest and Great Lakes regions, for example, have led to vigilantism and violence. The following discussion mentions the major controversies and gives general answers to the basic jurisdictional questions which are at their foundation. Information is taken from Benzie Fishery Coalition (1999), Canby (1981), Cohen (1982), Getches, Rosenfelt, and Wilkinson (1998), and O'Brien (1989).

Four themes are commonly heard from opponents of Indian treaty hunting and fishing rights: (1) they are unfair to non-Indians, (2) they are basically illegal, (3) they interfere with the hunting and fishing regulatory function of a state, and (4) they are contrary to conservation goals. On the unfairness claim, things may seem unfair to non-Indian hunting and fishing interests when a local tribe has equal or "superior" rights to their own. But, such a view is taken out of context. The Indian tribes in the lower 48 states gave up 98 percent of the land area through treaties and agreements with the colonial, state, and federal governments. Retaining two percent of the land base and some locally or regionally significant hunting and fishing rights does not generally appear to the tribes, Congress, or the courts as an unfair trade. However, to the non-Indian who is subject to state laws and game limits, it might naturally seem unfair. Nonetheless, controversies over the issue of Indian rights cannot be divorced from their historical and legal contexts.

Five essential points need to be emphasized before moving on to the regulatory and conservation questions. First, it is well settled in the law that establishment of a federal reservation includes a right of Indians to hunt and fish on their reservation, free of state interference.

Second, when some of the tribes gave up lands, they retained the rights to continue hunting and fishing on all or parts of their former homelands. These rights were retained through both explicit and implicit language in the treaties. Such rights can be likened to easements. Many Washington state tribes, several Chippewa tribes, the Crow Tribe, the Navajo, the Southern Cheyenne, and a few other groups retained off-reservation rights. These and the on-reservation rights are part of the "reserved rights doctrine" mentioned elsewhere with regard to Indian water rights. The doctrine is tied to the well-founded legal concept that, when Indian land rights were reserved, other associated rights (e.g., hunting, fishing, trapping, gathering of plant materials, water use, etc.) were reserved for the tribes' continued cultural and economic well-being.

A third point is that, under its plenary (near absolute) power over Indian affairs regarding federally recognized tribes, Congress, and not the states, has the ultimate authority to regulate all aspects of Indian hunting and fishing pertaining to reserved rights. It has rarely exercised this authority, however, leaving most regulatory responsibility to the tribes.

Fourth, on a few former reservations where the U.S. "terminated" the tribes' federal status and extinguished their aboriginal title to the reservations, Indian hunting and fishing rights continue to be in effect unless specifically extinguished by Congressional action.

Finally, in the absence of acknowledged treaty rights, Indians outside of legally defined "Indian country" are subject to the same laws as everyone else.

Tribal authority over on-reservation hunting and fishing

When no federal law exists to the contrary, tribes can regulate the hunting and fishing of Indians and non-Indians on Indian-owned land. To do so, tribes must establish comprehensive hunting and fishing codes for management, licensing, and enforcement purposes. Many have done so. As part of their regulatory authority, tribes can bring *criminal* charges in tribal court against Indians who violate tribal game laws, but not against non-Indians. However, tribes can impose *civil* penalties for game and fish violations by non-Indians. These penalties might include fines, equipment confiscation (debatable), or ejection from the reservation. Tribes may also request federal prosecution of non-Indians for violating federal trespass and game laws.

State authority over on-reservation hunting and fishing

States may regulate on-reservation hunting and fishing in two circumstances. First, if no federal or tribal regulatory program has been established for Indian-owned reservation lands, the state may be able to step in and fill the regulatory void. The state, however, may not authorize non-Indians to hunt and fish on Indian-owned reservation lands without the affected tribe's permission. Second, states can allow and regulate non-Indian hunting and fishing on non-Indian land that is within the exterior boundaries of a reservation, whether or not the affected tribe agrees. That is, unless the conduct of non-Indians threatens or has some direct effect on the political integrity, economic security, or health and welfare of the tribe.

Tribal authority over off-reservation hunting and fishing

The several tribes that retained off-reservation hunting and fishing rights in their treaties have the authority to regulate their members in this off-reservation activity. Unless Congress changes existing law, the states affected cannot prohibit the tribes from exercising their treaty rights and cannot require tribal members to buy state game licenses. Furthermore, neither the state nor a private landowner can prevent tribal access to reserved sites. Tribal rights predate non-Indian acquisition of the land and are legally "attached" to it in the form of a treaty easement.

State authority over off-reservation hunting and fishing

There are two exceptions to exclusive tribal regulation of off-reservation hunting and fishing allowed by treaty. Tribes have a responsibility to conserve off-reservation fish and wildlife. If they do not, and conservation requires action, the federal courts will allow states to impose regulations. Also, at least one state court has successfully held that an Indian violating tribal game and fish laws at an off-reservation site could be arrested and prosecuted by the state because he had (1) also violated state law and (2) stepped beyond his tribally protected rights.

Conservation

The opposition argument that Indian treaty hunting and fishing causes much greater pressure on game and fish populations than is caused by other pressures—like loss of habitat, poor logging practices, general environmental degradation, or fishing and hunting by non-Indian interests—is generally not supported by the evidence. Where conservation becomes an issue, either the tribes or the federal government, or both, are obliged to take remedial action. If they fail to do so, and if a state can show a "necessity for conservation," the state may proceed to take appropriate and non-discriminatory regulatory action to address identified problems.

G-11. *What does "environmental racism" mean and how much of a concern is it in Indian country?*

"Environmental racism" was coined by the Reverend Benjamin Chavis, Jr., executive director of the Commission of Racial Justice of the United Church of Christ (Associated Press 1991c). In 1987, Dr. Chavis first used the term in describing results of a study done by his commission that found a very strong correlation between race and the selection of sites for hazardous industries and waste disposal facilities. Environmental racism is generally defined as racial discrimination in environmental policy making, regulation enforcement, and waste facility siting, and also includes the exclusion of people of color from the decision-making process as well as from leadership positions in the environmental movement. It is very much an issue in Indian country.

In recent years, waste disposal agencies and companies have increased their contracting efforts in Indian country to try to entice tribes to take advantage of potentially profitable agreements. As an example, in the 1990s the federal government's chief nuclear waste negotiator made a point of attending meetings of the National Congress of American Indians. He offered money and assistance programs to those tribes who would allow development of nuclear waste sites on tribal lands (Workman 1991).

While a few tribes, or factions within the tribes, are actively courting government agencies and private companies to consider tribal lands for profitable waste disposal projects of different kinds, others are adamantly opposed. Several of the concerns beyond the waste disposal issue include water quality and quantity issues, the environmental effects of oil and gas development, health and environmental damage caused by uranium mining, and the effects of ongoing air and ground training and testing by the military services.

In October 1991, the first "National People of Color Environmental Leadership Summit" was held in Washington, D.C. The 600 participants included American Indians, African Americans, Hispanic Americans, Pacific Islanders, Canadians, Mexicans, and Central and South Americans. Speakers like Wilma Mankiller, principal chief of the Cherokee Nation of Oklahoma, called for such things as (1) an end to the myth that people of color are not involved in the environmental movement, (2) education of Indian people on the dangers of economic development projects that involve hazardous wastes, and (3) environmental justice for all people (Tallman 1991).

G-12. *How do American Indians earn a living?*

> The mind of mainstream America bears its Native citizens back ceaselessly into the past. Whereas many feel that economic progress is fine for every other ethnic group (thinking the quicker the better) too many of us non-Indians prefer our Natives as living museum pieces, in the saddle or the dugout, living out some storybook version of "natural" subsistence. In this view, economic progress is corrupted into a fall from aboriginal grace.
>
> White 1990, p. 276

American Indians earn their livelihoods in as many and varied ways as do other people. For example, there are American Indian teachers, loggers, physicians, soldiers, carpenters, factory workers, pilots, ranchers, cooks, corporate executives, rodeo cowboys, secretaries, farmers, radio announcers, race car drivers, accountants, dentists, engineers, professional golfers, commercial fishermen, homemakers,

The motion picture industry is one area in which some American Indians have been able to obtain employment. For example, Nathan Chasing Horse (right) played the role of "Smiles a Lot" in *Dances With Wolves*. He and his father, Joseph Chasing Horse, are Sicangu (Brulé) Lakota from the Rosebud Reservation in South Dakota.

Many Indians make all or part of their living by selling arts and crafts. Authentically-made items are given a certain degree of protection under the Indian Arts and Crafts Act. Phil Garcia, a Laguna Pueblo carver displays some of the tools of his trade.

legislators, foresters, veterinarians, musicians, actors, salespeople, janitors, lawyers, truckers, authors, bureaucrats, service station attendants, police officers, and psychologists. The list goes on. It also includes some individuals and groups in Alaska who rely on subsistence hunting, fishing, and even occasional whaling for much of their livelihoods. Some tribal members are eligible for per capita payments from tribal resource, business, or investment income, or corporate investments, trust accounts, and judgments awarded by the Indian Claims Commission and the Court of Claims.

Unemployment on reservations has ranged from a low of 0 or 1 percent to a high of about 90 percent in recent decades (Bureau of Indian Affairs 1989b). In a 1986 BIA study, before a number of tribes had gaming enterprises, it was found that 41 percent of Indians on reservations lived below the poverty line. That number has reduced to approximately 33 percent of reservation Indians. On average, a reservation Indian family from a non-gaming tribe lives on 40 percent of the income of a non-Indian family in the U.S. (O'Brien 1989).

There is one occupation in which American Indians can work and others cannot. That is the production of authentic arts and crafts

Wilson Hunter, a Navajo, is Chief of Interpretation at Canyon de Chelly National Monument, on the Navajo Reservation in Arizona. He is shown here (left) while on a tour of the Monument in 1992. As an employee of the National Park Service, Wilson has developed a national reputation for his ability to interpret the natural and cultural heritage of Canyon de Chelly to its thousands of annual visitors.

items. It is a violation of federal law for non-Natives to willfully offer for sale or display imitation "Indian" arts and crafts, while representing them as authentic. Some Indians and Alaska Natives make their entire livings from arts and crafts, while many thousands supplement their incomes in this way. Annual retail sales of Native arts and crafts total up to a billion dollars, but non-Native interests currently control most of the retail market (Andrews 1991; Indian Arts and Crafts Association 2000).

G-13. *May Indians qualify for the major social services and assistance programs offered by non-BIA agencies?*

Generally, yes. But overviews and comparisons of relevant Bureau of Indian Affairs and other programs (like those given in Cohen 1982 and Walke 1991) can clarify the sometimes confusing aspects of this issue.

BIA programs

The BIA has had programs to assist needy Indians since the 19th century. Until 1944, however, general assistance funds for the needy were routed through Indian agents on behalf of eligible Indian people. In that year, BIA welfare payments were authorized to be paid directly to individuals who were eligible for them. Until 1977, the BIA generally refused to make payments to Indians in need who lived outside the boundaries of a reservation. The exceptions were in parts of Alaska and Oklahoma. Some difficulties arose because many potentially eligible Indians lived *just outside* reservations. Today, needy Indians who live on "or near" a reservation may apply for general assistance from the BIA. Title 25 of the Code of Federal Regulations, Sec. 20.1(r), specifically defines the important term "near a reservation." The BIA's general assistance and child welfare programs are designed to provide social service assistance to needy American Indians who do not receive similar benefits from state or federal programs. The federal government's position is that the overall Social Security program (discussed below), and not the BIA, has the *primary* responsibility for providing financial support for economically disadvantaged American Indians.

Social Security programs

Indians and Alaska Natives who have worked under and contributed to the Social Security system have the same coverage as other people. This includes the "old age" benefits, for those 65 and over, that most people think of when social security is mentioned. The Social Security Act, however, also provides both federal and state financial assistance, administered in large part by the states and their subdivisions, to impoverished United States citizens. Under various programs, the act authorizes welfare payments to the poor and direct aid to disadvantaged senior citizens, dependent children, and disabled citizens. American Indians in need, like other citizens and state residents, may qualify for benefits under the Social Security Act. According to the BIA, general assistance is not available to Indians receiving social security benefits.

USDA programs

The Department of Agriculture's food stamp program aims to help economically disadvantaged or low income households, including those of American Indians, obtain a nutritious diet. Uniform eligibility requirements are established by the USDA. The overriding rule states that food stamps are for "those households whose incomes and other financial resources . . . are determined to be a substantial limiting factor in permitting them to obtain a more nutritious diet" (7 USC, Sec. 2014(a)). States normally administer the food stamp program. However, a tribal government may administer the program on its reservation if the Secretary of Agriculture determines that the state government is not doing an adequate job. Surplus food commodities that the USDA stores and then distributes to communities around the country, to prevent waste, are also available to Indian communities.

Tribal programs

On a few reservations which have substantial resources, there are tribal social service programs funded through the tribes' own finances. The increase in tribal gaming enterprises over the past decade, for example, has expanded several tribes' abilities to fund some of their own social service programs.

Other assistance programs

During 1990 and 1991, Roger Walke of the Congressional Research Service, Library of Congress, compiled a 331-page report for the Senate Select Committee on Indian Affairs titled *Federal Programs of Assistance to Native Americans* (102nd Congress, 1st Session, S. Prt. [sic] 102-162). It provides basic information on all government programs that specifically serve or are of particular interest to American Indians, Alaska Natives, and Native Hawaiians. This very important report, with a publication date of December 1991, is for sale by the Superintendent of Documents, U.S. Government Printing Office, Washington, D.C. 20402; phone (202) 783-3238.

G-14. *What can be said about the state of the economy in Indian country?*

Only general statements can be made because of the great diversity, nationwide, in the economic circumstances of tribes and individual American Indians. Indian country, like everywhere else, is affected by changing national economic trends.

Starting with perhaps the most successful situation, there seems to be at least one tribe in the country in which everyone is doing exceedingly well, financially. It is the Manshautucket Pequot Tribe of Connecticut, which operates the largest casino in the world, Foxwoods Resort Casino (see www.foxwoods.com). Another financial success story is that of the tiny Cabazon Tribe of Indio, California. The 30-plus members have a 1,700-acre reservation located 20 miles east of Palm Springs on a creosote-flats desert. When the author first visited there in 1970, some of the people were living under very poor conditions. Now, with a few controversial non-Indian business managers (who are government-wise and extremely effective at what they do), each tribal member is reported to have an annual income of perhaps $500,000 or more. This is derived from several hundred million dollars' worth of development that has been taking place on the reservation since the early 1980s. It has included gaming enterprises, a 1,300-unit housing project for non-Indians, a Canadian-backed electrical power plant, and possible military hardware and international trade projects (Littman 1991).

In contrast to the Indians of the Cabazon Reservation, thousands of individual Native people, from Florida to Alaska and Maine to California, are still mired in poverty. In 1995 the Census Bureau reported that approximately 33 percent of *all* American Indians lived below the poverty line. In 1999, the National Academy of Public Administration reported that this number had improved to 31 percent, compared to 13 percent of the general population, living below the poverty line. These statistics show that little has changed for most Indians, despite the widespread increase in Indian gaming during recent years. More than half of the Native population resides in and around urban areas, and perhaps a quarter of these Americans are unemployed, or underemployed, and impoverished.

On the brighter side, a number of Indian tribes and communities have businesses and resource-based enterprises—like electronics plants, fishing interests, cattle ranches, casinos, oil and gas wells, coal mines, resorts, retail outlets, waste disposal businesses, industrial parks, or sawmills—that generate steady and respectable returns. These now include the Passamaquoddies of Maine, the Mississippi Band of Choctaws, various Native corporations in Alaska, the Ak-Chin Community near Phoenix, the Confederated Tribes of the Warm Springs Reservation of Oregon, the Navajo Nation, the Cherokee Nation of Oklahoma, the Pascua Yaqui Tribe near Tucson, the Mescalero Apache Tribe of New Mexico, the Oneidas of New York, and many others. But even among these comparatively successful tribal groups and communities, there are often unemployment rates of 20 to 50 percent or higher. The point is that, although numerous tribes' businesses may be successful, this does not necessarily mean those businesses create nearly enough job opportunities for all or even a majority of the members of the tribe.

Most non-gaming reservation tribes have no substantial formal economy of their own to generate operating capital. Their revenues are derived primarily from outside the reservations. An average non-gaming reservation tribe obtains 30 percent of its revenue from tribal businesses, taxes, investments, etc., or from annuities relating to former land sales or court-awarded judgments on property claims. The remaining 70 percent of tribal income enters the reservation as federal program dollars. These federal funds, in combination with tribal monies, are important not only to tribes but to local off-reservation communities which provide goods and services to the tribes and their members. Thus, federal Indian programs, tribal enterprises, and off-reservation activities constitute the major interacting elements of the economy in that part of Indian country not involved in gaming.

On the issue of unemployment, while the nation as a whole is mildly concerned with a current unemployment rate of about 4.3 percent—going as high as 5 percent or slightly higher in several states—the numbers in Indian communities are so much higher as to be shocking. Labor force statistics available from the Bureau of Indian Affairs have shown the nationwide unemployment rate for the one million American Indians counted in the BIA's service population has been at 48 percent at times over the last 10 years. In 1999 it was 49 percent (National Academy of Public Administration). It is common to find individual Native community unemployment rates that go to 50 or 80 percent. Even Alaska Natives, with their many successful corporate businesses, have had unemployment rates of 57 percent in the 1990s. But the highest unemployment rate in the country is frequently reported from the Rosebud Reservation in South Dakota, where an incredible 93 percent of the work force has been unemployed in the 1990s. At various times, up to 90 percent of these people were looking for work, which shows the rather poor opportunities for employment on that particular reservation. As bad as all of these statistics may seem, they are still better than they used to be decades ago.

What is being done about the problem? Plenty, but it is not always effective. Roughly eight billion dollars a year are pumped through various federal programs devoted to American Indians. Almost two billion dollars a year goes into the Bureau of Indian Affairs alone. But, as much as a third of it used to be absorbed into the agency before the funds got out to any reservation. According to Arizona Senator John McCain, former Vice Chairman of the Select Committee on Indian Affairs, in the early 1990s only 12 cents of every dollar appropriated for Indian programs ever reached an American Indian. This has changed substantially, with hundreds of tribes now managing government programs themselves under the self-determination and self-governance legislation. It is also important to note that federal and tribal jobs, most with relatively good salaries, account for half of American Indian incomes on many reservations. This leaves little incentive for change in the bureaucratic system. But change is occurring and has been since the 1970s. Furthermore, it seems to be developing an accelerating pace for the new millenium.

Policy failures, corruption, bureaucratic incompetence, and politics have gone far toward holding American Indians back economically since the U.S. became a nation. The many, well-educated Native people of today, however, are very familiar with the laws, economics, and government bureaucracies that so thoroughly affect their lives. They and fellow Indians and Alaska Natives appear to be moving in a determined way to take control of their economic destiny. This process is a palpable happening. It may take years for some communities, or generations for others, but it is an ongoing trend.

The worst thing that non-Indian America can do is to presume—as it has so often done in the past, with such disastrous results—that it knows what is "right" for American Indians. As Wilma Mankiller, former principal Chief of the Oklahoma Cherokee Nation, has stated on this subject, "The best solutions to our problems are within our own communities" (White 1990, p. 275).

All who are concerned should also remember that tribal business and other economic development are not panaceas for the various problems facing Indian country. Native culture and the hundreds of Indian nations are not so simplistic as that. Better business and job opportunities, however, will go a long way toward improving economic self-determination, to which American Indians seem to be firmly dedicated.

G-15. *Is there a single best source for research information on economic development in Indian country?*

Although there are a number of different sources, the best single source with a national perspective is probably "The Harvard Project for American Indian Economic Development," in Cambridge, Massachusetts. Begun in 1987, the Project "is directed at understanding the conditions under which sustained, self-determined socio-economic development is achieved on American Indian reservations" (March 3, 2000, from the website, www.ksg.harvard.edu/hpaied).

The Harvard Project is perhaps best known for the 1992 publication *What Can Tribes Do? Strategies and Institutions in American Indian Economic Development*, edited by its two founders, Stephen Cornell and Joseph Kalt. The project also offers seminars around the country, useful publications, and tribal executive education.

A helpful academic entity that works closely with the Harvard Project is the Udall Center for Studies in Public Policy at the University of Arizona in Tucson. The center has a program for American Indian Policy that studies reservation economic development, tribal sovereignty, tribal governance, reservation environmental issues, and Indian health (March 3, 2000, from the website, www.udallcenter. arizona.edu/programs/aip).

One national publication that serious students of economic development in Indian country should make a habit of reading is *American Indian Report*, a monthly news magazine produced by the Falmouth Institute of Fairfax, Virginia (www.falmouthinst.com). A second necessary source is *Indian Country Today*, with corporate offices in Oneida, New York, and editorial headquarters in Rapid City, South Dakota (www.indiancountry.com). Both publications carry relevant articles and they also direct readers to other beneficial sources. The thoughtul work by Smith (2000) on modern tribal development is also worth reviewing.

SECTION H: LEGAL STATUS AND TRIBAL SELF-GOVERNMENT

H-1. *What were the facts of the famous federal court case of* **Standing Bear v. Crook** *(1879), and what aspect of the legal status of Indians did the case address?*

> *Webster describes a person as "a living soul; a self conscious being; a moral agent; especially a living human being; a man, a woman or child; an individual of the human race." This is comprehensive enough, it would seem, to include even an Indian. . . . I must hold then that the Indians . . . are persons.*
>
> U.S. District Court Judge Elmer S. Dundy
> in *Standing Bear v. Crook,* May 12, 1879

Because the case involved a decision of only a U.S. district court (i.e., a trial court) rather than the U.S. Supreme Court, *Standing Bear v. Crook* is sometimes ignored or only touched upon by scholars of federal Indian law. This is understandable, because lawyers concerned about federal questions focus on those cases that have the greatest precedent value under the U.S. legal system—cases that reach the Supreme Court.

Although *Standing Bear v. Crook* had a limited direct effect on federal courts around the country, it had an enormous impact on U.S. public opinion. The case was front-page news in the *New York Times* and many other nationally and regionally important newspapers on more than one occasion between 1877 and 1879. Authors like Thomas Henry Tibbles (1972) and John M. Coward (1999) have made the powerful story of *Standing Bear,* and the associated newspaper coverage of the time, readily available to us today.

The *Standing Bear* case can be traced to a fatal error made by the United States negotiators in the Treaty of Fort Laramie (1868), when the U.S. included as part of the original 22,000,000-acre Sioux Reservation some 96,000 acres that the government had already reserved to the Poncas of northern Nebraska in an earlier treaty.

Because the various Sioux tribes and the Poncas were traditional enemies, and the Sioux greatly outnumbered the Poncas (who had around 2,350 tribal members) and were more aggressive about protecting the territory they now had legal claim to, the Poncas found themselves in a dangerous situation. To make matters worse, the federal government was not interested in correcting its treaty blunder—its agents were too concerned about angering the powerful Sioux tribes.

Thus, in the fall of 1876, an order was issued by federal authorities for the Poncas to prepare to remove south to the Indian Territory (modern-day Oklahoma). The Poncas refused, declaring that they had built farms and homes on their reservation, they went to church, they followed the white man's ways, and they had never violated their treaty. Some white men appeared at the Reservation and represented themselves to the Poncas as the federal authorities in charge of their removal. These white men continued to demand removal and convinced Standing Bear and some other Ponca leaders to journey with them to Indian Territory to see how good it was and to decide if there was some land there that they would be willing to trade for their Nebraska land.

The Poncas made the trip, but were disappointed with the land they were shown in Indian Territory. They refused to accept a trade and demanded to go to Washington to talk with higher authorities, including the President. Their "federal" hosts, who turned out to be nothing more than land speculators, then refused the Ponca requests and abandoned them, without food, money, or horses, in Indian Territory. It was winter, and the small band of Ponca leaders began the long walk home. It took them 50 days to get to the Otoe Indian Agency in southern Nebraska, where they were fed, rested, and provided with horses.

Standing Bear and his group finally made it back to their northern Nebraska reservation, but the turmoil continued. The pressure on the Poncas to remove to Indian Territory grew until Standing Bear and the rest of his people finally were forced to leave in the spring of 1877. The journey proved to be terrible, and many Poncas died along the way. Once in the Indian Territory, they had no great improvement in their conditions. Poncas continued to die from disease and despair.

A few midwestern newspapers carried stories of the Poncas plight, but there was no substantial interest until a delegation of Poncas went to Washington to meet with the President. The *New York Times* announced, "PEACEFUL INDIANS AT THE CAPITAL," and made much ado about how friendly and assimilated the Poncas were compared to other tribes, such as the Sioux who had wiped out Custer's command the year before. Despite the sympathy, the Ponca trip to Washington did not result in any major change in their circumstances. They had to remain in Indian Territory. As Standing Bear later said: "We had nothing to do but sit still, be sick, starve and die" (Tibbles 1972, p. 24). By the end of their second year there, 800 Poncas had died, including several of Standing Bear's family members. His only son was among them.

As he lay dying, Standing Bear's son asked his father to take him north to be buried in their homeland. Standing Bear promised he would.

In early 1879 Standing Bear, and about 30 other Poncas who had had enough of Indian Territory, packed up and left. They headed north for the lands of their former reservation. Tired, ill, and starving, they made it as far as the Omaha Reservation in Nebraska. The Omahas, who spoke the same language as the Poncas, prevailed on their visitors to stay with them on their reservation, grow crops, build homes, and live a healthy and peaceful life, but then everything began to unravel.

Upon learning that the missing Poncas in Standing Bear's tiny band of thirty souls had taken up residence on the Omaha Reservation, Secretary of the Interior Carl Schurz issued a request to the Secretary of War to have Standing Bear and his people arrested and returned south to Indian Territory. General George Crook, Commander of the Department of the Platte, who was stationed at Fort Omaha, sent one of his lieutenants to the Omaha Reservation where he arrested the Poncas on March 27, 1879. The lieutenant and his detail then escorted the Poncas to Fort Omaha. However, church groups in the area immediately began to protest to federal officials in Washington. At the same time a newspaper editor with the *Omaha Daily Herald,* Thomas Henry Tibbles, took up the Ponca's cause, apparently with behind-the-scenes support from General Crook himself.

Standing Bear, the Ponca headman whose illegal arrest and confinement by federal authorities in 1879 created a public relations nightmare for the Interior Department and the Army. Studio photograph taken in Washington, D.C., 1877.

> *My boy who died down there, as he was dying looked up to me and said, I would like you to take my bones back and bury them there where I was born. I promised him I would. I could not refuse the dying request of my boy. His bones are in that trunk.*
>
> Standing Bear after his arrest and before his meeting with General Crook (Tibbles 1972, p. 25)

Tibbles helped the Poncas by beginning to telegraph regular news dispatches on their troubles to papers in New York, Chicago, and other cities. Soon thousands of newspaper readers around the country knew about the Poncas, who were being held by General Crook. Tibbles also helped the Ponca prisoners obtain legal counsel. A strategy was developed to seek a writ of habeas corpus in federal court, based on the theory that General Crook and the Army did not have jurisdiction over the peaceful group of Poncas. Therefore, the Poncas lawyer would argue that they were being illegally detained by General Crook and should be set free.

The arguments presented before the federal judge by the Poncas' lawyer and by the lawyer for General Crook (who was really arguing for the Interior Secretary) were relatively straightforward. The Poncas' lawyer argued that Standing Bear's band had severed their tribal ties with the Poncas remaining in Indian Territory, they were peaceful, they were living on the Omaha Reservation at the invitation of that tribe, and they were churchgoers and farmers. The small group had broken no civil or criminal laws, had violated no treaties, and had done much to take up the white man's way of life. He added that the order of arrest that had originated in the Interior Department and was then executed by the War Department was invalid, and that General Crook, as the War Department's representative, lacked any jurisdiction to hold the Poncas. The Poncas' lawyer concluded that therefore, under the federal habeas corpus statute, the court was compelled to grant the writ and order the Poncas released.

The argument by the attorney for the government went on for approximately five hours, but it can be summarized as a single assertion: that Standing Bear and his fellow Poncas were not entitled to the protection of the writ of habeas corpus because they were not "persons" under the law.

Judge Dundy disagreed. The judge was impressed with the fact that the Poncas had severed their tribal ties and were trying to live as white men, and he ended the summary of his opinion as follows:

> The military power of the government may be employed to effect such removal [of persons illegally within a reservation]. But when removal is effected, it is the duty of the troops to convey the persons so removed by the most convenient and safe route, to the civil authorities of the judicial district in which the offense may be committed, to be proceeded against in due course of law.
>
> In time of peace, no authority, civil or military, exists for transporting Indians from one section of the country to another, without the consent of the Indians, nor to confine them to any particular reservation against their will, and where officers of the government attempt to do this, and arrest and hold Indians who are at peace with the government, for the purpose of removing

Standing Bear with his wife and a son, who was born after the son who died soon after the Poncas' forced removal to Indian Territory from northern Nebraska. Photograph circa 1890, and taken in Nebraska.

them to, and confining them on, a reservation in the Indian Territory, they will be released on *habeas corpus*.

Although thoughtfully stated for his time, Judge Dundy's ruling that Indians were "persons" who had basic rights protected under law, was for decades often ignored throughout the West. Still, Standing Bear and his people were released from custody on May 19, 1879, much to the delight of the editors, and many of the readers, of newspapers like the *New York Times* and *Tribune*, and the *Chicago Tribune*. Standing Bear took care of his son's remains, and then he and editor Tibbles went on a well-received speaking tour of the East. After a couple of years, Standing Bear and his few followers settled on an island in the Niobrara River in northern Nebraska that was next to, but not included in, the Sioux Reservation. In 1890 he took an allotment of land in the region.

Also in 1890, Standing Bear briefly returned with his band to Indian Territory to visit with relatives. While there he irritated the Indian agent and missionary-school teacher, who thought he was a bad influence on the local Poncas because he was still too Indian.

> Similar complaints about "retrograde" leaders were voiced at [Indian] agencies throughout the West as it became apparent that even those Indians who seemed most willing to accommodate to white culture were not about to give up all their traditional practices. Standing Bear died in obscurity in 1908. He and many counterparts in other tribes never did adopt the white way of life exactly as the humanitarians had envisioned. (Tibbles 1972, p. 137)

(For a later case that used *Standing Bear v. Crook* as a precedent, see question F-10.)

H-2. *Are Indians wards of the federal government?*

> *These Indian tribes are the wards of the nation.*
> U.S. Supreme Court in *United States v. Kagama* (1886)
> [emphasis added]

No. The Government is not the guardian of individual Indians but, as indicated in the *Kagama* quote above, it is the guardian of Indian *tribes*. It is also the trustee of certain kinds of Indian property. Such "trust" property is most frequently associated, in one way or another, with current and former reservation lands and resources and with proceeds derived therefrom. The government only holds property in trust for federally recognized tribes. This property may be tribal or individual, depending on the circumstances.

Consider a general comparison of what is trust property and what is not. Navajo reservation land, for example, is held in trust by the United States. Therefore, major decisions involving reservation land require approval by the Bureau of Indian Affairs. In contrast, a home lot purchased by a Navajo Indian in the far-away city of Phoenix is not trust property. It is entirely private property, the same as for any non-Indian. It would be purchased with private—not tribal—resources, and it would be done without government involvement.

From the early 1800s to the early 1900s, reservation Indians were often referred to and often treated as wards by the three branches of the federal government. Frequently, the term "wards" was employed to mean non-citizen Indians. This situation began to be corrected with policy changes in the 1920s and 1930s which resulted from passage of the Indian Citizenship Act (1924) and the Indian Reorganization Act (1934). The latter act ended the destructive land allotment system which had begun in earnest in 1887. Allotment had progressively dismantled numerous reservations and forced the affected tribes into a more dependent or ward-like status. The self-determination policies of the '20s and '30s, fortunately, began to reverse that trend. To assure that there will be no turning back, additional reforms have been adopted. They were rightfully demanded by American Indians and their supporters in the 1960s and later years.

H-3. *Are Indians U.S. citizens?*

> *The Wyandot Indians, having become sufficiently advanced in civilization, and being desirous of becoming citizens . . . are hereby declared to be citizens of the United States.*
>
> Treaty with the Wyandots
> 1855

Yes. Indians born in the U.S., or born of citizens who are outside the country at the time of birth, are American citizens. They are also citizens of their states of residence. In addition, most Indians are also citizens, or members, of federally recognized Indian tribes, which are political bodies that exercise substantial powers of self-government.

In the 19th century, the prevalent opinion was that an Indian could not be both a tribal member and a U.S. citizen. This notion has long since been refuted by federal law. Therefore, Indian citizenship is not in any way inconsistent with tribal membership (Cohen 1982).

The road to citizenship was long and bumpy. A few early treaties offered citizenship options, e.g., the Treaty with the Cherokees (1817), the Wyandot treaty quoted above, and the Treaty with the Senecas, et al. (1867). Individual Indians were required to make a choice between (1) staying with their tribes which were being removed to a distant part of the country or (2) severing their tribal ties and remaining behind to accept citizenship and a small land allotment.

Besides treaties, roughly a dozen congressional acts have directly addressed the Indian citizenship issue in some way. The General Allotment Act of 1887 was one of the most significant. It conferred citizenship on Indians who were born within the U.S. and to whom the government made individual land allotments, of usually 80 to 160 acres, from tribal reservation lands. Another significant act, passed in 1888, declared that, "Every Indian woman . . . who may hereafter be married to any citizen of the United States is hereby declared to become by such marriage a citizen of the United States" (25 U.S. Code, Sec. 182). This piecemeal process of selectively conferring citizenship on the U.S. Indian population came to an end in 1924 with passage of the one-sentence law titled The Indian Citizenship Act. It reads: "[A]ll non-citizen Indians born within the territorial limits of the United States . . . are hereby declared to be citizens of the United States." At the time the act was passed, perhaps one third of the U.S. Indian population did not have citizenship.

As with much Indian legislation, many non-Indians still questioned the effect of the Citizenship Act, suggesting that it did not apply to Indians born after passage of the act on June 24, 1924, or to Alaska Natives. Subsequent amendments contained clarifying language granting citizenship "at birth" and including Alaska Natives. (See 8 U.S. Code, Sec. 1401.)

In 1983, Congress enacted what will probably be the last Indian citizenship legislation ever passed in this country. The act involved a band of Kickapoo whose ancestors had fled the central plains in the 1800s to live in isolation along the Texas-Mexico border area. For over a century, these Indians and their descendants moved back and forth between Mexico and the U.S., with no citizenship status in either country. The Texas Band of Kickapoo Act (1983) established federal recognition of the tribe, provided for the acquisition of a small reservation near Eagle Pass, Texas, and authorized tribal members to "apply for United States citizenship" within a five-year period after passage of the act.

> A few of the more traditional Indians, retaining views consistent with pre-1924 law, do not regard themselves as American citizens, but as citizens only of their own tribes (Deloria and Lytle 1983). In addition, a few tribes issue passports. Traditional leaders of the Hopi Nation and the Iroquois League, for example, have traveled to international meetings using only passports issued by tribal governments (O'Brien 1989). Historically, in the late-1700s and early-1800s, federal law required U.S. citizens traveling in Indian country to have passports.

H-4. *Can American Indians vote and hold public office?*

Voting Rights

The general right to vote comes with citizenship and state residency. Therefore, American Indians have the same rights to vote in federal, state, and local elections as do other U.S. citizens. But, getting the vote in *every* state was a long time in coming.

Even after the Indian Citizenship Act of 1924, a number of states continued to prohibit Indians from voting. The states' legal arguments were (1) that Indians were "under guardianship" and therefore not competent to vote or (2) Indians were not residents of the states in which they lived if they resided on reservations. These arguments were progressively invalidated in each of the holdout states over the four decades following enactment of the citizenship law.

The last states to fully extend voting rights to Indians were Arizona (1948), Maine (1954), Utah (1956), and New Mexico (1962).

Two of the most instructive court cases on the issue were Arizona's *Harrison et al. v. Laveen* (1948) and New Mexico's *Montoya v. Bolack* (1962). Indian voting rights cases that have arisen since 1962 have generally involved local issues such as county residency and school district expenditures (e.g., *Little Thunder et al. v. State of South Dakota* 1975 and *Prince v. Board of Education* 1975, respectively).

Public Office

Besides being able to serve in tribal government, American Indians have the same rights as other citizens to hold public office at all levels of government, whether elected or appointed. Nationwide, Native people now hold municipal, county, state, and national office.

The highest elected office ever held by an Indian in the U.S. was the vice presidency. Charles Curtis was a quarter-blood Kaw from Kansas who became an attorney and had a remarkable political career. He served as a Republican county attorney, U.S. Representative, U.S. Senator and majority leader, and finally vice president under Herbert Hoover. Often referred to as an example of Indian achievement, he was *very much* an assimilationist. His major Indian policies were vigorously opposed by many tribes (Harlow 1935). Even among his own tribe, some considered Curtis as something other than a supporter of Indian causes (Heat-Moon 1991; for a brief but revealing biography of Curtis, see Unrau 1985).

A few other Indians have been elected to Congress over the past century, but American Indians have always been underrepresented. The only Indian serving in Congress is Ben Nighthorse Campbell. He became a member of the House of Representatives from Colorado in 1986 and was elected to the U.S. Senate in November 1992. Senator Campbell is an enrolled member of the Northern Cheyenne Tribe of Montana.

Also, during the 1992 campaign, Ms. Ada Deer, a Menominee and widely respected Indian rights advocate from Wisconsin, ran unsuccessfully for the House of Representatives. And, Oklahoma State Senator Enoch Haney, a Seminole, entered the race for U.S. Senate. He also was unsuccessful in his election bid. There has been a notable absence of American Indian candidates in more recent congressional campaigns, but it is obvious that more Indian interest and activity in the national political scene will develop over the coming decade.

The following list shows American Indians who have served in the United States Congress:

AMERICAN INDIANS WHO HAVE SERVED IN THE U.S. CONGRESS

U.S. Senate:

Hiram R. Revels, Lumbee from Mississippi, 1870–1871

Mathew Stanley Quay, Abenaki or Delaware from Pennsylvania, 1887–1899 and 1901–1904

Charles Curtis, Kaw from Kansas, 1907–1912 and 1915–1929 (then vice president, 1929–1933)

Robert L. Owens, Cherokee from Oklahoma, 1907–1925

Ben Nighthorse Campbell, Northern Cheyenne from Colorado, 1993–

U.S. House of Representatives:

Charles Curtis, Kaw from Kansas, 1893–1907

Charles D. Carter, Choctaw from Oklahoma, 1907–1927

W.W. Hastings, Cherokee from Oklahoma, 1915–1921 and 1923–1935

Will Rogers, Jr., Cherokee from California, 1943–1944

William G. Stigler, Choctaw from Oklahoma, 1944–1952

Benjamin Reifel, Rosebud Sioux from South Dakota, 1961–1971

Clem Rogers McSpadden, Cherokee from Oklahoma, 1972–1975

Ben Nighthorse Campbell, Northern Cheyenne from Colorado, 1986–1992

Source: Congressional Research Service. The CRS cautions that this list may be incomplete.

H-5. *Do Indians pay taxes?*

Yes. Depending on specific residency and employment circumstances, and also the legal status of specific property, individual Indians are subject to most, and frequently all, of the same tax laws and liabilities that non-Indians are. Various income, estate, gift, sales, employment, property, business, and excise taxes are levied against Indians, just as they are against non-Indians. In the limited situations

Ben Nighthorse Campbell, U.S. Senator from Colorado.

where taxation exceptions exist, they relate to (1) the retained sovereignty of tribes over their members and territory and (2) the trust status of some Indian property.

Several basic tenets apply to the general subject of Indian taxation. First, tribes have the power to lay and collect certain taxes from Indians and non-Indians within reservation boundaries. States, however, generally lack jurisdiction to tax Indians within tribal lands unless they have specific federal authorization. Also, federal trust status over certain Indian property inside and outside reservations precludes some state taxes. The federal government, on the other hand, has broad authority under existing law to tax Indians. Treaties and federal statutes, however, have been interpreted to exempt Indians and tribes from a number of tax scenarios the government could devise, beyond those already in place. The major reasoning behind tribal exemptions is expressed by the maxim, "With the power to tax comes the power to destroy." The federal government is legally and morally bound to see that the tribes are not taxed out of political existence (Cohen 1982).

Seven general exceptions to taxation pertain to Indians (Bureau of Indian Affairs 1991a; Cohen 1982). Listed below, they deal with government activity, trust property, and transactions that occur within reservations. Recall from earlier in Part II that under 25 percent of the Indian population reported in the census resides within reservations.

1. Federal income tax provisions do not apply to the income of tribal governments, just as they do not apply to the states and other units of government.
2. Federal income taxes are not levied against that portion of an individual Indian's income that is derived from trust land, legal title to which is held by the U.S., or other trust property.
3. State income taxes are not assessed against the income of tribal governments.
4. State income taxes are not assessed against an individual Indian's income that is earned on a reservation.
5. State income taxes are not assessed against an individual Indian's trust property income.
6. State sales taxes are not paid by Indians for transactions they enter on their reservations.
7. Local property taxes are not paid on tribal trust land or individually owned trust land.

Here is a caveat regarding Indian taxation. Beyond the issue of trust property, what the rule of law is today may not be the rule tomorrow. Indian taxation topics seem to be among those fluid issues, changing with the times and the mood of the U.S. Supreme Court—which is now almost hostile to Indian cases. The complexity of Indian taxation issues always requires a cautious approach because minor variations in the facts from case to case can have major consequences.

H-6. *Why are Indian tribes and their members treated differently from other citizens by the federal government, and what is the "trust relationship" that influences their federal treatment?*

> *Tribes remain quasi-sovereign nations which, by government structure, culture, and source of sovereignty, are in many ways foreign to the constitutional institutions of the federal and state governments.*
>
> U.S. Supreme Court
> *Santa Clara Pueblo v. Martinez* 1978

At its inception, the United States recognized the power and influence of the Indian nations within its territory. It, therefore, negotiated treaties and passed laws which acknowledged the special rights and responsibilities of Indian tribes and their members, apart and distinct from other American residents and citizens (Kickingbird and Kickingbird 1977). The tribes were treated as separate political entities and their members were not U.S. citizens. The lack of citizenship has been changed but the tribes remain separate political entities with limited powers of self-government.

Some form of special federal relationship was implicit in the decision, made after the Revolutionary War, to keep Indian affairs in the hands of the federal government. This was justified as a means of protecting the tribes from the states and unscrupulous citizens, thereby avoiding Indian wars (Canby 1981, 1998). An early foundation for federal over state authority appears in Article IX of the Articles of Confederation (ratified in 1781). It declares "The United States in congress assembled shall have the sole and exclusive right and power of . . . regulating the trade and managing all affairs with the Indians." This concept was carried over to Article I, Section 8, Clause 3 of the Constitution when the latter superceded the Articles in 1789. It reads: "The Congress shall have power . . . to regulate commerce with foreign nations, the several states, and with the Indian tribes. . . ." The meaning attributed to "commerce," of course, is extremely broad. In summary, the doctrine that Indian affairs are subject to control by the federal government and not the states (except in specific instances approved by Congress) is based on the general constitutional powers which empower Congress to (1) ratify treaties, (2) regulate commerce with the Indian tribes, (3) admit new states, (4) administer federal property, and (5) enact legislation in pursuance of these enumerated powers (*Martinez v. Southern Ute Tribe* 1957).

The "trust relationship" portion of the question can be understood more easily by considering the following quotation from federal judge and author William Canby (1998, p. 33).

> Much of American Indian Law revolves around the special [trust] relationship between the federal government and the tribes. Yet it is very difficult to mark the boundaries of this relationship, and even more difficult to assess its legal consequences. At its broadest, the relationship includes the mixture of legal duties, moral obligations, understandings and expectancies that have arisen from the entire course of dealing between the federal government and the tribes. In its narrowest and most concrete sense, the relationship approximates that of trustee and beneficiary, with the trustee (the United States) subject in some degree to legally enforceable responsibilities.

The United States government "has charged itself with moral obligations of the highest responsibility and trust" toward the Indian tribes (*Seminole Nation v. United States* 1946). This trust responsibility was first formally addressed by the Supreme Court in *Cherokee Nation v. Georgia* (1831). Chief Justice Marshall found that, under U.S. dominion, tribes were no longer foreign nations. He determined that they constituted "distinct political" communities "that may, more correctly . . . be denominated domestic dependent nations" whose "relation to the United States resembles that of a ward to his guardian."

Some might assume Marshall's statement to mean that individual Indians are "wards" of the government, in conflict with the answer to question H-2. A clear reading shows that he wrote about Indian *tribes* or "nations," not individual Indians. So, the Indian tribe-to-U.S. trust relationship is one of government-to-government which "resembles" that of ward to guardian. *Protection* of the tribes as political entities is the key (Hall 1981; United Effort Trust 1979).

The American Indian Policy Review Commission (1977, p. 130) outlined the modern concept of the trust relationship, or responsibility, in its final report to the Congress.

The scope of the trust responsibility extends beyond real or personal property which is held in trust. The U.S. has the obligation to provide services, and to take other appropriate action necessary to protect tribal self-government. The doctrine may also include a duty to provide a level of services equal to those services provided by the states to their citizens [e.g., educational, social, and medical]. These conclusions flow from the basic notion that the trust responsibility is a general obligation which is not limited to specific provision in treaties, executive orders, or statutes; once the trust has been assumed, administrative action is governed by the same high duty which is imposed on a private trustee.

However, noble statements about trust are frequently disregarded by the U.S. Supreme Court (Johnson and Martinis 1995) and the other federal courts.

The government-to-government relationship of American Indian tribes and the United States is a truly unique one in the world system of governments. It is inexorably tied to the uninvited extension of U.S. dominion over all ancestral lands of the formerly independent tribes, bands, and similar groups of American Indians. The "different" treatment of Indians that is referred to on occasion is actually a different legal, not racial, treatment of the tribes and their members. It is based on the tribes' continuing political existence as "Quasi-Sovereign Domestic Dependent Nations" (Bush 1991), and the U.S. responsibility to those nations.

As additional questions and answers in this section indicate, this does not leave Indian people immune from the general rights and responsibilities of other citizens. It does, however, affect some of those rights and responsibilities. It is not unlike the way being a citizen of Arizona, Alaska, American Samoa, or Guam would have varying effects due to different laws, regulations, rules, and government services applicable to residents of these respective American states and territories. (See questions H-9 and H-13 on sovereignty and self-determination.)

H-7. *What different criminal jurisdiction can be applicable to Indians?*

This and the following question on civil jurisdiction are among the toughest of all to answer. Often referred to as a jurisdictional maze, questions arising from jurisdictional disputes among the federal government, tribes, and states are the most complex in the field of Indian law. Many jurisdictional questions remain unsettled, and mildly different facts between cases can have substantial effects on jurisdiction. Basic precepts, however, have developed over the years and serve as guidelines to relevant questions. These precepts are summarized in a table, at the end of this answer, following several paragraphs which are necessary to understand the table. The reader is cautioned that the text and table are not definitive. They should be considered introductory in nature and as basic examples of complexity.

It is necessary to understand the definitions of "Indian" and "Indian country" before it is possible to understand the topic of criminal (or civil) jurisdiction. The answer to "Who is an Indian?" will vary according to applicable statutes, court rulings, and tribal membership requirements and records. (See the shaded box below, as well as the answer to question A-1.) "Indian country," on the other hand, is legally defined as: (a) land within the exterior boundaries of a federal Indian reservation, (b) land outside reservation boundaries that is owned by Indians and held in trust or restricted status by the

---

For the purpose of criminal jurisdiction, an Indian is a person who has some ethnic connection and some degree of Indian blood. The definition of "Indian" varies according to the statutes, case laws, and administrative enactments that have formulated different definitions. Often, the definition of Indian appears in the individual constitution [or] legal codes of a tribe. In general, however, certain considerations are relevant in order to be considered an Indian. These include: an individual's residence, the particular law involved, a person's degree of Indian blood, tribal enrollment, and an individual's opinion as to his own status.

Flowers 1983, p. 5

federal government, and (c) all other lands set aside by whatever means for the residence of tribal Indians under federal protection, e.g., "dependent Indian communities" (Cohen 1982). Tribal jurisdiction is largely restricted to Indian country, and Indian country is where most jurisdictional disputes originate. (See the answer to question H-12 for non-legal definitions of Indian country.)

At the time of early European contact, American Indian tribes, bands, and clans had exclusive "jurisdiction," in fact and theory, over all people in their territory (Canby 1981, 1998). This gradually changed as the power of the Euro-American governments grew and their populations expanded. By the height of the reservation period, in the early-1880s, U.S. law enforcement policy for Indian country had evolved to where federal officers and courts had exclusive jurisdiction over *non-Indian* and *interracial* crimes. In other words, the jurisdiction applied to federal criminal offenses involving only non-Indians or where both Indians and non-Indians were involved. The General Crimes Act (now codified as 18 U.S. Code, Sec. 1152) embodied the early 1880s policy for Indian country. At the same time, Indian-to-Indian crime was still left to tribal jurisdiction. Congress began to change this in 1885, however, by passing the Major Crimes Act which significantly reduced the tribes' sovereign authority over law enforcement regarding their members or other Indians.

The early version of the act specified only seven crimes, but today's Major Crimes Act includes 14 offenses. Such offenses are often subjected to federal jurisdiction only. Their investigation is handled by the FBI and is prosecuted by the U.S. Department of Justice. The list of crimes which follows is quoted from the Major Crimes Act (18 U.S. Code, Sec. 1153). It is self-explanatory.

> Any Indian who commits against the person or property of another Indian or another person any of the following offenses, namely, murder, manslaughter, kidnaping, maiming, a felony under chapter 109A, incest, assault with intent to commit murder, assault with a dangerous weapon, assault resulting in serious bodily injury (as defined in section 1365 of this title), an assault against an individual who has not attained the age of 16 years, arson, burglary, robbery, and a felony under section 661 of this title within the Indian country, shall be subject to the same law and penalties as all other persons committing any of the above offenses,

within the exclusive jurisdiction of the United States. ["Chapter
109A" refers to sexual abuse and "section 661" deals with theft.]

Another of the many incursions into tribal criminal jurisdiction
resulted from the Supreme Court's 20th century application of the
Assimilative Crimes Act to Indian country (*Williams v. United States*
1946). The act, first passed in 1825 and periodically amended (18 U.S.
Code, Sec. 13), borrows state-defined crimes not otherwise covered
by federal law (such as the Major Crimes Act) and incorporates them
into federal law applicable to "federal enclaves." Before the court's
1946 ruling, the term "enclaves" did not include Indian country, but
it did include areas like post offices, national parks, and military
reservations. The act's practical function is to allow the federal
government to apply minor state criminal laws to Indian country and
the other enclaves (Deloria and Lytle 1983). It is effectively limited to
crimes that involve non-Indians, or both Indians and non-Indians,
and reads "whoever . . . is guilty of an act or omission which,
although not made punishable by an act of Congress, would be
punishable if committed or omitted within the jurisdiction of the
State . . . in which such place [e.g., Indian country] is situated, . . .
shall be guilty of a like offense and subject to like punishment."

A significant change in jurisdiction in parts of Indian country
developed in 1953 with passage of Public Law 280. This law, a child
of the "termination" era, gave six states mandatory and substantial
criminal and civil jurisdiction over Indian country within their
borders. The key criminal provision gave those states power to
enforce the great majority of their regular criminal laws inside Indian
country, just as they had been doing elsewhere. The "mandatory"
states were Alaska (added in 1958, except for Metlakatla Reservation),
California, Minnesota (except Red Lake Reservation), Nebraska,
Oregon (except Warm Springs Reservation), and Wisconsin (Canby
1998). When Public Law 280 was applied to these states, the General
Crimes Act and the Indian Major Crimes Act, specifically, and the
Assimilative Crimes Act, by default, no longer applied to Indian
country within the states—except for the reservations just named.

Other federal statutes have granted a few states certain criminal
jurisdiction in Indian country, but none has been so broadly applicable as Public Law 280. Even so, Public Law 280 does not grant

unlimited jurisdiction. Limitations on state criminal as well as civil jurisdiction continue in such areas as water rights, taxation of trust property, regulatory control over trust property, regulatory control over tribal activity otherwise protected by treaty or statute, and federally protected hunting, trapping, and fishing rights.

From the outset, Public Law 280 was criticized by tribes and states. The latter resented being directed to provide new law enforcement services with no financial assistance, and tribes resented state jurisdiction being forced upon them without their consent. This joint dissent stimulated later amendments to the act which now allow states to retrocede, or transfer back, jurisdiction to the federal government. A number of retrocessions have occurred since the 1960s, usually on a piecemeal or reservation-by-reservation basis.

The 1953 version of Public Law 280 also permitted other states, beyond the original six, to acquire similar jurisdiction in Indian country. The choice was theirs and it did not require tribal approval. (The law was amended in 1968 to require tribal consent.) Ten states opted to accept some degree of Public Law 280 jurisdiction. They were Arizona, Florida, Idaho, Iowa, Montana, Nevada, North Dakota, South Dakota, Utah, and Washington. The authority they assumed varied from limited jurisdiction over things like air and water pollution only (Arizona), to slightly greater jurisdiction over criminal offenses and civil causes of action arising on highways (South Dakota), to full Public Law 280 jurisdiction (Florida). Some of these 10 states have now returned at least part of their jurisdiction to the federal government (Cohen 1982).

Several authors have devised useful tables to simplify understanding of criminal jurisdiction in Indian country. The one by Deloria and Lytle (1983, p. 179), shown on page 260 in slightly modified form, follows introductory remarks by the authors:

> The jurisdictional maze that has clouded the Indian system of justice has confused layperson, lawyer, judge, and bureaucrat alike. The basic question to be resolved is which level of government assumes jurisdiction over criminal offenses in Indian country. . . . The answer to this question revolves around the interrelationship of three factors: (a) the location where the crime is committed, (b) the particular statute that has been violated, and (c) the type of persons involved in the crime (Indian/non-Indian).

GUIDELINES FOR CRIMINAL JURISDICTION

Location Where Crime Committed	*Federal Jurisdiction*	*State Jurisdiction*	*Tribal Jurisdiction*
I. Outside Indian Country			
A. Federal Law Involved	Yes	No	No
B. State Law Involved	No	Yes	No
C. Tribal Law Involved	No	No	Maybe
II. Inside Indian Country (in P.L. 280 state, or one given similar jurisdiction)	No	Yes	No
III. Inside Indian Country (no P.L. 280 or similar jurisdiction)			
A. Crimes by Indian v. Indian			
1. Major Crimes Act crimes	Yes	No	No[a]
2. Other crimes	No	No	Yes
B. Crimes by Indian v. non-Indian			
1. Major Crimes Act crimes	Yes	No	No[a]
2. General Crimes Act	Yes	No	Yes[b]
3. Assimilative Crimes Act	Yes	No	Yes
C. Crimes by non-Indian v. Indian			
1. General Crimes Act crimes	Yes	No	No
2. Assimilative Crimes Act	Yes	No	No
D. Crimes by non-Indian v. same	Yes	Yes	No
E. Victimless and consensual crimes			
1. Crimes by Indians	No	No	Yes
2. Crimes by non-Indians		Yes[c]	
a. General Crimes Act	Yes	Yes[a]	No
b. Assimilative Crimes Act	Yes	Yes[a]	No

[a]The law is unsettled in this area.

[b]If there has been prior punishment by tribal court, or if tribal jurisdiction is otherwise established by treaty or statute, federal jurisdiction under General Crimes Act is withheld.

[c]Some statutes permit concurrent jurisdiction.

Source: Deloria and Lytle (1983, p. 179, citing Getches, Rosenfelt, and Wilkinson 1979). Table is for basic reference only.

H-8. *What different civil jurisdiction can be applicable to Indians?*

[Author's note: The answer to the preceding question on criminal jurisdiction contains information necessary to the understanding of the answer which follows.]

Civil jurisdiction involves private rights, as opposed to the public wrongs which are covered by criminal law. Everyday civil issues include lawsuits and other legal actions pertaining to topics like auto accidents, child custody, probate, and divorce or other domestic relations. For the great majority of Americans the rule of law governing civil matters are those developed by the states. For American Indians, however, very different jurisdictional rules can apply (Canby 1998; Getches, Wilkinson, and Williams 1998).

In some ways, questions of civil jurisdiction, as applied to Indians and their property, are more complicated than those which relate to criminal jurisdiction. A major reason is that the federal government has not played as large a role in this arena as it has in criminal law. With a lesser federal role, the laws of several hundred tribes and the different states add a special complexity to civil jurisdiction.

A table summarizing answers to civil jurisdiction questions is shown on page 262. It relates only to those states where civil jurisdiction under Public Law 280 is *not* in effect. As the table makes plain, answers to questions on civil jurisdiction in "non-280" states turn on such issues as (a) who initiates an action (Indian or non-Indian plaintiff), (b) who is defending an action (Indian or non-Indian defendant), (c) the geographic origin of a claim (inside or outside Indian country), (d) the nature of a claim, (e) the nature of property at issue, and (f) the locations of the legal domiciles of the parties involved (inside or outside Indian country). Information in the table is from Canby (1981). As with the previous table, the reader is cautioned that this table should be considered as being representative but not definitive for all cases.

Although Public Law 280 conferred both criminal and civil jurisdiction on the six "mandatory" states, and allowed options for the same jurisdiction in others, the criminal law provisions were clearly the most important to Congress. Civil jurisdiction, it appears, was added as an afterthought, but a powerful one where applicable (Goldberg 1975). The civil section of the statute reads:

Each of the States . . . listed . . . shall have jurisdiction over civil causes of action between Indians or to which Indians are parties which arise in the areas of Indian country listed . . . to the same extent that such State . . . has jurisdiction over other civil causes of action, and those civil laws of such state . . . that are of general application to private persons or private property shall have the same force and effect within such Indian country as they have elsewhere in the State . . . [28 U.S. Code, Sec. 1369(a)].

In the several states where Public Law 280 is in effect, a number of tribal jurisdictions would no longer apply. As stated in the answer to the criminal jurisdiction question, however, state civil authority under Public Law 280 is excluded from encumbering trust property or interfering with treaty rights.

GUIDELINES FOR CIVIL JURISDICTION
(STATES OUTSIDE PUBLIC LAW 280)

I. General Civil Litigation

Plaintiff	Defendant	Origin of Claim	Jurisdiction
Indian	Indian	Indian country	Tribal (exclusive)
		Not Indian country	Tribal or state (concurrent)
Non-Indian	Indian	Indian country	Tribal (exclusive)
		Not Indian country	State; possibly tribal (concurrent)
Indian	Non-Indian	Indian country	Tribal, if tribe's code allows; State (concurrent)
Non-Indian	Non-Indian	Anywhere	State (exclusive)

II. Divorce

Plaintiff	Defendant	Domicile of Parties	Jurisdiction
Indian	Indian	Indian country	Tribal (exclusive)
		Not Indian country	State; Tribal, if tribe's code allows (concurrent)
Non-Indian	Indian	Indian country	State (probable); Tribal (concurrent)
		Not Indian country	State (exclusive)
Indian	Non-Indian	Indian country	Tribal (exclusive)
		Not Indian country	State (exclusive)
Non-Indian	Non-Indian	Anywhere	State (exclusive)

III. Adoption and Child Custody (Not Divorce Custody)

[Indian Child Welfare Act applies (25 U.S. Code, Sec. 1911).]

Proceeding	Domicile or Residence of Child	Jurisdiction
Adoption and all non-divorce custody	Indian country	Tribal (exclusive)
Adoption or adoptive placement	Not Indian country	Tribal; State (concurrent)
Foster care or termination of parental rights	Not Indian country	Tribal preferred; State (concurrent)

IV. Probate

Decedent	Decedent's Domicile	Property	Jurisdiction
Indian	Indian country	Trust assets	Federal (exclusive)
		Land outside Indian country	State (exclusive)
		Movables	Tribal (primary)
	Not Indian country	Trust assets	Federal (exclusive)
		Land outside Indian country	State (exclusive)
		Movables	State (primary); possibly tribal (concurrent)
Non-Indian	Anywhere	All assets	State (exclusive)

Source: Canby (1981, p. 153–154). Under section "I", wherever state jurisdiction is shown, federal jurisdiction may be acquired if "a federal question" or "diversity of citizenship" (parties from different states) are involved. For the latter, the controversy must exceed $10,000. Where the subject matter of a section "I" claim particularly affects Indian interests, state jurisdiction may be precluded.

H-9. *What is tribal sovereignty?*

If you don't understand tribal sovereignty,
you don't understand Indians.

John Echohawk, Director, Native American Rights Fund.
In Seldon 1999, p. B-4

At its most basic level, *sovereignty is separateness*. In the United States, this was proclaimed in the first paragraph of the Declaration of Independence:

> WHEN in the course of human events, it becomes necessary for one People to dissolve the Political Bands which have connected them with another, and to assume among the Powers of the Earth, the *separate* and equal Station to which the Laws of Nature and of Nature's God entitle them, a decent Respect to the Opinions of Mankind requires that they should declare the causes which impel them to the *Separation*. [Emphasis added.]

Thus, anything that threatens an Indian nation's separateness also threatens its sovereignty. Included among the most common threats are: suppression of culture; assimilative education; assimilative tribal government structure; destructive federal legislation; damaging state and federal court decisions; language loss; and Indian nations' acceptance of capitalism as *the* primary worldview, to the exclusion of tribalism.

Beyond separateness, *sovereignty also means the inherent right or power of self-government*. Sovereignty means many things to many people.

Sovereignty is the supreme power from which all specific political powers are derived.

Kiowa attorney Kirke Kickingbird
(Kickingbird et al. 1977, p. 1)

Sovereignty *is the force that binds a community together and repre-sents the will of a people to act as a single entity.*

Sharon O'Brien, *American Indian Tribal Governments*
(O'Brien 1989, p. 14)

If sovereignty means anything, it means that we Indian people have the right to choose our own future regardless of what the United States thinks is in our best interest. If in fact this choice ever does come into conflict with the law that the United States says must govern our relationship, I believe that any final resolution of this conflict can come about through rational discourse and legal reason-ing of the issues.

Seneca attorney Robert Porter (1998, p. 28)

Do NOT play with our sovereignty. We have very little sovereignty and freedom left. . . . Tribes are under siege from State, Federal, and sometimes local governments, and are bombarded daily with proposed legislation that will weaken Tribal governments and reduce them to nothing more than voluntary associations or municipalities. Remind the dominant culture and its governments that Indian people . . . have aboriginal rights, a Trust relationship with the USA, and that very few Tribes . . . are rich from gaming. The needs are still there.

Ronnie Lupe, former Chairman of the
White Mountain Apache Tribe, in his message to new
tribal attorneys. *In* Getches, Wilkinson, and Williams 1998,
Teacher's Memorandum 2000, p. 26

Hold fast to your sovereignty and self-governance, while improving mainstream America's image of Indians. . . . You better make certain that your sovereignty remains intact. Once you lose that, then, as President Reagan said, "You'll be one of us."

Senator Daniel K. Inouye, in a speech on "Building American
Indian Nations," Tucson, Arizona, Fall 1999

Sovereignty . . . is a relationship, essentially intangible, between human groups and their environment, a measure of a people's claimed and recognized right to think, organize, and act freely to meet their own needs as they see them.

Professor Steve Cornell (1988, p. 45)

I heard the word "sovereignty." It is getting pretty scarce these days. You don't hear it much anymore. There was a time when we used to talk about sovereignty all the time, used to hear it as the standard position. People talk about it and ask, "What is sovereignty?" I note that sovereignty is probably the most used and misused word as it relates to Indian nations. Self-recognition, that's first. Self-determination, the ability and right to govern oneself, exercising national powers in the interest of the nation and its peoples, is fundamental to sovereignty. This, along with the jurisdiction over the lands and territories that we live and exist on, is sovereignty. Simply put, sovereignty is the act thereof. It is a state of mind and the will of the people. No more, no less. That is sovereignty as we understand it, sovereignty is freedom. Sovereignty, as I heard the word, is responsibility. I think that the United States would have been much better off if, instead of making a Bill of Rights, it made a bill of responsibilities, because that is what is lacking in this country today and in the world at large. . . .

The Haudenosaunee are a separate, sovereign nation. We have our own passport, and we travel about the world independently. That is an act of sovereignty. We didn't go to the federal government and ask them, "Can we have a passport?" We issued it, and we traveled. And we continue to do so. It's hard work, but we do it.

Oren Lyons (1993, p. 209), a traditional chief of the
Onondaga Nation, Iroquois Confederacy

Sovereignty is like a muscle. If you don't exercise it, it gets weak.

Ken Meshigaud, Chairman,
Hanahville Indian Community, Escanaba, Michigan
In O'Brien 2000a, p. 1

Within the Europe of old, sovereignty was vested in monarchs and was considered to be God-given. When the U.S. constitutional system was established, the power was determined to be in the people and it was to be exercised through their chosen representatives. U.S. sovereignty was therefore comparable to the inherent sovereignty of Indian tribes (Canby 1981; Deloria and Lytle 1983), except that while U.S. sovereignty was simply declared overnight, tribal sovereignty evolved from the beginning of time.

When Europeans arrived in the hemisphere, the hundreds of Indian nations were sovereign by nature and necessity. They conducted their own affairs and depended on no outside sources of power—Europeans or anyone else—to legitimize their acts of government. Indian tribes east of the Rockies all had some form of tribal organization. Among the largest and most sophisticated was the Iroquois league, within which clan mothers chose the leaders. The so-called Five Civilized Tribes of the Southeast organized governments based on cities. The majority of the plains tribes, like the Sioux and the Cheyenne, established the tribal organizations that have become so familiar to non-Indians.

The Pueblos of the Southwest lived in sizable organized villages governed by theocracies. Less centralized tribal organizations existed throughout the rest of the Southwest, California, and the Northwest Coast, where family groups, or clans, or even larger bands from among extensive nations of related peoples, like the Navajos, tended to be the principal political units. In regions like the Great Basin, the Arctic, and the Sub-Arctic, which had less concentrated life-sustaining resources, political organization was usually limited to extended family or clan-sized groups (Canby 1981; Cohen 1982).

Contact with Euro-Americans irrevocably changed the original nature of tribal governments. Some tribes' traditions, like the general tribal council or the village government, continue to survive. But most tribes have adopted written constitutions or legal codes. Primary laws are now made through tribal councils. And internal conflicts or tribal initiatives are addressed through the actions of tribal courts and tribal legislative bodies that are modeled after the male-dominated political institutions of non-Indians.

As always declared by the tribes—and confirmed by Congress, the Executive, and the Supreme Court—the present rights of Indian nations to govern their members and remaining territories derive from sovereignty that predates European arrival. In fact, as suggested above, it traces back to time immemorial in almost all cases. It was this original sovereignty that once made the tribes fully independent nations. However, tribal sovereignty has since been limited by the tribes' inclusion within the territorial boundaries of the United States.

As outlined by Cohen (see Getches, Rosenfelt, and Wilkinson 1979, p. 254) the three fundamental principals behind contemporary tribal powers, defined under federal law, are: "(1) An Indian tribe possesses, in the first instance [i.e., before European contact], all the powers of any sovereign state. (2) Conquest renders the tribe subject to legislative power of the United States and, in substance, terminates the external powers of sovereignty of the tribe, e.g., its power to enter into treaties [or go to war] with foreign nations, but does not by itself affect the internal sovereignty of the tribe, i.e., its powers of local self-government. (3) These [internal] powers are subject to qualification by treaties and by express legislation of Congress, but [unless expressly qualified] full powers of internal sovereignty are vested in Indian tribes and in their duly constituted organs of government." It is important to note that most tribes were never "conquered" in the strict sense of the term. They were compelled to acquiesce in federal control over their destinies, due to the superior numbers and superior military power of the Americans and their government.

The principal attributes of tribal sovereignty today can thus be summarized as follows: (1) Indian tribes possess inherent power over all internal affairs, (2) states are precluded from interfering with tribes' self-government, and (3) Congress has plenary (near absolute) power to limit tribal sovereignty and thereby limit the first two attributes. It has often done so (Canby 1981, 1998).

This power of Congress is indeed extensive, and solemn pledges made by the U.S. can be eradicated even without the consent of the tribes. Congress can unilaterally abrogate treaty promises, alter tribes' powers of self-government, extinguish aboriginal and trust title to land, and even terminate the primary legal existence of a tribe, i.e., end the special political or "government-to-government" relationship between an Indian nation and the United States (*United States v. Wheeler* 1978). (Some 109 tribes and small bands were terminated between 1953 and 1970.) There is no *legal* recourse tribes can pursue when such things happen. They can only appeal to Congress to change its mind. This is because the relationship between Indian nations and the U.S. has been recognized by Congress and the courts to be a political one—between sovereigns—and not a legal one. The ultimate reason behind the reality that what the U.S. says is what goes is the United States' military power.

The federal policy of tribal self-determination, however, with its beginnings in the 1930s and a renewal in the 1970s, has created opportunities for tribes to retain limited amounts of their original sovereignty and to overcome some of the restraints arbitrarily or improperly placed on that sovereignty over the past 200 years. Still, it seems an inter-governmental tension will always be present and the Indian nations' sovereignty will always be under attack from various quarters.

O'Brien (1989, p. 292) has a fitting closing statement about some of the tension just noted: "Many Indian people argue that tribal sovereignty remains total, even today—that Indian nations have never been conquered and that all federal or state laws limiting tribal sovereignty are illegal. The federal government's familiar argument is that Indian tribes today are quasi-sovereigns, or domestic dependent nations."

H-10. *What have been the general characteristics of traditional tribal governments?*

Historically, only a few tribes had formal governments or written laws. There were exceptions, such as the Iroquois Confederacy. . . . But most Indian societies were oral cultures, a tradition that has by no means disappeared. This does not mean that "law" was absent. . . . Clearly understood rules developed by consensus and were strengthened by the tribes' pantheism which blended religion into all aspects of Indian life. The result was a "complex and smooth-working social organization of the tribes which functioned without need for written laws or the paraphernalia of European Civilization" (W. Washburn, The Indian in America 40, 1975).

Getches, Rosenfelt, and Wilkinson 1979, p. 300

When Europeans first arrived, there were perhaps 600 tribal entities in what is now the U.S. These Native people had many complex and pervasive forms of government and social control, on both large and small scales. On the large scale, the most highly developed tribal government was that of the powerful Iroquois league of the near Northeast. Even before Columbus sailed, the Iroquois had a constitution in the form of the Ne Gayaneshagowa, or Great Binding Law. The constitution was embodied in the symbolized writing of sacred wampum belts made of patterned sea shell beads. Specialized patterns were read aloud at ceremonies as a recitation of the Great Law, which was acknowledged as the instrument of Iroquois nationality. Their government provided for such sophisticated procedures as tribal confirmation of council representatives, initiative, recall, referendum, equal suffrage, a system of checks and balances, and specific delegations of wartime and peacetime responsibilities to tribes of the League. Other large Indian confederacies, like the Creeks of the Southeast, also developed extensive and complex governments (Deloria and Lytle 1983; Kickingbird, et al. 1977).

Less sophisticated but socially pervasive governments were found among native peoples in areas like the Great Basin deserts and the Arctic. Environmental limitations in such areas prevented the coming together of substantial numbers of people in organized living groups. This, in turn, reduced the need for highly developed governments. Relying on less formal traditions, mores, and social pressures was better suited to the needs of family and clan living. For basic government, a small group might have met daily to discuss matters of general importance. Leadership naturally fell to elders who were respected for their wisdom (O'Brien 1989). Despite the contrast with tribes like the Iroquois, there were still important characteristics common to the small and grander forms of Native government.

An idea like separation of church and state would have been inconceivable to *all* traditional governments. They made little distinction between the political and the religious. All aspects of life were inextricably bound together. Political and religious power were often the same. Government actions were pursued with spiritual guidance and were oriented toward combined spiritual and political fulfillment (O'Brien 1989).

At the base of individual and tribal life was the belief that a spirit force resided within every natural being. The concept of "beings" who peopled the tribe's world included the land, plants, animals, and humans. Native people were not superior to the natural world but were an integral part of it. Therefore, it was incumbent upon their combined religious and political governments to strive for harmony among the many elements of life important to their specific tribal groups. The tribe was primary and individuals secondary (O'Brien 1989; Underhill 1965).

Power to govern came from the community and flowed upwards. Rights of birth, so important to European rulers, were generally insignificant—with some exceptions. The great tribal leaders, who sometimes served only during times of special need or crisis, were those who proved themselves by deed and ability, and who demonstrated an overriding concern for the welfare of the community. They lacked dictatorial power; therefore, they depended on their persuasive and other abilities—and the respect of the people—to achieve governmental goals. Powers of persuasion were often of paramount importance, for tribes generally made decisions based not on mere majority rule but on consensus. Dissension and disharmony within the tribe, and spiritual or physical imbalance with the living environment, were things to be avoided. Thus, unusually broad concepts of balance and harmony, with a strong religious foundation, were the common primary tenets of Native government (O'Brien 1989; Owen, Deetz, and Fisher 1967).

H-11. *What are the characteristics of modern tribal governments?*

There are two important changes that time has brought on the form and nature of tribal governments. First, whereas the traditional form functioned primarily as an adjudicatory body settling disputes within the tribes, today tribal bodies have become legislative in their outlook and bureaucratic in their operations. . . . Second, tribal governments have taken on the cloak of Anglo-American institutional forms. The structures, the functions, the technologies, the politics,

> *and even the goals of the* [non-Indian] *community are in many ways
> displacing the traditional ways of the Indians. The unanswered ques-
> tion . . . is how much of the traditional Indian culture and values can
> survive if tribal government continues to develop along these lines.*
>
> Deloria and Lytle 1983, p. 109

The dwindling number of traditional Native governments which
survived into the 1800s were almost totally disrupted by the end of
the century. The principal causes were (1) contact with European
culture, (2) removal and placement of tribes within confining reservations, and (3) establishment of the powerful Indian agent system
by the federal government. Only a few groups, most notably the
Pueblos, escaped this political fate and have been able to continue
their traditional governments largely intact to the present.

Federal erosion of tribal organization was at its peak during the
land allotment period (1887–1934), when official policy was to destroy
Indian tribalism (Canby 1981). But a dramatic policy change came in
1934 with passage of the Indian Reorganization Act (IRA). The act was
purposely designed to help re-establish self-government and restore
to tribes sufficient powers to represent tribal interests in a variety of
political and economic circumstances. Much of the bureaucratic stran-
glehold and paternalism of the Bureau of Indian Affairs was reduced.
However, the majority of new governments that emerged under the
act (181 of 258 tribes voted to accept reorganization) became constitutional governments organized on a legalistic European model. The
two main reasons for this were (1) by the 1930s, most of the tribes'
traditional governments and customs had been dormant too long or
were too badly eroded to resurrect in short order and (2) all tribal
governments that were developed under the IRA had to be approved
by the Secretary of the Interior. So, the change wrought in the 1930s
was positive but it was obviously not a panacea. The decades since
passage of the IRA have seen the continuation and evolution of a variety of governments (Deloria and Lytle 1983).

Quoting the National American Indian Court Judges Association,
Deloria and Lytle list the categories of government into which most
tribes fall:

Representative: Here the tribe elects a governing body that operates under a constitution which the tribal members have approved [e.g., Jicarilla Apache of New Mexico].

Representative/Traditional Combination: Under this system, governmental officials are elected by tribal members, but some governmental positions are reserved for traditional leaders by virtue of their traditional lineage. The officials operate under a written constitution voted on by the tribal members [e.g., Warm Springs Tribes of Oregon].

General Council: The tribal membership adopts bylaws which govern and control the tribal officers, but these tribal officials have no substantive authority. When a substantive issue arises, officers call a General Council meeting of the tribe and the members vote on the issue [e.g., Crow Tribe of Montana].

Theocracy: Both the civil leaders and officers of the tribe are selected by the religious leaders. This is the most traditional form of tribal government [e.g., the Pueblos of New Mexico].

To this contemporary list must be added the ongoing Iroquois government mentioned above, the town corporation government of several eastern tribes under state rather than federal supervision, and the Alaska Native corporations for villages and regions. The latter are technically not governments but, with passage of the Alaska Native Claims Settlement Act in 1971, they supplanted most existing Native governments by assuming control over management of finances, lands, and resources.

The many—and complicated—activities of today's tribal governments include defining conditions of membership, regulating domestic relations of members, prescribing rules of inheritance for reservation property not in trust status, levying taxes, regulating property under tribal jurisdiction, controlling conduct of members by tribal ordinance, administering justice, conducting elections, developing tribal health and education programs, managing tribal economic enterprises, managing natural resources, and maintaining inter-governmental relations at the federal, state, and local levels (American Indian Lawyer Training Program 1988; Bureau of Indian Affairs 1991a).

Reflecting on the opening quotation, scattered but dedicated attempts are now being made in Alaska and the lower 48 states to restore more traditional ways into tribal governments.

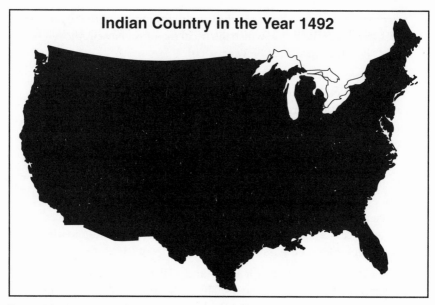

Figure 7. When Columbus landed in the Western Hemisphere, all the land of what is today the United States was "Indian Country."

H-12. *What is Indian country?*

The term "Indian country" has been around for more than two hundred years. It originated in popular designations for lands beyond the frontier that were mostly unknown and inhabited by Native peoples who were deemed "uncivilized" (Deloria and Lytle 1983). The term has developed to the point where it is now commonly heard in three contexts—legal, socio-political, and military.

Legal

The first definition is the most important and complex. Whether an area is legally classified as Indian country is the basic question in legal jurisdiction issues involving federal Indian law. The term denotes those geographic areas in which tribal and federal laws normally apply and state laws do not (Getches, Rosenfelt, and Wilkinson 1979). (See Figures 7 and 8.) The statutory definition of Indian country that is relevant today was enacted by Congress in 1948 as part of a criminal statute (18 U.S. Code, Sec. 1151). The U.S. Supreme Court, however, has found it also applies to questions involving civil jurisdiction. The definition reads:

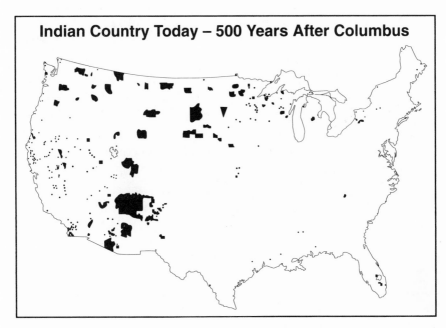

Indian Country Today – 500 Years After Columbus

Figure 8. The shaded areas on this map represent all that is left of Indian country today in the lower 48 states. It represents less than 3 percent of the total land area. There are no reservations left in Oklahoma, but there are many small parcels of trust land, which still qualify as "Indian country." These are not represented on the map.

> The term "Indian country," . . . means (a) all land within the limits of any reservation under the jurisdiction of the United States government, . . . (b) all dependent Indian communities within the borders of the United States, . . . and (c) all Indian allotments, the Indian titles to which have not been extinguished.

Subsection (a) refers to *all* territory within the exterior boundaries of a designated Indian reservation, whether a parcel in question is currently Indian-owned or not, as long as it was, at one time, a legal part of the reservation. Subsection (b) refers to reasonably defined areas occupied by dependent Indian communities that are federally recognized, e.g., Reno, Nevada, Indian Colony. Subsection (c) deals with individual Indian land allotments still held in trust by the U.S., whether the allotments are in or outside a reservation, e.g., Indian-owned land originally acquired under the homestead laws and held in trust by the U.S. (Cohen 1982).

A significant development concerning legal application of the term "Indian country" arose in 1998 regarding Alaska. In the case of *Alaska v. Native Village of Venetie* (1998) the Supreme Court essentially ruled that the millions of acres of lands held by Alaska Native corporations are not *Indian country*, as had once been ruled in 1992 by the 9th Circuit Court of Appeals in the case of *Native Village of Tyonek v. Puckett et al*. The 9th Circuit's opinion in the *Venetie* case, which the Supreme Court overturned in 1998, had been consistent with that circuit's earlier *Tyonek* ruling. By way of its *Venetie* decision, the Supreme Court moved Alaska Native villages one step further along the path of "judicial termination" (see the end of Part III on page 409).

Socio-political

In this context, Indian country is the Indian equivalent of terms like "African American community," "Hispanic community," "Jewish community," etc., and is frequently used to refer to the national American Indian population.

Military

Indian country is a colloquialism, considered inappropriate by many, that has long been used by U.S. Army soldiers to mean "enemy territory." It was very commonly heard in Viet Nam and was sometimes invoked in the war with Iraq.

H-13. *What is the meaning and derivation of the term "Indian self-determination?"*

> *Self-determination: Decision-making control over one's own affairs and the policies that affect one's life.*
>
> O'Brien 1989, p. 319
>
> *Self-determination means that tribal governments should shape the development of federal policy.*
>
> Senator Daniel K. Inouye, in a speech on "Building American Indian Nations," Tucson, Arizona, Fall 1999

"Self-determination" is a catch-all term that covers a variety of concepts including tribal restoration, self-government, cultural renewal, reservation resource development, self-sufficiency, control over education, and equal or controlling input into all policies and programs arising from the American Indian–federal government trust relationship (Waldman 1985).

The present movement toward heightened self-determination had its recent beginnings in the early 1960s with the growth of pan-Indian organizations that demanded meaningful control of programs affecting the Indian community (Kelly 1988). There had been an earlier start toward self-determination, however, in the era surrounding the Indian Reorganization Act (IRA) of 1934. (Discussed in Part III of this book.)

By the 1920s, the growth of the administrative power of the Bureau of Indian Affairs had effectively destroyed most pre-existing forms of tribal government. The agency had evolved into the role of colonial administrator and directed programs and services on reservations under a policy which later became known as "paternalism." A dictionary-like definition of paternalism would be "a policy or practice of treating or governing a people in a fatherly manner, especially by providing for their presumed needs without giving them representation or responsibility."

In the early 1930s, the power brokers in Washington had to admit that paternalism was doing a great disservice to American Indian tribes and their people. The response at the congressional level was the IRA, which was referred to as the Indian "New Deal" by the Roosevelt administration. Revolutionary for its time, the IRA fell far short of the current policy of "Indian self-determination without termination." It nonetheless provided a number of opportunities for renewed tribal self-government and the exercise of certain dormant powers of sovereignty.

But, the momentum that began in the 1930s dwindled into the unconscionable termination era of the 1950s, which sought to terminate entirely the federal recognition—or government-to-government relationship—of the Indian tribes through legislative and administrative fiat. More than 100 Indian tribes and communities were "terminated" and a renewed paternalism took hold over the rest of Indian country.

The turn-about started in the 1960s and got an official boost in 1970 from Richard Nixon in his July 8th congressional "Message from the President of the United States Transmitting Recommendations for Indian Policy."

> It is long past time that the Indian policies of the Federal government began to recognize and build upon the capacities and insights of the Indian people. Both as a matter of Justice and as a matter of enlightened social policy, we must begin to act on the basis of what the Indians themselves have long been telling us. The time has come to break decisively with the past and to create the conditions for a new era in which the Indian future is determined by Indian acts and Indian decisions.

Congress subsequently debated and eventually passed the Indian Self-Determination and Education Assistance Act of 1975. This act authorizes federal agencies to contract with and make grants directly to Indian tribal governments for federal services, much like it does with state and local governments. The legislative logic is that the tribes know best their own problems and can better allocate their resources and energies in the necessary direction, compared with decisions made by distant federal bureaucrats (Deloria and Lytle 1984). The broader effect of the act is that it has set the statutory climate for the rejuvenation of tribal governments by admitting, rejecting, and countering yesteryear's paternalistic policies.

> [T]he prolonged Federal domination of Indian service programs has served to retard rather than enhance the progress of Indian people and their communities by depriving Indians of the full opportunities to develop leadership skills crucial to the realization of self-government, and has denied to the Indian people an effective voice in the planning and implementation of programs for the benefit of Indians which are responsive to the true needs of Indian communities . . . (Sec. 2 (2) (1).).

> The Congress declares its commitment to the maintenance of the Federal Government's unique and continuing relationship with and responsibility to the Indian people through the establishment of a meaningful Indian self-determination policy which will permit an orderly transition from Federal domination of programs for and services to Indians to effective and meaningful participation by the Indian people in the planning, conduct, and administration of these programs and services . . . (Sec. 3. (b).).

SECTION I: THE BUREAU OF INDIAN AFFAIRS

I-1. *What are the administrative roots, current mission, objectives, and program responsibilities of the Bureau of Indian Affairs?*

Roots

In August 1786, the Secretary of War was placed in charge of Indian affairs by Congress (Horsman 1988). General authority over Indian matters, though shared on specific issues with other involved agencies, remained with the War Department for decades. However, there was little in the way of a formalized administrative structure for Indian matters most of that time.

In 1824, Secretary of War John C. Calhoun created a Bureau of Indian Affairs (BIA) in the War Department and assigned a superintendent and two clerks to operate the fledgling agency. The duties of these employees included administering appropriations for treaty annuities, approving expense vouchers, managing funds used to "civilize" the Indians, managing official correspondence regarding Indian affairs, and deciding on trespass, damage, and other claims arising between Indians and non-Indians (Taylor 1984).

Eight years after the founding actions of Secretary of War Calhoun, an act of Congress officially authorized an Office of Indian Affairs within the War Department. In 1849, the Office of Indian Affairs was transferred to the newly created Department of the Interior, where it obtained bureau status and where it has remained for nearly 150 years.

Mission

The BIA's mission and policy responsibilities, as defined by Congress and the Executive, have evolved since the 1820s from removal of eastern tribes to the West, to reservation confinement, to land allotment and assimilation, to termination, and finally to tribal self-government and self-determination. The current basic mission of the BIA is (1) to act as the principal agent of the United States in carrying on the government-to-government relationship that exists between the United States and federally-recognized Indian tribes and (2) to act as

279

the principal agent in carrying out the responsibilities of the United States as trustee for property it holds in trust for federally-recognized tribes and individual Indians (Bureau of Indian Affairs 1987a, March 12, 2000, www.doi.gov/bureau-indian-affairs.html.)

With the advent of the internet, the BIA has taken advantage of the opportunity to reformulate its image in electronic "print" by developing an additional mission statement for its internet site, along with a "VISION" statement and a list of "GUIDING PRINCIPLES." The mission statement is:

> The Bureau of Indian Affairs' mission is to enhance the quality of life, to promote economic opportunity, and to carry out the responsibility to protect and improve trust assets of American Indians, Indian tribes, and Alaska Natives. We will accomplish this through the delivery of quality services, maintaining government-to-government relationships within the spirit of Indian self-determination.

Objectives

The primary objectives of the BIA are to (1) encourage and assist Indian and Alaska Native people to manage their own affairs (under the trust relationship with the federal government), (2) help them facilitate full development of their human and natural resource potentials, (3) mobilize all public and private aids to the advancement of Indians and Alaska Natives, and (4) utilize the skills and capabilities of these people in the direction and management of programs established for their benefit (United States Government Manual 1997).

Responsibilities

The BIA is the largest and most complex bureau in the Department of the Interior. Its general administrative responsibilities are numerous and varied. They include: a 40,000-student education program, a 50,000-client social services program, law enforcement, mining and mineral leasing, forestry, agriculture and irrigation programs, power systems development and management, road construction and maintenance of a 20,000-mile road system, and management of a combined trust fund valued at over $2 billion. The agency's service population includes about 1.2 million individuals who are members of some 300 tribes and 200 Alaska Native villages and corporations (Bureau of Indian Affairs 1992b, 2000b).

I-2. *How is the BIA administered?*

It is an agency run by Indians. Of the approximately 10,200 Bureau employees, almost 90 percent are American Indians (National Academy of Public Administration 1999). This is not a recent phenomenon. Indians have made up the majority of personnel in the BIA at least since 1950 (Taylor 1984). The high percentage of Native employees holds true for the Washington office and the 12 BIA regions. The regional offices, and the 83 smaller "field" offices within the regions, have the majority of the BIA's direct contact with the tribes and often pride themselves on the high percentage of Native people hired at all levels. The Juneau Area office in Alaska, for example, reported that by the early 1990s 95 percent of the BIA's Alaska employees were American Indian and Alaska Native (Tundra Times 1991). Also, the top administrators in the Bureau's Washington, D.C., headquarters are American Indian.

The most significant factor contributing to the high percentage of BIA Indian employees is an employment preference for qualified Indians and Alaska Natives that was established by Congress in the Indian Reorganization Act of 1934. It was administratively expanded in the early 1970s by the Secretary of the Interior. Questioned by some, this preference has been declared by the Supreme Court as being a political and not a racial policy under the broad constitutional authority of Congress over Indian affairs (*Morton v. Mancari* 1974).

I-3. *Is there a single best contemporary source for learning about the BIA's organizational structure, administration, and management?*

Yes. Without doubt, it is the recent study of BIA management and administration done by the National Academy of Public Administration (1999). The academy is a congressionally chartered nonprofit and nonpolitical institution that works with all levels of government in the U.S. to help governments and agencies address and resolve problems of public administration.

The academy's 130-page BIA report was commissioned by the BIA itself to help the agency identify, analyze, and begin to resolve some of the many problems it has implementing its duties and responsibilities.

A complete copy of the report can be found through the BIA website (see Question I-1), or may be obtained from the academy at 1120 G. Street, N.W., Suite 850, Washington, D.C. 20005.

I-4. *How many American Indians are* **directly** *affected by programs administered by the BIA and where are the BIA's major administrative offices?*

Although the Census Bureau reports an Indian population of nearly 2.4 million in its preliminary figures for 2000, the BIA estimates that its "service population" is approximately 1.2 million individual Indians and Alaska Natives (National Academy of Public Administration 1999). These are American Indians who have on-going relations with the agency, either through social service, education, trust property, or related programs. They are also people who meet the agency's general qualifying criteria of living on or near a reservation, being a member (or descendant of a member) of a federally recognized tribe, and having a Native blood quantum of one-fourth or more (Bureau of Indian Affairs 1989b).

The BIA has one national office, a dozen geographic regional offices, 83 field offices, and another two dozen special offices distributed throughout the 12 geographic regions. (See Figure 9.) The mailing addresses and main telephone numbers for the national and regional offices are given below. (For correspondence, insert "Bureau of Indian Affairs" as a second line for each regional address.) Although the BIA recently changed the names of its administrative units from "areas" and "agencies" to "regions" and "field offices," the geographic boundaries did not change. The regional names in the list below are followed by their old "area" designations.

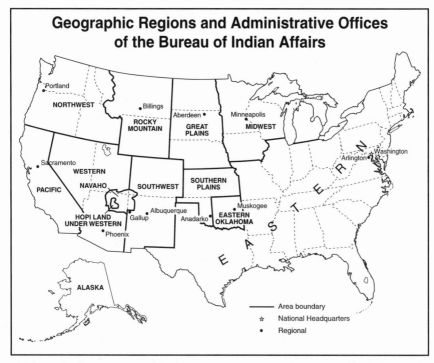

Figure 9. The Bureau of Indian Affairs has twelve main geographic regions, each of which has an office to serve American Indians in that region. National headquarters is in Washington, D.C. (After Nash 1988.)

Bureau of Indian Affairs
1849 C Street, N.W.
Washington, DC 20240
(202) 208-3711

Alaska Region (Juneau Area)
P.O. Box 25520
Juneau, AK 99802
(907) 586-7177

Eastern Region (Eastern Area)
3701 N. Fairfax Drive
MS: 260-VASQ
Arlington, VA 22203
(703) 235-2571

Eastern Oklahoma Region
  (Muskogee Area)
101 North 5th St.
Muskogee, OK 74401-6206
(918) 687-2296

Great Plains Region (Aberdeen
  Area)
115 4th Ave. S.E.
Aberdeen, SD 57401-4384
(605) 226-7343

Midwest Region
  (Minneapolis Area)
One Federal Drive, Room 550
Minneapolis, MN 55111-4007
(612) 713-4400

Rocky Mountain Region
  (Billings Area)
316 North 26th Street
Billings, MT 59101
(406) 247-7943

Navajo Region (Navajo Area)
P.O. Box 1060
Gallup, NM 87305
(505) 863-8314

Southern Plains Region
  (Anadarko Area)
W.C.D. Office Complex
  P.O. Box 368
Anadarko, OK 73005
(405) 247-6673

Northwest Region (Portland
  Area)
Federal Building
911 N.E. 11th Avenue
Portland, OR 97232
(503) 231-6702

Southwest Region (Albuquerque
  Area)
P.O. Box 26567
Albuquerque, NM 87125-6567
(505) 346-7590

Pacific Region (Sacramento Area)
Federal Building
2800 Cottage Way
Sacramento, CA 95825
(916) 978-6000

Western Region (Phoenix Area)
P.O. Box 10
Phoenix, AZ 85001-0010
(602) 379-6600

I-5. *What is the BIA's annual budget for its various programs?*

It has changed over the years. Throughout the lean, eight-year period of the Reagan era in the 1980s, the Bureau's annual budget averaged about one billion dollars. In 1987, for example, the amount was 1.02 billion (Bureau of Indian Affairs 1987b). With a change in administrations, the budget began to increase substantially in important areas like education. BIA data from 1992, for example, showed that Congress made an annual appropriation of slightly more than 1.5 billion dollars.

The 2000 budget of dollars appropriated by Congress amounted to $1,869,052,000. The proposed budget for 2001 was $2,200,956,000. These amounts can be broken down into several major categories:

Budget Category	2000 Appropriations	2001 Proposed Approp.
Tribal Priority Allocations		
(Direct-to-Tribes Funds)		
Tribal Gov't	$352,899,000	$374,634,000
Human Services	149,511,000	165,964,000
Education	50,867,000	52,662,000
Pub. Safety & Justice	1,384,000	1,364,000
Comm. Development	39,698,000	43,963,000
Resource Mgmt.	54,595,000	55,321,000
Trust Services	28,605,000	43,723,000
Gen. Administration	23,164,000	23,549,000
Subtotal	**$700,723,000**	**$761,180,000**
Education	502,216,000	544,773,000
Resource Mgmt.	39,830,000	37,184,000
Non-recurring Programs	64,231,000	71,405,000
Central Office (Wash., D.C.)		
Operations	52,637,000	57,864,000
Regional Office Operations	42,241,000	56,794,000
Special Programs/Pooled	237,657,000	265,810,000
Construction	197,404,000	365,912,000
Land & Water Claims	27,128,000	34,026,000
Guaranteed Loans	4,985,000	6,008,000
Total of Direct Appropriations	**$1,879,052,000**	**$2,200,956,000**

Source: March 12, 2000, www.doi.gov/bueau-indian-affairs.html.

I-6. *Including BIA funds, what is the combined total amount of federal appropriations for the Indian programs of all federal agencies?*

In 1998 the amount was approximately $7.5 billion (National Academy of Public Administration 1999), but only about 25 percent of this went through the BIA. In 2000, the total amount of Indian program appropriations had increased to approximately $8.2 billion (Maniaci 2000).

For 2001, President Clinton proposed a $1.2 billion increase (Rolo 2000a), which, if passed by a reluctant Congress, would have raised the total federal appropriations for federal Indian programs to an unprecedented $9.4 billion.

People who do not follow Indian country issues were very surprised by the seemingly large amount of the proposed increase. However, it was common knowledge before the president's announcement was made in February 2000 that there was a $1.2 billion shortfall in Indian country in base funding for vital services—ranging from fire protection and land and water rights protection to social programs and law enforcement (Howarth 1999a).

Not long after Clinton's proposal was made public, Kevin Gover, Assistant Secretary of the Interior for Indian Affairs, remarked that there will continue to be "dire needs in Indian country," due to long-overlooked problems, and that "[c]ertainly 1.2 billion cannot be the last increase" (Rolo 2000b, p. 1).

I-7. What are the most frequent complaints about the BIA?

> *To us, the situation with the bureau is often that "we can't live with it and we can't live without it."*
>
> Phillip Martin 1984, Chief
> Mississippi Band of Choctaw Indians

Complaints about the BIA are legion. They vary from time to time, depending upon the politics of the day, and they come from all quarters—including individuals, tribes, the public, Congress, and the Executive branch. Whenever anything goes wrong concerning any Indian or Alaska Native issue, there is a good probability that finger-pointing will begin or end with the BIA, whether or not the agency is ultimately at fault.

Sometimes the agency escapes unscathed, however, as when Congress, the White House, interest groups, land owners, state government, and the Passamaquoddy tribe took the initiative in hammering out a solution to the Maine land claims issue of the 1970s. In 1972, the tribe claimed two-thirds of the state, based on a land cession made in 1791 which was in violation of the 1790 Non-intercourse Act. In 1980, through the Maine Indian Claims Settlement Act, the tribe gave up its legal claims to most of the state in exchange for retained rights to 120,000 acres and a $40 million settlement (White 1990). The BIA officially entered the arena only *after* the settlement act was passed and then only to comply with the provisions in the act which required BIA administration.

Several selected newspaper headlines and column quotes follow. They give the general flavor of some of the major complaints surfacing (or resurfacing) in the early 1990s and then again in 1999 and 2000. There is no intention here to apologize for administrative shortcomings which do arise within the BIA. Nevertheless, it is important to remember that *Congress*, and not the BIA, is ultimately and constitutionally responsible for *all* the federal government's Indian affairs policies and programs.

BIA Blames Sloppy Bookkeeping For $23.8 Million In Lost Equipment

WASHINGTON—The federal Bureau of Indian Affairs can't find $23.8 million in equipment it is supposed to own and has overestimated the value of other machinery by $536 million, officials say . . . BIA spokesman Carl Shaw said the audit does not show any intentional wrongdoing, just sloppy accounting . . . (Associated Press 1991b)

Probe Blames Government For Deficient Indian Schools

WASHINGTON—The government has managed its Indian schools so poorly that students score well below their grade level on standardized tests, an Interior Department investigation concludes.

Only two schools run by the Bureau of Indian Affairs performed at the national median, the Department's Inspector General said in a recent report . . . (Associated Press 1991f)

BIA Mismanagement Blasted

WASHINGTON—Calling Bureau of Indian Affairs management of the $2 billion Indian trust fund "a continuing crisis" and "a national disgrace," a House committee is urging greater tribal control in trust fund administration . . . (Anquoe 1992a)

Brown Defends Budget

WASHINGTON—The House Subcommittee on Interior Appropriations chastised Bureau of Indian Affairs officials [e.g., Dr. Eddie Brown, Assistant Secretary for Indian Affairs] for proposed 1993 budget cuts in Indian programs.

"This administration doesn't like Indians, does it?" charged Rep. Sidney Yates, D-Ill., subcommittee chairman, during the April 2 hearing . . . (Anquoe 1992b)

BIA: Can It Be Fixed?

WASHINGTON—A critical study of the management and administration of the Bureau of Indian Affairs (BIA) concludes that budget cuts, and a huge reduction in force in 1996, have disabled the agency's ability to carry out basic planning and managerial functions. . . .

In 1980, the BIA work force numbered 19,000. Today there are 10,000 employees country-wide. [Assistant Secretary Kevin Gover said] "Congress has disabled the organization to the point where it cannot operate properly" . . . (Howarth 1999b)

TAAMS new computer, will it work?

WASHINGTON—The General Accounting Office, the investigative arm of Congress, has charged the Department of the Interior is about to waste millions on a computer system that won't work—its much-lauded "fix" for years of BIA mismanagement of Indian trust funds . . . (Hill 1999). ["TAAMS" stands for "Trust Asset Accounting and Management System."]

U.S. Reveals Trust-Fund Fix Delays

WASHINGTON—The Interior Department has admitted drastic setbacks in its plans to fix mismanagement of a $500 million trust system for American Indians, meaning years of more financial uncertainty for some 300,000 account holders, many of them poor. . . .

A group of Indians sued the federal government in 1996 over the mismanagement of their accounts, which hold proceeds of leases for grazing, logging or oil drilling on Indian land. . . .

[Judge] Lamberth held Interior Secretary Bruce Babbitt, Bureau of Indian Affairs head Kevin Gover and then Treasury Secretary Lawrence Summers in contempt of court last year for failing to turn over documents . . . (Kelley 2000)

Saginaw PR blitz blasts BIA leadership

WASHINGTON—When Kevin Gover came to Washington nearly two years ago to head up the beleaguered Bureau of Indian Affairs, he knew he was going to take his share of hits from his detractors—every politician does.

But a few weeks ago, when he found himself the target of a nasty political media campaign that threatened to reduce his reputation to rubble, he decided to come out swinging with a counter media punch of his own . . . (Rolo 1999b)

I-8. *What were the results of the study of BIA management and administration that was published by the National Academy of Public Administration in 1999, and what is the BIA doing about the recommendations?*

The academy found significant difficulties in almost all areas of management and administration within the agency. The most serious problems were found in the areas of policy, the budget system, human resource management, financial management, information resource management, records management, and procurement management. In a generalized summary statement on "Managing for Success," the academy panel had this to say:

> The panel believes the current management and administration of the BIA are not fully adequate to meet all of its trust responsibilities to American Indians and Alaska Natives, to carry out the numerous statutory responsibilities, and to operate an effective and efficient agency. Specifically, there is no existing capability to provide budget, human resources, policy, and other types of management assistance to the Assistant Secretary-Indian Affairs and the Bureau. Staff do not receive adequate training in management and administrative skills and techniques, and BIA does not have adequate standards by which to determine its management and administrative requirements for resources and staffing. Strategic planning, yearly performance planning, and program analysis are not institutionalized. Important policy manuals and implementation handbooks are out of

date. In short, neither the Office of the Assistant Secretary-Indian Affairs nor the Bureau has the internal staff capabilities that typically support managerial and administrative excellence.... (p viii)

BIA has been unable to meet the basic requirements for administrative systems within the federal government. BIA does not, for example, have a unified approach to human resources management. The budget structure and process do not provide the information necessary to estimate or justify actual needs. The financial management systems do not permit matching funding to changing requirements, and the BIA has been unable to obtain an unqualified audit. Since 1991 DOI has declared the procurement system a material weakness, but there has been little improvement.

The large number of recommendations spawned by the study are too numerous and extensive to present here, but they can be reviewed through the BIA website (www.doi.gov/bureau-indian-affairs.html). The report's key suggestions include: significantly increasing managerial discipline; developing a new office of policy, management, and budget; greatly improving strategic and annual performance planning; establishing a human resource management unit; developing a budgeting system that has sufficient flexibility to adapt to changing allocations of funds; significantly improving financial management; establishing an information resource management system that links the BIA together and greatly improves communication and information technology training; substantially improving records management; establishing a new and much improved procurement policy; and establishing clearly defined management "milestones," and specific plans for achievement of tangible results.

In response to the academy's report, Assistant Secretary of the Interior for Indian Affairs Kevin Gover said that there are now new opportunities to improve the BIA (Rolo 2000c). But any major repairs to the agency will take a number of years and will require the commitments of future federal administrations.

SECTION J: HEALTH

J-1. *What are the goals, mission, structure, and function of the Indian Health Service?*

The primary federal health resource for American Indians is the Indian Health Service (IHS). It is located within the U.S. Public Health Service, which is part of the Department of Health and Human Services. With a current annual budget of more than $2.2 billion, the IHS developed out of very meager beginnings in 1954. At that time, Congress transferred the badly ailing Indian health program out of the BIA and into the Public Health Service. Improvement of the amount and quality of medical service available to American Indians was the reason behind the transfer, and it worked. But, as with the BIA, the IHS has had its share of problems regarding waste, mismanagement, and fraud. (See also the IHS website, www.ihs.gov.)

Mission and overall goal

As stated by the Director of the Indian Health Service (Trujillo 2000, p. 1):

> Our mission, in partnership with American Indian and Alaska Native people, is to raise their physical, mental, social, and spiritual health to the highest level.

> Our goal is to ensure that comprehensive, culturally acceptable personal and public health services are available and accessible to all American Indian and Alaska Native people.

The Indian Health Service (2000, "Fact Sheet") explains that:

> To carry out its mission and to attain its goal, IHS:
> (1) Assists Indian tribes in developing their health programs through activities such as health management training, technical assistance, and human resource development;
> (2) Facilitates and assists Indian tribes in coordinating health planning, in obtaining and utilizing health resources available through Federal, State, and local programs, in operating comprehensive health care services, and in health program evaluation;
> (3) Provides comprehensive health care services, including hospital and ambulatory medical care, preventive and rehabilitative

291

services, and development of community sanitation facilities; and

(4) Serves as the principal Federal advocate for Indians in the health field to ensure comprehensive health services for American Indian and Alaska Native people.

Further goals and objectives

The Indian Health Care Improvement Act of 1976, as reauthorized by the Indian Health Amendments of 1992, establishes two primary goals for the IHS. They are (a) to raise the health status of American Indians and Alaska Natives to the highest possible level and (b) to encourage the maximum participation of Indians in the planning and management of IHS services. This second goal is an extension of self-determination policies.

The IHS has three ongoing objectives, also grounded in the 1976 legislation. Rhoades, Reyes, and Buzzard 1987 (p. 353–354) list them as:

1. To assure Indian people access to high-quality, comprehensive health services appropriate to their needs.
2. To assist Indian tribes and Alaska Native corporations to develop their capacity to staff and manage health programs and provide these tribal organizations with the opportunity to assume operational authority for IHS programs serving their communities.
3. To act as advocate for the Indian people in health-related matters and help them gain access to other Federal, State, and local programs to which they are entitled.

Service operations

A decentralized agency, the IHS is comprised of 12 geographic "area offices" which administer programs officially covering 34 states. The central office, area offices, cities where headquartered (with office phone numbers), and the states covered by each are as follows (Indian Health Service 1991a, 1997, 2000).

The areas are subdivided into approximately 150 geographic "service units." These are the basic health care administration units which the IHS serves within each of the 12 geographic areas. Recent reports show that 66 of the service units are operated by the IHS and 84 are operated by tribes. In the lower 48 states, the service units are

IHS HEADQUARTERS
Rockville, MD
(301) 443-3593

Area	Headquarters	States Covered
Aberdeen	Aberdeen, SD (605) 226-7581	IA, NE, ND, SD
Alaska	Anchorage, AK (907) 257-1153	AK
Albuquerque	Albuquerque, NM (505) 248-5429	NM, CO, TX (part)
Bemidji	Bemidji, MN (218) 759-3412	MI, MN, WI
Billings	Billings, MT (406) 247-7248	MT, WY
California	Sacramento, CA (916) 566-7001	CA
Nashville	Nashville, TN (615) 736-2441	AL, CT, FL, LA, MA, ME, MS, NC, NY, PA, RI, TN, TX (part)
Navajo	Window Rock, AZ (520) 871-5811	AZ (northeast), parts of UT, CO, NM
Oklahoma City	Oklahoma City, OK (405) 951-3820	OK, KS, TX (part)
Phoenix	Phoenix, AZ (602) 640-2052	AZ (most), UT (most), NV
Portland	Portland, OR (503) 326-2020	ID, OR, WA
Tucson	Tucson, AZ (520) 295-2406	AZ (south central)

usually centered around one or more Indian reservations, pueblos, rancherias, colonies, or former reservations. In Alaska they are centered around population concentrations. Both urban and rural programs are included. Service units function like county and city health departments, answering to area offices much like such departments would answer to states (Indian Health Service 1997).

The San Xavier Health Clinic, near Tucson, Arizona, serves some of the more than 20,000 Indians who live in the Tucson metropolitan area.

IHS operations are managed locally by the service units. Within each unit are a number of individual bases of operation. Typically, they are small hospitals or health centers with a number of clinics. An IHS policy of seeking community input into identification of needs and delivery of services affects how these bases of operation function. Individual patient care and community health are their points of focus (Indian Health Service 1988, 1991c, 1997).

In the opening years of the 2000s, the IHS has a service population of around 1.5 million. This number has increased from 1.2 million in 1990. (Indian Health Service 1991b, 2000). The average increase is about 2 percent per year. The various health services available are classified as preventive, curative, rehabilitative, and environmental, e.g., safe drinking water and sanitation. Added to "traditional" physician-patient encounters, there are emergency services, mental health programs, community outreach programs, and additional support services. These are provided through three modes of delivery—direct, tribal, and contract. Clinical services at facilities operated directly by the IHS, or through IHS agreements with tribes, are often the only sources of care reasonably available to many Indian people. When additional care is needed, or in areas beyond the normal reach of IHS and tribal programs, contract services are often relied on. As the name suggests, contract care is purchased through contracts with community hospitals and private practitioners (Rhoades, Reyes, and Buzzard 1987).

The IHS does not pay for all health care needs of its service population, but it does cover about 70 percent. The other 30 percent is covered by additional sources, including the same types of entitlement programs, or insurance, available to non-Indian citizens. When adequate IHS services are available, the agency prefers that program beneficiaries use IHS staff and facilities first. If additional care is needed, then a patient may be authorized by the IHS to use an outside health care facility or a private practitioner contracted by the IHS. For more than 30 years, IHS policy has been that the agency should be the payor of last resort when contract health care is obtained. In other words, for contract care, applicable federal, state, local, or private health payment programs, which Indian patients are otherwise entitled to, should be the primary payors (U.S. Public Health Service 1991, Sec. 36.61). There is occasional conflict over this rule. It usually comes from non-IHS health care providers who feel that the IHS should pay most or all coverage in all cases.

Staff

The IHS has about 15,800 employees, of whom 62 percent are American Indians. This relatively high percentage of Native employees is attributable to an Indian hiring preference comparable to that of the BIA. In recent years, the IHS has employed a medical staff of approximately 840 physicians, 100 physician assistants, 2,580 nurses, 350 pharmacists, 380 dentists, 60 optometrists, 45 physical therapists, 7 nutritionists, 80 dieticians, and 285 medical technologists. Vacancy rates of from three to 10 percent, high turnover among physicians, and serious regional staff shortages present significant challenges to the Service's health care effort (Indian Health Service 1988, 1992a, 1997, 2000).

A major support program, begun in 1968, is the one involving community health representatives (CHRs). They are Native paraprofessional health care providers who are selected, employed, and supervised by their tribes and communities. Their services include home visits, hospitalization follow-up, medication monitoring, health promotion, and disease prevention, incorporating traditional Native concepts whenever appropriate. About 1,400 CHRs work in Indian communities throughout the 12 IHS areas.

In 1991, when the Bush administration proposed cuts in health programs, the IHS director told Congress that the agency actually needed to double the number of physicians it employs. The director also stated that the number of health care workers in the agency was inadequate. He declared that, if improvements were not made, the IHS could not reach its immediate goal of providing the level of health care for American Indians that is normally available to the general public (Hazard 1991). By 2000 some improvements had been made, but the number of physicians remained unchanged.

Eligibility

IHS regulatory "principles" describe persons for whom the agency provides health care services (U.S. Public Health Service 1991, 1997). These include "Indians" (which incorporates Alaska Natives) who (a) are bona fide members of federally recognized tribes, bands, nations, villages, communities, organized groups, or Alaska Native Corporations and (b) reside in a geographically designated Health Service Delivery Area. Beneficiaries also include minor children who are not directly eligible but who have at least one parent who is.

Non-Indian women who are pregnant with an eligible Indian's child are also eligible, but only during the pregnancy and for about six weeks after birth. Non-Indian members of an eligible Indian's household may be eligible for service if it is necessary to control an acute infectious disease or other immediate public health hazard. Public Health Service and other federal beneficiaries may also be eligible under certain circumstances.

Ineligible non-Indians may receive emergency treatment on a fee-for-service basis. Also, on reservations or in remote settings where tribes will approve it, non-Indians living in an IHS area may receive medical services if (a) they pay for them and (b) providing the service does not interfere with delivery of services to Indian beneficiaries.

Facilities

The IHS system has 49 hospitals and 492 outpatient facilities. Among the outpatient facilities, health centers offer the most service and clinics generally the least. Operational control between the IHS and

Indian tribes or other groups breaks down in the following manner (Indian Health Service 1991a).

Type of Facility	IHS	Tribal
Hospital	37	12
Outpatient		
Health Centers	61	134
School Health Centers	4	4
Health Stations	48	73
Alaska Village Clinics	—	168

FEDERAL INDIAN HEALTH PROGRAM—A BRIEF HISTORY

Federal health services for Indians began in the early nineteenth century when Army physicians took steps to curb smallpox and other contagious diseases among tribes living in the vicinity of military posts. Treaties committing the federal government to provide health services to Indians were introduced in 1832 when members of the Winnebago Tribe were promised physician care as partial payment for rights and property ceded to the U.S. government. Transfer of the Bureau of Indian Affairs (BIA) from the War Department to the Department of the Interior in 1849 extended physician services to Indians by emphasizing non-military aspects of Indian administration and developing a corps of civilian field employees. The first federal hospital built to care for Indian people was constructed in the 1880s in Oklahoma. Nurses were added to the staff in the 1890s. Professional medical supervision of health activities for Indians began in 1908 with the establishment of the BIA position of Chief Medical Supervisor. Dental services began in 1913. Pharmacy services were organized in 1953. In 1955, responsibility for American Indian and Alaska Native health was transferred from the Department of the Interior's BIA to the Public Health Service (PHS) within the Department of Health, Education and Welfare (currently the Department of Health and Human Services). On January 4, 1988, the Indian Health Service was elevated to agency status and became the seventh agency in the PHS.

Indian Health Service 1992a

J-2. What are the major health-related statistics for the Indian population, and how do they compare with those for the general population?

In 1997, the Indian Health Service published its latest *Trends in Indian Health*. Most of the limited information presented below came from that relatively comprehensive document. The remainder was taken from the IHS companion document, *Regional Differences in Indian Health*. The agency used a number of sources for its data. Some are from the 1990 census and others are from compilations done in the mid 1990s. Readers requiring specifics on the sources and limitations of the data should review these two publications. They may be available in a local library, or they can be requested from the IHS. They are also available on the IHS website (www.ihs.gov). Year of collection and general population comparisons are provided with the statistics. Also, when the Indian population is referred to, it does not include all Indians and Alaska Natives counted in the nationwide census. It does include the approximately 1.5 million Native people in the 12 IHS service areas described in the previous answer.

Only national rates for the combined service areas are presented in the table on the following page. Rates for individual areas vary considerably. For example, the accident mortality rate given in the table, for Indians as a whole, is 94.5 per 100,000 population. The rate for the Oklahoma Area, however, is around 50 (the lowest of all 12 areas); but it has been 220 for the Tucson Area (the highest of all 12 areas).

Summarizing the table, the Indian birth rate is 65 percent higher than the national average, and infant survival is slightly lower than in the general population. An Indian child is also more likely than someone in the general population to suffer and die from a variety of causes, including all types of accidents (3.1 times as likely), liver disease (4.4 times), diabetes (3.3 times), pneumonia and influenza (1.3 times), suicide (1.6 times), homicide (1.4 times), and tuberculosis (5.7 times).

Does this mean that the IHS has not been doing the improved job which Congress expected when it transferred Indian health care responsibility from the BIA to the Public Health Service in 1954? No. Although there is room for improvement, the IHS has not been treading water since the 1950s. Past efforts have brought about some remarkable changes. Ongoing programs exist to further reduce the disparities in statistics shown in the table. Such programs include the

MAJOR INDIAN HEALTH STATISTICS

	Indian*	U.S., All Races
Birth Rate (mid-1990s)	25.6	15.5
(per 1,000 people)		
Infant Mortality	10.9	8.4
(per 1,000 live births)		
Life Expectancy at Birth	71.1	75.5
(in years)		
Leading Causes of Death		
(age-adjusted, per 100,000 people)		
All causes	612.4	513.3
Major cardiovascular disease	194.6	181.8
Disease of the heart	157.6	145.3
Cerebrovascular disease	27.8	26.5
Atherosclerosis	2.3	2.4
Malignant neoplasms	112.2	132.6
Accidents	94.5	30.3
Motor vehicle	53.3	16.0
All other	41.2	14.3
Chronic liver disease		
and cirrhosis	35.0	7.9
Diabetes mellitus	41.1	12.4
Pneumonia and Influenza	21.7	13.5
Suicide	19.2	11.3
Homicide	15.1	10.7
Chronic obstructive		
pulmonary diseases	17.4	21.4
HIV	3.9	13.8
Tuberculosis, all forms	2.3	0.4

*The term "Indian" includes Alaska Natives.

upgrading of equipment and facilities, more training of staff, recruitment of career staff, awareness and prevention of injury, treatment of substance abuse, nutrition counseling, mental health counseling, expanded dental services, upgrading of water and sanitation facilities, and so on. Budget limitations, staff shortages, and staff turnover, however, seem to be significant perennial problems.

MAJOR PROGRAM ACCOMPLISHMENTS SINCE 1973

	Percent Decrease in Mortality Rate
Infant	61
Maternal	86
Pneumonia and influenza	48
Tuberculosis	78
Gastrointestinal disease	77
Accidents	56
Suicide	18
Homicide	45
Alcoholism	33

J-3. *How serious is alcoholism among American Indians?*

> *Indian drinking is a particularly sensitive issue because it is also a major theme in anti-Indian prejudice and stereotyping. However, alcoholism and its effects are too important to be ignored, whether they involve* [non-Indians] *or Indians.*
>
> Price 1978, p. 188
>
> *There is a tremendous pressure in this country to conform. And when a group like the Indian doesn't, there's a sense of failure. Wouldn't it be nice if* [non-Indians] *were right that Indian alcoholism is a genetic weakness? This ignores their tremendous cultural depression over many, many years. Their alcohol problems are huge. But the reasons are so perplexing. You hear . . . the sadness.*
>
> Dale Walker, M.D., Cherokee, *In* Gibbons 1992, p. 34

Alcoholism, a world-wide plague, is indeed a major problem in many Indian communities. As with non-Indians, the causes are numerous and varied. Dr. Walker's quotation refers to one of the most common.

The most serious statistic kept on the topic of alcoholism by the Indian Health Service (IHS) is the alcoholism *mortality* rate. Among the population served by the IHS (roughly 1.5 million Native people in 34 states), the alcoholism mortality rate is 32.7 per 100,000 population. This is about 5.5 times the rate for the general U.S. population, but it is still 38 percent lower than it was a decade earlier (Indian Health Service 1991c, 1997, 2000; May 1994). There are, however, marked regional differences in alcoholism mortality rates in Indian country. They range from a low of 9.5 per 100,000, in the Oklahoma Area of the IHS, to a high of about 70 in the Aberdeen Area. Alcohol is also implicated in three-fourths of all traumatic American Indian deaths. (See the answer to question J-1 for a delineation of IHS "areas.")

ALCOHOL BEFORE COLUMBUS

Prior to European contact, Native use of alcoholic beverages was concentrated in areas of intensive agriculture in Mexico and Central and South America. Such beverages were also made and consumed in the American Southwest, in the area of the Carolinas, and around the Chesapeake Bay region. Alcoholic drinks were most often made by fermenting maize or tapioca, but in northern Mexico and parts of the Southwest U.S., wines were also produced from agave, dasylirion, saguaro and pitahaya cacti, and mesquite or screwbean. In the eastern U.S., Native people made a persimmon wine.

Price 1978; Waldman 1985

In much of the Southwest, among the Zunis, Yuman groups, and Apaches, as well as in the Southeast, alcohol use was mostly nonreligious. The Tohono O'odham and Pimas of the Southwest, however, believed that intake of alcoholic beverages could bring rain. For the Aztecs, intoxication served to induce meditation and prophecy. But, public drunkenness was taboo and, in some instances, could be punished by death.

Waldman 1985

Fetal Alcohol Syndrome, or FAS, is another major alcohol-related concern. This term describes the damage some unborn children can suffer when their mothers consume alcohol during pregnancy. In the bloodstream, alcohol can be toxic to the fetus. It depends on the stage of pregnancy and how much is consumed. Damage can range from subtle to severe—causing clumsiness, behavioral problems, stunted growth, disfigurement, and mental retardation (Steinmetz 1992). Specific data on FAS among Indian people are not readily available, but the incidence is relatively high. The rate for the general population is a little higher than 1 per 100,000 births. Some Indian communities may have a rate of 6 per 100,000 births, or greater (Stillman 1991, Indian Health Service 2000).

Even though the alcoholism *rate* among the Native population as a whole is comparatively high, the fact remains that a relatively small minority of American Indians are alcoholics. The very complex problem of alcoholism (or other substance abuse) among Indians or non-Indians goes well beyond simple comparisons of cold statistics. It also goes beyond the narrow confines of this book. (For general information on alcohol abuse and alcoholism see the *Journal of Studies on Alcohol*. More references on Indians and alcohol include Mancall (1995), May (1994), May and Smith (1988), and Navarro et al. (1997).)

J-4. *Do Indians metabolize alcohol differently or more slowly than do people of other ethnic groups?*

No. There is a persistent myth that Indians have a biophysical reason for "not being able to hold their liquor" (May 1994, p. 124). In his important article on the epidemiology of alcohol abuse among American Indians, May (p. 124) reported, "not only do non-Indians believe this, but many Indians also believe that their ethnic group has a biological deficit in metabolizing alcohol." He also firmly declares that "the myth has no basis in fact," and concludes:

> No basis at all for this myth is found in the scientific literature, and it should not be a consideration in current prevention and intervention programs. Major reviews of alcohol metabolism

among ethnic groups usually conclude that alcohol metabolism and alcohol genetics are traits of individuals and that there is more variation within an ethnic group than there is between ethnic groups. Further, when biophysiological investigators attempt to explain major alcohol-related behaviors, they generally point to sociocultural variables as the major factors.

(Also see Question D-4 on the myth of Indian genetic susceptibility to alcohol intoxication.)

J-5. *Is AIDS a major concern in Indian country?*

Spread the News—Not the Disease. AIDS Kills Indians Too.
> AIDS Awareness Poster
> Inter Tribal Council of Arizona, Inc. 1993

It is my fear and my belief that AIDS and HIV infection present an unprecedented threat to the future of all Native Americans.
> Josiah Moore, Chairman
> Tohono O'odham Nation, 1991

This is not a disease that only happens somewhere else, that only happens to someone else.
> Daris Hayes
> Lakota man with AIDS, 1991

How we respond to AIDS will tell a lot about us as a people.
> Carole LaFavor
> Ojibwa woman with AIDS, 1991

AIDS is obviously very much a concern in Indian country. AIDS experts consider many Indian people to be at high risk of HIV infections because of "unsafe" sex habits, alcohol use and related poor judgment, IV drug use, and the inter-migration between urban centers and Indian country (Erikson 1991). Statistics on the rate of HIV infection and full-blown AIDS among Native people have, in the past, been sketchy and confusing. One reason is that people being tested by doctors and laboratories generally have not been asked if they are American Indian or Alaska Native. Reporting techniques are now improving.

The federal Centers for Disease Control is currently maintaining separate records on AIDS with regard to American Indians. At the end of the 1990s, the figures stood as shown in the box on page 305.

Education and the halting of destructive or high risk behaviors are the keys to controlling the AIDS epidemic. Only these actions can reduce the rates or probabilities of infection. There is something that everyone should remember, however. Whenever AIDS or any other tragedy strikes someone, society's ever-important statistics—so coveted by the media, medical experts, and politicians—all go to a 100% reality for the victim. He or she is more than a number.

To obtain additional information, contact the National AIDS Information Hotline at 1-800-342-AIDS, or the National Native American AIDS Prevention Center in Oakland, California at (510) 444-2051.

AIDS STATISTICS FOR AMERICAN INDIANS—1998

Total number of AIDS cases   1,783
(No firm numbers exist for those who may be HIV positive.)

Breakdown of reported cases by sex of adult patient
      Cases among females   292
      Cases among males   1,491

Number of those affected who are children (under 13)   36

Probable means of infection among the reported cases:

Sex between gay men	49%
IV drug use	20%
Sex with men who inject drugs	14%
Hemophiliac blood transfusions	1%
Heterosexual sex or sex with bisexuals	8%
Receipt of blood transfusions or blood products	1%
Mother who had HIV or was at risk	1%
Unknown	6%

NOTE: These data are from the Centers for Disease Control (CDC) and are current through March 1998. Completely reliable data are still difficult to obtain because of highly variable reporting. For updates on data and sources, contact the CDC through the National AIDS Hotline at 1-800-342-AIDS and the IHS's HIV Center of Excellence in Phoenix, Arizona at (602) 263-1502.

    In June 1999, the CDC announced that the total number of reported AIDS cases among American Indians had reached 2,034 (National Native American AIDS Prevention Center website, March 15, 2000 www.nnaapc.org).

J-6. *Where can more in-depth historical and contemporary Indian health data be obtained?*

The Indian Health Service and the University of New Mexico Health Sciences Center Library have collaborated in the development of the

"Native Health Research Database." According to the IHS, this database includes various Indian health documents and other materials that have been published since about 1970. Additionally, the IHS has developed the "Native Health History Database," which is a computerized resource that contains bibliographic information and abstracts on historical Indian medical and health research reports and covers the remarkable period from 1652 to 1970. These two databases can be accessed through the IHS's website at www.ihs.gov/MedicalPrograms/HealthCare/info.asp (March 18, 2000). (For more on the Indian Health Service and its history, policy, and performance, see Boyum 1989 and Pfefferbaum et al. 1996. For a classic on Indian medicine, see Vogel 1970.)

SECTION K: EDUCATION

> The quotation which follows is a reply from Conassatego, of the Iroquois League, to an offer from the Virginia Legislature, in 1744, inviting the Iroquois to send six youths to be educated at the College of William and Mary, in Williamsburg (from O'Brien 1989, p. 239).
>
> *We know you highly esteem the kind of Learning taught in these colleges, and the maintenance of our young men, while with you, would be very expensive to you. We are convinced, therefore, that you mean to do us Good by your proposal; and we thank you heartily. But you who are so wise must know that different Nations have different conceptions of things; and you will not therefore take it amiss, if our Ideas of this kind of education happen not to be the same with yours. We have had some experience of it. Several of our young People were formerly brought up in the colleges of the Northern Provinces; they were instructed in all your Sciences; but, when they came back to us, they were bad Runners, ignorant of every means of living in the woods, unable to bear either cold or hunger, knew neither how to build a Cabin, take a deer, or kill an enemy, spoke our language imperfectly, were ther[e]fore neither fit for Hunters, Warriors, nor Counsellors; they were totally good for nothing. We are however not the less obliged for your kind offer, tho' we decline accepting it; and to show our grateful Sense of it, if the Gentlemen of Virginia shall send us a Dozen of their Sons, we will take care of their Education, instruct them in all we know, and make Men of them.*

K-1. *What is the general history of education programs for American Indians?*

The hundreds of tribes, bands, clans, and extended family groups of Native people which inhabited North America in the late 15th century had their own forms and concepts of education. These "systems" had evolved with their cultures over the millennia. The broad focus of pre-European education was to facilitate a child's acquisition of environmental and cultural knowledge necessary to (1) survive in a subsistence lifestyle and (2) contribute meaningfully to the overall socio-economic welfare of the group (Bureau of Indian Affairs 1988). The 1490s, however, marked the beginning of the end of an epoch of complete Indian self-determination in the education of their children.

The first time Indian education was formally addressed by a European colonial government was in 1512 in the Laws of Burgos. This was a legal code developed by the Spanish government whereby the Indians under Spanish rule were to have impressed upon them the virtues of Christianity and civilization (Williams 1990). Not many Indians were formally educated under these early laws—only a few Indian leaders' sons, who were entrusted to Franciscan missionaries for four years, received formal training. By and large, the Laws of Burgos functioned to legitimize forced labor and assimilation. In 1568, however, the Jesuits began the long history of non-Indian education of Indian children when they established a school in Havana, Cuba (O'Brien 1989). The purpose of this school, like nearly all of the others for hundreds of years to come, was to "civilize" the Indians. This meant conversion to Christianity, learning reading and writing, developing agricultural and other skills, and adopting "white" values. These included individualism (versus tribalism), materialism, competitiveness, and conquest of the natural world.

British colonial education of Indians took numerous forms. At the simplest level, colonists took Indian children into their homes and educated them in the ways of Euro-American civilization. At the more sophisticated level, small schools were established for basic Indian education. In 1619, for instance, the first British Indian school was established by the Virginia Company near present-day Richmond. More advanced schools were later developed for the "more promising," or better assimilated, students. The College of William and Mary, chartered in 1693, was partly dedicated to Indian education. Dartmouth College in New Hampshire was also established originally to educate Indians. And still other colonial institutions, such as Harvard and the College of New Jersey, provided for Indian education, as did religious organizations (Szasz and Ryan 1988).

The federal government made its first appropriation for Indian education in 1776, when the Continental Congress provided for a minister, a blacksmith, and two teachers to live among some of the Indians in New York. For decades, sporadic, and not very substantive, attempts to address Indian education were made by the federal government through different treaties, executive orders, and limited legislation. At the same time, religious groups increased their efforts in this area by establishing hundreds of missionary schools and several academies. A few of the Indian tribes, most notably the Cherokees, developed flourishing school systems of their own in the late 18th and early 19th centuries, based to a large degree on the Euro-American models of the time (Harlow 1935; Szasz and Ryan 1988).

In 1860, the BIA opened its first Indian school, on the Yakima Reservation in the state of Washington. By the turn of the century, the BIA was operating 147 reservation day schools, 81 reservation boarding schools, and 25 off-reservation boarding schools for Indians in various parts of the country as a part of the government's trust responsibility. The most famous of the boarding schools was Carlisle, in Pennsylvania, the first off-reservation government boarding school. It was established in 1879 by Henry Pratt, a Civil War veteran, whose goal was complete assimilation. "Kill the Indian and save the man" was his motto. Regimentation, reading, writing, arithmetic, the manual trades, and home economics were drilled into the students until the school closed in 1918 (Bureau of Indian Affairs 1988; O'Brien 1989; Szasz and Ryan 1988).

While the mission schools declined in influence, from the 1870s through the 1890s, "contract" schools developed. The government employed religious denominations by contract to run part of its expanding network of schools. Before the practice was ended in 1897, Catholic and Protestant denominations had operated as many as 60 of the government Indian schools.

From the turn of the century through the 1920s, the government's poorly funded and woefully inadequate Indian education system was focused solely on assimilation. This involved federal schools as well as state schools paid by the government. A new attitude toward cultural pluralism, and increased awareness of the bleak conditions at most Indian schools, led to passage of the Johnson-O'Malley Act in 1934. The act, as amended in 1936, permitted the government to contract with states, territories, corporations, private institutions, agencies, and political subdivisions to provide education and other services (Cohen 1982). Despite this act, thirty years later Indian education remained far below national standards. In Alaska, the U.S. Office of Education controlled the education of Alaska Natives from 1887 until the BIA took over in 1931 (Szasz and Ryan 1988).

In 1969, the Special Senate Subcommittee on Indian Education published a report titled *Indian Education: A National Trugedy—A National Challenge.* The upshot of this report, numerous other studies, and contemporary tribal input was that there was a need for cultural relevance and that Indians must be given greater control over the education of their children. Congress soon passed the Indian Education Act of 1972, which has been amended during each of the decades since its passage. This legislation established funding for special bilingual and bicultural programs, culturally relevant teaching materials, proper training and hiring of counselors, and establishment of an Office of Indian Education in the U.S. Department of Education. Most importantly, the act required participation of American Indians in the planning of all relevant educational projects (Cohen 1982; O'Brien 1989).

In 1975, the Indian Self-Determination and Education Assistance Act provided for and encouraged the contracting out of BIA education functions to Indian tribes themselves. The long-term goal of the act is the assumption of managerial and policy-making responsibilities by the tribes for their own affairs. More than 50 tribes have taken over the operation of their own schools under contract with the BIA, affecting about 75 institutions and 30 percent of the total enrollment in BIA-funded schools. The great majority of other Indian students attend BIA-run or regular public schools (Bureau of Indian Affairs 1988, 1991a, and 1991b; O'Brien 1989).

Indian education has improved remarkably in the past three decades. This has come about through periodic increases in funding, updating of legislation, greater cultural relevance, and expanding tribal involvement. Much remains to be accomplished, however. Ongoing problems include deterioration of BIA facilities, poor program management in some areas, higher than average dropout rates, and substandard student achievement in various locales. Despite these problems, there are bright spots which bode well for the future betterment of the tribes and their members. Increased Native emphasis on, involvement in, improvement of, and control over education will continue to be major contributors to the improving situation. Education's influence goes far beyond the classroom and the tribes recognize this increasingly.

K-2. *What are the best sources for information on Indian education?*

> *We are challenged to make sure our grandchildren's grandchildren know who they are as Indian people. If we don't do that now, we will simply be another racial minority in this country. And I pray I will never live to see that day.*
>
> *Indian children should be pledging allegiance to their own tribes when placing their hands over their hearts at school each morning. . . .*
>
> *We have to make our children good citizens of the governments that control their destinies, and that should be the Indian tribes.*
>
> Claudine Bates Arthur, former Attorney
> General of the Navajo Nation
> (*In* Norell 1999, p. A-3)

This question is difficult to answer because there are many excellent sources on the subject, but the best internet sources on Indian education can be easily identified.

One can begin with the website for the BIA: www.doi.gov/ bureau-indian-affairs. Although not always functional, the BIA's education sub-site contains information on BIA education programs, budgets, statistics, reports, and so on.

The best website on Indian education may be the one posted by the National Indian Education Association (NIEA): www.niea.org. The NIEA is more than 30 years old, and its membership is intensely interested and actively involved in Indian education issues from the national to the local level.

The U.S. Department of Education (USDOE) has an Office of Indian Education (OIE) that is involved in Indian education at all levels. There is a website for the USDOE, at www.ed.gov, where some

Indian education information can be obtained. The phone number for the OIE office in Washington, D.C., is (202) 260-3774.

The National Advisory Council on Indian Education in Washington, D.C., can be reached by phone at (202) 205-8353.

Because there are literally thousands of books, articles, dissertations, and theses that have some relevance to Indian education, it is a great challenge to list the most useful printed material on Indian education. But a classic overview of the subject is Szasz (1999), *Education and the American Indian: The Road to Self-Determination Since 1928*. Now in its third edition, this book provides an excellent starting place for interested readers and covers Indian education policy and programs from 1870 to the 1990s.

Another recently published book by Swisher and Tippeconnic (1999), *Next Steps: Research and Practice to Advance Indian Education*, is a compilation of essays by a dozen Indian scholars responding to the two cogent questions: "What is Indian education today?" and "How will it look in the future?" And there are two works by Mihesuah (1992, 1998) about academic research and writing on Indian issues.

Some additional useful sources are: Deloria (1991a), *Indian Education in America*; Deloria (1999), *Spirit and Reason*, part III; Noriega (1992), *American Indian Education in the United States: Indoctrination for Subordination into Colonialism*; Prucha (1979), *The Churches and the Indian Schools, 1888–1912*; Reyhner (1992), *Teaching American Indian Students*; Reyhner and Eder (1989), *A History of Indian Education*; Stago's (1998) dissertation on Navajo student dropout issues; and the *Journal of Indian Education*.

Harvey and Harjo's (1994) book, *Indian Country: A History of Native People in America*, is a well-structured and usable text for elementary and middle school students. Its tone, information, and lesson plans have been praised by such Indian country notables as U.S. Senator Ben Nighthorse Campbell and author Joseph Bruchac.

K-3. *What are the basic data on federal Indian education facilities and programs?*

Bureau of Indian Affairs

At the end of the 1990s, the BIA was funding 185 education facilities. These included 50 day schools, 40 on-reservation boarding schools, five off-reservation boarding schools, and eight Bureau-operated dormitories which enable Indian students to attend public schools. In addition, under the provisions of the Indian Self-Determination Act of 1975, the BIA has contracted with various tribes to operate more than 60 day schools, 11 on-reservation boarding schools, one off-reservation boarding school, and six dormitories. Enrollment in all of the schools and dormitories exceeds 50,000 or roughly 10 percent of the total Indian student population. The rest of the student population attends regular public, private, or parochial schools.

The BIA also provides support funding to many public school districts around the country, under the Johnson-O'Malley Act of 1934. Such financial support is designed to aid in the educational needs of more than 260,000 eligible Indian students who attend public school. Under its handicapped children program, the Bureau also provides financial support for the educational costs of approximately 300 children in at least 28 different institutions.

Two post secondary schools are operated by the BIA. Haskell Indian Nations University, in Lawrence, Kansas, has an enrollment of about 1,000 students; and Southwestern Indian Polytechnic Institute, in Albuquerque, New Mexico, has more than 400 students (see the Haskell website at www.haskell.edu).

Approximately 15,000 Indian students receive scholarships under BIA programs to attend colleges and universities each year. About 500 of these students are in law school and other graduate programs. Altogether, it is estimated that 70,000 Indian students are attending college. Those who do not obtain BIA assistance are eligible to apply for other assistance programs, just as similarly situated non-Indian students can. The BIA also provides funding for the operation of 22 tribally controlled community colleges which have a combined enrollment of more than 7,000 students. Diné College, on the Navajo Reservation in Arizona, and Sinte Gleska (Spotted Tail) University, on the Rosebud Reservation in South Dakota, are two of the better-known of these institutions.

U.S. Department of Education

The Office of Indian Education (OIE), in the U.S. Department of Education, oversees programs and funding to provide educational opportunities for Indian children and adults, and to address culturally related academic needs of Indian children. Grants to local education agencies supplement services to over 400,000 American Indian and Alaska Native students and also assist in the establishment or operation of Indian controlled schools on or near reservations. "Special programs" grants are also available for (1) planning, pilot, and demonstration programs, (2) educational services, (3) personnel development, (4) student fellowships, (5) gifted and talented programs, and (6) Indian education technical assistance centers. There is also an OIE educational services program which provides grants for adult education (Office of Indian Education 1991; 2000).

Indian Health Service

Pursuant to the Indian Health Care Improvement Act of 1976, as amended, and relevant regulations (U.S. Public Health Service 1998), the IHS makes scholarships and grants available to recruit and educate eligible Indians in various health care professions. The purpose of the overall program is to encourage Indians and Alaska Natives to enter the health professions and insure the availability of Native health professionals to serve Native people.

K-4. *Is it true that federal efforts at Indian education did much to destroy Indian families?*

> *The purpose of the first boarding school on the Navajo Reservation as stated in its charter in the 1890s was "to remove the Navajo child from the influence of his savage parents."*
>
> Robert Bergman (1977, p. 34)

> *Tribal relations should be broken up, socialism destroyed, . . . and the*
> *autonomy of the individual substituted. . . . At San Carlos are the*
> *Apaches. . . . These people decline to send their children to school;*
> *but I have within the last twelve months taken from that reservation*
> *about two hundred* [children].
>
> Thomas Morgan, Commissioner of
> Indian Affairs, 1889
>
> *We all wore white man's clothes and ate white man's food and went*
> *to white man's churches and spoke white man's talk. And so after a*
> *while we also began to say Indians were bad. We laughed at our own*
> *people and their blankets and cooking pots and sacred societies and*
> *dances.*
>
> Sun Elk, Taos Pueblo, in a statement about his
> boarding school experience
> (*In* Josephy 1994, p. 434)
>
> *The real tragedy . . . is . . . the disruption of family life and its effect*
> *on the character of both parents and children.*
>
> Lewis Meriam, in his renowned 1928 report on
> "The Problem of Indian Administration"
> (*In* Unger 1977, p. 14)

Yes. The general pattern for the destruction of Indian culture began, of course, with European arrival in the Western hemisphere. In the U.S., the destruction was piecemeal at first, but started in earnest in the 1870s with establishment of the first off-reservation boarding school at Carlisle, Pennsylvania (Adams 1995). As recently as the late 1970s the Association on American Indian Affairs published the book *The Destruction of American Indian Families* (Unger 1977), which addressed several different causes for this destruction, including the educational and family separation policies of the federal and state governments. The book is significant because it was one of the important documents considered by Congress when it passed the Indian Child Welfare Act in 1978. This act was to help reverse the destruction of Indian families in the areas of child placement and adoption. The destruction and separation that occur today usually are caused by the general influence of the larger society, rather than by direct policies.

Today's Indian education is still overwhelmingly dominated by the non-Indian world, despite all the politically correct terms and programs being used and espoused. American Indian homelife is similarly dominated—except in the few homes that do not have television and that are far away from the every-day influences of American cities and towns. Yet even in these more remote locations the children attend schools that necessarily are geared, like every other school in the country, toward "mainstreaming" their students. As Vine Deloria suggests (Simonelli 1999) these children are taught by teachers who are also, for the most part, products of the mainstreaming process.

There *are* schools that try to reverse the loss of Native culture, including the famous Rough Rock Community School on the Navajo Nation. But the fact remains that after more than 30 years of operation, Rough Rock continues to be famous not only for its innovation, but because it is still one of the few schools of its kind in the country. Rough Rock Community School can be reached by phone at (520) 728-3503, or through their website (April 2000) at: www.roughrock.bia.edu.

On the destruction of American Indian families, Unger (1977) contains a descriptive essay about "Kid Catching" on the Navajo Reservation that was originally written in the 1930s by Dane Coolige. Mr. Coolige began with a statement describing how the children in more remote parts of the Navajo Reservation, and those whose parents resisted letting them be taken far away to school, were forcibly removed from their families.

> I am making a brief statement of my experience with what I consider the greatest shame of the Indian Service [BIA]—the rounding up of Indian children to be sent away to government schools. . . . Stockmen, Indian police, and other mounted men are sent ahead [of the trucks] to round them up. The children are caught, often roped like cattle, and taken away from their parents, many times never to return.

It is one thing to read about such things, but it is another to hear of them from the families that were affected. One of my Navajo friends has told me how his mother, who I'll call Desbah (a woman's traditional war name), ended up going to the Albuquerque Indian school in the early 1920s.

Desbah was herding sheep one fall day out away from the family hogan, which was located in the northwest region of New Mexico. She was about eight years old and her smaller sister, who was about six, was with her. Not long before sunset, when they had decided to herd the sheep back north in the direction of the corral near their hogan, they saw a strange man man riding down on them, at a gallup, along the wagon trail from the west. He was about a mile away. Desbah, who was standing, knew what he was up to. She hid her little sister, who was sitting on the ground, in the brush and told her to tell their parents what happened after it was over. Then Desbah ran to the southeast as fast as she could.

It didn't take the white BIA man long to catch up with her, but she kept running—darting in and out of stands of juniper trees. He yelled "stop" at her in Navajo. It seemed to be the only Navajo word he knew, because that was all he said, over and over.

When the man's horse bogged down briefly in some sand, Desbah ran out from the trees and across a clearing. She was hoping to run up the side of a small hill nearby and get away from the man on horseback by climbing through a jumble of rocks. But he chased her down on his horse and roped her. He then tied her hands and put her in front of him in the saddle.

They headed back in the direction he had come from. Desbah didn't scream or struggle because she didn't want to do anything that might cause her little sister to reveal herself.

The man now said many words in English, but the only one she understood was "truck." Desbah and the man continued to ride west and, on the way, they passed within about 100 yards of her little sister, who was still hiding. By this time the sun was already below the horizon. As it was getting dark, a livestock truck came down the wagon trail in their direction, and they met it about three miles from where she had been captured.

When they stopped at the truck, Desbah could hear children's voices and crying coming from inside the back of the truck. While the truck driver opened up the back of the truck, the BIA man untied her hands and then put her in the back with the other children. There were eight of them. The youngest was a boy who seemed to be five or six years old. The oldest was a girl, who looked 12 or 13. Desbah recognized most of the children, but she only knew the names of two.

The truck started moving. It turned south and drove into the dark night. They rode in the back of the truck all night, but the driver stopped once to sleep for awhile. The children spent the time in the truck crying softly, talking, and missing their families. They were let out once, to relieve themselves and to get a drink of water. They could not tell where they were going, and the driver didn't say.

After the sun came up they crossed over a big river. They would soon learn that the river was the Rio Grande and they were in Albuquerque, New Mexico. The driver delivered the children to the Albuquerque Indian school, where they were promptly showered and then covered with delousing powder. They were then warned not to speak Navajo and were herded off to different dormitories, where they were finally allowed to sleep.

> *Did I want to be an Indian? After looking at the pictures of the Indians on the warpath . . . Oh! Such ugly faces. No! Indians are mean people—I'm glad I'm not an Indian, I thought. And so the days passed by and the changes slowly came to settle with me. . . . Gone were the vivid pictures of my parents, sisters and brothers. Only a blurred vision of what used to be. Desperately, I tried to cling to the faded past which was slowly being erased from my mind.*
>
> Mertha Bercier, Chippewa, a boarding school student
> (*In* Josephy 1994, p. 434)

Desbah did not go home for 10 years. Though her family visited a few times, they were not allowed to take her home. In the summer when school was out, like many of the other children, she was made to participate in a "placement" program. Boarding school officials "placed" her with a white minister and his family in a small town some distance outside Albuquerque. When she was younger, the man touched her inappropriately. When she was 15, he raped her. She never went back to that home but was placed in others, during the summers, until she graduated. Then she moved back home.

Her mother had died, and her father had a new wife. Her sisters and brothers did not really know her, including the little sister she had protected. The sister had avoided being captured when her parents moved her further out into the backcountry to live with her grandparents.

Desbah, who later married a good Navajo man and had a large family, never really got over the pain, betrayal, and trauma that her boarding school experience brought to her life. She outlived her husband, who had also been forced to go to boarding school and had lived through his own tough experiences. Desbah died in the 1980s.

> *I remember one evening when we were all lined up in a room and one of the boys said something in Indian to another boy. The man in charge . . . caught him by the shirt, and threw him across the room. Later we found out that his collar-bone was broken.*
>
> Lone Wolf, a Blackfoot and
> former boarding school student
> (*In* Josephy 1999, p. 435)

K-5. *How do tribes integrate traditional Indian philosophy with Western educational systems?*

Particular methods vary with different tribes, reservations, institutions, and settings. A good example of one of the better-developed approaches comes from Diné College in Arizona, as described below by McNeley (1990, p. 1–12).

The traditional *Diné* (Navajo) philosophy of learning is embedded in oral traditions accounting for the creation and evolution of the Navajo world. This philosophy is based upon a view of man in nature—of the Navajo people deriving the powers of life, thought, speech and motion from the forces underlying the workings of the natural world. Knowledge is identified with the cardinal directions. The values and other principles by which people live are identified with dawn and the east; knowledge for making a living, with daylight and the south; planning for social well-being is identified with evening twilight and the west; contentment and reverence for all life, with darkness and the north. Knowledge from all of these sources is essential for a balanced life. The goal of life is to live in harmony with others in society and in nature—a condition called *hozho*—resulting from balancing the four categories of knowledge.

Herbert John Benally's paper describing this "*Diné* philosophy of learning" (1987) challenges educators with the revolutionary proposal that, instead of attempting to fit Navajo knowledge into a Western conceptual organization—an approach which has heretofore characterized Navajo bicultural education—Western knowledge must be fit into the traditional Navajo organization of knowledge referred to above. It will no longer suffice, in this view, to merge bits of the Navajo world view into existing courses of the standard curriculum, fragmented as the latter usually is along lines defined by the academic disciplines which have evolved in the Western world. Rather, the subject matter of Western education must now be accommodated to the traditional Navajo view that all knowledge must be integrated so as to promote the development of harmonious relationships of the individual with his social and natural environment.

. . . The object of learning as well as of life generally is "a state of being and a society called *hozho*, a state of much good in terms of peace, happiness and plenty" (Benally 1987). The philosophy also provides a set of guiding principles for a program of general education for attaining this shared goal of the Navajo community. The categories of knowledge identified with the cardinal directions are the basis for this program of general education. An adequate general education, in this view:

> . . . *requires balancing all four categories of Navajo knowledge so that the individual will have sound beliefs and values to make the best possible decisions, will possess skill to provide the best living for the family and provide good leadership to the family and community, and will have a reverence for the earth and for all living things. (Benally 1987).*

The *Diné* philosophy of education, in addition to establishing a clear purpose and guiding principles for general education, also provides an epistemology which eminently facilitates "seeing the connectedness of things," by conceptually placing the individual "at the focus where the four great branches of Navajo knowledge meet to produce the desired condition, *hozho.*" (Benally 1987). It expresses the concept that all of these aspects of knowledge are relevant to all courses and programs of study: "Each course and program at NCC will reflect the thematic areas of the *Diné* philosophy of learning . . ." (Navajo Community College Presidential Task Force). For example, the course Principles of Economics, if taught in accordance with this philosophy, would place economics in the context of broader life values, would show its relevance to making a livelihood, would relate it to social well-being, and would consider issues of economic impacts on the natural environment. The student educated in accordance with the traditional philosophy would emerge from such a course with enhanced knowledge and understanding of the economic system and of its relevance to the overall goal of *hozho.*

. . . Certainly, there are universally important aspects of higher education that must not be omitted even from unique programs, including the mastery of communication and numerical skills as well as scientific and technological literacy. Similarly, there are "ways of knowing" which should be encouraged across the curriculum including the processes of inquiry, historical consciousness, the experience of diverse cultures, the exploration of values, and the processes involved in studying a subject in depth.

. . . [Nonetheless,] at the local level, pedagogical approaches . . . need to be better adapted to Navajo styles of learning. Becktell (1986) argues that even more important than incorporating Navajo content in the curriculum is the need for educators "to understand the Navajo style of learning and develop teaching strategies that address that style." Reservation instructors typically base their teaching methods on the Anglo style of learning in which the learner is expected to act before competency is achieved. One is to "learn by doing." This approach, however, causes major problems for the Navajo student who generally learns by observation and by internal thought until he or she feels competent to act overtly:

> *The Navajo seem uncomfortable when they are expected or asked to perform before they feel mentally prepared for the performance. . . . This . . . causes stress in the Navajo learner and sets in motion the endless cycle of premature performance, sense of failure, no confidence, poor performance. (Becktell 1986).*

Becktell recommends that teachers of Navajo students adopt teaching strategies that are better attuned to Navajo learning styles including greater use of example and metaphor, increased opportunity for learning by observation, and greater opportunities for self-discovery and self-correction. She cites the need for a "handbook of teaching strategies" for Navajo teachers.

. . . [T]raditional Navajo thought provides the philosophical basis for a potentially effective way of addressing many concerns expressed nationally about American . . . education. It provides a culturally-focussed purpose for Navajo education which relates well to concern for student character and moral development as well as establishing principles for a program of general education which, if implemented, will provide for integration of the curriculum. The traditional Navajo philosophy of education . . . provides us with a useful tool for addressing urgent educational concerns.

K-6. *What was the goal of President Clinton's Executive Order on Indian education?*

Executive Order (E.O.) 13096, *American Indian and Alaska Native Education,* was issued on August 6, 1998. It was a major policy declaration on Indian education with six stated goals:

(1) improving reading and mathematics; (2) increasing high school completion and post-secondary attendance rates; (3) reducing the influence of longstanding factors that impede educational performance, such as poverty and substance abuse; (4) creating strong, safe, and drug-free school environments; (5) improving science education; and (6) expanding the use of educational technology.

Clinton's E.O. also had a strategy statement, the substance of which was a directive for an interagency task force to (1) develop a plan to carry out the president's order, (2) improve interagency participation in implementing the government's Indian education programs, (3) develop a federal research agenda to help improve Indian education, and (4) draft and publish a *Comprehensive Federal Indian Education Policy* within two years of the date of the order.

The President mandated his task force to "consider the ideas in the Comprehensive Federal Indian Education Policy Statement proposal developed by the NIEA [National Indian Education Association] and the NCAI [National Congress of American Indians]."

This "policy statement" is an exceptional pronouncement because of its importance, its representation of an "Indian view," its direct acknowledgment by the president, and the NIEA's desire that it be widely distributed to promote public support for the outlined ideals (now and in the future). (The proposed policy statement can be found on the NIEA website at www.niea.org/policystm.htm.)

In our current educational system we are producing people who are professionals in a certain subject, but they are not developing themselves as people. . . .

Highly educated Indians can't talk about Indian problems because they often don't know anything about reservations. They fall back on jargon like "decolonization," "indigenization," and so on. But if you ask them to go before an Indian audience and talk for half an hour on a major topic, they are totally lost. That's a result of their education. They have pushed their way through school to the Ph. D., but they are out of touch with grass roots Indians or Indian issues. . . .

An awful lot of people in higher education are genetically Indians but don't really have an emotional connection to tribes. . . .

To solve the problem of being colonized you've got to stop thinking like the colonizers. You've got to think like Indians. If you're going to be an Indian you've got to think like an Indian. And you've got to live a simple humble life with people. To be straightforward. If you go around trying to impress people with the use of technical jargon, which may be useful at the big universities, you'll never reach people on the reservations or in the tribal council. They are going to look at you like you're crazy. . . .

Schools of education are the worst things that ever happened to American education. Teacher training for Indians suffers from the same difficulty as that for non-Indians. . . . It would be far better for Indians entering post secondary education with an eye on teaching to think about majoring in a certain substantial field and then picking up teacher's credentials at the end. . . .

A new teacher ought to intern with these community folks, even if its an old grandmother who comes to school three hours in the morning and then goes home and makes soup for her grandchildren. She knows about talking to an audience. And that's what teaching really is—talking to an audience. Otherwise, all these gimmicks and techniques are not going to help. . . .

I'd like to see Indians in the future get so involved with what the tribe really means, with what the community means, and with what elders mean, that they will be able to get up and articulate things very clearly. . . .

But if you are going to be a minority you've got to have some edge against the majority to act as your foundation. Indian oratorical style and its ability to capture history, religion and culture all in one set of words, holds a lot of power in areas Indians don't realize. . . .

The best example of that kind of orator is Oren Lyons. He can get up and speak in very simple sentences which cover the whole subject, convincing the opponents that they have got to do the right thing. If Indians could re-develop that style by observing people like Oren, and how they do these things, you wouldn't be afraid at all for the Indian future.

Vine Deloria Jr.
(quoted in Simonelli 1999)

SECTION L: OTHER AGENCIES AND NATIONAL INDIAN ORGANIZATIONS

L-1. *What other government agencies, besides the BIA and IHS, have missions or programs relating to American Indians?*

Within the U.S. government, scores of agencies have what are called "Indian desks." These are not full-fledge agencies; rather they are usually small administrative units consisting of one or several employees who deal with Indian issues and programs that are peripheral to the overall mission of the larger agency. Walke (1991) presents an excellent source list of agencies with Indian desks. There are, however, additional non-BIA and non-IHS agencies with missions that are specifically related to Native issues. Several of the more notable agencies are describe briefly below, in alphabetical order.

Administration for Native Americans

The Administration for Native Americans (ANA) is a little-known but very active agency. It is located within the Administration for Children and Families, in the U.S. Department of Health and Human Services. The mission of the ANA is to promote social and economic self-sufficiency for American Indians, Alaska Natives, Native Hawaiians, and Native American Pacific Islanders (American Samoa Natives, indigenous peoples of Guam, and Natives of the Commonwealth of the Northern Marianas Islands and the Republic of Palau). The agency's activities include provision of financial assistance grants, technical assistance and training, research, demonstrations, and pilot projects (Administration for Native Americans 1991b). The agency can be contacted by phone at (202) 690-7776; the website (March 3, 2000) is: www.acf.dhhs.gov/programs/ana/index.

Indian Arts and Crafts Board

Congress established the Indian Arts and Crafts Board (IACB) in 1935 as an independent agency located within the U.S. Department of the Interior. The Board serves the Indian, Eskimo, and Aleut communities, and the general public, as an informational, promotional, and advisory clearinghouse for all matters pertaining to the development of authentic Native arts and crafts of the U.S.

The IACB administers the Southern Plains Indian Museum in Anadarko, Oklahoma, the Sioux Indian Museum in Rapid City, South Dakota, and the Museum of the Plains Indian in Browning, Montana.

Misrepresentation or imitation of American Indian arts and crafts is a major concern of the Board. Besides providing consumer information about how to avoid these problems, the Board has a responsibility to refer reported cases to proper federal and state law enforcement agencies (Andrews 1991; Vanwey 2000).

The IACB can be contacted by phone at (202) 208-3773; the website (March 3, 2000) is: www.iacb.doi.gov.

National Indian Gaming Commission

The National Indian Gaming Commission (NIGC) is a federal regulatory agency, within the Department of the Interior, established by Congress through the Indian Gaming Regulatory Act (IGRA) of 1988 (see also Section N, on gaming). Among the Commission's various and complicated powers and responsibilities are the promulgation and implementation of federal regulations for the Indian gaming industry, consistent with the mandates of the IGRA. For further information on the complex and controversial nature of this agency and its mission, one can refer to the IGRA and the federal regulations the Commission is charged with implementing, which are available from the NIGC.

The NIGC can be contacted by phone at (202) 632-7003; the website (March 3, 2000) is: www.nigc.gov.

National Museum of the American Indian

One of the national museums that is part of the Smithsonian Institution, the National Museum of the American Indian (NMAI), was established by an act of Congress in 1989. It is

> dedicated to the preservation, study, and exhibition of the life, languages, literature, history, and arts of Native Americans. . . . The museum works in collaboration with the Native peoples of the Western Hemisphere to protect and foster their cultures by reaffirming traditions and beliefs, encouraging contemporary artistic expression, and empowering the Indian voice. (National Museum of the American Indian 2000)

The Smithsonian has acquired the enormous George Gustav Heye collection of Indian artifacts in New York, and it is still in the process of cataloging the many thousands of items in the collection and adding them to the already large national collection. The vast majority of the Heye items will eventually be housed in the NMAI's Cultural Resources Center, established in Suitland, Maryland, but this will not be fully accomplished until approximately 2005. The George Gustav Heye Center, located in the Manhattan borough of New York City, was opened in 1994 and will remain a permanent part of the NMAI. The Heye Center will serve as an education and exhibition facility and will be used as a venue for a wide range of public programs.

The National Museum of the American Indian building is being constructed on the Mall in Washington, D.C., and is scheduled for completion in 2002.

For more information, contact the executive offices of the NMAI in Washington, D.C., by phone at (202) 357-3164; or the exhibition and programs offices of the Heye Center in New York at (212) 668-6624. For ongoing communications about the NMAI's activities, one can subscribe to their journal, *American Indian,* by calling 1-800-242-6624. The website (April 1, 2000) for the National Museum of the American Indian is: www.si.edu/nmai.

Office of Indian Education

The Office of Indian Education (OIE), in the U.S. Department of Education, was created under the Indian Education Act of 1972. The OIE oversees funding distribution for special programs designed to provide educational opportunities for Indian children and adults and to address culturally related academic needs of Indian children. (See Section K of this book, on Education.)

The OIE can be contacted by phone at (202) 260-3774; their website can be located through the Department of Education's website at www.ed.gov.

Congressional Committees

The U.S. Senate and House committees which deal directly with Indian affairs and policy development are exceptionally important and powerful government entities, although they are not "agencies" as such. The committees may be contacted as follows:

Senate Select Committee on Indian Affairs
Room SH 838
Hart Senate Office Building
Washington, DC 20510
Phone (202) 224-2251

Committee on Natural Resources
1522 Longworth House Office Building
Washington, DC 20515
Phone (202) 225-2761

State Indian Commissions

At least 40 states have some form of commission, agency, or office of Indian Affairs (Giago 1991d). Missions and activities vary, but those of the Arizona commission of Indian Affairs (1991; 1999) are typical.

> MISSION AND PURPOSE. [T]he mission of the Arizona Commission on Indian Affairs is "to cooperate with and support State and Federal Agencies in Assisting Indian Tribes in developing mutual goals, in designing projects for these goals and in implementing their plans." In this liaison capacity the Commission on Indian Affairs gathers data and facilitates the exchange of information needed by Tribal, State, and Federal Agencies; assists the state in its responsibilities to Indians and Tribes of this State by making recommendations to the governor and the Legislature; confers and coordinates Indian needs and goals with various Government Officials; works for greater understanding and improved relationships between Indians and Non-Indians by creating an awareness of the legal, social and economic needs of Indians in this State; promotes increased participation by Indians in local and State affairs; and assists Tribal groups in developing increasingly effective methods of self-government.

In 1999, the mission statement of the Arizona Commission was refined to "Build partnerships to enhance tribal-state relations and economic prosperity for the 21 Indian Tribes/Nations in Arizona."

See Appendix 6 for a listing of the Indian commissions in the various states.

L-2. *What are some of the major Indian organizations?*

More than 200 national associations, societies, and organizations of all kinds are active in Indian affairs. Perhaps the best general source for basic information about these organizations is the internet. However, an excellent printed source is Klein's 1997 *Reference Encyclopedia of the American Indian*. Another good source is *The American Indian and the Media* (Giago 1991d). Listed and described below are some of the more notable and active of the major Indian organizations.

American Indian Movement

The story of the American Indian Movement is one that deals with an evolution of events. In July 1968, Clyde Bellecourt, Eddie Benton Bonai, George Mitchell, and Dennis Banks founded an organization known as "Concerned Indian Americans" in Minneapolis. Because of the acronym CIA, the name was quickly changed to American Indian Movement (AIM). Russell Means later became a prominent member of the organization (American Indian Movement 1991, 2000).

The original purpose of AIM was to assist Indians in urban ghettos who had been displaced by the government's programs of termination and relocation. These programs had effectively forced thousands of Indians from their reservations to unfamiliar and hostile urban environments.

One of the earliest and most successful of AIM's projects was the establishment, in 1972, of a "survival school" in Minneapolis. The concept of a survival school, which spread to other regions of the country, was an attempt to help Indian youths adjust to non-Indian society without losing what was most valuable from their own culture.

AIM's goals have developed over time and now encompass the entire spectrum of Native concerns. They include such topics as economic independence, religious freedom, treaty rights, sovereignty, self-determination, cultural revitalization, environmental protection, land and resource management, education, racism, and fair administration of justice.

AIM and its members have been involved in numerous and highly publicized protests and related activities since its founding. It was one of the groups involved in the occupation of Alcatraz Island (1969–1971), the occupation of Mount Rushmore (1970 and 1971), the march on Washington and occupation of the BIA office (1972), the occupation of Wounded Knee (1973), and the controversial firefight between AIM members and federal officers that resulted in the deaths of two FBI agents and one Indian man (1975).

By the late-1970s, with many of its leaders in exile or prison, considerable pressure from law enforcement agencies, and dissention among members, the national leadership disbanded. Attempts were being made in 1992 to reform a national AIM council, while state and regional AIM organizations have, since the start, maintained active roles in a wide range of Native issues. Still troubled by internal strife, the national organization nonetheless remains active in Indian affairs issues throughout North, Central, and South America.

For additional information, the AIM can be contacted by phone in Minneapolis, Minnesota, at (612) 721-3914; the website (March 30, 2000) is: www.aimovement.org.

Association on American Indian Affairs

The Association on American Indian Affairs (AAIA), founded in 1922, is a nonprofit corporation with 15,000 Indian and non-Indian members and more than 40,000 contributors (Association on American Indian Affairs 1991 and 1992). The Association is organized as an advocacy group for American Indians and Alaska Natives. It prides itself on working closely with American Indian people to deal with issues that they identify as being of greatest urgency. These often include issues for which there is no other aid available.

The AAIA works to perpetuate the well-being of Native people through efforts that (1) help sustain cultures and languages, (2) protect sovereign, constitutional, legal, religious, and human rights, (3) protect natural resources, and (4) improve health, education, and economic and community development. Association staff members respond to observed problems and requests for assistance through a variety of means, including:

Direct advocacy	Public education	Policy development
Grants	Legislation drafting	Technical support
Legal assistance	Research	Congressional testimony
amicus curiae briefs	Advice to agencies	Scholarship programs

For additional information, contact the AAIA headquarters in South Dakota by phone at (605) 698-3998, or 3787; the website (March 30, 2000) is: www.indian-affairs.org.

Columbia River Inter-Tribal Fish Commission

The Columbia River Inter-Tribal Fish Commission (CRITFC) was established in 1977 to provide technical support and serve as the coordinating agency for fishery management policies of the four mid- and upper-basin tribes that have treaty fishing rights: the Confederated Tribes of the Warm Springs Reservation of Oregon, the Confederated Tribes and Bands of the Yakama Indian Nation, the Confederated Tribes of the Umatilla Indian Reservation, and the Nez Perce Tribe. The commission's mission is:

> to ensure a unified voice in the overall management of the fishery resources and, as a manager, to protect reserved treaty rights through the exercise of the inherent sovereign powers of the tribes.

The CRITFC staff consists of scientists, administrators, policy analysts, and public information specialists who assist the tribes, and work with other governments, on such issues as research, advocacy, planning, interagency cooperation, harvest control, and law enforcement.

The commission, which is headquartered in Portland, Oregon, is respected for its efforts and approach and has been used as a model for several other intertribal resource organizations around the country.

For additional information, contact the CRITFC by phone at (503) 238-0667; the website (March 3, 2000) is www.critfc.org.

International Indian Treaty Council

The International Indian Treaty Council (IITC) was established in 1974 as an advocacy and educational organization concerned with issues affecting indigenous people from all areas of the world (Scheurkogel 1992). Besides having a mission of countering the negative effects of 500 years of Euro-American influence, the Council is involved in a variety of specific issues important to Native people, including the environment, religious freedom, protection of sacred sites, and other socio-political issues. IITC is a non-governmental organization, in consultative status (category II), with the United Nations Economic and Social Council. Representatives annually present testimony and documentation on Native issues before the U.N. Commission on Human Rights (International Indian Treaty Council 1992; 2000). In the San Francisco Bay area, the Council is also active in hosting noted speakers, sponsoring a regular radio broadcast on news in Indian country, distributing timely information on Native issues to the media, and holding fund-raising events (Stanley 1992).

For additional information, contact the council in San Francisco by phone at (415) 512-1501. Or, contact the Council's "Speaker's Bureau" through the telephone number they share with AIM in Minnesota at (612) 721-3914. The council also shares AIM's website at: www.aimovement.org.

Leonard Peltier Defense Committee

The Leonard Peltier Defense Committee (LPDC) is a national and international support group organized for the purpose of gaining the release of Leonard Peltier, a Dakota-Ojibwa, from federal prison. Mr. Peltier is serving two consecutive life sentences in Leavenworth Federal Penitentiary for the deaths of two FBI agents in 1975 (Leonard Peltier Defense Committee 1991; 2000).

On June 26, 1975, two FBI agents drove onto private Indian land on the Pine Ridge Reservation in South Dakota, where Peltier and other AIM members were staying at the invitation of the owners. Confusion remains as to why the agents were there and what happened to precipitate the shootout. The LPDC asserts the incident was the culmination of an FBI conspiracy against AIM and its members. The agents' abrupt appearance and behavior, LPDC suggests, directly caused the shootout, and Peltier and others were acting in self-defense. The FBI, however, claims the agents were ambushed by distant gunfire from AIM members and were subsequently executed at close range. Initially, four Indian men were charged equally with aiding and abetting in the deaths of the agents. Two were acquitted and the government dropped the charges on the third. Concentrating its efforts on Peltier, the government obtained a conviction in April 1977 in U.S. District Court in North Dakota (Matthiessen 1991).

U.S. Circuit Court Judge Gerald W. Heaney (1991), who served as a member of the appellate court in two of the Peltier appeals (in 1984 and 1986), has concluded that "the United States government must share the responsibility with the Native Americans for the June 26 [1975] firefight. . . . The government's role in escalating the conflict into a firefight . . . can properly be considered as a mitigating circumstance. . . . The FBI used improper tactics in securing Peltier's extradition from Canada and in otherwise investigating and trying the Peltier case."

Although his name has not been that widely known in the United States, Leonard Peltier is known to millions of Europeans as a "political prisoner" who was targeted by the FBI, in its efforts in the 1970s, to disintegrate AIM and other activist groups of the era (Savilla 1991; Leonard Peltier Defense Committee 2000). Currently, LPDC is campaigning to obtain Peltier's freedom through Executive Clemency by the President. This campaign has many who oppose it, including some members of the Indian community, but also has had the support of Judge Heaney, several important members of Congress, and numerous U.S. and foreign citizens who believe Leonard Peltier was the victim of an abuse of the justice system. Peltier's latest parole application was denied on June 12, 2000. Ramsey Clark, one of Peltier's attorneys and a former U.S. Attorney General, responded by saying, "There is a simple and sad lesson in what happened today . . . the United States is still at war with the American Indian." (Pierpoint 2000, p. A-1).

The motion picture, *Incident at Oglala,* is a docu-drama on Leonard Peltier's story and the broader issues surrounding it.

For additional information, contact the Leonard Peltier Defense Committee in Lawrence, Kansas, by phone at (785) 842-5774; the website (April 1, 2000) is: www.freepeltier.org.

National Congress of American Indians

The National Congress of American Indians (NCAI) was founded in 1944. The dual purposes of this nonprofit organization are to (1) provide unity and cooperation among American Indian governments for the protection of individual and tribal rights and (2) promote the common welfare of American Indians. NCAI began with fewer than 100 members, from a small number of tribes. It now has 136 member tribes with a constituency of approximately 600,000 Native people. Organized as a confederation of member tribal governments, NCAI is now the largest, second oldest (the Association on American Indian Affairs is the oldest), and perhaps most representative national American Indian and Alaska Native organization in the country (National Congress of American Indians 1991, 1992, 2000).

The five operating principles of the NCAI are:

1. Protect Indian and Native traditional cultural and religious rights.
2. Seek appropriate, equitable, and beneficial services and programs for Indian and Native governments and people.

3. Secure and preserve Indian and Native rights under treaties and agreements with the United States, as well as under federal statutes, case law, and administrative decisions and rulings.
4. Promote the common welfare and enhance the quality of life of Indian and Native people.
5. Promote a better understanding among the general public concerning Indian and Native governments, Native sovereignty, and Native people and their rights.

For additional information, contact the NCAI by phone at (202) 466-7767; the website (March 3, 2000) is: www.ncai.org.

National Indian Education Association

The National Indian Education Association (NIEA) is a nonprofit organization that was chartered in 1970. With a nationwide membership of approximately 2,000 individuals actively concerend with Indian education, it is considered by many to be the foremost voice for Indian education in the U.S. The Association is dedicated to promoting high quality education for American Indian and Alaska Native people, while protecting traditonal cultures and values. The NIEA's chartered goals are:

1. Communication—to conduct an annual National Conference on American Indian education and hold specific workshops in conjunction with the conference; to disseminate specific issue alerts; to issue a bimonthly newsletter and other presentations; to conduct hearings and surveys; to construct position papers.
2. Advocacy—to evaluate and improve delivery of state and local educational services; to intercede and establish liaison with state and federal agencies; to issue analysis and reaction strategies; to define issues in anticipation rather than in reaction; to work in the area of legislative analysis; and to work in the area of employment opportunities.
3. Technical Assistance—to assess and coordinate existing technical assistance sources; to add services where needed, given NIEA resources and capacity.
4. Long-Range Issues and Goals of NIEA—to perform a clearinghouse function; to coordinate NIEA efforts closely with

state, tribal, and local Indian education associations; to maintain a directory of Indian professionals; to conduct education workshops on Indian education for non-Indians; to improve the quality of education in both Bureau of Indian Affairs and Public Schools. [National Indian Education Association 1991, p. 2, 2000]

For additional information, contact the NIEA in Alexandria, Virginia, by phone at (703) 838-2870; the website (March 22, 2000) is: www.niea.org.

National Indian Youth Council

The National Indian Youth Council (NIYC) is one of the country's oldest national Indian organizations. It was founded in 1961 to help protect traditional tribal rights and values through education and litigation. Since then it has grown to a national membership of more than 15,000 (National Indian Youth Council 1991a).

In the 1960s, the Council was primarily a civil rights organization, pressing such issues as treaty rights for northwestern tribes and coordinating Indian aspects of the "Poor Peoples' Campaign" in Washington, D.C. In the 1970s, the NIYC was chiefly an environmental organization, aiding tribes beset by problems associated with environmental issues such as coal strip mining and uranium mining. As times have changed, the Council has expanded its activities to encompass other concerns, including freedom of religion, increased Indian political participation, voting rights protection, Indian education, job training and placement, education of the general public about Indian issues, and international Indian issues (National Indian Youth Council 1991b). Regarding the latter topic, the NIYC now has Non-Governmental Organization status with the Economic and Social Council of the United Nations. The Youth Council works with the U.N. to promote Indian interests and causes throughout the hemisphere. Its representatives attend relevant international meetings, disseminate information to U.S. tribes about indigenous people in other countries, and promote cultural exchanges among Indians of different countries (National Indian Youth Council 1991c).

For additional information, contact the NIYC in Albuquerque, New Mexico, by phone at (505) 247-2251.

Native American Journalists Association

The Native American Journalists Association (NAJA), based in Minneapolis, Minnesota, states that its primary goal is "to improve communications among Native people and between Native Americans and the general public" (Native American Journalists Association 2000). Their primary focus is the vast array of issues relating to the survival and development of Native media and communications.

NAJA began as the Native American Press Association, which was an outgrowth of a 1984 meeting of Native journalists at Pennsylvania State University. In 1990 the association took on its current name.

NAJA is a nonprofit organization which endeavors to enrich the journalism profession and promote Native cultures. It also strives to educate its membership and the public on numerous Native issues. NAJA has the additional objectives of promoting diversity and defending challenges to free press, free speech, and freedom of expression on Native lands.

For more information, contact NAJA by phone at (612) 729-9244; the website (March 25, 2000) is: www.naja.com.

Native American Rights Fund

The Native American Rights Fund, affectionately referred to as "NARF," is a nonprofit organization that was incorporated in 1971. NARF is headquartered in Boulder, Colorado, and specializes in protection of the rights of Indians and Alaska Natives. Its principal activities involve (a) preservation of tribal existence, (b) protection of tribal resources, (c) promotion of human rights, (d) accountability of governments to Native Americans, (e) development of Indian law, and (f) education of the public about Indian rights, laws, and issues (Native American Rights Fund 2000).

NARF is known primarily for its legal research and advocacy roles. In its 30 years of operation, the organization and its sophisticated legal staff have successfully represented Indian tribes and individuals in nearly every state in the country. Through its involvement in hundreds of cases, it has touched on every area and issue in the complex field of Indian law. NARF has also developed an Indian law library of significant national stature.

For additional information, contact NARF by phone at (303) 447-8760; the website (March 23, 2000) is: www.narf.org.

Other Important American Indian Organizations

American Indian Science and Engineering Society. Main offices in Albuquerque, New Mexico, (505) 765-1052. Editorial offices for *Winds of Change* in Boulder, Colorado, (303) 444-9099. Websites: www.aises.org and www.colorado.edu/AISES.

Indian Law Resource Center. In Washington, D.C., (202) 547-2800; in Helena, Montana, (406) 449-2006; in Anchorage, Alaska, (907) 258-5811. Website: www.indianlaw.org.

Intertribal Bison Cooperative. Main offices in Rapid City, South Dakota, (605) 394-9730. Website: www.intertribalbison.org.

Native American Public Telecommunications. Main office in Lincoln, Nebraska, (402) 472-3522. Website: www.nativetelecom.org.

National Indian Gaming Association (see also Section N, on gaming). Main offices in Washington, D.C., (202) 546-7711. Website: www. indiangaming.org.

SECTION M: ALASKA

M-1. *How did Euro-American control and influence over Alaska and its Native people begin and evolve?*

The vast majority of the history of contact between Alaska Natives and Euro-American nations involves only two countries—Russia and the United States. The general experience of Alaska Natives with the Russians and the Americans contrasts greatly, in several respects, from that of other Native groups in the lower 48 states. For example, there was little armed conflict between whites and Alaska Natives. No formal treaties were made by the U.S. government with Native groups. Except for Russian enslavement of Aleuts in the 1700s, neither government assumed the type of control over Native lives that developed in other parts of the U.S. And, although there is one remaining reservation in far southeastern Alaska, a reservation system was never permanently instituted (Spicer 1982). Because specifics of Alaska history are unfamiliar to many people, the two eras of Russian and American possession of Alaska merit some review.

The Russian Era

Spanish and Portuguese explorers may have ventured into Alaskan waters in the late-1500s. However, it wasn't until the mid-1700s, 250 years after Columbus landed in the Bahamas, that Alaska was officially "discovered" in the name of Russia.

Vitus Bering, a Danish navigator sailing on behalf of Russia in 1728, traveled through the strait that now bears his name. He landed on and named the Diomede Islands, but heavy fog prevented him from reaching the Alaska mainland which lay just 30 miles to the east. On his second voyage, in 1741, however, Bering and his expedition sighted Mt. St. Elias, in the southeast region of Alaska, and briefly explored the coastal area. One of the first of several Russian reconnaissance parties was lost near present-day Sitka in a hostile encounter with Native people, probably Tlingit warriors. Bering died from poor health and depression during the latter portion of this second voyage. Nonetheless, his voyages established Russia's claim to Alaska. The second expedition had returned to Russia with an impressive collection of valuable sea otter furs, thus launching what proved to be a remarkably rich fur trade (Rogers 1990).

By 1763, independent Russian trading companies and adventurers had moved across the Aleutian Island chain and penetrated as far east as Kodiak Island. It was there, at Three Saints Bay, that the first permanent Russian settlement was established in 1784 (Lynch 1990). During their tenure, the Russians went on to occupy most of the economically strategic areas of coastal Alaska, except for the northern part of the territory.

Apart from one or two locations, like Kodiak and Sitka, permanent Russian settlements were very small, often having only a dozen inhabitants. Most locations were simple trading posts that were manned by one or two Russians who dealt primarily with Aleuts, Koniags, Chugachmuit, some of the southwestern Eskimos, and perhaps a few Tanainas. The Athapaskans and Russians had almost no contact. (The principal Native cultural areas are shown in Figure 10.)

The first 50 years of Russian activity in Alaska were marked by murder and enslavement of the peaceful Aleuts and, probably, some of the Pacific Eskimo people. It was also a period when the formerly vast populations of fur-bearing animals were plundered. The brutal fur traders had simple reasons for the way they treated the Aleuts. Because the Aleuts were excellent hunters of the valuable sea otter, the traders wanted their service. When the Aleuts resisted enslavement, the Russians frequently killed whole groups of them to induce the remaining people to submit (Arnold 1976).

To establish some kind of constructive control, the Czarist government chartered the Russian American Company in 1799 as the sole trading enterprise, with absolute domination over all aspects of Russian America. For more than two decades, relative peace, order, systematic exploration, and expansion of the fur trade occurred. At any one time, probably fewer than 800 Russians were found in all of

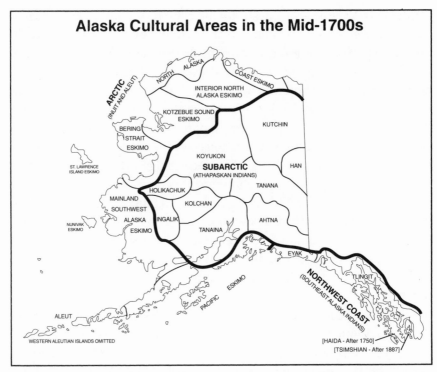

Figure 10. This map shows the principal Native cultural areas in Alaska at the beginning of Russian occupancy in the mid-18th century. (After Prucha 1990a)

Alaska (Lynch 1991). They and their hundreds of Aleut "employees" accomplished the work for the Russian American Company. Many Aleuts even joined the Russian Orthodox Church, learned Russian, and made a career out of working for the Company. (Even today, some older Aleuts speak English, Russian, and Aleut.) Most of the other Alaska Natives were largely left to themselves, though many along the coastal regions did engage in regular activity with non-Indian trading interests.

In the 18th and 19th centuries, English, French, Spanish, and American explorers and whalers charted Alaskan waters, explored much of the coastline, and traded with some of the Native groups along the coast. The Russians, in the meantime, tried repeatedly to expand their operations eastward to control southeast Alaska. They never quite succeeded, however. For example, all the residents of one early settlement near Yakutat were killed by Tlingits. The first

Russian settlement at Sitka in 1802 had the same fate. The Russians resorted to a combined naval-ground operation to drive the Tlingits out of Sitka in 1804. After that, the Tlingits merely tolerated the Russian presence in the immediate Sitka area and remained a serious threat to the intruders through the 1850s.

Continued intrusions by British and American fur traders forced the Russians to grant equal trading rights to these interests in an 1824 agreement. That resulted in an increase in multi-national contact for most coastal and near-interior Native people. By 1839, the Hudson's Bay Company had encroached on southeastern Alaska territory to such an extent that Russians were forced to lease the entire region to this competitor (Rogers 1990).

Over the next three decades, Russian profits from Alaska declined steadily while costs of administration kept rising. The adverse economic situation, disastrous effects of the Crimean War (1853–1856), and the lingering threat of further armed conflict in Europe caused Russia to try to interest the United States in purchasing Alaska in 1859. Preoccupied with domestic problems, the U.S. declined the offer until after the Civil War. A treaty of purchase was signed on March 30, 1867, ratified by the Senate on April 9, and signed by President Andrew Johnson on May 28. A formal transfer of the territory was made during a ceremony at Sitka on October 18, 1867. The purchase price was an incredibly low $7.2 million, or roughly two cents an acre (Lynch 1990).

The American Era

Even prior to the payment of the money for Alaska, Americans began moving in to take control of the assets of the Russian American Company. These included forts, schools, foundries, coal mines, farms, livestock operations, and, of course, the Native trade infrastructure (Lynch 1990).

As was similar with other Euro-American land transfers, the Native people of Alaska were not consulted in any way regarding the change in "ownership" of their land and resources—or their overnight change in nationality. The 1867 land cession treaty with Russia, hastily negotiated and drawn, did not clearly define the legal status, basic rights, and matters of land ownership relevant to Alaska Natives (Arnold 1976). Article III of the treaty did mention them however.

The uncivilized tribes will be subject to such laws and regulations as the United States may, from time to time, adopt in regard
to aboriginal tribes of that country.

In the beginning years of U.S. control of Alaska, the area was
commonly viewed as being useless and was referred to as "Seward's
Folly" or "Seward's Icebox." This was because Secretary of State
William Seward had championed the land purchase. Although some
limited economic development took place in the early period of U.S.
possession, the region was generally neglected by the government.
For 17 years, Alaska was successively under the nominal administration of the War Department, Treasury Department, and the Navy.
The government largely stayed out of the everyday lives of Natives
and non-Natives, with the exception of several forced intrusions by
the Army and Navy into Tlingit affairs (Arnold 1976; Lynch 1990).

In 1884, Congress passed an Alaska "Organic Act" establishing a
civilian government for the area, which was declared to be a "civil
and judicial district." The "general laws of the State of Oregon" and
the mining laws of the U.S. were to be applied. A gold discovery near
Juneau prompted this legislative action. Its main purpose was the
legal control of mining activity and adjudication of disputes over
land. Significantly, the general land laws of the U.S. were not applied
to Alaska, and the issue of Native land claims was deferred.

The Indians or other persons in said district shall not be disturbed in the possession of any lands actually in their use or
occupation or now claimed by them, but the terms under which
said persons may acquire title to such lands is reserved for future
legislation by Congress. [Organic Act, p. 26]

From 1880 to 1910, establishment of fish canneries, discoveries of
gold, the large influx of non-Natives, the increased importation of
outside influences, and the spread of diseases like influenza and
tuberculosis greatly disrupted the Native population. Many of the
best of the traditional fishing and hunting sites were taken by non-
Natives, food became scarce as the fish and game populations
decreased, and living conditions deteriorated. Many Native people
simply did not survive the transition.

When the Russians arrived in Alaska in the mid-1700s, it is estimated that the Native population consisted of 74,000 Indians,

Eskimos, and Aleuts (Arnold 1976). When the U.S. took possession in 1867, the Native population, including 1,400 mixed-bloods, had fallen to an official count of 28,254 (Case 1984). In 1880, at the beginning of three decades of feverish economic development, there were 32,996 Natives and only 430 non-Natives in Alaska. By the end of the gold rush era, in 1910, the Native population had fallen 23 percent from the 1880 level, to 25,331. The non-Native population, however, had increased 9,000 percent, to 39,035. The non-Native population had done well enough during that time period to enable them to push Congress to move Alaska's status one step up from a "judicial district" to a United States territory in 1912.

Where was the BIA all this time? The primary legal status of Alaska Natives—following the 1867 purchase and the 1884 Organic Act, and up until Congressional action in 1905—was presumed by most people to equate with non-Native legal status. That is, Natives were not considered to have separate "Indian" status such as that held by Native people in the lower 48 states. The BIA, therefore, did not get involved. Significantly, there had been no distinction between Native and non-Native residents of Alaska with regard to federal educational services. There was no Indian agency in Alaska, and the

PHOTO COURTESY OF THE SMITHSONIAN INSTITUTION

This photo from the Smithsonian archives shows Eskimos and store houses at Togiak, Alaska, about the beginning of the twentieth century.

Bureau of Education—not the Bureau of Indian Affairs—provided educational services "without regard to race" (Case 1984).

In 1905, Congress passed an education bill, called the Nelson Act, in which it recognized Alaska Natives as a separate group of Alaska residents and specifically allowed for appropriations for the "education and support of the Eskimos, Indians and other Natives of Alaska." This was one of the first of a number of legislative, judicial, and administrative developments which finally led to assumption of responsibility for Alaska Native affairs by the Bureau of Indian Affairs in 1931. Seven years earlier, Alaska Natives had also gained U.S. citizenship under the Indian Citizenship Act of 1924.

As described in Part III of this book, the Indian Reorganization Act of 1934 provided American Indians with increased opportunities for land retention, self-government, and economic development. Originally, the act did not fully apply to Alaska. A 1936 amendment, however, applied the bill to the unique circumstances of Alaska. Numerous Native village governments were organized under the act, a few reservations were established (later to be dissolved), and some Native businesses were chartered or financed.

World War II brought change to Alaska and its Native people. The Japanese invaded the Aleutian Islands in 1942, even taking a small group of Aleuts back to Japan as prisoners of war. Military personnel numbering 200,000 were sent by the U.S. to the territory. The Alcan Highway was completed. Many Native people were displaced for security reasons or voluntarily left their homes to work in defense-related jobs. Military construction boomed, bringing in more civilians; and many military personnel remained in Alaska after their tours of duty or else later retired to the territory. As the population increased, so did the desire for statehood. On January 3, 1959, Alaska became the 49th state.

Alaska Native government, BIA administration, and efforts at defining and protecting Native rights limped along through the 1940s, the 1950s, and the early-1960s. One very positive development was the beginning of widespread provision of health care services to Native people, initiated in the 1950s. A growing "background noise," however, was the long-ignored question of Native land claims. In the 1960s, it rose to a thunder and resulted in passage of the revolutionary and far-reaching Alaska Native Claims Settlement Act (ANCSA) of 1971 (see also question M-4).

M-2. *What is the legal definition of an Alaska Native?*

The Alaska Native Claims Settlement Act (1971) contains the definition shown below. It combines a blood quantum and document standard, and it includes the more socially realistic community standard for "Indians" put forth by Cohen (1982) (see also question A-1).

> (b) "Native" means a citizen of the United States who is a person of one-fourth degree or more of Alaska Indian . . . Eskimo, or Aleut blood, or combination thereof. The term includes any Native as so defined either or both of whose adoptive parents are not Natives. It also includes, in the absence of proof of a minimum blood quantum, any citizen of the United States who is regarded as an Alaska Native by the Native village or Native group of which he claims to be a member and whose father or mother is (or, if deceased, was) regarded as Native by any village or group. [43 USC 1602]

Technical definitions are also given in the act for "village" and "group." The act further states that, in any questions regarding eligibility for enrollment (i.e., whether or not someone is a Native), the decisions of the Secretary of the Interior are final.

M-3. *What is the Alaska Federation of Natives, and what are its history, mission, and current concerns?*

The Alaska Federation of Natives, or AFN, is the major advocacy and lobbying organization for the Native people of Alaska. It is a corporation formed largely to represent the concerns of Alaska Natives before Congress, the Alaska State Legislature, and federal and state government agencies. AFN's board of directors includes representatives of Native nonprofit regional associations, Native regional corporations, and the Alaska Native village corporations formed under the Alaska Native Claims Settlement Act, or ANCSA (1971).

In 1966, more than 400 Alaska Natives, representing 17 Native organizations, gathered in Anchorage for a conference. Their purpose was to address aboriginal land rights and other common problems and to begin the process of organizing AFN. From 1966 to 1971, AFN worked primarily to achieve a fair land claims settlement, which resulted in the signing into law of ANCSA on December 8, 1971.

After passage of ANCSA, the AFN provided technical assistance to Native groups to help implement the terms of the act, including the establishment of corporations mandated by ANCSA. Subsequently, the AFN managed several statewide human service programs, which were later transferred to regional associations, as the latter grew in strength and independence.

In the late-1970s and the 1980s, AFN was a key figure in passage of the Alaska National Interest Lands Conservation Act (1980) and the very important 1987 amendments to ANCSA, known as the "1991 legislation." In the 1990s the AFN intensified its involvement in the "subsistence" issue (see question M-7). Today the Federation continues to work at the federal, state, and local levels on pressing social, tribal, and economic issues.

The overall mission of the AFN is to enhance and promote the cultural, economic, and political voice of the entire community of Alaska Natives. The Federation's declared goals for 2000 and beyond are to:

- Serve as an advocate for Alaska Native people, their governments and organizations with respect to federal, state and local laws;
- Foster and encourage preservation of Alaska Native cultures;
- Promote understanding of the economic needs of Alaska Natives and encourage development consistent with those needs;
- Protect, retain, and enhance all lands owned by Alaska Natives and their organizations; and
- Promote and advocate programs and systems which instill pride and confidence in individual Alaska Natives.

All information for this answer was provided courtesy of the Alaska Federation of Natives, Inc. (1991a; 1991c; 2000). For further information, contact the AFN, 1577 "C" Street, Suite 300, Anchorage, Alaska 99501; phone (907) 274-3611. AFN's two websites, which are sometimes difficult to access, are (March 3, 2000): www.akfednatives. org and http://akfednatives.org.

M-4. *What is the best single source of contemporary information on Alaska native cultural issues of all kinds?*

Without doubt, it is the internet site cooperatively established by the Alaska Federation of Natives and the University of Alaska, Fairbanks. This site (March 25, 2000) at www.ankn.uaf.org must be visited to be appreciated. It also provides links to other sites for indigenous groups such as Native Hawaiians, the Saami of Scandinavia, First Nations of Canada, and the Maori of New Zealand.

M-5. *What is the history of the Native land claims issue, and what is the Alaska Native Claims Settlement Act?*

Background

When Alaska was purchased by the U.S. in 1867, and again when the first civil government was organized by Congress in 1884, the issue of Native land claims was put on hold. As stated earlier, no treaty was ever entered into with Alaska Natives. The coming decades of economic and military development led to increasing encroachment on what had always been Native land. Little of real substance was done to address the land and resource rights of Alaska Natives until the 1960s. A series of significant events then brought the land claims issue to a head.

In 1957, major oil fields were discovered in the Kenai Peninsula and Cook Inlet regions. The associated population increase helped lead to Alaskan statehood in 1959. The statehood act granted the State of Alaska the right to select 103 million acres of federal public domain land for itself. In 1961, state land selections were threatening lands which Native peoples considered to be their own. Native protests and complaints to the government began in earnest. At the same time, proposals for federal land withdrawals also threatened land claims by Natives.

A statewide conference of Native groups in 1966 resulted in formation of the Alaska Federation of Natives (AFN) which helped spearhead the land rights battle. Also in 1966, Secretary of the Interior

Stewart Udall stopped the transfer, to the State of Alaska, of lands claimed by Natives until Congress could act upon the claims. By then, the amount of land claimed had grown to 380 million acres. The first bills designed to settle land claims were introduced in Congress in 1967.

In 1968, huge oil and gas reserves were discovered along Alaska's North Slope. That same year a state-supported Land Claims Task Force recommended a 40 million-acre settlement, and a newly published government study supported the validity of Native land claims. Sales of oil leases in the North Slope area brought the State $900 million in 1969. Also in 1969, oil companies and other business interests placed their full support behind efforts to reach a land settlement quickly so the Alaska pipeline project could get in motion.

A land claims bill passed the Senate in 1970, but the legislation provided only the relatively small amount of 10 million acres of land. Native interests protested successfully in the House. In 1971, Congress passed the Alaska Native Claims Settlement Act (ANCSA) and it was signed into law by President Nixon on December 18. (For additional background on ANCSA, see Arnold 1976; Lynch 1990 and 1991; Rogers 1990; Tundra Times 1991; Alaska Federation of Natives 2000.)

Basic Provisions of ANCSA

Arnold (1976) summarized the provisions of the Alaska Native Claims Settlement Act. Alaska Natives were to receive full title to 44 million acres of the 380 million acres they had claimed. Native claims based on aboriginal title were said to be "extinguished." The several existing reservations, except for the Annette Island Reserve in far southeast Alaska, were revoked. In addition, monetary compensation for the extinguished land claims was set at $962.5 million. Congress authorized $462.5 million of the monetary award to be appropriated from the federal treasury and to be paid into the Alaska Native Fund over an 11-year period. The remaining $500 million was to be paid into the fund from a percentage of oil and gas revenues as these minerals were developed on federal and state lands. Payments from the Alaska Native Fund were to be made only to regional Native corporations. They, in turn, were to retain part of the funds and pay out part to village corporations and individual Natives. The amount of money each regional corporation received was to be based on the proportion which its enrolled Natives represented to the total number enrolled for all regional corporations.

All U.S. citizens of one-fourth or more Alaska Native blood, and who were alive on December 18, 1971, were qualified to participate in the settlement—unless they were members of the Annette Island Reserve community (which had no relevant claims to be settled).

Unique to federal Indian law, benefits under the settlement were to accrue to eligible Natives through modern Native corporations, and *not* through the traditional entities of tribes, clans, families, or similar communities. All eligible Natives were to become stockholders of their appropriate corporations. Those Natives born after December 18, 1971, were barred from corporate membership and from obtaining stock, except through inheritance.

The initial step for Natives to become stockholders was for them to be enrolled as corporate members. This involved the registering of names, communities, and regions of permanent residence, and the required proving of Indian, Inuit, or Aleut heritage. Based upon the region of one's permanent residence, he or she would be enrolled in one of 12 regional corporations created under the act. ANCSA was later amended to allow the formation of a 13th "regional" corporation for those Alaska Natives living outside the state.

Regarding land distribution, 22 million acres of the total were to be for Native village selection. Just as with the monetary distribution, the number of acres to which a village was entitled was to be determined by its enrollment. Village corporations would own only the surface rights to their land selections. The subsurface of the village corporation land, and most of the remaining land of the 44 million acres, went to the 12 regional corporations. The comparatively small amount of remaining acreage was allocated for a few special corporations that were organized in largely non-Native communities. These lands were intended for Natives or groups of Natives residing away form villages, for pending Native allotments, and for cemeteries and historic sites.

Afterthoughts

When ANCSA was passed, it was heralded as a monumental piece of legislation and the most generous land claims settlement ever

Delegates in Anchorage, Alaska, at the 1991 convention of the Alaska Federation of Natives. The banner marks the 20th anniversary of enactment of the Alaska Native Claims Settlement Act. Photo by Jeff Silverman, Alaska Federation of Natives.

made with American Indians (including Inuit and Aleut people). Alaska Natives were granted title to more land than was held in trust for all tribes, combined, in the rest of the United States. In addition, compensation for lands surrendered by the Native people was about four times greater than the amount which all the tribes in the lower 48 states had won from the Indian Claims Commission over its 25-year history (Worl 1988).

Alaska Natives were, at first, elated with the settlement. Only five years later, however, it was seen as a flawed victory. Some analysts questioned if ANCSA was actually a new form of termination—the disastrous 1950s policy of "terminating" the legal existence of tribes and their reservations. At the base of Native apprehension was the novel corporate approach employed in settling the land claims. The potential long-term effects of the corporate approach had somehow gone unchallenged until after passage of the act (Getches 1985).

The settlement was a distinct departure from previous Indian settlements. ANCSA land would be held by the Native corporations under fee simple title rather than as tribal reservation land held in trust by the federal government. Thus, the Alaska lands would not be protected under trust status. Congress clearly intended that ANCSA assets would provide a means for economic development and native assimilation into the larger society (Worl 1988).

Traditional cultures and Native subsistence hunting and fishing were now seen as being threatened by potential development at the hands of Native corporations. These "for profit" corporations were designed to make money for shareholders. It soon became evident that the removal of restrictions on the alienation of corporate stock to non-Natives could result in the loss of Native ownership and control of their own corporations. Ironically, some Native leaders are now looking for legislative, judicial, and administrative means of establishing reservation status, tribal governments, sovereignty, and federal trusteeship over lands and resources to help protect their land settlement legacy and traditional cultures (Alaska Federation of Natives 1992, 2000; Getches 1985; Worl 1988).

ANCSA hasn't been a failure, but it has been a disappointment in some ways. A number of flaws have been addressed in amendments and related legislation, including the Alaska National Interest Lands Conservation Act (ANILCA) of 1980, the ANCSA Amendments of 1987, the 1990 act authorizing a Joint Federal-State Commission on Policies and Programs Affecting Alaska Natives, and a more recent bill (Title III of Public Law 102-201) that extended certain protections against alienation of stock and hostile corporate takeovers. The Joint Commission's activities and investigations, which were under way in the early 1990s, were intended to lead to additional corrective actions relating to ANCSA as well as to other actions relating to non-ANCSA issues.

Discord between Native villages and the state, and between the federal government and the state—primarily over resource management issues like subsistence—have detracted from some of the positive results of the commission, and a vast amount of work remains to be done.

Delegates of the Alaska Federation of Natives meet in caucus, during their 1991 convention, to discuss the issue of hostile corporate takeovers. Photo by Jeff Silverman, Alaska Federation of Natives.

M-6. *How much land is held by the Native people of Alaska?*

To be able to put the Native landholdings of Alaska into perspective, one should first understand just how large Alaska is. The total area of the state, including land and interior water, covers 591,000 square miles. That is 378,240,000 acres—more than twice the size of Texas and a dozen times the size of New York state. Border-to-border distances are also immense. Measuring the north-to-south and east-to-west extremities, Alaska stretches roughly 1,400 and 2,400 miles, respectively, including the Aleutian Island chain.

The Native landholding situation in Alaska is quite different from that in the lower 48 states. Whereas the great majority of Indian land in the 48 states is reservation-related trust land, 98 percent of the Native land in Alaska is privately owned, non-reservation land that is not held in trust by the United States. There are three categories of Native land in Alaska and they are discussed separately below.

Tribal trust land

Annette Island Indian Reservation, also known as Metlakatla, is the only remaining Indian reservation in the state. It contains all of the tribal trust land in Alaska—86,741 acres (Bureau of Indian Affairs 1985a). Again, title to this category of land is held in trust by the U.S. The reservation is located in the far southeastern tip of Alaska, where it is home to the Tsimshian Indians. They migrated to Annette Island from nearby British Columbia, Canada, in 1887, under the leadership of the Anglican missionary, William Duncan. In 1891, Congress enacted legislation making the Island a reservation (Case 1984).

Individually owned trust land

Some 884,100 acres of numerous, individually owned, allotments of trust land are located in several areas of Alaska (Bureau of Indian Affairs 1985). This acreage is the legacy of federal land policies predating the Alaska Native Claims Settlement Act (ANCSA) of 1971.

Native corporation land

The provisions of ANCSA led to the formation of 12 Native regional corporations, a 13th "regional" corporation for non-resident Alaska Natives (without a defined area), and just over 200 village corporations distributed throughout the 12 regional corporations. (See Figure 11.) These are all for-profit entities. Full private ownership of 40 million acres was promised to the Native corporations as partial compensation for the extinguishing of aboriginal title to the state. In addition, seven village corporations, on five revoked reservations, voted to accept full title to their former reservations and forego other benefits of the settlement act. This brought the total ANCSA land to 43.7 million acres of widely distributed parcels for the Native corporations, or 11.6 percent of the state. About 80 percent of the land selections and title transfers had been completed as of December 1991 (Silverman 1991b), and the distribution is now nearly complete. Much of the allocation of ANCSA land to the Native corporations is based on corporate enrollment numbers which relate to eligibility requirements at the time the act was passed (Arnold 1976).

The U.S. Bureau of Land Management (BLM) is the agency responsible for the ANCSA land distribution process. Data originating from the Anchorage office of the BLM are presented in the table on the next page. This shows how the 43.7 million acres will have been allotted when the process is completed.

ALASKA NATIVE LAND ALLOCATIONS

Region	Regional Corporation Lands	Village Corporation Lands	Former Reservation Village Lands	Totals
		(to the nearest acre)		
Ahtna	1,038,256	691,200		1,729,456
Aleut	142,533	1,221,120		1,363,653
Arctic Slope	4,177,586	852,480		5,030,066
Bering Straits	293,420	1,820,160	1,433,932	3,547,512
Bristol Bay	234,303	2,718,720		2,953,024
Calista	570,132	5,644,800		6,214,932
Chugach	427,976	460,800		888,776
Cook Inlet	1,590,667	668,160		2,258,827
Doyon	8,748,591	3,248,640	2,543,087	14,540,317
Koniag	116,756	923,520		1,040,276
NANA	954,523	1,198,080		2,152,603
Totals	18,294,743	19,447,680	3,977,019	*41,719,442

*Total excludes a 2,000,000-acre land fund from which land is conveyed to Natives (not corporations) pursuant to ANCSA for special purposes, i.e., for cemetery sites and historical places; for Natives living in Sitka, Kenai, Juneau, and Kodiak; for primary places of residence of Natives; and for individual allotments. The excess between the 2,000,000 acres and the total special purpose conveyances will be distributed pro-rata to the regional corporations based on their Native populations. Sealaska Corporation was not entitled to any land under ANCSA because of a pre-ANCSA government settlement with the Tlingit and Haida people. The Thirteenth Regional Corporation received only cash in the ANCSA settlement. [Table information is from Getches 1985.]

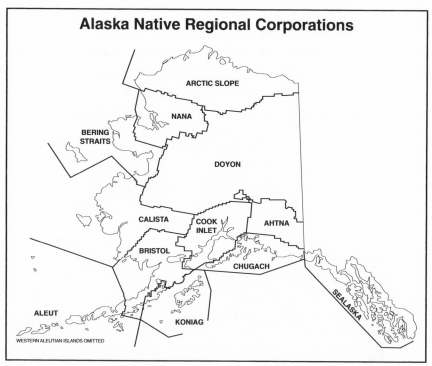

Figure 11. Geographic limits of the 12 Native regional corporations established under provisions of the Alaska Native Claims Settlement Act are shown here.

M-7. *What is the conflict known as the subsistence issue?*

In the eyes of Native people, "subsistence" is not primarily a question of animals, or their habitats, or the efficiency of their management by public agencies, or even the constitutionality of their allocation among competing user groups. For us, subsistence is a critical part of a much broader historical question about the status, rights, aspirations and future development of the people who are from Alaska. Subsistence law is social policy on a grand scale. It poses the fundamental question of cultural tolerance in modern society; whether all citizens must be made identical in order to be made equal.

Alaska Federation of Natives 1991b, p. 6

Since the early 1990s, the subsistence issue has been the dominant political concern for the statewide Native community (Alaska Federation of Natives 1991c, 2000). From an all-Alaska perspective, including the views of non-Natives, *the* issue is actually several very emotion-packed issues. In one way or another, all are related to hunting and fishing rights and activities (Burch 1984; Alaska Federation of Natives 2000).

One issue involves the question of whether Alaska lands should be developed—and thus cause interference with fish and wildlife populations—or left in a natural or nearly natural state. Concerns about development of oil and gas in the Alaska National Wildlife Refuge have been the most public of recent development conflicts.

A second issue, being hotly contested in the political arena and in the courts, concerns who should legally control hunting and fishing. Should it be the federal government, the state government, organized regional user groups, or a combination thereof? The Alaska Federation of Natives (AFN) favors management of all fish and game by the state government. However, in October 1999, after the state legislature failed to provide for a vote on a state constitutional amendment for a rural subsistence priority, the federal government

Village elder testifies on the subsistence issue at a public meeting. The earphone is for translation into Yupik Eskimo language. Photo by Jeff Silverman, Alaska Federation of Natives.

Fish drying at Kotzebue Sound, Alaska, in the spring. Photo by Jimmy Evak, Maniilaq Association.

"took over." A new "Federal Subsistence board" took over fishing and hunting regulatory control for the federal lands and waters within the state, which include the majority of the land and water areas in Alaska (Office of Subsistence Management 2000).

Another heated issue focuses on the question of who is to be permitted to hunt and fish in a state where (1) the population has grown too large for everyone to hunt and fish at a substantial harvest level and (2) important fish and game populations have declined or been threatened with decline in recent decades. AFN has always urged the legislature and the people of Alaska to adopt a constitutional amendment allowing a statutory subsistence preference for rural residents, but they have not received much support.

Some of the more prominent interest groups involved in the various aspects of the subsistence issue include sport hunting and fishing organizations, commercial hunting and fishing interests (Native and non-Native), conservation groups, development interests, Native organizations, rural communities, state and federal agencies, and the statewide Native community. Natives believe it is important that others understand they do not view subsistence as an "issue" but, rather, as a cultural and economic fact of life (Silverman 1991a; Alaska Federation of Natives 2000).

M-8. *What are the most pressing socio-economic problems of Alaska Natives, and how are they going to be addressed?*

In 1989, the Alaska Federation of Natives (AFN) produced a startling document titled "The AFN Report on the Status of Alaska Natives: A Call for Action." The report declared that "the fundamental issue confronting Alaska Natives is the struggle of previously self-sufficient individuals and family units to adjust to rapid social change largely imposed from the outside." It also publicized several significant findings. Among them:

1. A plague of alcohol abuse, violence, and self-destruction is afflicting Alaska Natives.
2. Alaska Natives are more vulnerable to serious injury, infectious disease, and death than non-Natives.
3. Alaska Natives have a growing "at risk" population. (Young adult Natives are adrift between cultures and are often excluded from meaningful and gainful employment.)
4. The village economy cannot meet the needs of the growing Native population.
5. Villages are precariously dependent upon public sector spending, and the cost of living in villages is exorbitant.
6. Native children enter and exit village schools with serious educational handicaps, and their education is worse than mediocre.

Existing efforts directed toward issue definition, analysis, and resolution—by Native groups and state and federal agencies—were found to be inadequate for the severity of the problems and the rapid social change at their core. AFN approached the U.S. Senate Select Committee on Indian Affairs for advice on what should be done and asked the committee to make some recommendations. The result was

ALEUT MONTHS

January—Month of the black cormorant

February—Month when last stored food is eaten

March—Month of hunger, gnawing thongs and straps

April—Month of near hunger

May—Month of flowers

June—Month seals are born

July—Month when young amphibians flourish

August—Month when the grass begins to wither
and animals grow thin

September—Month when animals shed fur

October—Month of Autumn

November—Month devoted to hunting

December—long month

Oliver 1988

an important piece of legislation that was added as a rider to the Indian Law Enforcement Reform Act of 1990.

Section 12 of this act (1) acknowledged the existence of "a growing social and economic crisis" among Alaska Natives, (2) declared it was timely and essential to conduct a comprehensive review of federal and state policies affecting these Native people, and (3) authorized establishment of the "Joint Federal-State Commission on Policies and Programs Affecting Alaska Natives." The Commission has 14 voting members, seven appointed by the President and seven by the Governor. All appointments have now been made to the commission and it is now undertaking its responsibilities. As charged by Congress:

    (c) The Commission shall—

        (1) conduct a comprehensive study of—

            (A)the social and economic status of Alaska Natives, and

            (B) the effectiveness of those policies and programs of the United States, and the State of Alaska, that affect Alaska Natives,

(2) conduct public hearings on the subject of such study,

(3) recommend specific actions to the Congress and to the State of Alaska that—

(A) help to assure that Alaska Natives have life opportunities comparable to other Americans, while respecting their unique traditions, cultures, and special status as Alaska Natives,

(B) address, among other things, the needs of Alaska Natives for self-determination, economic self-sufficiency, improved levels of educational achievement, improved health status, and reduced incidence of social problems,

(4) in developing these recommendations, respect the important cultural differences which characterize Alaska Native groups,

(5) submit, by no later than the date that is eighteen months after the date of the first meeting of the Commission, a report on the study, together with the recommendations developed under paragraph (3), to the President, the Congress, the Governor of the State of Alaska, and the legislature of the State of Alaska, and

(6) make such a report available to Alaska Native villages and organizations and to the public.

Expectations were running high in Alaska and Washington, D.C., in the early 1990s that much would come from the Joint Commission's endeavors. Many studies have since been conducted under the auspices of the Commission, and overall results and recommendations from them have recently been submitted to Congress for consideration (Pass 2000). Whether Congress will act remains to be seen.

SECTION N: GAMING

> *Gaming is the best economic opportunity since the arrival of the white man.*
>
> Philip Martin, 1995, Chief, Missippi Band
> of Choctaw Indians, during a speech at
> Arizona State University
>
> *The members of the Commission agree that there is a need for a "pause" in the growth of gambling. The purpose of the pause is not to wait for definitive answers to the subjects of dispute, because those may never come. Instead the purpose of this recommended pause is to encourage governments to do what, to date, few, if any, have done: to survey the results of their decisions and to determine if they have chosen wisely; to ask if their decisions are in accord with public good, if harmful effects could be remedied, if benefits are being unnecessarily passed up. Because the search for answers takes time, some policymakers may wish to impose an explicit moratorium on gambling expansion while awaiting further research and assessment.*
>
> From the 1999 Report of the National
> Gambling Impact Study Commission

Many scholars of law and history now say we are in the self-determination era, but our times and the profound events surrounding them may eventually show that we have entered what may become known as "The Gaming Era."

N-1. *How did gaming evolve into an Indian country economic and political issue?*

Only since the early 1980s has gaming (the "politically correct" term for gambling) become a significant economic activity and a sensitive

361

political issue in Indian country. Revenues derived from gaming by non-Indians, on Indian land, now supplement tribal government incomes on a number of reservations throughout the U.S. Headlines are also being made as federal, tribal, and state governments argue, in the courts and in the press, over who is going to regulate what in tribal gaming enterprises. Gaming is currently the most politically charged economic issue in Indian country.

Background of the issue

In 1979, the Seminole Tribe of Florida was the first tribe to enter into the bingo gaming industry in a major way (Sokolow 1990). By 1982, their bingo operation was annually netting $2.7 million. This, and a few other success stories around the country, caused many additional tribes (and the Reagan administration) to encourage more gaming enterprises on reservations to stimulate economic development. Economic self-sufficiency was a cornerstone of the administration's Indian policy. Gaming enterprises were seen by many, then as now, as a quick fix for the difficult economic conditions on numerous reservations with limited resources.

Immediately upon the expansion of gaming in Indian country, conflicts arose among federal, state, and tribal governments as to what was legal and what was not—and who had jurisdiction. What resulted from the conflict was the Indian Gaming Regulatory Act (IGRA) of 1988. The meaning and application of this act is now the focus of most of the conflict over Indian gaming.

The stated multiple purposes of the act are: (1) to provide a legislative basis for the operation and regulation of gaming by Indian tribes; (2) to establish a National Indian Gaming Commission as a federal agency to meet congressional concerns and protect gaming as a means of generating tribal revenue; (3) to promote economic development, self-sufficiency, and strong tribal governments; (4) to shield tribes from organized crime; and (5) to assure fairness to operators and players.

Three classes of gaming and related jurisdiction are treated by the IGRA. Class I includes social, traditional games in connection with tribal ceremonies, pow wows, or celebrations. These are under the exclusive jurisdiction of the Indian tribes.

Class II gaming includes such things as bingo, lotto, pull tabs, punch boards, tip jars, and certain card games. Excluded from this class are baccarat, chemin de fer, blackjack, all slot machines, and all electromechanical facsimiles of any game of chance, such as video poker and video bingo. The IGRA permits Class II gaming on Indian lands if the gaming is located in a state which allows it for any purpose, by any person or entity. Only four states (Arkansas, Hawaii, Indiana, and Utah) criminally prohibit all types of gaming, including bingo. The tribes involved and the National Indian Gaming Commission share regulatory jurisdiction over Class II gaming activities.

Class III includes all gaming that is not covered in Classes I and II, i.e., the usual casino games of baccarat, blackjack, roulette, and craps, as well as slot machines, video poker, horse and dog racing, etc. Before Class III games can be offered legally, a tribe and the state involved must first negotiate a tribal-state regulatory compact. It must then be approved by the Secretary of the Interior.

Much of the current news about the Indian gaming issue involves the topic of state-tribal compacts. Some states have been almost immovable in their attitudes toward negotiating compacts. According to many tribes, the states have not engaged in "good faith" negotiation as language of the IGRA requires. Some tribes took their complaints to federal court. But the end result has been a declaration by the U.S. Supreme Court that the 11th amendment of the Constitution

Freeway sign on the Gila River Indian Reservation, south of Phoenix, Arizona.

Newspaper advertisement for an Indian casino operation in Sault Ste. Marie, Michigan.

bars suits by tribes against states without state consent, in other words, the states have sovereign immunity from tribal lawsuits (*Seminole Tribe of Florida v. Florida* 1996).

Although data on the Indian gaming industry varies, in 2000 there were reported to be 310 Indian gaming operations involving Type II gaming or Types II and III gaming. However, only 260 of these "operations" were casinos. Some tribes have more than one casino or "other" gaming operations, which include bingo halls. (For comparison purposes, Nevada alone has approximately 215 non-Indian casinos.)

Class III or "Las Vegas" style gaming requires tribal-state compacts, and although there were 198 such compacts in place at the beginning of 2000, it was reported that only about 140 of the compact tribes were actually operating Class III gaming establishments. The reported number may be low, but the count is bound to increase in the near future, especially now that the California constitutional issue restricting slot machines has moved toward resolution. Most of California's

107 tribes will now be able to expand their current operations or begin new ones (Howarth 1999b, 1999c; National Indian Gaming Association 2000; National Indian Gaming Commission 2000).

Estimates of *gross* revenues from Indian gaming for 2000 reached as high as 7.5 billion dollars. This compares with the $150 billion dollar a year state lotteries and the $15 billion non-Indian casino businesses. Even if *net* returns were on the low end of a reasonable 10 to 15 percent, the $750 million would be more than 60 times the amount annually appropriated directly for the BIA economic development program over the past decade. Obviously, Indian gaming will continue to play a major and increasing role in the tribal economies in the foreseeable future. (See the award-winning work by Mason (2000) on the issues of Indian gaming, tribal sovereignty, and politics.)

The debate

In the late 1980s and early 1990s, much of the debate surrounding Indian gaming dealt with whether or not it should be allowed. Now that the phenomenon has swept across many parts of the county, the emphasis of much of the discussion has shifted to how to control gaming—not just in Indian country but all across America. The following quotations from selected recent news stories provide revealing "snapshots" of the variety of media messages that seem to directly influence the voting public and state and federal officials in various quarters of the country.

> We thought [our casino] would be successful, but we didn't last seven months. Most of the tourists come here from Las Vegas. Who wants to come out and play piddly machines when their main concern is visiting the natural beauty of the [Grand] Canyon?
>
> Edgar Walema, Vice Chairman, Hualapai Tribe
> of Arizona, Associated Press article
> November 8, 1998

> Three in 10 registered [New Mexico] voters know someone who has had financial or family problems brought about by gaming.
>
> Brian Sanderhoff, opinion pollster
> *Albuquerque Journal*
> March 24, 2000

The [New Mexico] tribes agreed to pay 16 percent in revenue sharing [to the state] from their casino slot-machine profits. The tribes argue that is too high, and some have refused to pay. . . . In recent negotiations, the tribes sought to lower the revenue sharing payments to 7.5 percent.

Albuquerque Journal
March 23, 2000

As quid pro quo for sitting down to discuss amending South Dakota's compact with the Oglala Sioux to permit 50 more slot machines to the 200 already authorized, state negotiators suggested to the impoverished Pine Ridge leaders that they fork over 34 percent of their net revenues.

American Indian Report
August 1999

The legal age to gamble on Arizona reservations could rise to 21 [from 18] and ATMs could be banned in casinos under agreements to be negotiated over the next four years with the state's 15 gaming tribes.

Arizona Republic
November 13, 1999

Gov. John Engler [of Michigan] . . . said that with 18 casinos in the state and three in Detroit, he will not give approval for more casinos.

Record-Eagle
Traverse City, Michigan
October 1, 1999

The Department of the Interior announced Friday that it plans to work out gaming compacts with tribes in states where legislatures have not negotiated in good faith, but where other tribes already have casinos.

Record-Eagle
Traverse City, Michigan
January 17, 1998

In the last few years, the federal agency charged with regulating the Indian gaming industry has grown into what some say are the beginnings of another overblown bureaucracy.

Many in the industry are concerned that growth of the National Indian Gaming Commission may be a sign of greater infringement on tribal sovereignty.

Indian Country Today
February 23, 2000

Casinos are a good way of making money if you're not interested in ethical concerns. Personally, I think gambling is a horrible thing. As a human being, I detest it. As an advocate for an Abenaki renaissance, I think it has advantages.

Fred Wiseman, Abenaki
Indian Country Today
May 17, 1999

Nine of Arizona's 15 gaming tribes are among others nationwide forking over casino profits to fight compulsive gambling, a problem receiving increasing national attention.

Arizona Republic
July 6, 1999

According to the National Opinion Research Center report, 2.5 million adults are pathological gamblers, another three million are considered to be problem gamblers. An additional 15 million gamblers are considered at risk and 148 million are low risk gamblers.

Indian Country Today
April 12, 1999

The tribal leadership [of the National Congress of American Indians and the National Indian Gaming Association] have taken the position that we do not support any amendments to [the IGRA] unless those amendments include provisions intended to create a "Seminole" remedy [a "waiver" of state sovereign immunity] so that states no longer have the power to unilaterally defeat the good faith negotiation requirement of the original IGRA process.

Richard Hill, Chairman of the NIGA, in written testimony
on S. 399, proposed amendments to the IGRA, presented
to the U.S. Senate Committee on Indian Affairs
March 24, 1999

The tribal council [of the Salt River Pima–Maricopa Indian Community, Arizona] informally rejected giving 25 percent of the community's casino profits directly to members but pledged to work toward a compromise agreement. About 1,000 members [of the 6,200-member tribe] . . . signed a petition seeking such payments.

Indian Country Today
January 5, 2000

Dipping revenue since the opening of the Salt River Tribe's first of two [competing] casinos in October 1998 has forced cutbacks [for the Fort McDowell Yavapai Nation of Arizona], including reducing annual dividends of $36,000 to $30,000 for each tribal member.

Arizona Republic
January 28, 2000

Foxwoods Resort Casino's slot machines have earned $4 billion since the Mashantucket Pequot tribe entered into a special agreement with the state [of Connecticut] seven years ago. More than $1 billion of that revenue has gone back to the state. The tribe announced January 14 that they now have paid $1,007,482,922 to the state under an agreement whereby the tribe pays Connecticut 25 percent of its slot revenue in return for semi-exclusive rights to operate the machines in their casino.

Indian Country Today
February 2, 2000

In a move reminiscent of the labor campaigns that empowered auto, steel and farm workers a decade ago, unions are trying to organize employees at casinos on Indian reservations, a campaign that could test the limits of tribal sovereignty.

Associated Press
May 24, 1999

FOR TRIBES, CASINO MONEY MEANS CLOUT

Headline in the *Reno Gazette-Journal*
July 12, 1999

A federal commission studying gaming in the United States completed its two-year inquiry calling for a national "pause" in the growth of casinos, lotteries and slot machines.

Indian Country Today
June 21, 1999

> If we are to restore our traditional government, it has to mean the end of gaming.
>
> Doug George, Mohawk
> *Indian Country Today*, May 2000

> We've had gambling forever. [It's] not new to the Oneidas.
>
> Dale Rude, Oneida
> *Indian Country Today*, May 2000

N-2. *Where can copies of the Indian Gaming Regulatory Act and the federal Indian gaming regulations be obtained?*

The Indian Gaming Regulatory Act of 1988 (IGRA), which had not been amended as of 2000, can be found in several ways. In libraries that receive U.S. government documents, the Act can be found in the *U.S. Statutes at Large*, either through the Act's public law number (P.L. 100-497) or through its volume and page number (102 Stat. 2467).

The Act can also be found in its codified form in Title 25 of the United States Code at Section 2701. If the IGRA is ever amended, researchers should look for the most current version in the U.S. Code, because the U.S. Code is the only officially published source of federal legislation that incorporates later amendments in one location with the original act.

Gaming regulations can be found on the website of the National Indian Gaming Commission (NIGC). Go to the site, at www. nigc.gov, and click on "Laws and Regulations," which links users to a site with the complete text of the Act. A direct website (April 1, 2000) for the IGRA is: www.4.law.cornell.edu/uscode/25/2701.text.

The Indian gaming regulations can also be located in libraries that receive federal documents at Title 25 of the Code of Federal Regulations, Part 501. A more direct website (April 1, 2000) for the regulations is www.4.law.cornell.edu/cfr/25cfrIII.

N-3. *What is the difference between the National Indian Gaming* **Commission** *and the National Indian Gaming* **Association?**

The Commission (see Question L-1) is a federal regulatory agency housed within the U.S. Department of the Interior. The Commission was created by the 1988 Indian Gaming Regulatory Act. Its stated mission is "to insure that Indian gaming is regulated, to shield it from organized crime and other corrupting influences, to insure that the Indian tribe is the primary beneficiary of the gaming operation and to insure that gaming is conducted fairly and honestly by both the operator and the player" (National Indian Gaming Commission 2000, "About the Commission," p. 1).

The Association, on the other hand, is a private nonprofit organization that was established in 1985. It has approximately 170 regular member tribes, and additional non-voting members representing other organizations, additional tribes, and businesses involved in Indian gaming. The common purpose of the Association and its membership is to "advance the lives of Indian peoples economically, socially and politically" (National Indian Gaming Association 2000, "About NIGA," p. 1). The Association also strives to serve "as a clearinghouse and educational, legislative, and public policy resource for tribes, policy makers, and the public on Indian gaming issues and tribal community development."

The NIGA states that its mission is "to protect and preserve the general welfare of tribes striving for self-sufficiency through gaming enterprises in Indian country." The Association endeavors to work with the federal government and Congress to develop sound gaming policies and practices and to provide technical assistance and advocacy on gaming-related issues. In addition, the NIGA seeks to protect the sovereignty of Indian governments within Indian country.

The National Indian Gaming Association is headquartered in Washington, D.C., and has two main telephone numbers: (202) 546-7711 and (800) 286-6442; the website is: www.indiangaming.org.

N-4. *What was the National Gambling Impact Study Commission?*

In August 1996, Congress passed the "National Gambling Impact Study Commission Act." In the "findings" section of the Act, Congress declared that:

1. the most recent Federal study of gambling in the United States was completed in 1976;
2. legalization of gambling has increased substantially over the past 20 years, and State, local and Native American tribal governments have established gambling as a source of jobs and additional revenue;
3. the growth of various forms of gambling, including electronic gambling and gambling over the Internet, could affect interstate and international matters under the jurisdiction of the Federal Government;
4. questions have been raised regarding the social and economic impacts of gambling, and Federal, State, local, and [N]ative American tribal governments lack recent, comprehensive information regarding those impacts; and
5. a Federal commission should be established to conduct a comprehensive study of the social and economic impacts of gambling in the United States. (National Gambling Impact Study Commission 2000a)

Section 3 of the Act established the nine-member commission. Three members each were chosen by the President, the Speaker of the House, and the majority leader of the Senate.

The Commission was charged with conducting a comprehensive factual and legal study of the social and economic impacts of gambling on the four levels of governments mentioned in the findings: federal, state, local, and tribal. It was also to study the impacts of gambling on communities and social institutions.

On June 18, 1999, the Commission completed its work and issued its final report and recommendations, which were delivered to the president, Congress, state governors, and tribal leaders. Sixty days later, as required by Section 10 of the Act, the Commission was terminated.

For more information on the Commission, the names and backgrounds of its nine members (including photographs), and its responsibilities, see the August 1997 issue of *American Indian Report*, which is published by the Falmouth Institute. Available in some libraries, it may also be obtained from the institute's editorial offices in Fairfax, Virginia, phone: (800) 992-4489 or (703) 352-2250; the website is: www.falmouthinst.com.

N-5. *What did the National Gambling Impact Study Commission finally report about Indian gaming, and what did it recommend?*

> *Federally-recognized Indian tribes are grouped under the legal status of "defeated nations." . . . These tribes, both as collective units and their individual members, are wards of the federal government.*
>
> National Gambling Impact Study Commission 2000b

The quote above indicates the commission's unfortunate ignorance about Indian country, despite the fact that one member was an Alaska Native. The commission's final report is far too lengthy to reproduce, or even adequately summarize here, but it is available on the internet at: www.ngisc.gov/reports/fullrpt.html.

In general, the majority of the commission felt that legalized gambling in the U.S. had grown much too far and too fast in little more than a decade, and it issued a call for a "pause" in gambling. The commission's final report was not seen as oppressive to Indian gaming. In fact, when compared to their findings on the non-Indian gaming industry, Indian gaming fared relatively well. Jacob Coin (Hopi), Executive Director of the National Indian Gaming Association, responded: "On balance, the tribes are pleased with the outcome. They [the commission] recognized tribal sovereignty, they recognized the tribes' right to engage in gaming for economic development, [and] they recognized the role of the National Indian Gaming Commission to regulate us" (Flowers 1999, p. 1). However, the commission did point out problems in (1) the definitions of Class II and Class III gaming, (2) the labor laws governing employees at Indian casinos, and (3) the means of resolving disputes over gaming between states and tribes.

The commission issued a total of 76 gaming and gaming-related recommendations (National Gambling Impact Study Commission 2000c). This unwieldy number of recommendations was reviewed by the public interest group "Stand Up For California" (2000) and summarized in 16 general recommendations:

1. All legal gambling should be restricted to those who are at least 21 years of age.
2. Betting on Collegiate and amateur events . . . [should be] banned altogether.
3. The Federal government should prohibit Internet gambling within the United States.
4. States should not allow the expansion of gambling into homes through technology, and should not allow the expansion of account wagering.
5. States should refuse to allow the introduction of casino style gambling into parimutuel facilities.
6. States, tribal governments, and parimutuel facilities should ban credit card cash advance machines from their premises.
7. There should be a ban on aggressive gambling promotion strategies, especially those that target people in impoverished neighborhoods, or youth anywhere.
8. State lotteries are urged to reduce their sales dependence on low-income neighborhoods.
9. There should be enforceable advertising guidelines, and application of the federal truth-in-advertising laws, to include Indian gambling operations and state lotteries.
10. States should not authorize any further convenience gambling operations, and should cease and roll back existing operations.
11. There should be warnings required regarding the dangers and risks of gambling, as well as the odds of success where feasible. And, these should be posted in prominent locations in all gambling facilities.
12. Comprehensive gambling impact statements (somewhat like environmental impact statements) should be developed prior to decision making for new or enlarged forms of gambling.
13. Gamblers should have procedures for "voluntary self-exclusion" from gambling facilities.

14. States should adopt tight restrictions on contributions to state and local campaigns by gambling entities.
15. There needs to be future research into the effects of gambling on family members, to include, but not be limited to, issues of divorce, spousal and child abuse, severe financial instability, and suicide.
16. There should be much broader research into the social, personal, economic, and crime-related costs of gambling.

Indian gaming recommendations

The commission also issued 15 specific recommendations for the Indian gaming industry:

6.1 The Commission acknowledges the central role of the National Indian Gaming Commission (NIGC) as the lead federal regulator of tribal government gambling. The Commission encourages the Congress to assure adequate NIGC funding for proper regulatory oversight to ensure integrity and fiscal accountability. The Commission supports the NIGC's new Minimum Internal Control Standards, developed with the help of the National Tribal Gaming Commissioners and Regulators, as an important step to ensure such fiscal accountability. The Commission recommends that all Tribal Gaming Commission work ensures that the tribal gambling operations they regulate meet or exceed these Minimum Standards, and that the NIGC focus special attention on tribal gambling operations struggling to comply with these and other regulatory requirements.

6.2 The Commission recommends that the IGRA's classes of gambling be clearly defined so that there is no confusion as to what forms of gambling constitute Class II and Class III gambling activities. Further, the Commission recommends that Class III gambling activities should not include any activities that are not available to other persons, entities or organizations in a state, regardless of technological similarities. Indian gambling should not be inconsistent with the state's overall gambling policy.

6.3 The Commission recommends that labor organizations, tribal governments, and states should voluntarily work together to ensure the enforceable right of free association—including the right to organize and bargain collectively—for employees of tribal casinos. Further, the Commission recommends that Congress should enact legislation establishing such worker rights only if there is not substantial voluntary progress toward this goal over a reasonable period of time.

6.4 The Commission recommends that tribal governments, states and, where appropriate, labor organizations, should work voluntarily together to extend to employees of tribal casinos the same or equivalent (or superior) protections that are applicable to comparable state or private-sector employees through federal and state employment laws. If state employee protections are adopted as the standard for a particular tribal casino, then they should be those of the state in which the tribal casino is located. Further, the Commission recommends that Congress should enact legislation providing such protections only if there is not substantial voluntary progress toward this goal over a reasonable period of time.

6.5 The Commission recognizes that under IGRA, Indian tribes must annually report certain proprietary and non-proprietary tribal government gambling financial information to the NIGC, through certified, independently audited financial statements. The Commission recommends that certain aggregated financial, Indian gambling data from reporting tribal governments, comparable by class to the aggregated financial data mandatorily collected from commercial casinos and published by such states as Nevada and New Jersey, should be published by the National Indian Gaming Commission annually. Further, the Commission recommends that the independent auditors should also review and comment on each tribal gambling operation's compliance with the Minimum Internal Control Standards (MICS) promulgated by the NIGC.

6.6 The Commission recommends that, upon written request, a reporting Indian tribe should make immediately available to any enrolled member the annual, certified, independently audited financial statements and compliance review of the MICS submitted to the NIGC. A tribal member should be able to inspect such financial statements and compliance reviews at the tribal headquarters or request that they be mailed.

6.7 The Commission recommends that tribal and state sovereignty should be recognized, protected, and preserved.

6.8 The Commission recommends that all relevant governmental gambling regulatory agencies should take the rapid growth of commercial gambling, state lotteries, charitable gambling, and Indian gambling into account as they formulate policies, laws, and regulations pertaining to legalized gambling in their jurisdictions. Further, the Commission recommends that all relevant governmental gambling regulatory agencies should recognize the long overdue economic development Indian gambling can generate.

6.9 The Commission has heard substantial testimony from tribal and state officials that uncompacted tribal gambling has resulted in substantial litigation. Federal enforcement has, until lately, been mixed. The Commission recommends that the federal government fully and consistently enforce all provisions of the IGRA.

6.10 The Commission recommends that tribes, states, and local governments should continue to work together to resolve issues of mutual concern rather than relying on federal law to solve problems for them.

6.11 The Commission recommends that gambling tribes, states, and local governments should recognize the mutual benefits that may flow to communities from Indian gambling. Further, the Commission recommends that tribes should enter into reciprocal agreements with state and local governments to mitigate the negative effects of the activities that may occur in other communities and to balance the rights of tribal, state and local governments, tribal members, and other citizens.

6.12 IGRA allows tribes and states to negotiate any issues relating to gambling. Nothing precludes voluntary agreements to deal with issues unrelated to gambling either within or without compacts. Many tribes and states have agreements for any number of issues (e.g., taxes, zoning, environmental issues, natural resources management, hunting and fishing, etc.). The Commission recommends that the federal government should leave these issues to the states and tribes for resolution.

6.13 The Commission recommends that Congress should specify a constitutionally sound means of resolving disputes between states and tribes regarding Class III gambling. Further, the Commission recommends that all parties to Class III negotiations should be subject to an independent, impartial decisionmaker who is empowered to approve compacts in the event a state refuses to enter into a Class III compact, but only if the decision-maker does not permit any Class III games that are not available to other persons, entities, or organizations of the state and only if an effective regulatory structure is created.

6.14 The Commission recommends that Congress should adopt no law altering the right of tribes to use existing telephone technology to link bingo games between Indian reservations when such forms of technology are used in conjunction with the playing of Class II bingo games as defined in the IGRA.

6.15 The Commission recommends that tribal governments should be encouraged to use some of the net revenues from Indian gambling as "seed money" to further diversify tribal economies and to reduce their dependence on gambling.

The National Gambling Impact Study Commission's 1999 recommendations are important because they will directly and indirectly affect the $200 billion-a-year legalized gambling industry in America, including Indian gaming, for at least two decades.

SECTION O: THE FUTURE

What is the greatest issue facing American Indians in the future?

The major issues we face now are [about] *survival . . .*

N. Scott Momaday, Kiowa
In Nabokov 1991, p. 438

Of course Momaday is correct, and when he talks about survival, he means two kinds—environmental and cultural.

Environmental survival

This subject is common to us all, as we face what some have chosen to describe as the end of nature. Without denying the seriousness of the many Native issues that require ongoing attention, it is absolutely clear that, unless the planet's immense environmental problems are solved, all other concerns, save nuclear conflagration, won't matter.

> *Respect the Earth or all is a waste.*
>
> *Lakota Times*
> June 3, 1992
>
> *I think we're on the brink of disaster on many fronts. . . . At one time I was more optimistic than I am now, but I think we have to operate on hope, that it is possible to reverse this march toward annihilation that we have begun on the nuclear front and on the ecological front. . . . We're very comfortable. We have committed ourselves to a technological society in such a way that it is hard for us to understand that we are . . .* [destroying the world]. *We know we are, but we have a tendency to think that we are so intelligent as a people and we have achieved such a high degree of civilization that the solutions will come about in the course of time. That's a dangerous attitude.*
>
> N. Scott Momaday, Kiowa
> Nabokov 1991, p. 437

> *The* [white men's] *love of possessions is a disease among them.*
>
> Sitting Bull, Lakota
>
> *Because of the almighty dollar, I guess we've kind of grown apart....*
> *I don't think we can leave our culture behind as we move forward*
> *economically.*
>
> George Bennett, Chairman, Grand Traverse
> Band of Ottawa and Chippewa Indians
> *In* O'Brien 2000b, p. 1
>
> *The lesson which seems so hard to learn is that of dignity and*
> *respect.... The land itself must be seen to have a measure of dignity*
> *and respect and when it does not receive these accommodations,*
> *human beings who live on the land are accordingly incomplete.*
>
> Vine Deloria, Jr.
> (1991, p. xviii and xix)

At the time of the first Earth Day in 1970, many of us naively thought the overall environmental problem had hit bottom and that the only direction we could reasonably choose to travel from there was up. Instead, following the "me generation" of the 1970s and the selfish decade of the 1980s, things have deteriorated much more than anyone in 1970 would have wanted to imagine. We are now regularly updated by the media with stories that essentially go like this: "Remember how very bad we said it was a little while back? Well, we were wrong. It's much worse."

In early October 1991, Oren Lyons, an Onondaga elder, appeared in an interview on a segment of the CBS television magazine "Sunday Morning." Describing his concerns about environmental degradation, he first made the point that there is plenty of blame to be shared by "all of us." He went on to make a very graphic statement summarizing the effect of environmental damage on the future. He simply said, "We have taken our grandchildren by the hair, tilted their heads back, and slit their throats."

This statement startles and even offends some people. But, unless the reality that caused its expression startles and offends them—and the rest of us—even more, we will continue to go precipitously down the road to virtual destruction of the world's biosphere.

Potentially, the *one* issue over which Indian and non-Indian Americans can most strongly come together—and through which we can positively contribute to each others' futures—is environmental cleanup and protection.

> The days of tea-and-crumpets conservation are over. We are talking about deadly issues here, issues that necessitate a most courageous, sweeping, and accelerated solution in order for the world's environment to be fit for habitation. . . .
>
> The causes of the environmental crisis are well-known, as are the solutions. . . . [K]ey social institutions, primarily national governments, lack the direction and high level of motivation necessary to implement solutions. It is therefore imperative, and exceedingly appropriate . . . that "We the People" of the world's nations [including the Indian nations] begin to resolutely provide our leaders with the strong motivation and direction so desperately needed.
>
> Utter, Valen, and Cantu 1989

In the new millennium, we must honestly admit that we continue to give mere lip service to most environmental issues. We know the direction we're headed in, and if there is no reversal, Oren Lyons's words could prove prophetic.

Cultural survival

N. Scott Momaday, Kiowa, provides a poignant answer to the question on the survival of American Indian culture:

> Part of [survival] is how to remain Indian, how to assimilate without ceasing to be an Indian. I think some important strides have been made. Indians remain Indian, and against pretty good odds. They remain Indian and, in some situations, by a thread. Their languages are being lost at a tremendous rate, poverty is rampant, as is alcoholism. But still there are Indians, and the traditional world is still intact. . . . It's a matter of identity. It's thinking about who I am. I grew up on Indian reservations, and

then I went away from the Indian world and entered a different context. But I continue to think of myself as Indian, I write out of this conviction. I think this is what most Indian people are doing today. They go off the reservations, but they keep an idea of themselves as Indians. That's the trick.

In Nabokov 1991, p. 438

PART III

A SUMMARY HISTORY

OF

UNITED STATES INDIAN POLICY

One of the enduring issues facing the government and the people of the United States through two centuries of existence is the place of American Indians in American society.

Francis Paul Prucha 1985
In *The Indians in American Society*

History is the essential foundation for an understanding of American Indian law and policy.

American Indian Lawyer Training Program 1988

COLONIAL BEGINNINGS

At its earliest stages, United States Indian policy was most directly influenced by two things: (1) former policies of the British Empire and (2) Indian-U.S. conflicts of the Revolutionary War (Prucha 1985).

British policies toward Indians in what is now U.S. territory evolved over more than a century and a half, from the time of the empire's first permanent settlement in North America in 1607 to the American takeover. Unlike the Spanish, who relied heavily on Native labor and economic activity in their colonization of the Western Hemisphere, the British did not consider indigenous people as particularly necessary to colonial life (United States Commission on Civil Rights 1981). During most of their tenure, the British viewed the Indians that were under their influence as trading partners and as potential allies against the ambitions of other European powers. When international intrigue grew during the early- and mid-1700s, however, the Indian tribes were seen to represent a strong balance of power among Spain, France, and England (Bureau of Indian Affairs 1975). Accordingly, the tribes were treated as sovereign nations with whom binding agreements could be made for the benefit of the signatory tribes and European powers.

> *European states were obliged to respect Indian sovereignty and utilize the practice of diplomacy to form consensual relations. The hallmark of the epoch was the treaty process. Seventeenth- and eighteenth-century treaties, in the aggregate, bear compelling witness to the presence of Indian nations as independent actors on the international plane.*
>
> Howard Berman, professor of
> international law (1992, p.187)

Until 1755, each of the English colonies had its own policy on Indian affairs. In that year, however, control over Indian affairs was placed directly under the British government. This was in response to competing policies of the French, who were attracting the loyalties of frontier tribes. The British government established a policy intended to (1) protect the tribes from unscrupulous traders and speculators,

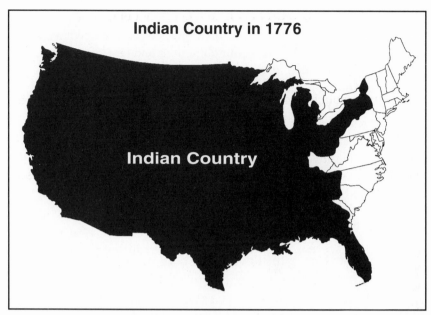

Figure 12. The shaded area was considered to be Indian country at the time of the American Revolution. An earlier boundary line, proclaimed in 1763 by King George III of England, ran along the Appalachian crest. It lay somewhat to the east of the boundary shown here.

(2) negotiate boundaries by treaties, (3) enlist tribes on the side of the British in the French and Indian War, and (4) exercise as much control over the fur trade as possible (Bureau of Indian Affairs 1975).

Shortly after the conclusion of the French and Indian War, King George III issued the Proclamation of 1763. It established a boundary along the crest of the Appalachian Mountains, separating "Indian country" to the west from the white settlement territory to the east. (See Figure 12.) The proclamation represented, for the first time in the history of European colonization of the hemisphere, the concrete formalization of the concept of Indian land titles. It prohibited issuance of colonial patents to any lands claimed by a tribe unless the Indian or "aboriginal" title had first been extinguished by treaty or purchase. This policy remained in effect through the end of British rule and set the tone for some of the subsequent U.S. approach.

> And whereas it is just and reasonable, and essential to our interest, and the security of our colonists, that the several nations or

tribes of Indians, with whom we are connected, and who live under our protection, should not be molested or disturbed in the possession of such parts of our dominions and territories as, not having been ceded to, or purchased by us, are reserved to them or any of them, as their hunting grounds; we do therefore . . . declare it to be our royal will and pleasure, that no governor . . . do presume, upon any pretense whatever, to grant warrants of survey, or pass any patents for lands beyond the bounds of their respective governments, . . . or upon any lands whatever, which not having been ceded to, or purchased by us, as aforesaid, are reserved to the said Indians, or any of them.

Proclamation of 1763
In O'Brien 1989, p. 48

In the first years of the Revolution, both sides wanted to keep the friendship of the tribes. The British were able to enlist much Indian support because the royal policies offered greater protection for Indian lands. Siding with the British was, therefore, seen by many tribes as siding against the land-grabbing frontiersmen. The enmity that developed during the fighting of the Revolution continued to influence some of the bureaucrats and politicians who later shaped Indian policy in the early years after the war (Horsman 1988).

THE U.S. LEGACY

Numerous works have been published to describe the complex and often fickle history of federal Indian policy. Some are extremely detailed and serve the scholar well (e.g., Prucha 1984). Others are more appropriate as introductory summaries of the subject matter. One such summary has been selected for use as the core of this third part of the book and is reproduced here almost in its entirety. The material is taken directly from the second chapter of a report by the United States Commission on Civil Rights (1981), and it makes up the first six sections of the U.S. Legacy. This is supplemented with additional information from Canby 1998; the Falmouth Institute 1992; Getches, Wilkinson, and Williams 1998; Prucha 1986 and 1990b; and Washburn 1975. The final section, "Self-Determination: Post-1960," represents my effort to update this brief summary of U.S. Indian policy to the year 2000.

Early United States-Indian Relations: 1776–1820

Conflict regarding relations with Indian tribes was not resolved by the outcome of the Revolutionary War. The United States replaced the Crown, and the States replaced the colonies, but the issue of local versus national interest and control was not settled. The newly formed Continental Congress reserved to itself the power of "managing all affairs with the Indians not members of any of the States," but also provided that the "legislative right of any State, within its own limits, be not infringed" (Articles of Confederation 1781). This essentially codified a dichotomy between national and local views on Indian affairs.

Both the emerging central government and the states agreed that the Indians were needed as allies in the Revolutionary War. As a military imperative they sought to maintain friendly relations with as many tribes as possible. By 1778 the American government had negotiated its first written treaty, with the Delawares.

The role of the central government with respect to the tribes and the policy it would follow toward them was a much debated issue in revolutionary times. George Washington played an important role in formulating policy and made clear in his writings that the Federal Government would need to intercede on behalf of the tribes:

> To suffer a wide extended Country to be over run with Land Jobbers, Speculators, and Monopolisers or even with scattered settlers, is, in my opinion, inconsistent with that wisdom and policy which our true interest dictates, or that an enlightened People ought to adopt and, besides, is pregnant of disputes both with the Savages, and among ourselves, the evils of which are easier, to be conceived than described; and for what? but to aggrandize a few avaricious Men to the prejudice of many, and the embarrassment of Government.
>
> Washington 1783

The policy that General Washington would ultimately recommend was both pragmatic and coldly racist:

> I am clear in my opinion, that policy and economy point very strongly to the expediency of being upon good terms with the Indians, and the propriety of purchasing their Lands in preference to attempting to drive them by force of arms out of their Country; which as we have already experienced is like driving

Wild Beasts of the Forest which will return as soon as the pursuit
is at an end and fall perhaps on those that are left there; when
the gradual extension of our Settlements will as certainly cause
the Savage as the Wolf to retire; both being beasts of prey tho
they differ in shape. . . . In a word there is nothing to be obtained
by an Indian War but the Soil they live on and this can be had
by purchase at less expence, and without that bloodshed.

Washington 1783

Washington's advice, accepted by a Nation that was exhausted
and weak, was codified as a proclamation of the Continental Congress
on September 22, 1783. The Ordinance for the Regulation of Indian
Affairs followed in 1786, and in 1787, the Northwest Ordinance. This
often quoted and much violated document expresses the following:

The utmost good faith shall always be observed towards the
Indians; their lands and property shall never be taken from them
without their consent; and, in their property, rights, and liberty,
they shall never be invaded or disturbed, unless in just and lawful wars authorized by Congress; but laws founded in justice
and humanity shall from time to time be made for preventing
wrongs being done to them, and for preserving peace and
friendship with them.

When the Revolutionary War ended in 1783, the United States
embarked on a round of treaties with its former allies as well as with
the tribes that had aligned themselves with the British. The United
States Constitution, ratified in 1789, confirmed the federal role in
Indian policy by assigning Congress the authority to involve itself in
Indian affairs. Through the treaty process the United States would
acquire both lands and legal responsibilities; the tribes would cede
lands and obtain federal commitments in return. It was believed to
be in the clear interest of both the United States Government and the
Indian nations, under the military circumstances of the era, to live
without war and by contract. Between the end of the French and
Indian War (1763) and the end of the War of 1812, the Indian nations
were said to have been made *secure* in the use and occupancy of their
lands. But what this really meant was that the U.S. was secure in its
ability to eventually take those lands. The tribes "in effect parlayed
their claims to land into claims for services from the new American

government" (Kickingbird and Ducheneaux 1973). The treaty process would continue for almost a hundred years and would acquire millions of acres of land for the U.S. Government to provide to non-Indian settlers. The treaties also built a reservoir of material and political promises to the tribes.

The quest for land for the use of non-Indian settlers took on new impetus at the turn of the 19th century. The Louisiana Purchase in 1803 and the acquisition of Florida in 1812–1819 doubled the United States in size. With this expansion, coupled with the consolidation of military and political strength by the new government and the development of the philosophy of "manifest destiny," Indian tribes faced a dramatic and damaging change in Federal Indian policy.

> *When the United States came into being, it joined a political reality and a received tradition that determined the practice of its relations with Indian nations. In seeking to consolidate its own political existence, one of the first imperatives for the United States was the negotiation of treaties of peace with many of the same Indian nations that had been actively involved in European diplomacy and whose hostility posed a serious threat to the stability of the new state. Indeed, many of those same Indian nations continued to maintain independent relations with European powers until the end of the Napoleonic era [1815], despite United States claims of territorial superiority.*
>
> Berman 1992, p. 187

The Removal Era: 1820–1850

Beginning with Spain's withdrawal from the U.S.'s newly-acquired Florida, the eastern tribes, particularly those in Georgia, faced rapidly increasing pressures from state and local authorities to give up their lands and political status. Major court battles were fought. (See *Cherokee Nation v. Georgia* 1831 and *Worcester v. Georgia* 1832.) Influential leaders of the day proposed moving the eastern tribes to the western territories. In the early 1800s Thomas Jefferson proposed a constitutional amendment to exchange the Indian land east of the Mississippi for land west of that boundary. This amendment failed, but congressional authorization was obtained on the same question in 1804. The western area to which Indians were to be moved was then considered uninhabitable by white people.

The political-military realities between the tribes and the United States had shifted by this period, and the tribes were unable to resist removal. The euphemistic "exchange of lands" began in 1817 and continued until mid-century. Thousands of Indian people, including nearly the entire Indian population that had existed in the southeastern United States, were moved west. (See Map 13.) The first major removal treaty was the Treaty of Doak's Stand (1820) with the Choctaws. The first removal treaty to follow passage of the Indian Removal Act of 1830, however, was the Treaty of Dancing Rabbit Creek, also with the Choctaw Nation (1830). Although removal was theoretically based on the consent of those removed, it is clear that the eastern tribes were coerced. The ideal of "progress" was invoked to rationalize the forced migrations as inevitable and to obscure the material greed of American expansionism. This period has been described as one of the blackest chapters in American history:

> Tens of thousands of helpless Indians, many of whom had white blood, were wholly or partly civilized, and owned homes, livestock, and farms, suffered incredible hardships. . . . All their efforts to halt or reverse the government's policy failed, and in the end almost all the members of each of the tribes were removed to different areas in the present State of Oklahoma. Some of them went reluctantly but without defiance; others went in chains. Most of them streamed westward under the watchful eyes of troops who made sure that they kept moving.
>
> Josephy 1968, p. 323

Some tribes did remain in the East. The U.S. for the most part, however, acted from this time on as if no Indians existed east of the Mississippi.

The assimilationist movement grew in tandem with the policy of removal. Thomas Jefferson was one of the major supporters of the view that, with adequate resources and coaxing, Indians could be "civilized" and live in harmony with their white neighbors. The responsibility of civilizing Indians fell to the various benevolent societies and missionary organizations. Until the end of the War of 1812 the missionary effort had been hampered by a lack of funding and no clear sense

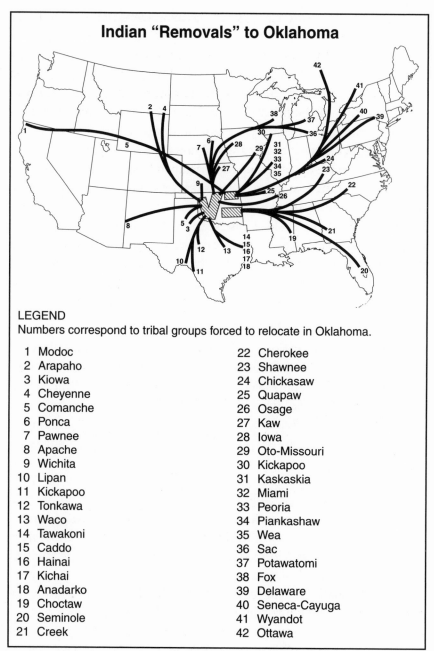

Figure 13. Major "removals" or relocations of Indians to Oklahoma ("Indian Territory") from all across the United States are indicated on this map. Tribal groups were forced to relocate in Oklahoma, beginning in 1817 and continuing into the 1880s.

of direction. The change in national mood accompanying removal led to the establishment in 1819 of a Civilization Fund, which provided an annual appropriation from Congress to these organizations and gave impetus to the assimilationist movement. The removal period saw the massive movement of missionary stations to west of the Mississippi. From this vantage the missionaries "directed their attention to Indians indigenous to the Indian territory as well as to regaining the confidence of their former eastern charges" (Berkhofer 1967, p. 2).

Indians were seen as being historically anterior and morally inferior to Protestant Christian settlers, and with expectations of their demise as a people, there was pressure to "civilize" and Christianize them before it was too late. Large and small missions were strung out across America. They were to provide the Indians with European concepts of work, time, savings, and Christian orthodoxy to the end that "as tribes and nations the Indians must perish and live only as men!" (Berkhofer 1967, p. 7).

Mid-Century–Reservations and Wars: 1850–1887

Although land reservations had existed since colonial times, they did not become a primary ingredient in federal Indian policy until the mid-19th century. Reservations were defined as areas of land, usually within former Indian land holdings, that were set aside for the exclusive use and occupancy of individual tribes or groupings of tribes. Government policy had been to move the tribes westward from areas of white settlement into unsettled territories denoted as Indian country. Areas without white occupation and trade were to become scarce after the mid-19th century. Expansion brought newcomers to all parts of the continent. Wagon trains trekked to Oregon and California as early as 1841. Texas joined the Union in 1846, and the Treaty of Guadalupe Hidalgo in 1848 extended the United States' dominion to the Pacific.

The western tribes and the relocated eastern tribes were challenged for land and resources, such as Black Hills gold, by the new white settlers. The United States embarked on an aggressive policy of establishing Indian reservations by treaty. The treaties would secure land for the settlers, set aside preserves for the tribes, and once again promise material and political assistance to the tribes. Between 1853 and 1856, 52 treaties were negotiated, sometimes peacefully, sometimes not. The desperate saga of the Indian tribes of the Great Plains, the Northwest, and the Southwest has been told in detail elsewhere (Brown 1970). It is clear that in the taking of Indian lands any device that was deemed effective was used, including theft, fraud, deceit, and military force. Even those tribes that had been friendly toward the United States were unable to protect their lands.

Throughout the first half of the 19th century Indian tribes, individuals, and their allies had used the political and legal system of the United States to redress grievances. Sometimes this path proved effective. But even in the face of setbacks, the tribes continued to pursue constitutional mechanisms for grievances.

Congress established in 1855 a Court of Claims that allowed private parties to sue the United States for violations of contracts. A number of Indian tribes and individuals subsequently filed suits for treaty violations involving the taking of land. As the suits progressed, Congress perceived the danger of potential Indian claims and amended the Court of Claims statute to exclude those deriving from treaties. Another century would pass before any systematic process would be available for hearing claims of illegal land taking.

Nothing ultimately prevented the taking of Indian lands. Their holdings were reduced, and the tribes were placed firmly in the reservation system. Indians refusing to stay within reservation boundaries were dealt with by military measures. Reservation occupants were placed under total control of a federal agent-in-charge whose duty was to acculturate and foster the assimilation of the Natives. Christian churches also played a major role on reservations. President Ulysses Grant delegated to the churches the right to nominate Indian agents and direct educational activities on reservations. The direct result manifested itself in later years:

> [M]any reservations had come under the authority of what had amounted to stern missionary dictatorships whose fanatic zealousness had crushed Indian culture and institutions, suppressed religious and other liberties, and punished Indians for the least show of independence.
>
> Josephy 1968, p. 340

Assimilation and Allotment: 1887–1934

The drive to assimilate Indians into the mainstream of American life by changing their customs, dress, occupations, language, religion,

and philosophy has always been an element in federal-Indian relations. In the latter part of the 19th century and the early part of the
20th century, this assimilationist policy became dominant.

A major thrust of assimilation efforts was to educate Indians in
"American" ways. In 1879 the Carlisle Indian Training School was
established by a former military officer. Its philosophy of separating
Indian children totally from their Indian environment and forcing them
to adopt white ways became the basis for a widescale boarding school
movement that eventually removed thousands of Indian children from
their cultural settings and families. In addition, traditional tribal governing systems, particularly justice systems, came under strong attack
during this period. The Bureau of Indian Affairs established tribal police
forces and courts under the administrative control of its agents, the
reservation superintendents. These and other efforts were designed to
erode the power and influence of Indian leaders and traditions.
Everything "Indian" came under attack. Indian feasts, languages, certain
marriage practices, dances, and any practices by medicine or religious
persons were all banned by the Bureau of Indian Affairs.

The Great Sioux Nation was a focus of much of the assimilation
activity, and Black Hills gold provided much impetus for reducing
the size of the Sioux Reservation as non-Indians flocked by the thousands into South Dakota. The defeat of Custer and his troops at Little
Bighorn in 1876 was a direct outgrowth of the discovery of gold in
the Black Hills and tribal resistance to the miners who came seeking
it. The Sioux were ultimately forced to cede the Black Hills in 1876.
Pressure on the Sioux to give up more land continued up to the time
of the allotment legislation, and even then it did not end. In 1889 the
Great Sioux Nation was divided into six smaller, generally noncon-
tiguous reservations.

Concurrently, the Bureau of Indian Affairs banned Ghost Dancing.
The new Ghost Dance religion had gained prominence by promising
an Indian messiah. The 1890 Wounded Knee massacre is now clearly
understood as a tragic overreaction on the part of the United States in
its efforts to suppress Indian religious practices. Soldiers participating in the massacre, however, were awarded medals at the time.

The latter part of the 19th century was also a period when the
traditional Indian means of economic support were no longer viable.

Subsistence hunting and gathering, which had supported many nomadic tribes, were precluded by the advent of reservations and the mass destruction of wildlife, particularly buffalo, that had accompanied white westward expansion. Many tribes were forced into economic dependency and a dole system of goods and supplies operated by the Bureau of Indian Affairs. This period of economic hardship was accompanied by widespread and severe health problems.

Even those tribes whose economies were strong were unable to escape efforts to subjugate them. The Five Civilized Tribes, removed from the Southeast in the 1820s and 1830s, had organized themselves economically and politically in a manner similar to the American states and territories. By the latter part of the 19th century, these tribes were at least as self-sufficient as the states and territories, but they were nevertheless stripped of most of their governmental powers in 1898. (See the Curtis Act of 1898.)

All of these factors played critical roles in undermining tribal self-sufficiency, but the single most devastating development was the allotment system. Allotment was advocated as a means of further "civilizing" Indians by converting them from a communal land system to a system of individual ownership. It was argued that ownership would make farmers out of the "savages."

In 1887 Congress passed the General Allotment Act, also known as the Dawes Act. Although many other acts of Congress would follow, the general formula of the Dawes Act set the pattern for allotting Indian reservations. Each family head was to receive 160 acres, and a single person was to receive 80 acres. Title to the land was to be held in trust for at least 25 years. "Civilized" Indians could end the trust period and receive United States citizenship and fee simple title to their land. Citizenship would be unilaterally granted all Indians in 1924 by the Indian Citizenship Act. Surplus lands within the reservation boundaries, lands not allotted or otherwise set aside, were to be sold to the United States and then opened for homesteading. Proceeds from the sales were also to be placed in trust and used by the United States as an account for supplies provided to the Indians.

Allotment and other assimilationist practices received strong support from "friends" of the Indians. Many believed that these policies represented the only alternative to Indian extinction. Not everyone defended the policies of the government, however. Dissenters in

INDIAN LAND FOR SALE

GET A HOME
OF
YOUR OWN
⁂
EASY PAYMENTS

PERFECT TITLE
⁂
POSSESSION
WITHIN
THIRTY DAYS

FINE LANDS IN THE WEST

IRRIGATED
IRRIGABLE   **GRAZING**   **AGRICULTURAL**
DRY FARMING

IN 1910 THE DEPARTMENT OF THE INTERIOR SOLD UNDER SEALED BIDS ALLOTTED INDIAN LAND AS FOLLOWS:

Location.	Acres.	Average Price per Acre.	Location.	Acres.	Average Price per Acre.
Colorado	5,211.21	$7.27	Oklahoma	34,664.00	$19.14
Idaho	17,013.00	24.85	Oregon	1,020.00	15.43
Kansas	1,684.50	33.45	South Dakota	120,445.00	16.53
Montana	11,034.00	9.86	Washington	4,879.00	41.37
Nebraska	5,641.00	36.65	Wisconsin	1,069.00	17.00
North Dakota	22,610.70	9.93	Wyoming	865.00	20.64

FOR THE YEAR 1911 IT IS ESTIMATED THAT **350,000** ACRES WILL BE OFFERED FOR SALE

For information as to the character of the land write for booklet, "INDIAN LANDS FOR SALE," to the Superintendent U. S. Indian School at any one of the following places:

CALIFORNIA:	MINNESOTA:	NORTH DAKOTA:	OKLAHOMA—Con.	SOUTH DAKOTA:	WASHINGTON:
Hoopa.	Onigum.	Fort Totten.	Sac and Fox Agency.	Cheyenne Agency.	Fort Simcoe.
COLORADO:		Fort Yates.	Shawnee.	Crow Creek.	Fort Spokane.
Ignacio.	MONTANA:	OKLAHOMA:	Wyandotte.	Greenwood.	Tekoa.
IDAHO:	Crow Agency.	Anadarko.	OREGON:	Lower Brule.	Tulalip.
Lapwai.	NEBRASKA:	Cantonment.	Klamath Agency.	Pine Ridge.	WISCONSIN:
KANSAS:	Macy.	Colony.	Pendleton.	Rosebud.	Oneida.
Horton.	Santee.	Darlington.	Roseburg.	Sisseton.	
Nadeau.	Winnebago.	Muskogee, ⸤⸤ ⸥⸥	Siletz.		
		Pawnee.			

WALTER L. FISHER,
Secretary of the Interior.

ROBERT G. VALENTINE,
Commissioner of Indian Affairs.

Congress and elsewhere pointed out the underlying reality of the period: whites were securing vast quantities of Indian land.

Toward the end of the allotment period, the federal government commissioned a major study of conditions on Indian reservations. The study, known as the Meriam Report (1928), enumerated the disastrous conditions afflicting Indians at that time: high infant death

rates, high mortality rates for the entire population, appalling housing conditions, low incomes, poor health, and inadequate education.
The policy of forced assimilation was judged a failure. The failure
was that it had not worked. "It has resulted in much loss of land and
an enormous increase in the details of administration without a com-
pensating advance in the economic ability of the Indians" (Meriam
Report 1928, p. 41). But such criticism did not challenge ultimate
assimilationist goals.

> *If I stand alone in the Senate, I want to put upon the record my*
> *prophecy in this matter, that when thirty or forty years shall have*
> *passed and these Indians shall have parted with their* [land] *title,*
> *they will curse the hand that was raised professedly in their defense*
> *to secure this kind of legislation, and if the people who are clamor-*
> *ing for it understood Indian character, and Indian laws, and Indian*
> *morals, and Indian religion, they would not be here clamoring for*
> *this at all.*
>
> U.S. Senator Henry M. Teller of Colorado,
> in his unsupported January 20, 1881, speech
> against the allotment of Indian lands

In the wake of the damaging results of the reservation allotments
and assimilation efforts, some Indians moved to use the American
legal system on behalf of their people. By 1910 a small group of
Indian lawyers had emerged to do battle in the courts over the questions of Indian lands, citizenship, allotment procedures, and the
enforcement of treaty rights. Even though reservations were originally conceived of as a means to deprive Indians of their lands, they
represented the last remnants of Indian land and, as such, were held
sacred by the tribes. Despite the prison-like aspects of life on many
reservations, Indian advocates moved to protect this land base.

Indian Reorganization: 1934–1953

The Meriam Report and several other investigations produced major
changes in federal Indian practices. Federal policy would ultimately
favor restoration of some measure of tribal self-government and tribal
resources. The strategy was to use tribal culture and institutions as

transitional devices for the complete assimilation of Indian life into the dominant white society. The major instrument for this policy was the Indian Reorganization Act of 1934, which, with companion legislation affecting the Oklahoma tribes, essentially provided for an end to allotment, for measures to restore Indian land bases, and for establishment of a revolving credit fund to promote economic development. Also included were the regulation of resources, mechanisms for chartering and reorganizing tribal governments, and the establishment of an employment preference policy for Indians within the federal government.

The Indian Reorganization Act, however, did not go as far as its advocates would have liked, and several key features were not in the legislation as it finally was passed. The elements lost included an appellate Indian court system, mechanisms to assure tribal independence from bureaucratic control, and a national policy to promote and support the study and understanding of Indian cultures.

Another major development during this period was the passage by Congress of the Johnson-O'Malley Act (1934) as a means to promote federal and state cooperation in the provision of services to Indians, particularly in education. This development involved states more aggressively in Indian affairs and was a natural outgrowth of the Meriam Report's view that the federal government had performed poorly as a service provider and that the states had a better record.

Finally, during the Great Depression, the Department of the Interior assisted hundreds of tribes in drafting new constitutions, codes, and governmental structures. These efforts produced essentially standardized approaches promoted by Department of the Interior lawyers. Some land was purchased and returned to tribal control during this time, but the Indian land base remained essentially unaltered. This period for reviving tribal governments was a relatively short one.

The Termination Period: 1953–1968

Probing examination of the living conditions of Indians has periodically served as a stimulus to promote change in the manner in which the federal government deals with tribes. The United States Senate in 1943 conducted a survey of Indian conditions and found serious and troubling problems. The Bureau of Indian Affairs and federal bureaucracy were held culpable for these conditions. The administrative and financial costs of achieving slow progress toward assimilation were viewed as excessive.

Criteria began to be developed by the Commissioner of Indian Affairs to identify Indian tribal groups that could be removed from Federal aegis. The theory was that some tribes were sufficiently acculturated and that the federal protective role was no longer necessary. But another development of the same period suggests a less benign interpretation of events—some 133 separate bills were introduced in Congress to permit the transfer of trust land from Indian ownership to non-Indian ownership. There was also pressure to terminate particular tribes, such as the Klamaths, who possessed valuable timber resources, and the Agua Caliente, who owned much of the area in and around Palm Springs, California. In 1949, the Hoover Commission (although not established to deal with Indian issues) recommended the full and complete integration of Indians into American society.

In 1953 Congress officially adopted a policy of termination, indicating that its goal was: "as rapidly as possible, to make the Indians within the territorial limits of the United States subject to the same laws and entitled to the same privileges and responsibilities as are applicable to other citizens of the United States, [and] to end their status as wards of the United States" (House Concurrent Resolution 108). Federal Indian policy became a three-pronged program of: (1) termination of tribes over which federal responsibility was thought unnecessary, (2) transfer of federal responsibility and jurisdiction to state governments (e.g., under Public Law 280), and (3) physical relocation of Indian people from reservations to urban areas.

The three-pronged policy was aggressively carried out by Dillon Myer, former director of detention camps for Japanese Americans, who became the Commissioner of Indian Affairs in 1950. The Bureau of Indian Affairs, which had been a target of congressional criticism in 1943, grew in budget and staff as it administered terminationist policies. Between 1954 and 1962, statutes were passed authorizing the termination of 109 tribes, bands, or Indian rancherias. Most of those affected were small bands on the West Coast, but two sizable tribes, the Klamaths and Menominees, were also terminated. In all, approximately 12,000 individual Indians lost tribal affiliations that included political relationships with the United States. Approximately 2.5 million acres of Indian land were removed from protected status.

Self-Determination: After 1960

The foundations of the self-determination era can be traced back to the presidential election campaign of 1960 (Sanders 1985). Candidates John Kennedy and Richard Nixon both pledged there would be no change in treaty or contractual relationships without tribal consent. They also declared there would be protection of the Indian land base, credit assistance, and encouragement of tribal planning for economic development.

The newly-elected President Kennedy further promised the inclusion of Indians in legislative programs for segments of the nation's population that were depressed and impoverished. He also appointed Stewart Udall as Secretary of the Interior, and Udall promptly commissioned a task force on Indian affairs. The task force recommended a shift away from termination of the federal trust relationship and toward the development of human and natural resources in Indian country (Cohen 1982).

Kennedy's promise of Indian inclusion in social programs only began to take shape in a substantial way during President Johnson's administration. Johnson's "Great Society" programs made Indians an integral part of the expanding human concern of the times (Deloria and Lytle 1983). In 1968, President Johnson proposed

> . . . a new goal for our Indian programs: A goal that ends the old debate about "termination" of Indian programs and stresses self-determination; a goal that erases old attitudes of paternalism and promotes partnership self-help. (p. 336)

Also in 1968, the Indian Civil Rights Act was passed—the first major piece of legislation enacted during the post-termination era that dealt specifically with Indian matters. Although the Act received mixed reviews, the relevant and significant part of it prohibited states from assuming jurisdiction over Indian country, under Public Law 280, without first obtaining tribal consent (Deloria and Lytle 1983).

President Johnson came close to being the first federal official to formally repudiate the termination policy. It didn't happen under his administration, however. It was President Nixon, in a speech on July 8, 1970, who said:

> This policy of forced termination is wrong. . . . The special relationship between Indians and the Federal government is the

result . . . of solemn obligations which have been entered into by the United States Government. . . . To terminate this relationship would be no more appropriate than to terminate the citizenship rights of any other American. . . . Self-determination among the Indian people can and must be encouraged. . . . This, then, must be the goal of any new national policy toward the Indian people. . . . (p. 564–567)

President Nixon reinforced his message by declaring that it was necessary to strengthen Indian autonomy without any threat of ending federal concern and federal support. He asked Congress to repeal House Concurrent Resolution 108, passed in 1953, which embodied the termination mentality. Ironically, it took Congress 18 more years to *officially* repeal the resolution. This was accomplished through the addition of the following short paragraph to section 5203 of the Tribally Controlled Schools Act of 1988.

(f) TERMINATION.—The Congress hereby repudiates and rejects House Concurrent Resolution 108 of the 83rd Congress and any policy of unilateral termination of Federal relations with any Indian Nation.

Nixon also made a number of specific legislative recommendations. Following upon his urgings, along with those of growing numbers of Indian activists, traditional tribal leaders, and an American public that was reawakening to Native needs, a flurry of Indian legislation was passed into law in the 1970s.

Several pieces of legislation among the many passed during this period are notable because they are indicative of the change in federal policy from the days of termination. The Indian Education Act of 1972 set a statutory foundation for more comprehensive funding of Indian education and greater focus on Indian education at the local level (Sanders 1985). The act provided for special training programs for teachers of Indian students, for fellowships for students in certain fields of study, and for basic research in Indian education (Deloria and Lytle 1983). Not a panacea for the many problems in Indian education, it was a start in the right direction.

A second and very significant statute is the Indian Self-Determination and Education Assistance Act of 1975. It is often referred to in Indian country as "638" legislation, because it was passed as Public

Law 93-638. Through grants and contracts, the act, as amended, encourages tribes to assume responsibilities for federally funded Indian programs formerly administered by employees in the Departments of Education, Interior, and Health and Human Services. Tribes decide if they wish to participate in a particular program. If they do, then funds and management decisions are subject to tribal control. This is similar to the ways other local governments participate in federal revenue sharing programs. It means that participating tribal governments can now control their own housing, education, law enforcement, social service, health, and community development programs (American Indian Lawyer Training Program 1988; Cohen 1982; Kelly 1988; O'Brien 1989).

In 1978, Congress enacted two additional laws of major significance. The Indian Child Welfare Act addressed the long-standing problem in which as many as a third of Indian children were taken from their natural parents and adopted out to non-Indian parents pursuant to state adoption and guardianship laws. This act provided that many adoption and guardianship cases were to take place in tribal court, and it established a preference for Indian guardians over non-Indian guardians when Indian guardianship cases were heard in state courts. The second law, the American Indian Religious Freedom Act (AIRFA), while much less successful in its implementation, nonetheless recognized the government's obligation to maintain tribal cultural existence. Its language specifically recognized the importance of traditional Indian religious practices. Furthermore, it directed that all federal agencies were to make sure that their policies do not interfere with the free exercise of Native religions (American Indian Lawyer Training Program 1988; O'Brien 1989; Unger 1977).

The self-determination movement was accelerated through a series of decisions by the Supreme Court in the 1970s and early 1980s. The Court emphasized "Indian sovereignty" and the inherent power of tribes to assert their economic, political, and cultural authority in appropriate areas (Kelly 1988). (See, for example, *McClanahan v. Arizona State Tax Commission* 1973, *Santa Clara Pueblo v. Martinez* 1978, and *Merrion v. Jicarilla Apache Tribe* 1982.) Other sovereignty-related cases, however, limited tribal powers in various areas, such as law enforcement, regulation of hunting and fishing by non-Indians on non-Indian land within reservation boundaries (if no significant tribal interest is at stake), and litigation of reserved water rights barred by prior court decrees (American Indian Lawyer Training Program 1988). (See, for example, *Oliphant v. Suquamish Tribe* 1978, *Montana v. United States* 1982, and *Nevada v. United States* 1983.)

Overall, the 1980s represented an era of mixed outcomes for Indian self-determination, with some notable results on both the positive and negative sides. The Reagan administration gave strong vocal support for programs developed for Indian self-betterment and tribal development, but the number of these programs actually soon declined because of the administration's cutbacks (Waldman 1985). Still, the federal policies of the 1980s affirmed many of the sovereign powers of tribes and continued to enunciate the concept of a government-to-government relationship among the federal government, the states, and the tribes (Kelly 1988). During the decade, it became apparent that another dramatic shift to some "new" unilateral and damaging policy—akin to the old one of forced assimilation—was not going to happen anytime soon. The tribes, however, know to "never say never." The publicly stated, positive attitude of Congress and the administration toward the issue of self-determination and the trust relationship at the end of the 1980s was demonstrated by House Concurrent Resolution 331 (see Appendix 7), which was passed by the House of Representatives on October 4, 1988.

Although the controversial Indian Gaming Regulatory Act became law in 1988, it was not until the 1990s that the Act, its provisions, and its regulatory implementation began to be so hotly debated. Indian gaming business activities and related policies have become and will continue to be among the most public of issues on Indian policy in the 2000s. As the controversy rages, clashes will continue among the various governmental units—federal, state, and tribal—and private gaming entities. Each party with a vested interest will continue its attempts to acquire (or to maintain) a piece of the lucrative "economic pie" associated with gaming.

If another major "shift" in federal Indian policy is to occur in the new century, conflict over Indian gaming will no doubt be a major cause, but gaming is *not* the only Indian country issue. The more "common" issues from past years will still require serious attention, evaluation, and problem resolution. Major issues continue to include:

housing, health services, environmental concerns, AIDS awareness and prevention programs for the highly vulnerable communities in Indian country, economic development, education, natural resource protection and management, corruption in tribal government, basic issues of sovereignty and self-government, land rights, water rights, hunting and fishing rights, preference for Indians in contracting, alcohol and drug abuse programs, Indian youth at risk, federal recognition of unrecognized tribes, racism, Native suicide, mismanagement of trust accounts, crime and law enforcement, cultural and religious freedom, child welfare, tribal autonomy, sufficiency of government appropriations, general relations among federal, state, and tribal governmental units—including unresponsiveness of government at all levels.

The Joint Federal-State Commission on Policies and Programs Affecting Alaska Natives presented its findings and recommendations to Congress, the President, and the State of Alaska, and much non-gaming work needs to be done for the Native people of that state alone. Congress, the state, and Native people in Alaska need to work hard for policy changes on a grand scale that will address the serious socio-economic challenges faced by Alaska Natives.

Native Hawaiian rights and land claims are beginning to receive more attention in the new century. At the same time, conflict is developing over whether to (1) leave Native Hawaiian affairs under state control, (2) include their rights, land claims, and social services under federal Indian programs, or (3) develop a separate federal program or independent classification for their unique needs for status, culture, socio-political concerns, and a viable land base.

In 1989, after two years of investigation and hearings, the Special Committee on Investigations (a subcommittee of the Senate Select Committee on Indian Affairs) published its final, bipartisan report. The report was a general indictment of the handling of Indian affairs at all levels. Consider the following excerpts:

> We indeed found fraud, corruption and mismanagement pervading the institutions that are supposed to serve American Indians. (p. 4)

> Paternalistic federal control over American Indians has created a federal bureaucracy ensnarled in red tape and riddled with fraud, mismanagement and waste. Worse, the Committee found

that federal officials in every agency knew of the abuses but did little or nothing to stop them. (p. 5)

In every area it touches, the BIA is plagued with mismanagement. (p. 8)

Free from tough criminal laws and energetic prosecution, some tribal officials have engaged in corrupt practices. (p. 6)

Like so many of the federal agencies responsible for Indian affairs, mismanagement is pervasive at the Indian Health Service. . . . (p. 153)

Like other federal agencies involved in Indian preference contracting, HUD (U.S. Department of Housing and Urban Development) has been vulnerable to fraud and abuse, making it a haven for phony Indian companies that successfully bid contracts away from legitimate Indian firms. (p. 171)

Since Congress has ultimate responsibility for federal Indian policy, we in the Senate and House must accept the blame for failing to adequately oversee and reform Indian affairs. Rather than becoming actively engaged in Indian issues, Congress has demonstrated an attitude of benign neglect. (p. 7)

Needless to say, the report shook things up in Washington and in Indian country at the time, but it didn't really change things. Thus the 1989 report still seems timely today.

Besides reporting its findings, the committee had also called for some sweeping legislative changes in several areas and "A New Federalism for American Indians." The proposed foundation of the "New Federalism" was (1) the establishment of an Office of Federal-Tribal Relations (OFTR) within the Executive Office of the President and (2) negotiation by the OFTR, on behalf of the United States, of new formal agreements with federally recognized tribes to promote greater tribal self-government.

As frequently happens in big government, reactions to the report settled down, in many cases, after the initial jolt of publication. Even so, some agencies took major internal steps to address the shortfalls and accusations outlined in the report. Reform attempts were made within the BIA itself that are likely to continue for some time to come.

In fact, many observers have commented that the BIA now seems to be in perpetual reorganization.

In 1990, Secretary of the Interior Manuel Lujan formed an Advisory Task Force on reorganization of the BIA. The task force was composed of 36 tribal leaders, two Interior Department officials, and five BIA officials. This group held meetings in different parts of Indian country for several years. Among other things, it attempted to come up with an administrative design for an "ideal" Indian agency, to possibly replace some of the agency offices in the BIA's 12 geographically-defined administrative areas (Bureau of Indian Affairs 1991c). The task force, in its preliminary report, had proposed a revolutionary budget system, transferring more than 86 percent of BIA funds to tribal control (Anquoe 1992c). The tribes then controlled about 27 percent of the budget. Other suggested measures included staff cuts in the BIA and shifting of some BIA staff members to tribal employment, maximizing the distribution of funding, delegating more authority from Washington to field offices, increasing administrative flexibility at the tribe or agency level, and establishing an independent "National Indian Advisory Board." Congress, of course, did not fully approve implementation of the task force recommendations. However, some significant changes in BIA structure, funding and administrative functions came from Secretary Lujan's efforts.

Time will tell how well the BIA, other federal agencies with Indian responsibilities, and the Congress will respond to the policy challenges of the future.

TWO BRIEF POLICY PREDICTIONS

The Gaming Era

During an April 2000 conversation that I had with Phil Stago, Jr., a former long-time member of the White Mountain Apache Tribal Council, Phil remarked: "It's unfortunate, but the national and international images of Indian people seem to be focused on one or the other of two major stereotypes—the museum image, which is trapped in the 19th century, and the gaming image, which is much less flattering, mostly artificial, and is becoming more predominant."

I thought for a few moments and then replied that I remembered listening to KTNN (the Navajo Nation radio station) in the fall of '97, when they aired interviews with several British citizens. The interviews had originally been broadcast by the British Broadcasting Network (BBC). The BBC reporter in the interviews was doing some kind of impromptu survey of British perceptions of Indian gaming in America. The last person who was interviewed said, "I think the view of many of us in Britain is that nearly every American Indian owns a slot machine and a Cadillac." I told Phil that I thought the story underscored, very strongly, what he had said. He gave me a knowing yet frustrated look.

The British citizen's view indicates the rapidly and radically changing images of Indian country in the U.S. and elsewhere, due in part to the exponential growth of gaming over the past decade. In light of the changing images, and the changes in public and political attitudes that go along with them, it is difficult to imagine that there will not eventually be another major shift, or "backlash" of some kind, in federal Indian policy that is fueled by widely held stereotypical views of Indian gaming.

A sterotyped Indian country image of privileged casino operators will make it easier for non-Indians to change federal Indian law and policy in more than the gaming arena, because there will be much less guilt on the part of the larger society if it chooses to further reduce or even eliminate tribal autonomy. It is important to remember that the United States has *never* allowed Indian country to have an advantage in anything for an extended period of time.

The desire of many non-Indian interests to share in the dollars that are now going to the gaming tribes is bound to contribute to significant modifications in gaming laws and in federal attitudes toward Indian country. These modifications will probably lead to reductions in sovereignty and reversals of the advances in self-determination that have occurred since the 1960s. Ideas like tribal sovereignty and *real* self-determination will likely be considered too quaint, archaic, and economically inconvenient for a modern America that has married itself to an exploding world economy.

> *Indian tribes have always been at risk when the avaricious urges of the nation desired their . . . resources, whether they be land, water, minerals from the earth, or gambling.*
>
> Dale Mason (Mason 2000, p. 236)
>
> *Our adversaries have used the illusion of rich Indians to justify cutting BIA and IHS budgets to the bone and reducing funds available to even the neediest tribes.*
>
> Kevin Gover, Pawnee,
> Assistant Secretary of the Interior for Indian Affairs
> from a speech made October 20, 1998

Euro-American capitalism is ultimately what crushed the tribes from the "outside." I have been told by a number of elder tribal members that capitalism and consumerism and their joint influence on Indian people and their governments—if not culturally counterbalanced—will also crush what is left from the "inside."

My Indian country contemporaries frequently complain that without a very strong counterbalance, Indian nations may, over time, remain genetically Indian, but will culturally and philosophically cease to be. If this occurs, it will not be so much the fault of Indian people, but a tribute to the success and overwhelming power of the larger society in its relentless obsession to assimilate American Indians, even when politically correct "self-determination" policies are espoused.

Phil Stago makes it clear that the highly capitalistic Indian gaming enterprises, in and of themselves, are not bad. He points out that gaming revenues provide Indian tribes with opportunities long denied them, "and the dollars also help tribes overcome the great poverty that has haunted Indian people since the coming of the white man." But Phil hastens to add that "unless American Indian governments and their citizens can still 'think like Indians' as they engage in gaming enterprises and other aspects of a modern economy, they may lose the ability to do so."

If gaming and nongaming tribes are to survive as distinct sovereign entities, it will probably be necessary for them to have perpetually activist governments and "mixed" economies that balance *capitalism* with *tribalism*.

Judicial termination

Today many Indian nations are obviously concerned about the debate over gaming, about new types of regulations that might be passed by Congress, and about several perceived "enemies" of Indian country in the Congress who are actively proposing major policy changes in such areas as Indian gaming regulation and tribal sovereign immunity. What is equally important, however, and what seems to get much less attention from rank-and-file members of the public and the media, is the profound role and cumulative impact of the Supreme Court on federal Indian law.

The Supreme Court under Chief Justice William Rehnquist deserves particularly close scrutiny of its actions in the arena of federal Indian law, because it has been relatively destructive to tribes.

> *Although Congress has rejected the policy of termination, Rehnquist and the Court seem to have adopted it. Chief Justice Rehnquist has made it his policy to chip away at the sovereignty of Indian nations. His policy contradicts not only the will of Congress, but also a long line of Supreme Court decisions affirming inherent tribal sovereignty. . . . An examination of the Chief Justice's opinions in each of* [the key subject areas relating to sovereignty and the trust relationship] *illustrates the devastating impact his legal philosophy has had, and continues to have, on Indians. . . .*
> *One can only hope that Rehnquist loses his majority* [on the court] *before his judicial agenda completely devastates tribal sovereignty.*
>
> Ralph Johnson and Berrie Martinis,
> Indian law attorneys (1995, p. 7–8, 25)

I agree with Johnson and Martinis that the judicial termination activity of the Rehnquist Court is likely to continue. Although Chief Justice Rehnquist will eventually leave the Court, his influence will not, nor will the damaging decisions that have and will result from the Court he oversees. The decisions will stand as precedents, ready to rise and strike down future efforts by tribes to protect their sovereignty. Tribes will have to take the initiative to force any change.

> *What is absolutely necessary now and in the future is the kind of determined activism that many Indian country leaders have displayed since first contact with Europeans. Modern-day Sitting Bulls, Geronimos, Josephs, Annie Waunekas, and Crazy Horses—Indian people with 'attitudes' for their nations—are needed.*
>
> Phil Stago, Jr., White Mountain Apache
>
> *No matter how well-intentioned we are in Washington, no matter how dedicated we are, all too often, the solutions we make are the wrong ones.*
>
> Senator Daniel K. Inouye, in a fall 1999 speech
on "Building American Indian Nations,"
Tucson, Arizona

The future of "Sovereignty Man"

In 1970 the Hollywood movie *Little Big Man*, with Dustin Hoffman in the lead role, was released to rave reviews by non-Indian critics. It was also received with widespread appreciation in Indian country, despite the fact that a few of the "Indian" actors were Italians or Hispanics wearing less-than-real wigs. The main character was Jack Crabb, also known as "Little Big Man," who, at 121 years of age, claimed to be the sole non-Indian survivor of Custer's Last Stand.

The film is based on Crabb's narrative of his colorful life on the plains, his adoption by Cheyenne Indians, his multiple marriages, his encounters with Custer, his friendship with Wild Bill Hickock, and the tragic drama of the so-called "war for the plains" in the 1860s and 1870s.

One of the characters who drifts in and out of the film at strategic times is an odd pioneer figure who is part entrepreneur, part opportunist, and part showman. He goes by the name of Mr. Meriweather. I have begun to refer to Mr. Meriweather as "Sovereignty Man," not because of his philosophy, but because of the things that happen to him over the course of the film. Meriweather suffers a series of losses that serve as a metaphor for what I have seen happening to tribal sovereignty over the last 25 years.

Mr. Meriweather is driven by his never-ending desire to profit in the economic invasion of the American West. Each time he shows up, he is missing another body part—lost to the dangerous world in which he lives. But he always shrugs it off. At first he has lost his left ear. Then his left hand. Next an eye is missing. In his final appearance, Meriweather has lost a leg and is walking on an ivory peg. At this point Dustin Hoffman's down-and-out drunken character, Jack Crabb, looks up while sitting hip deep in mud in a rain-soaked alley, and says, "You better watch out Mr. Meriweather. They're whittlin' you down pretty serious. You can't afford to lose any more of your parts." The same is true for tribal sovereignty.

> *By any objective standard, the doctrine of tribal sovereignty is a badly leaking ship in need of urgent repairs.*
>
> Russel Lawrence Barsh, Indian
> law attorney (1994, p. 55)
>
> *Great nations, like great men, should keep their promises.*
>
> Supreme Court Justice Hugo Black's famous dissent remark in
> *Federal Power Commission v. Tuscarora Indian Nation* (1960)

APPENDIX 1

BACKGROUND ON NATIVE HAWAIIAN ISSUES

[The opinion of the United States is] *that the Government of the* [Hawaiian] *Islands ought to be respected, that no power ought either to take possession of the islands as a conquest, or for the purpose of colonization, and that no power ought to seek for any undue control over the existing Government, or any exclusive privileges or preferences in matters of commerce.*

U.S. Secretary of State Webster, 1842
(Cohen 1982, p. 799)

Native Hawaiians are descended from Polynesians who arrived in the Islands between 1,000 and 1,500 years ago. By the time Captain James Cook first landed in 1778, perhaps 300,000 Hawaiians resided there. He found these people to be living under a well established political system and a feudal land tenure system controlled by various chiefs. The clear existence of these cultural/governmental institutions, the islanders' demonstrated ability to defend themselves, and their relative remoteness all worked together to negate application of the discovery doctrine to Hawaii. The Islands were soon recognized as an independent nation by the world community.

Most of the credit for this early recognition of Hawaiian sovereignty goes to king Kamehameha I. Starting in 1782, through conquest and coercion, he progressively consolidated all of the islands under a single monarchy ruled by him. By 1810, he had complete control of Hawaii. Even after Kamehameha's death, in 1819, the monarchy grew in sophistication, and a written constitution was developed in 1840. But the toll from disease, cultural disintegration, and meddling by foreign nations and their resident merchants mounted steadily.

By 1890, the total island population of 90,000 had only 34,000 full-blood Hawaiians and 6,000 mixed-bloods. Foreigners, mostly American merchants, now owned 25 percent of the kingdom's 4,100,000 acres of land. These foreigners also controlled another 25 percent of the country through leasehold interests. But, they wanted more.

413

In 1893, a coup d'état, sponsored primarily by American businessmen, overthrew the constitutional government of Queen Liliuokalani. The coup was successful only because the U.S. Minister to Hawaii, without authorization from the President, ordered U.S. Marines ashore from nearby war ships and strategically located them to prevent the Queen and her loyalists from putting down the coup. (In November 1993, the U.S. formally apologized to Native Hawaiians for the 1893 overthrow of their government [see Public Law 103-150].)

The coup's conspirators, known as "The Annexation Club," negotiated an annexation agreement with U.S. officials, but President Grover Cleveland refused to submit the agreement to the U.S. Senate for ratification. He adamantly opposed the annexation attempt, declaring Queen Liliuokalani's overthrow to be a stain on U.S. honor; and he called for restoration of the rightful monarchy.

The insurrectionists had to put annexation on hold for awhile and decided to try establishing a republic. They did, and they included Native Hawaiians as citizens. Five years later, with the blessings of the new president, William McKinley, Congress annexed Hawaii to the United States. The Islands were incorporated as a U.S. territory in June 1900.

In the early 1900s, Congress took notice of the terrible social and economic conditions among Native Hawaiians. It was widely acknowledged that loss of the land base which had sustained them in the past was at the heart of the problem. Congress reacted by passing the Hawaii Homes Commission Act of 1921. This act was intended to allow the leasing of certain public lands for Native homesteads—supposedly to "rehabilitate" people of at least one-half Hawaiian ancestry—while ownership of the lands remained in trust status. About 200,000 acres of federal lands were designated as being available for the homestead leasing program. However, Territorial administration of the act failed badly in providing agricultural lands and residential lots for the betterment of Native Hawaiians.

When Hawaii became a state in 1959, the Hawaii Homes Commission lands, and administrative responsibility for them, were transferred to the state by the federal government. Administration improved notably under state control, and increasing numbers of Hawaiian families were provided leased homesteads for some agricultural and residential purposes. However, 60 years after its inception, the program had accommodated only 15 percent of Native Hawaiians and only about 25 percent of the designated lands had been utilized for homesteads.

The statehood act of 1959 included a provision which allowed, at state discretion, use of income from state lands "for the betterment of conditions of Native Hawaiians. . . ." The state generally opted, however, to make other uses of state land proceeds. This changed in 1978 when a provision was added to the Hawaiian Constitution calling for at least partial contribution of state land income toward improvement of conditions among Native Hawaiians.

Today, despite the constitutional change, large numbers of Native Hawaiians continue to be acutely disadvantaged. Statistics on health, education, crime, unemployment, and underemployment graphically bear this out. Many Hawaiians are convinced that these adverse conditions would not exist if they had not been deprived of their land base and other pre-1893 elements of their heritage.

Concerned for their people's well being, more Hawaiians are becoming politically active. They are pursuing a variety of issues including redress of past American conduct, land rights, subsistence hunting and fishing rights, inclusion within federal service programs for other Native Americans, access to beaches and other traditional sites, and federally recognized political status with some level of self-government or "sovereignty." Several initial successes have been achieved in Congress, such as inclusion of Native Hawaiians in the Native American Programs Act of 1975, the American Indian Religious Freedom Act of 1978, the Elementary and Secondary Education Act Amendments of 1988, and the Native American Graves Protection and Repatriation Act of 1990. In addition, Congress has passed specific legislation pertaining to Native Hawaiians, namely the Native Hawaiians Study Commission Act of 1980 and the Native Hawaiian Health Care Act of 1988.

The 1990 Census reported that 138,742 individuals with Native Hawaiian ancestry accounted for 12.5 percent of the total Hawaii state population of 1,111,800. (The Native ancestry number included an estimated 9,400 full-blood Hawaiians, which was down from an estimated 11,000 for 1980.) These people clearly constitute a significant minority and they will no longer allow themselves to be left out of the state or national political scenes. Many will continue to press further to reclaim some of the numerous rights of which they and their ancestors were deprived following Euro-American contact. Unless they falter in their resolve, additional gains are sure to be achieved for Native Hawaiians in the future. In fact, in September 2000, the U.S. Senate Committee on Indian Affairs approved proposed legislation (S.2899) that would formally recognize sovereign rights of Native Hawaiians (Stokes 2000b). This will be the major issue for Native Hawaiians for the next 10–20 years.

NOTE: Primary sources for this appendix are: American Indian Lawyer Training Program 1988; Cohen 1982; State of Hawaii 1991; Sutton 1985; and Wilkinson 1988.

Additional useful sources include Laenui (1993), Trask (1991), and Wutzke (1998), and the Internet websites of the Center for Hawaiian Studies, www.hawaii.edu/chs (March 28, 2000) and the Office of Hawaiian Affairs, http://hoohana.aloha. net/~oha/ (March 29, 2000). In addition, see the U.S. Supreme Court case *Rice v. Cayetano* (2000), wherein the Court struck down a state policy that had limited participation in state elections for the trustees of the Office of Hawaiian Affairs to Native Hawaiians. Also, see the case of *Hou Hawaiians v. State of Hawaii* (1985) where an organized group of Native Hawaiians unsuccessfully attempted to gain federal recognition under laws and regulations pertaining to Indian tribes. Houghton (1989) also addressed this issue. With respect to population figures, it is instructive to note that the total "Pacific Islander" population of Hawaii (more than 200,000) is sometimes confused with the Native Hawaiian population (State of Hawaii 1991). Beyond Hawaii, legitimate concerns being expressed by Natives of current and former Pacific island territories of the United States (American Samoa, Guam, Bikini Atoll, etc.) merit full consideration by the U.S. government.

Appendix 2

Procedures for Establishing that an American Indian Group Exists as an Indian Tribe
BIA Summary of 25 CFR, Part 83, Sec. 83.7 (1998)

The regulations contain seven specific criteria which must be met for a group to qualify as a "tribe." The petitioner (the group) must be traceable as an identifiable Indian group, containing a membership core which has exerted a governing influence over its members from historic times to the present. Briefly, to gain acknowledgment, the mandatory criteria are:

(a) The petitioner has been identified as an American Indian entity on a substantially continuous basis since 1900.

(b) A predominant portion of the petitioning group comprises a distinct community and has existed as a community from historical times to the present.

(c) The petitioner has maintained political influence or authority over its members as an autonomous entity from historical times until the present.

(d) A copy of the group's present government document, including its membership criteria.

(e) The petitioner's membership consists of individuals who descend from a historical Indian tribe or from Indian tribes which functioned as a single autonomous political entity.

(f) The membership of the petitioning group is composed principally of persons who are not members of any acknowledged North American tribe [though there are exceptions to this general rule].

(g) Neither the petitioner nor its members are the subject of congressional legislation that has expressly terminated or forbidden the Federal relationship.

The Assistant Secretary of the Interior for Indian Affairs evaluates each petition and the accompanying evidence and makes one of two determinations.

NOTE: The information in this appendix pertains to Indian groups not previously recognized as tribes by the federal government. CFR refers to the Code of Federal Regulations.

The petitioning group either meets the criteria or does not. Petitions that are denied can be reconsidered at the special request of the Secretary of the Interior. Only if the petitioners qualify, however, will they be acknowledged as a tribe. Otherwise, their pre-petition status remains the same or they must obtain special legislation from Congress—an unlikely event under their circumstances. Title 25 of the Code of Federal Regulations (CFR), Sec. 83.12, describes what takes place after a petition is successful:

> (a) Upon final determination that the petitioner is an Indian tribe, it shall be considered eligible for the services and benefits from the Federal Government that are available to other federally recognized tribes. The newly acknowledged tribe shall be considered a historic tribe and shall be entitled to the privileges and immunities available to other federally recognized tribes by virtue of their government-to-government relationship with the United States. It shall also have the responsibilities and obligations of such tribes. Newly acknowledged Indian tribes shall likewise be subject to the same authority of Congress and the United States as are other federally acknowledged tribes.
>
> (b–d [summary]) While the newly recognized tribe shall be eligible for benefits and services, acknowledgment of tribal existence will not create an immediate entitlement to existing Bureau of Indian Affairs programs. Such programs shall become available upon appropriation of funds by Congress. Requests for appropriations shall follow a determination of the needs of the newly recognized tribe.

APPENDIX 3

MEMBERSHIP IN THE NAVAJO NATION

GENERAL PROVISIONS

§ 501. Composition

The membership of the Navajo Tribe shall consist of the following persons:

(1) All persons of Navajo blood whose names appear on the official roll of the Navajo Tribe maintained by the Bureau of Indian Affairs.

(2) Any person who is at least one-fourth degree Navajo blood, but who has not previously been enrolled as a member of the Tribe, is eligible for Tribal membership and enrollment.

(3) Children born to any enrolled member of the Navajo Tribe shall automatically become members of the Navajo Tribe and shall be enrolled, provided they are at least one-fourth degree Navajo blood.

§ 502. Adoption as not possible

(a) No Tribal law or custom has ever existed or exists now, by which anyone can ever become a Navajo, either by adoption, or otherwise, except by birth.

(b) All those individuals who claim to be a member of the Tribe by adoption are declared to be in no possible way an adopted or honorary member of the Navajo people.

§ 503. Member of another tribe

No person, otherwise eligible for membership in the Navajo Tribe, may enroll as a member of said Tribe, who, at the same time, is on the roll of any other tribe of Indians.

§ 504. Authority of Advisory Committee

The Advisory Committee of the Navajo Tribal Council is authorized and directed:

NOTE: This information is from the Navajo Tribal Code (N.T.C.), courtesy of the Navajo Nation.

(1) to make and promulgate all necessary rules and regulations for establishing eligibility for membership and enrollment in the Navajo Tribe;

(2) to establish basic standards and requirements of proof required to determine eligibility for membership and enrollment;

(3) to prescribe forms of application for enrollment, and establish dates or designated periods for enrollment.

§ 505. Renunciation of membership

Any enrolled member of the Navajo Tribe may renounce his membership by written petition to the Chairman of the Navajo Tribe requesting that his name be stricken from the Tribal roll. Such person may be reinstated in the Navajo Tribe only by the vote of a majority of the Navajo Tribal Council.

ENROLLMENT PROCEDURE

§ 551. Application for enrollment

Anyone wishing to apply for enrollment in the Navajo Tribe may submit an application in the form set out in 1 N.T.C. § 556. Such application must be verified before a notary public.

§ 552. Enrollment Screening Committee; action by Advisory Committee

An Enrollment Screening Committee consisting of the Chairman, the Vice-Chairman, and the Director of Land Investigations, the Agency Census Clerk, and the Tribal Legal Advisor is established. The Enrollment Screening Committee shall consider all applications for enrollment in the first instance.

In all cases where the records of the Navajo Agency do not show that the applicant is of at least one-fourth degree Navajo blood or the applicant does not establish such fact by documentary evidence independent of his own statement, consisting of the affidavits of disinterested persons, certified copies of public or church records, or the like, the Screening Committee shall reject the application. In all cases where the applicant appears to be enrolled in another Indian tribe, the Screening Committee shall reject the application. In all cases the Screening Committee or any successor committee lawfully established shall inform the applicant of his rights of appeal under this section. The Committee or its successor shall establish a record of any hearing or proceeding on any application, and this record shall contain the evidence used by the Committee in making its decision, a statement of its decision, and its reasons therefore, and the date. The Committee or its successor shall transmit this record to an appropriate Trial Court of the Navajo Tribe, and a copy to the Office of the Prosecutor.

§ 553. Standards for Screening Committee recommendations

The Screening Committee shall be guided by the following standards in making its recommendations:

(1) If the applicant appears to be a Navajo Indian of full blood it shall recommend approval.

(2) If the applicant appears to have Navajo blood of one-fourth degree or higher, but not full blood, it shall base its recommendations on his degree of Navajo blood, how long he has lived among the Navajo people, whether he is presently living among them, whether he can be identified a member of a Navajo clan, whether he can speak the Navajo language, and whether he is married to an enrolled Navajo. The Screening Committee is authorized to make investigations to determine such facts, but the burden of proof in all cases shall rest on the applicant.

§ 554. Appeals from Screening Committee—Trial Courts

The Trial Courts of the Navajo Tribe shall have original jurisdiction to hear and decide appeals from decisions of the Enrollment Screening Committee or any successor committee lawfully established by the Advisory Committee of the Navajo Tribal Council pursuant to 1 N.T.C. § 504.

§ 560. Form of application

APPLICATION FOR ENROLLMENT IN THE NAVAJO TRIBE
OF INDIANS

STATE OF ....)
)
COUNTY OF ....) ss.
)

I hereby apply for enrollment in the Navajo Tribe. I am a man/woman. All the names by which I have ever been known are as follows:

....

....

....

My present address is..

....

I was born.. at...
                     (Date)   (Place)

My mother's name was...

Her degree of Navajo blood was ....

Census number, if any ....

Her clan was ....

She was born.................................... at..
               (Date)   (Place)

If living, her present address is..

....

My maternal grandmother's name was..

Her degree of Navajo blood was ....

Census number, if any ....

Her clan was ....

She was born.................................... at..
               (Date)   (Place)

If living, her present address is..

....

My maternal grandfather's name was ....

His degree of Navajo blood was...

Census number, if any ....

His clan was..

He was born.................................... at..
               (Date)   (Place)

If living, his present address is..

....

My father's name was..

His degree of Navajo blood was...

Census number, if any ....

His clan was..

He was born.................................... at..
               (Date)   (Place)

If living, his present address is..

....

My paternal grandmother's name was..

Her degree of Navajo blood was ....

Census number, if any ....

Her clan was ....

She was born.................................... at..
               (Date)   (Place)

If living, her present address is..

....

My paternal grandfather's name was ....

His degree of Navajo blood was..

Census number, if any ....

His clan was ....

He was born................................... at..
(Date)   (Place)

If living, his present address is..

....

I have lived among Navajo people during the following periods at the following places:

From .... to.......................... at..
(Year)   (Year)

From .... to.......................... at..
(Year)   (Year)

From .... to.......................... at..
(Year)   (Year)

From .... to.......................... at..
(Year)   (Year)

I can/cannot speak the Navajo language.

My wife's/husband's name is ....

She/he is/is not an enrolled member of the Navajo Tribe. If such a member, her/his census number is ....

I am not at the present time enrolled in any other Indian Tribe.

I have/have not been previously enrolled in the Navajo Tribe. If previously enrolled, my census number was..

If previously enrolled, I was dropped from the official roll of the Navajo Tribe on .... for the following reason

....

....

....

  (A person who has voluntarily renounced membership
  in the Navajo Tribe may be reinstated only by a vote of
  majority of the Navajo Tribal Council.)

Remarks:..

....

....

....

....

        Signature: ....
           (Use name in current use)

Subscribed and sworn to before me, a notary public, this.......................
day of .... , 19..................., by..
                                                    (Name of applicant)
My commission expires ....

                              ....
                                                    Notary Public

(SEAL)

NOTE: In all cases where the records of the Navajo Agency do not show that the applicant is of at least one-fourth degree Navajo blood, such fact must be established by documentary evidence independent of the applicant's own statement. Such evidence may consist of the affidavits of disinterested persons, certified copies of public or church records or the like.

Appendix 4

Treaty with the Delawares, 1778

Articles of agreement and confederation, made and entered into by Andrew and Thomas Lewis, Esquires, Commissioners for, and in Behalf of the United States of North-America of the one Part, and Capt. White Eyes, Capt. John Kill Buck, Junior, and Capt. Pipe, Deputies and Chief Men of the Delaware Nation of the other Part.

ARTICLE I.

That all offences or acts of hostilities by one, or either of the contracting parties against the other, be mutually forgiven, and buried in the depth of oblivion, never more to be had in remembrance.

ARTICLE II.

That a perpetual peace and friendship shall from henceforth take place, and subsist between the contracting parties aforesaid, through all succeeding generations: and if either of the parties are engaged in a just and necessary war with any other nation or nations, that then each shall assist the other in due proportion to their abilities, till their enemies are brought to reasonable terms of accommodation: and that if either of them shall discover any hostile designs forming against the other, they shall give the earliest notice thereof, that timeous measures may be taken to prevent their ill effect.

ARTICLE III.

And whereas the United States are engaged in a just and necessary war, in defence and support of life, liberty and independence, against the King of England and his adherents, and as said King is yet possessed of several posts and forts on the lakes and other places, the reduction of which is of great importance to the peace and security of the contracting parties, and as the most practicable way for the troops of the United States to some of the posts and forts is by passing through the country of the Delaware nation, the aforesaid deputies, on behalf of themselves and their nation, do hereby stipulate and agree to give a free passage through their country to the troops aforesaid, and the same to conduct by the nearest and best ways to the posts, forts or towns of the enemies of the United States, affording to said troops such supplies of corn, meat, horses, or whatever may be in their power for the accommodation of such troops, on the commanding officer's, &c paying, or engageing to pay, the full value of whatever they can supply them with. And the said deputies, on the behalf of their nation, engage to join the troops of the United States aforesaid, with such a number of their best and most expert warriors as they can spare, consistent with their own safety, and act in concert with them; and for the better security of the old men, women and children of the aforesaid nation, whilst their warriors are engaged against the common enemy, it is agreed on the part of the United States, that a fort of sufficient strength and capacity be built at the expense of the said States, with such assistance as it may be in the power of the said Delaware Nation to give, in the most convenient place, and advantageous situation, as shall be agreed on by the commanding officer of the troops aforesaid, with the advice and concurrence of the deputies of the aforesaid Delaware Nation, which fort shall be garrisoned by such a number of the troops of the United States, as the commanding officer can spare for the present, and hereafter by such numbers, as the wise men of the United States in council, shall think most conducive to the common good.

ARTICLE IV.

For the better security of the peace and friendship now entered into by the contracting parties, against all infractions of the same by the citizens of either party, to the prejudice of the other, neither party shall proceed to the infliction of punishments on the citizens of the other, otherwise then by securing the offender or offenders by imprisonment, or any other competent means, till a fair and impartial trial can be had by judges or juries of both parties, as near as can be to the laws, customs and usages of the contracting parties and natural justice: The mode of such trials to be hereafter fixed by the wise men of the United States in Congress assembled, with the assistance of such deputies of the Delaware nation, as may be appointed to act in concert with them in adjusting this matter to their mutual liking. And it is further agreed between the parties aforesaid, that neither shall entertain or give countenance to the enemies of the other, or protect in their respective states, criminal fugitives, servants or slaves, but the same to apprehend, and secure and deliver to the State or States, to which such enemies, criminals, servants or slaves respectively belong.

ARTICLE V.

Whereas the confederation entered into by the Delaware nation and the United States, renders the first dependent on the latter for all the articles of clothing, utensils and implements of war, and it is judged not only reasonable, but indispensably necessary, that the aforesaid Nation be supplied with such articles from time to time, as far as the United States may have it in their power, by a well-regulated trade, under the conduct of an intelligent, candid agent, with an adequate salary, one more influenced by the love of his country, and a constant attention to the duties of his department by promoting the common interest, than the sinister purposes of converting and binding all the duties of his office to his private emolument: Convinced of the necessity of such measures, the Commissioners of the United States, at the earnest solicitation of the deputies aforesaid, have engaged in behalf of the United States, that such a trade shall be afforded said nation, conducted on such principles of mutual interest as the wisdom of the United States in Congress assembled shall think most conducive to adopt for their mutual convenience.

ARTICLE VI.

Whereas the enemies of the United States have endeavored, by every artifice in their power, to possess the Indians in general with an opinion, that it is the design of the States aforesaid, to extirpate the Indians and take possession of the country: to obviate such false suggestion, the United States do engage to guarantee to the aforesaid nation of Delawares, and their heirs, all their territorial rights in the fullest and most ample manner, as it hath been bounded by former treaties, as long as they the said Delaware nation shall abide by, and hold fast the chain of friendship now entered into. And it is further agreed on between the contracting parties should it for the future be found conducive for the mutual interest of both parties to invite any other tribes who have been friends to the interest of the United States, to join the present confederation, and to form a state whereof the Delaware nation shall be the head, and have a representation in Congress: Provided, nothing contained in this article to be considered as conclusive until it meets with the approbation of Congress. And it is also the intent and meaning of this article, that no protection or countenance shall be afforded to any who are at present our enemies, by which they might escape the punishment they deserve.

In witness whereof, the parties have hereunto interchangeably set their hands and seals, at Fort Pitt, September seventeenth, anno Domini one thousand seven hundred and seventy-eight.

Andrew Lewis,
[L.S.]
Thomas Lewis,
[L.S.]

White Eyes, his x mark,
[L.S.]
The Pipe, his x mark,
[L.S.]
John Kill Buck, his x mark,
[L.S.]

In presence of—

Lach'n McIntosh, brigadier-general, commander the Western Department.
Daniel Brodhead, colonel Eighth Pennsylvania Regiment,
W. Crawford, colonel,
John Campbell,
John Stephenson,
John Gibson, colonel Thirteenth Virginia Regiment,
A. Graham, brigade major,
Lach. McIntosh, jr., major brigade,
Benjamin Mills,
Joseph L. Finley, captain Eighth Pennsylvania Regiment,
John Finley, captain Eighth Pennsylvania Regiment.

APPENDIX 5

A PUBLIC DECLARATION TO THE TRIBAL COUNCILS AND TRADITIONAL SPIRITUAL LEADERS OF THE INDIAN AND ESKIMO PEOPLES OF THE PACIFIC NORTHWEST

November 21, 1987

Dear Brothers and Sisters,

This is a formal apology on behalf of our churches for their long-standing participation in the destruction of traditional Native American spiritual practices. We call upon our people for recognition of and respect for your traditional ways of life and for protection of your sacred places and ceremonial objects. We have frequently been unconscious and insensitive and have not come to your aid when you have been victimized by unjust Federal policies and practices. In many other circumstances we reflected the rampant racism and prejudice of the dominant culture with which we too willingly identified. During the 200th Anniversary year of the United States Constitution we, as leaders of our churches in the Pacific Northwest, extend our apology. We ask for your forgiveness and blessing.

As the Creator continues to renew the earth, the plants, the animals and all living things, we call upon the people of our denominations and fellowship to a commitment of mutual support in your efforts to reclaim and protect the legacy of your own traditional spiritual teachings. To that end we pledge our support and assistance in upholding the American Religious Freedom Act (P. L. 95-134, 1978) and within that legal precedent affirm the following:

1) The rights of the Native Peoples to practice and participate in traditional ceremonies and rituals with the same protection offered all religions under the Constitution.
2) Access to and protection of sacred sites and public lands for ceremonial purposes.
3) The use of religious symbols (feathers, tobacco, sweet grass, bones, etc.) for use in traditional ceremonies and rituals.

The spiritual power of the land and the ancient wisdom of your indigenous religions can be, we believe, great gifts to the Christian churches. We offer our commitment to support you in the righting of previous wrongs: To protect your peoples' efforts to enhance Native spiritual teachings; to encourage the members of our churches to stand in solidarity with you on these important religious issues; to provide advocacy and mediation, when appropriate, for ongoing negotiations with State agencies and Federal officials regarding these matters.

May the promises of this day go on public record with all the congregations of our communions and be communicated to the Native American Peoples of the Pacific Northwest. May the God of Abraham and Sarah, and the Spirit who lives in both the cedar and Salmon People be honored and celebrated.

Sincerely,

The Rev. Thomas L. Blevins, Bishop
Pacific Northwest Synod –
    Lutheran Church in America

The Most Rev. Raymond G. Hunthausen
    Archbishop of Seattle
Roman Catholic Archdiocese of Seattle

The Rev. Dr. Robert Bradford,
    Executive Minister
American Baptist Churches of the
    Northwest

The Rev. Elizabeth Knott, Synod Exec.
Presbyterian Church
    Synod Alaska-Northwest

The Rev. Robert Brock
N.W. Regional Christian Church

The Rev. Lowell Knutson, Bishop
North Pacific District
    American Lutheran Church

The Right Rev. Robert H. Cochrane,
    Bishop, Episcopal Diocese of
    Olympia

The Most Rev. Thomas Murphy
    Coadjutor Archbishop
Roman Catholic Archdiocese of Seattle

The Rev. W. James Halfaker,
    Conference Minister
Washington North Idaho Conference
    United Church of Christ

The Rev. Melvin G. Talbert, Bishop
United Methodist Church –
    Pacific Northwest Conference

APPENDIX 6

STATE INDIAN COMMISSIONS

Individual states have developed commissions to address American Indian issues.

ALABAMA
Alabama Indian Affairs Commission
339 Dexter Ave., Suite 113
Montgomery, AL 36130

ALASKA
Assistant for Alaska Native Affairs
Office of the Governor
Pouch A
Juneau, AK 99811

ARIZONA
Arizona Commission on Indian Affairs
1645 W. Jefferson, Suite 433
Phoenix, AZ 85007

CALIFORNIA
California Native American Heritage
 Commission
915 Capitol Mall
Sacramento, CA 95814

COLORADO
Colorado Commission of Indian Affairs
130 State Capitol
Denver, CO 80203

CONNECTICUT
Connecticut Indian Affairs Council
Department of Environmental
 Protection
165 Capitol Ave.
Hartford, CT 06106

DELAWARE
Office of Human Relations
630 State College Rd.
Dover, DE 19901

FLORIDA
Florida Governor's Council on
 Indian Affairs
521 E. College Ave.
Tallahassee, FL 32301

GEORGIA
Office of Indian Heritage
330 Capitol Ave. S.E.
Atlanta, GA 30334

HAWAII
Hawaii Council of American
 Indian Nations
Box 17627
910 N. Vineyard Blvd.
Honolulu, HI 96817

IDAHO
American Indian Coordinator
State House
Boise, ID 83720

IOWA
Office of the Governor
State Capitol
Des Moines, IA 50319

LOUISIANA
Governor's Commission on
    Indian Affairs
Box 44455, Capitol Station
Baton Rouge, LA 70804

MAINE
Maine Indian Affairs Commission
State Health Station #38
Augusta, ME 04333

MARYLAND
Commission on Indian Affairs
45 Calvert St.
Annapolis, MD 21401

MASSACHUSETTS
Massachusetts Commission on
    Indian Affairs
One Ashburn Pl., Rm. 1004
Boston, MA 02108

MICHIGAN
Michigan Commission on
    Indian Affairs
Dept. of Management and Budget
Box 30026
611 W. Ottawa St.
Lansing, MI 48909

MINNESOTA
Minnesota Council on Indian Affairs
127 University Ave.
St. Paul, MN 55155

MONTANA
Governor's Office of Indian Affairs
1218 E. Sixth Ave.
Helena, MT 59620

NEBRASKA
Nebraska Indian Commission
Box 94914, State Capitol
Lincoln, NE 68701

NEVADA
Nevada Indian Commission
3100 Mill St., Suite 206
Reno, NV 89502

NEW HAMPSHIRE
New Hampshire Indian Council
913 Elm St., Room 201
Manchester, NH 03101

NEW JERSEY
New Jersey Indian Office
300 Main St., Suite 3F
Orange, NJ 07050

NEW MEXICO
New Mexico Office on Indian Affairs
La Villa Rivera Building
Santa Fe, NM 87501

NEW YORK
Dept. of Indian Services
Donovan State Office Bldg.
125 Main St., Rm. 471
Buffalo, NY 14203

NORTH CAROLINA
North Carolina Commission on
    Indian Affairs
Box 27228
227 E. Edenton St. #229
Raleigh, NC 27611

NORTH DAKOTA
North Dakota Indian Affairs
    Commission
State Capitol Bldg.
Bismarck, ND 58505

OHIO
Ohio Indian Affairs Coordinator
Outdoor Recreation Service
Fountain Square Bldg. E
Columbus, OH 43224

OKLAHOMA
Oklahoma Indian Affairs Commission
4010 N. Lincoln
Oklahoma City, OK 73105

OREGON
Commission on Indian Affairs
454 State Capitol Bldg.
Salem, OR 97310

RHODE ISLAND
Rhode Island Commission for
    Indian Affairs
444 Friendship St.
Providence, RI 02907

SOUTH CAROLINA
Assistant to the Governor
Box 11450
Columbia, SC 29211

SOUTH DAKOTA
South Dakota Office of Indian Affairs
Kneip Bldg.
Pierre, SD 57501

TEXAS
Texas Indian Commission
Box 2960
Austin, TX 78768

TENNESSEE
Tennessee Indian Council
1110 12th Ave. S.
Nashville, TN 30273

UTAH
Utah Division of Indian Affairs
6220 State Office Bldg.
Salt Lake City, UT 84114

VIRGINIA
Indian Affairs Coordinator
Secretary of Human Resources
9th Street Office Bldg., Rm. 622
Richmond, VA 23219

WASHINGTON
Washington Commission for
    Indian Affairs
1057 Capitol Way
Olympia, WA 98504

WISCONSIN
Wisconsin Governor's Indian Desk
Box 7863
Madison, WI 53701

WYOMING
Wyoming State Indian Commission
    2660 Peck Ave.
Riverton, WY 82501

Source: Giago, Tim, ed. 1991. *The American Indian and the Media.* The National
Conference on Christians and Jews. Minneapolis, Minn. 84 p.

APPENDIX 7

100th Congress 2d Session
H. Con. Res. 331

CONCURRENT RESOLUTION

To acknowledge the contribution of the Iroquois Confederacy of Nations to the development of the United States Constitution and to reaffirm the continuing government-to-government relationship between Indian tribes and the United States established in the Constitution.

Whereas the original framers of the Constitution, including, most notably, George Washington and Benjamin Franklin, are known to have greatly admired the concepts of the Six Nations of the Iroquois Confederacy;

Whereas the confederation of the original Thirteen Colonies into one republic was influenced by the political system developed by the Iroquois Confederacy as were many of the democratic principles which were incorporated into the Constitution itself; and

Whereas, since the formation of the United States, the Congress has recognized the sovereign status of Indian tribes and has, through the exercise of powers reserved to the Federal Government in the Commerce Clause of the Constitution (art. I, s. 2, cl. 3), dealt with Indian tribes on a government-to-government basis and has, through the treaty clause (art. II, s. 2, cl. 2) entered into three hundred and seventy treaties with Indian tribal Nations;

Whereas, from the first treaty entered into with an Indian Nation, the treaty with the Delaware Indians of September 17, 1778, the Congress has assumed a trust responsibility and obligation to Indian tribes and their members;

Whereas this trust responsibility calls for Congress to "exercise the utmost good faith in dealings with Indians" as provided for in the Northwest Ordinance of 1787, (1 Stat. 50);

Whereas the judicial system of the United States has consistently recognized and reaffirmed this special relationship: Now, therefore, be it

Resolved by the House of Representatives (the Senate concurring), That—

(1) the Congress, on the occasion of the two hundredth anniversary of the signing of the United States Constitution, acknowledges the contribution made by the Iroquois Confederacy and other Indian Nations to the formation and development of the United States;

(2) the Congress also hereby reaffirms the constitutionally recognized government-to-government relationship with Indian tribes which has been the cornerstone of this Nation's official Indian policy;

(3) the Congress specifically acknowledges and reaffirms the trust responsibility and obligation of the United States Government to Indian tribes, including Alaska Natives, for their preservation, protection, and enhancement, including the provision of health, education, social, and economic assistance programs as necessary, and including the duty to assist tribes in their performance of governmental responsibility to provide for the social and economic well-being of their members and to preserve tribal cultural identity and heritage; and

(4) the Congress also acknowledges the need to exercise the utmost good faith in upholding its treaties with the various tribes, as the tribes understood them to be, and the duty of a great Nation to uphold its legal and moral obligations for the benefit of all of its citizens so that they and their posterity may also continue to enjoy the rights they have enshrined in the United States Constitution for time immemorial.

Passed the House of Representatives October 4, 1988.

Attest: DONNALD K. ANDERSON,
Clerk.

BIBLIOGRAPHY

Aaseng, Nathan. 1992. *Navajo code talkers*. Walker and Company, New York. 114 p.

Abel, Annie Heloise. 1992a. *The American Indian as slaveholder and secessionist*. Univ. of Nebraska Press, Lincoln. 394 p.

———. 1992b. *The American Indian in the Civil War, 1862–1865*. Univ. of Nebraska Press, Lincoln. 403 p.

———. 1993. *The American Indian and the end of the Confederacy: 1863–1866*. Univ. of Nebraska Press, Lincoln. 419 p.

Adams, David Wallace. 1995. *Education for Extinction: American Indians and the Boarding School Experience, 1875–1928*. Univ. of Kansas Press, Lawrence. 396 p.

Administration for Native Americans. 1991a. Availability of financial assistance. 56 *Federal Register* No. 151, p. 37396.

———. 1991b. Fact sheet. Washington, D.C. 6 p.

———. 1998. 45 CFR Part 1336—Native American Programs.

Alaska Federation of Natives. 1989. *The AFN report on the status of Alaska Natives: A call for action*. Anchorage. 78 p.

———. 1991a. No title. Information pamphlet on history, mission, and organizational structure. Anchorage. 3-leaf fold-out.

———. 1991b. *AFN Newsletter*. Vol. IX, No. 4 (Dec.). 16 p.

———. 1991c. *ANCSA twenty years later*. Annual Report. Anchorage. 24 p.

———. 1992. *AFN Newsletter*. Vol. X, NO. 2 (Mar.). 8 p.

———. 2000. www.akfednatives.org (March 4).

Alaska National Interest Lands Conservation Act. 1980. P.L. 96-487, 94 Stat. 2371, 16 USC 3111 et seq.

Alaska Native Claims Settlement Act. 1971. P.L. 92-203, 85 Stat. 688, 43 USC 1601 et seq.

Alaska Native Claims Settlement Act Amendments of 1987. 1988. P.L. 100-241, 101 Stat. 1788.

Alaska v. Native Village of Venetie. 1998. 118 S. Ct. 948 (140 L.Ed.2d 30).

Ambler, Marjane. 2000. Honoring Native languages. *Tribal College* XI(3):8–9 (Spring).

American Indian Anti-Defamation Council. 1991. Mission statement. Denver, Colo. 1 p.

American Indian Lawyer Training Program. 1988. *Indian tribes as sovereign governments: A sourcebook on federal-tribal history, law, and policy.* AIRI Press, Oakland, Calif. 156 p.

American Indian Movement. 1991. Fact sheet. Leonard Peltier Defense Committee, Lawrence, Kans. 6 p.

———. 2000. www.aimovement.org (March 220.

American Indian Policy Review Commission. 1977. Final report. U.S. Govt. Printing Office, Washington, D.C. Vol. I, 624 p., Vol. II, 923 p.

American Indian Religious Freedom Act (Joint Resolution). 1978. P.L. 95-341, 92 Stat. 469, 42 USC 1996.

American Indian Religious Freedom Act Amendments. 1994. P.L. 103-344, 42 USC 1996 et seq.

American Indian Report. 1998. Dec.

Anderson, Edward F., 2nd ed. 1996. *Peyote: the divine cactus.* Univ. of Arizona Press, Tucson. 272 p.

Anderson, George E., W.H. Ellison, and Robert F. Heizer. 1978. *Treaty making and treaty rejection by the federal government in California, 1850–1852.* Ballena Press, Socorro, N.Mex. 124 p.

Andrews, Patsy J. 1991. Personal communication. Advisory Services Specialist, Indian Arts, and Crafts Board, Washington, D.C., Oct. 28.

Anquoe, Bunty. 1991b. Oklahoma tribes ink treaty. In *Lakota Times,* Oct. 16.

———. 1991a. Canadian Eskimos win fifth of Canada. In *Lakota Times,* Dec. 24.

———. 1992a. BIA mismanagement blasted. In *Lakota Times,* Apr. 8.

———. 1992b. Brown defends budget. In *Lakota Times,* Apr. 8.

———. 1992c. Task force reworks budgetary process. In *Lakota Times,* Feb. 4.

Antoine v. Washington. 1975. 420 U.S. 194.

Arizona v. California. 1963. 373 U.S. 546.

Arizona Commission on Indian Affairs. 1991. Legislative statement of executive director. Sept. 23. 6 p.

———. 1999. *Newsletter.* 12(2):1–8. (July–Sept.)

Arnold, Robert D. 1976. *Alaska Native land claims.* Alaska Native Foundation, Anchorage. 348 p.

Articles of Confederation. 1781. Art. IX. 1 Stat. 4, 7 (1845).

Associated Press. 1991a. Alaska churches apologize to Indians. In *Lakota Times*, Nov. 6.

———. 1991b. BIA blames sloppy bookkeeping for $23.8 million in lost equipment. In *Arizona Daily Star*, Nov. 3.

———. 1991c. Environmental racism claim to be studied at meeting. In *Arizona Daily Star*, Aug. 25.

———. 1991d. Eskimos to gain control of a fifth of Canada. Reprinted in *Arizona Daily Star*, Dec. 17.

———. 1991e. Indian gaming funds cited as aid to culture. In *Arizona Daily Star*, Aug. 25.

———. 1991f. Probe blames government for deficient Indian schools. In *Tucson Citizen*, Aug. 5.

———. 1991g. Thanksgiving no holiday for U.S. Indians. In *Arizona Daily Star*, Nov. 28.

———. 1991h. Tribal leaders may debate legislation of alcohol sales on Navajo Reservation. In *Arizona Daily Star*, Nov. 29.

———. 1992. Indian task force report to Congress urges BIA overhaul, tribal control of funds. In *Arizona Daily Star*, Feb. 2.

———. 1999a. New theory: N. America's 1st inhabitants may have crossed Atlantic. *The Albuquerque Journal*, Nov. 1.

———. 1999b. Archaeologist: First North Americans in Wisconsin. *The Gallup Independent*, Oct. 22.

———. 1999c. U.S. Army honors last Comanche 'code talker.' *The Gallup Independent*, Dec. 2.

———. 2000a. Mille lacs opens language center. *Indian Country Today*, Aug. 2.

———. 2000b. American Indian languages near extinction: Federal policies blamed for long-standing malaise. *Indian Country Today*, Aug. 2.

———. 2000c. Big settlement is rebirth for Cayugas, official says. *The Gallup Independent*, Jan. 28.

Association on American Indian Affairs. 1991. Annual report. New York. 20 p.

———. 1992. *Indian Affairs*, No. 125, Winter/Spring. 8 p.

Axtell, James. 1988. *After Columbus: Essays in ethnohistory of colonial North America*. Oxford Univ. Press, New York. 300 p.

Axtell James, and William C. Sturtevant. 1986. The unkindest cut, who invented scalping. *In* Nichols. 1986. p. 47–60.

Balikci, Asen. 1970. *The Netsilik Eskimo*. The Natural History Press, Garden City, N.Y. 264 p.

Barsh, Russel Laurence. 1994. Indian policy at the beginning of the 1990s: The trivialization of the struggle. *In* Legters and Lyden. 1994. p. 55–69.

Basso, Keith. 1996. *Wisdom sits in places.* Univ. of New Mexico Press, Albuquerque. 171 p.

Basso, Keith H., and Morris E. Opler, eds. 1971. *Apachean culture, history, and ethnology.* Anthropological Papers of the University of Arizona, Tucson. No. 21. 167 p.

Bataille, Gretchen M. and Kathleen Mullen Sands. 1984. *American Indian women: Telling their lives.* Univ. of Nebraska Press, Lincoln. 209 p.

Begay, David H., and Martha B. Becktell. 1990. These are ancient traditions and they don't grow old. Paper presented at Conference on Native American Voices: Culture and Learning. Prescott College, Prescott, Ariz. Aug. 4 p.

Begay, Manley. 2000. Harvard professor, and copetitioner in the case of *Harjo, et al. v. Pro-Football, Inc.* Personal communication. Feb. 22.

Benally, Ailema. 2000a. National Park Service interpreter, Canyon de Chelly National Monument, Navajo Indian Reservation, Ariz. Personal communication. Feb. 11.

Benally, Christine C. 2000. Community Health Educator, Flagstaff, Ariz. Personal communication. Jan. 28.

Benally, Herbert John. 1990. Navajo philosophy of learning. Paper presented at conference on Native American Voices: Culture and Learning. Prescott College, Prescott, Ariz. Aug. 15 p.

Benzie Fishery Coalition. 1999. *Benzie Fishery News.* Benzie County, Mich. Oct.

Bergman, Robert. 1977. The human cost of removing Indian children from their parents. *In* Unger 1977, p. 34–36.

Berkhofer, Robert F., Jr. 1967. *Salvation and the savage: An analysis of Protestant missions and American Indian response, 1787–1862.* Univ. of Kentucky Press, Louisville. 186 p.

———. 1979. *The white man's Indian: Images of the American Indian from Columbus to the present.* Vintage Books, New York. 261 p.

Berman, Howard. 1992. Perspectives on American Indian sovereignty and international law, 1600–1776. *In* Lyons et al. 1992. p. 125–188.

Biolsi, Thomas, and Larry J. Zimmerman. 1997. *Indians and anthropologists: Vine Deloria, Jr., and the critique of anthropology.* Univ. of Arizona Press, Tucson, 226 p.

Black's Law Dictionary. 1990. West Publishing Co., St. Paul, Minn. 1657 p.

Book Publishing Company. 1992. *How can one sell the air: Chief Seattle's vision.* The Book Publishing Company, Summertown, Tenn. 80 p.

Bordewich, Fergus M. 1996. *Killing the white man's Indian: Reinventing Native Americans at the end of the Twentieth Century.* Doubleday, New York. 400 p.

Boyum, William. Health care: An overview of the Indian Health Service. In *American Indian law Review* 14:241–267.

Bradford, Ernle. 1973. *Christopher Columbus.* Viking Press, New York. 288 p.

Brand, Stewart. 1988. Indians and the counterculture, 1960s–1970s. *In* Washburn. 1988. p. 570–572.

Brendale v. Yakima Indian Nation. 1989. 492 U.S. 408.

Britten, Thomas A. 1997. *American Indians in World War I: At war and at home.* Univ. of New Mexico Press, Albuquerque. 254 p.

———. 1999. *A brief history of Seminole-Negro Scouts.* Edwin Mellen Press, Lewiston, N.Y. 140 p.

Brodeur, Paul. 1985. *Restitution: The land claims of the Mashpee, Passamo-quoddy, and Penobscot Indians of New England.* Northeastern Univ. Press, Boston. 148 p.

Brooks, Drex. 1995. *Sweet medicine: Sites of Indian massacres, battlefields, and treaties.* Univ. of New Mexico Press, Albuquerque. 163 p.

Brophy, William A., and Sophie D. Aberle. 1966. *The Indian: America's unfinished business. Report of the commission on the rights, liberties, and responsibilities of the American Indian.* Univ. of Oklahoma Press, Norman. 236 p.

Brown, Dee. 1970. *Bury my heart at Wounded Knee—An Indian history of the American West.* Holt, Rinehart, and Winston, New York. 487 p.

Bruchac, Joseph, ed. 1991. *Raven tells stories: An anthology of Alaskan Native writing.* Greenfield Review Press, Greenfield Center, N.Y. 224 p.

Burch, Ernest S., Jr. 1984. The land claims era in Alaska. *In* Damas. 1984. p. 657–661.

Bureau of Indian Affairs. 1903. *Report of the Commissioner of Indian Affairs. Treaties made with Indian tribes in the United States which have been ratified by the Senate.* Annual Rept., Dept. of the Interior, Washington, D.C. 45 p.

———. 1964. *Answers to your questions about the American Indian.* Supt. of Documents, U.S. Govt. Printing Office, Washington, D.C. 38 p.

———. 1966. *Indians, Eskimos, and Aleuts of Alaska.* Washington, D.C. 18 p.

———. 1968. *Answers to your questions about American Indians.* Supt. of Documents, U.S. Govt. Printing Office, Washington, D.C. 42 p.

———. 1974. *The American Indians: Answers to 101 questions.* Supt. of Documents, U.S. Govt. Printing Office, Washington, D.C. 60 p.

———. 1975. *Federal Indian Policy.* Washington, D.C. 21 p.

———. 1978. *The American Indians: Answers to 101 questions.* Supt. of Documents, U.S. Govt. Printing Office, Washington, D.C. 61 p.

———. 1984. *Tribal enrollment.* Phoenix Area Office, Arizona. 172 p.

———. 1985a. *Annual Report of Indian Lands.* Washington, D.C. 89 p.

———. 1985b. *Information about acknowledgment.* Washington, D.C. 5 p.

———. 1987a. *American Indians today: Answers to your questions.* U.S. Dept. of the Interior, Washington, D.C. 24 p.

———. 1987b. *The Bureau of Indian Affairs.* (Mission Statement.) Washington, D.C. 1 p.

———. 1988. *Report on BIA education.* Washington, D.C. 261 p.

———. 1989a. *Indian Land Areas Map.* Washington, D.C.

———. 1989b. *Indian service population and labor force estimates.* U.S. Dept. of the Interior, Washington, D.C. 24 p.

———. 1990. *American Indian and Alaska Native education.* Washington, D.C. 2 p.

———. 1991a. *American Indians today.* Washington, D.C. 36 p.

———. 1991b. *Education fact sheet.* Washington, D.C. 6 p.

———. 1991c. Reorganization task force to meet in Anchorage; "Ideal agencies" to be discussed. *Indian News* 15(13):1–2.

———. 1992a. *Indian forestry career opportunities.* Washington, D.C. 5 p.

———. 1992b. *Tribal horizons.* In *Departmental Highlights,* p. 19–24. Washington, D.C. p. 19–24.

———. 1997. *Annual Report of Indian lands.* Bureau of Indian Affairs, Washington, D.C., www.doi.gov/bia/realty/consol/97.html (March 3, 2000).

———. 1999. *Report on tribal priority allocations.* U.S. Dept. of the Interior, Bureau of Indian Affairs, Washington, D.C. 148 p.

———. 2000a. www.doi.gov/aitoday/q_and_a.html. May 19.

———. 2000b. Public Affairs Office. Personal communication. February 1.

Burton, Lloyd. 1991. *American Indian water rights and the limits of law.* Univ. of Kansas Press, Lawrence. 174 p.

Bush, George. 1991. *President's policy statement on American Indians.* Bureau of Indian Affairs, Washington, D.C. June 14.

Callicott, J. Barid. 1983. Traditional American Indian and traditional western European attitudes towards nature: An overview. *In* Ellioh and Gore. 1983. *Environmental philosophy: A collection of readings.* Pennsylvania State Univ. Press, University Park. p. 230–259.

Calloway, Colin G. 1995. *The American Revolution in Indian Country: Crisis and diversity in Native American communities.* Cambridge Univ. Press, New York. 327 p.

———. 1997. *New worlds for all: Indians, Europeans, and the remaking of early America.* The Johns Hopkins Univ. Press, Baltimore. 229 p.

Camp, Carter. 1992. Sincere doubts: Tourism diminishes Lakota ceremonies. In *Lakota Times*, Aug. 12.

Campbell, Lyle, and Marianne Mithun, eds. 1979. *The languages of Native America: Historical and comparative assessment.* University of Texas Press, Austin. 1034 p.

Canby, William C., Jr. 1981. *American Indian law in a nutshell.* West Publ. Co., St. Paul, Minn. 288 p.

———. 1998. *American Indian law: In a nut shell* (3rd). West Group, St. Paul, Minn. 463 p.

Capps, Benjamin. 1973. *The Indians.* Time-Life Books, Chicago. 240 p.

———. 1975. *The great chiefs.* Time-Life Books, Chicago. 240 p.

Carillo, Jo, ed. 1998. *Readings in American Indian law: Recalling the rhythm of survival.* Temple Univ. Press, Philadelphia. 353 p.

Carroll, Margueritte D. 1998. Speaking out: supporters seek recognition for Indian code talkers. In *American Indian Report*, Nov., p. 8–9.

———. 1999. On top of the world: Inuit's aspirations realized in a new Canadian territory called Nunavut. *American Indian Report,* July, p. 12–15.

Carter, Kent. 1999. *The Dawes Commission—and the allotment of the Five Civilized Tribes, 1893–1914.* Ancestry.com, Inc., Orem, Utah. 284 p.

Case, David S. 1984. *Alaska Natives and American laws.* Univ. of Alaska Press, Fairbanks. 586 p.

Castañeda, Antonia I. 1992. Women of color and the rewriting of Western history—the discourse, politics, and decolonization of history. *Pacific Historical Review* 61(4):510–533.

Castile, George Pierre, and Robert L. Bee, eds. 1992. *State and Reservation: New perspectives of federal Indian policy.* Univ. of Arizona Press, Tucson. 259 p.

Ceram, C.W. 1971. *The first Americans: A story of North American archaeology.* Harcourt Brace Jovanovich, Inc., New York. 357 p.

Champagne, Duane. 1994. *Native America: Portrait of the peoples.* Invisible Ink Press, Detroit, Mich. 786 p.

Chasing Horse, Joseph. 1991. Personal communication. Sicangu Lakota, Rosebud Reservation, S.Dak. Dec. 28.

Checchio, Elizabeth, and Bonnie G. Colby. 1993. *Indian water rights: Negotiating the future.* Water Resources Research Center, Univ. of Arizona, Tucson. 91 p.

Cherokee Nation v. Georgia. 1831. 30 U.S. (5 Pet.) 1.

Churchill, Ward. 1991. *Jimmy Durham: An artist for Native North America.* Spirit of Crazy Horse, L.P.D.C., Lawrence, Kans. Oct.–Nov., p. 6, 12.

———. 1997. *A little matter of genocide: Holocaust and denial in the Americas 1492 to present.* City Lights Books, San Francisco, Calif. 531 p.

Civilization Fund. 1819. 3 Stat. 516 (1846).

Clark, Blue. 1994. *Lone Wolf v. Hitchcock: Treaty rights & Indian law at the end of the nineteenth century.* Univ. of Nebraska Press, Lincoln. 182 p.

Clifton, James A., ed. 1990. *The invented Indian: Cultural fictions and government policies.* Transaction Publishers, New Brunswick, N.J. 388 p.

Clinton, William Jefferson. 1996. Executive Order on Indian Sacred Sites. 61 FR 26.

Code of Federal Regulations. 1990. Title 25—Indians.

———. 1998. Title 25—Indians.

Coggins, George Cameron, and Charles F. Wilkinson. 1981. *Federal public land and resources law.* The Foundation Press, Mineola, N.Y. 849 p.

Cohen, Fay G. 1986. *Treaties on trial: The continuing controversy over Northwest fishing rights.* Univ. of Washington Press, Seattle. 229 p.

Cohen, Felix S. 1942a. *Handbook of federal Indian law.* U.S. Govt. Printing Office, Washington, D.C. 662 p.

———. 1942b. The Spanish origin of Indian rights in the United States. *Georgetown Law Journal* 31:1–21.

———. 1947. Original Indian title. *Minnesota Law Review* 32:28–59.

———. 1953. The erosion of Indian rights, 1950–1953. 62 *Yale Law Journal* 348.

———. 1971. *Handbook of federal Indian law.* (Reprint of 1942 edition.) Univ. of New Mexico Press, Albuquerque. 662 p.

———1982. *Felix S. Cohen's handbook on federal Indian law.* The Michie Company, Charlottesville, Va. 912 p.

Collier, John. 1934. *Memorandum, hearings on H.R. 7902.* House Committee on Indian Affairs, 73rd Cong., 2nd sess., p. 16–18.

Committee on Interior and Insular Affairs. 1964. *List of Indian treaties.* 88th Cong., 2nd sess. Committee Print No. 33. 45 p.

Conners v. United States. 1901. 180 U.S. 271.

Cornell, Stephen. 1988. *The return of the Native: American Indian political resurgence.* Oxford Univ. Press, New York. 278 p.

Cornell, Stephen and Joseph P. Kalt, eds. 1992. *What can tribes do? Strategies and institutions in American Indian economic development.* American Indian Studies Center, Univ. of California, Los Angeles. 336 p.

Correll, J. Lee. 1970. *BAI-A-LIL-LE: Medicine man—or witch?* Navajo Historical Publications, Biographical Series No. 3, Navajo Parks and Recreation, Window Rock, Ariz. 56 p.

Coward, John M. 1999. *The newspaper Indian: Native American identity in the press, 1820–1890.* Univ. of Illinois Press, Urbana. 244 p.

Crawford, James. 1994. *Endangered Native American languages: What is to be done?* Paper presented at the annual conference of the American Educational Research Association, New Orleans, La. April 5. www.ncbe.gwu.edu/miscpubs/crawford (March 28, 2000).

Curtis Act. 1898. 30 Stat. 495.

Dale, Edward Everett. 1949. *The Indians of the Southwest: A century of development under the United States.* Univ. of Oklahoma Press, Norman. 283 p.

Damas, David, ed. 1984. *Handbook of North American Indians—Arctic.* Smithsonian Institution, Washington, D.C. 829 p.

Davis, Tony. 1992. Apaches split over nuclear waste. *High Country News* 24(1):12–14. (Jan. 27)

Debo, Angie. 1970. *A history of the Indians of the United States.* Univ. of Oklahoma Press, Norman. 450 p.

———. 1968. *And still the waters run: The betrayal of the Five Civilized Tribes.* Princeton Univ. Press, Princeton, N.J. 417 p.

Deloria, Philip. 1998. *Playing Indian.* Yale Univ. Press, New Haven, Conn. 249 p.

Deloria, Vine, Jr. 1969. *Custer died for your sins: An Indian manifesto.* The Macmillan Company, Toronto. 279 p.

———. 1970. *We talk, you listen: New tribes, new turf.* Macmillan and Company, New York. 227 p.

———. 1973. *God is red.* Grosset and Dunlap, New York. 376 p.

———. 1974a. *Behind the trail of broken treaties: An Indian Declaration of Independence.* Univ. of Texas Press, Austin. 296 p.

———. 1974b. *The Indian affair.* Friendship Press, New York. 95 p.

———. 1979. *The metaphysics of modern existence.* Harper & Row, San Francisco. 223 p.

———. 1988. *Custer died for your sins.* Univ. of Oklahoma Press, Norman. 278 p.

———. 1989. A simple question of humanity—The moral dimensions of the reburial issue. *Native American Rights Fund Legal Review* 14(4):1–12.

———. 1991a. *Indian education in America: 8 essays by Vine Deloria, Jr.* American Indian Science & Engineering Society, Boulder, Colo. 70 p.

———. 1991b. Foreword. *In* Nabakov. 1991. p. xvii–xix.

———. 1995. *Red earth white lies: Native Americans and the myth of scientific fact.* Scribner, New York. 286 p.

———. 1997. *Red earth white lies: Native Americans and the myth of scientific fact.* Fulcrum Publishing, Golden, Colo. 271 p.

———. 1998. Revision and reversion. *In* Carillo. 1998. p. 146–151.

———. 1999a. *For this land: Writings on religion in America.* Routledge, New York. 311 p.

———. 1999b. *Spirit and reason: The Vine Deloria, Jr., reader.* Deloria, Barbara, Kristen Foehner, and Sam Scinta, eds. Fulcrum Publishing, Golden, Colo. 400 p.

Deloria, Vine, Jr., ed. 1971. *Of utmost good faith.* Straight Arrow Books, San Francisco. 262 p.

———, ed. 1985. *American Indian policy in the twentieth century.* Univ. of Oklahoma Press, Norman. 265 p.

Deloria, Vine, Jr., and Raymond J. DeMallie. 1999. *Documents of American Indian diplomacy: Treaties, agreements, and conventions, 1775–1979.* Univ. of Oklahoma Press, Norman. 2 vols. 1540 p.

Deloria, Vine, Jr., and Clifford M. Lytle. 1983. *American Indians, American justice.* Univ. of Texas Press, Austin. 292 p.

———. 1984. *The nations within: The past and future of American Indian sovereignty.* Pantheon Books, New York. 293 p.

DeMallie, Raymond J. 1977. *Comanche treaties with the Republic of Texas.* Institute for the Development of Indian Law, Washington, D.C. p. 1–4.

Denevan, William M. 1976. *The native population of the Americas in 1492.* Univ. of Wisconsin Press, Madison. 353 p .

Denver Post. 1992. *Chief Seattle given forked tongue?* April 22. *In* Harvey and Harjo. 1994. p. 298.

Devens, Carol. 1992. *Countering colonization: Native American women and Great Lakes missions, 1630–1900.* Univ. of California Press, Berkeley. 185 p.

Diaz, Elvia. 1998. *Statue of Spaniard loses foot.* In *Albuquerque Journal.* Jan. 8.

Dobyns, Henry F. 1976. *Native American historical demography: A critical bibliography.* Indiana Univ. Press, Bloomington. 95 p.

Dozier, Edward. 1970. *The Pueblo Indians of North America.* Holt, Rinehart, and Winston, Inc., New York. 224 p.

Drinnon, Richard. 1997. *Facing west: The metaphysics of Indian hating & empire building.* Univ. of Oklahoma Press, Norman. 572 p.

Driver, Harold E. 1969. *Indians of North America.* Univ. of Chicago Press, Chicago. 632 p.

Drucker, Philip. 1954. *Indians of the northwest coast.* The Natural History Press, Garden City, New York. 224 p.

Duro v. Reina. 1990. 495 U.S. 676.

Dutton, Bertha P. 1983. *American Indians of the Southwest.* Univ. of New Mexico Press, Albuquerque. 285 p.

Dvorchak, Robert. 1992. Without wampum or buffalo, Indians rely on blackjack, bingo. Associated Press article in *Prescott Courier,* Dec. 11.

Echo-Hawk, Roger C. and Walter R. Echo-Hawk. 1994. *Battlefields and burial grounds: The Indian struggle to protect ancestral graves in the United States.* Lerner Publications Company, Minneapolis, Minn.

Echo-Hawk, Walter. 1992. Native American religious liberty: Five hundred years after Columbus. *American Indian Culture and Research Journal* 17(3):33–52.

Edmunds, David R. 1980. *American Indian leaders: Studies in diversity.* Univ. of Nebraska Press, Lincoln. 257 p.

Elementary and Secondary Education Act Amendments. 1988. P.L. 100-297, 102 Stat. 358, 20 USC 4901.

Encyclopaedia Britannica. 1990. *American Indians.* Vol. 1, p. 318–320. Encyclopaedia Britannica, Inc. Chicago.

Erikson, Jane. 1991. La Frontera gets Indian AIDS grant. In *Arizona Daily Star,* Nov. 19.

Evans, G. Edward, and Jeffrey Clark. 1980. *North American Indian language materials, 1890–1965: An annotated bibliography of monographic works.* American Indian Studies Center, Univ. of California at Los Angeles. 154 p.

Falmouth Institute. 1992. *Historical review of federal Indian policy.* The Falmouth Institute, Fairfax, Va. 26 p.

Farb, Peter. 1968. *Man's rise to civilization as shown by the Indians of North America from primeval times to the coming of the Industrial State.* Dutton, New York. 332 p.

Federal Register. 1988. *Indian entities* [within the lower 48 states and] *Native entities within the state of Alaska recognized and eligible to receive services from the United States Bureau of Indian Affairs.* U.S. Govt., Washington, D.C. vol. 53(250):52829–52835.

Fehr-Snyder. 2000. Kennewick man was an Indian. *The Arizona Republic,* Jan. 14.

Feraca, Stephen E. 1990. Inside BIA: Or, "We're getting rid of all these honkies." *In* Clifton. 1990. p. 271–289.

Fischer, Roger. 2000. And the word is god. In *The Economist.* January 29. (from Fischer (1999), *A History of language,* Reaktion Books.)

Flowers, Charles. 1999. Impact study not expected to alter tribal gaming. In *Indian Country Today.* June 5.

Flowers, Ronald B. 1983. *Criminal jurisdiction allocation in Indian country.* Associated Faculty Press, Inc., Port Washington, N.Y. 121 p.

Fontana, Bernard L. 1994. *Entrada: The legacy of Spain and Mexico in the United States.* Southwest Parks and Monuments Association, Tucson, Ariz. 286 p.

Forbes, Jack D. 1993. *Africans and Native Americans: The language of race and the evolution of Red-Black Peoples.* Univ. of Illinois Press, Urbana. 344 p.

Foster, Martha Harroun. 1993. Of baggage and bondage: Gender and status among Hidatsa and Crow women. *American Indian Culture and Research Journal* 17(2):121–152.

Funke, Karl A. 1976. Educational assistance and employment preference: Who is an Indian. *American Indian Law Review* 4:1–47.

Gallatin, Albert. 1836. A synopsis of the Indian tribes within the United States east of the Rocky Mountains, and the British and Russian possessions in America. In *Archaeologia Americana: Transactions and Collections of the American Antiquarian Society* 2. Cambridge, Mass. p. 1–422,

Gamerman, Ellen. 1992. State blocked gaming pact, Indian chairman tells panel. In *Arizona Daily Star,* Jan. 10.

Geertz, Clifford. 1983. *Local knowledge: Further essays in interpretive anthropology.* Basic Books, Inc. New York. 236 p.

General Accounting Office. 1992. *Indian Programs: Profile of land ownership at 12 reservations.* U.S. General Accounting Office, Washington, D.C., GAO/RCED-92-96BR. 30 p.

General Allotment Act. 1887. 24 Stat. 388.

George Philip Limited. 1998. *The American desk encyclopedia.* Oxford Univ. Press, New York. 892 p.

Getches, David H. 1985. Alternative approaches to land claims: Alaska and Hawaii. *In* Sutton. 1985. p. 301–303.

———. 1997. *Water law: In a nut shell.* West Group, St. Paul, Minn. 456 p.

Getches, David H., Daniel M. Rosenfelt, and Charles F. Wilkinson. 1979. *Federal Indian law: Cases and materials.* West Publishing Company. St. Paul, Minn. 660 p.

Getches, David H., Charles F. Wilkinson, and Robert Williams, Jr. 1998. *Cases and materials on Federal Indian law.* (4th ed.). West Group, St. Paul, Minn. 1063 p.

Gonzales, Patrisia. 2000. Women's leadership in indigenous America. *Winds of Change* 15(2):36–40 (Spring).

Guest, Richard A. 1995. Intellectual property rights and Native American tribes. *American Indian Law Review* 20(1):111–139.

Giago, Tim. 1991a. Notes from Indian country. In *Lakota Times,* Sept. 11.

———. 1991b. What do you call an Indian. In *Lakota Times,* Dec. 14.

———. 1991c. Mascots, spirituality, and insensitivity. In *Lakota Times,* Oct. 23.

Giago, Tim, ed. 1991d. *The American Indian and the media.* National Conference of Christians and Jews. Minneapolis, Minn. 84 p.

Gibbons, Boyd. 1992. Alcohol: The legal drug. *National Geographic* 181(2):3–35.

Gibson, Ronald, ed. 1977. *Jefferson Davis and the Confederacy, and treaties concluded by the Confederate States with Indian tribes.* Oceana Publications, Inc., Dobbs Ferry, New York. 205 p.

Gillespie, Beryl C. 1981. Territorial groups before 1821: Athapaskans of the Shield and Mackenzie drainage. *In* Helm. 1981. p. 161–168.

Glaser, Lynn. 1973. *Indians or Jews.* Lorrin L. Morrison Press, Los Angeles. 85 p.

Goldberg, Carole E. 1975. Public Law 280: The limits of state jurisdiction over reservation Indians. 22 *U.C.L.A. Law Review* 535–594.

Graham, Colonel W.A. (USA Ret.). 1959. *The story of the Little Bighorn.* Bonanza Books, New York. 178 p.

Grinde, Donald A., Jr. 1977. *The Iroquois and the founding of the American nation.* American Indian Historian Press, San Francisco. 175 p.

Grinnell, George B. 1910. Coup and scalp among the Plains Indians. *American Anthropologist* 12:296–310.

Hafford, William E. 1989. The Navajo code talkers. *Arizona Highways* 65(2): 36–45.

Hagan, William T. 1981. Tribalism rejuvenated: The Native American since the era of termination. *In* Nichols. 1981. p. 295–304.

———. 1988. "To correct certain evils": The Indian land claims cases. In Vecsey, Christopher and William A. Atarna. 1988. *Iroquois land claims.* Syracuse Univ. Press, Syracuse, N.Y. p. 17–30.

———. 1993. *American Indians.* Univ. of Chicago Press. 239 p.

Hall, Gilbert L. 1981a. *An introduction to criminal jurisdiction in Indian country.* American Indian Lawyer Training Program, Oakland, Calif. 52 p.

———. 1981b. *The federal-Indian trust relationship.* Inst. Devel. Indian Law, Washington, D.C. 132 p.

Harjo, Joy, and Gloria Bird, eds. 1997. *Reinventing the enemy's language: Contemporary women's writings of North America.* W. W. Norton & Company, New York. 576 p.

Harjo, et al. v. Pro-Football, Inc. 1999. Trademark Trial and Appeal Board, Patent and Trademark Office, 1999 WL 329721 (P.T.O.) In Getches, Wilkinson, and Williams (1998), Teacher's Memorandum for 1999–2000. p. 29–40.)

Harlow, Victor E. 1935. *Oklahoma: Its origins and development.* Harlow Publ. Corp., Oklahoma City. 450 p.

Harring, Sidney L. 1994. *Crow Dog's case: American Indian sovereignty, tribal law, and United States law in the nineteenth century.* Cambridge Univ. Press, New York. 301 p.

Harrison et al. v. Laveen. 1948. 196 P.2d 456.

Harvey, Karen D., and Lisa D. Harjo. 1994. *Indian country: A history of Native people in America.* North American Press, Golden, Colo. 339 p.

Hausman, Gerald. 1992. *Turtle Island alphabet: A lexicon of Native American symbols and culture.* St. Martin's Press, New York. 204 p.

Hawaii Homes Commission Act. 1921. P.L. 67-42, 42 Stat. 108.

Hazard, Anne. 1991. Indians need more doctors, Senators told. In *Arizona Daily Star*, Nov. 13.

Heaney, Gerald W., Senior Judge on the U.S. Circuit Court of Appeals for the Eighth Circuit. 1991. Letter to Senator Inouye, Chairman, Senate Select Committee on Indian Affairs. Apr. 18.

Heat-Moon, William Least. 1991. *PrairyErth (a deep map).* Houghton Mifflin Company, Boston. 624 p.

Heinl, Robert Debs, Jr. 1962. *Soldiers of the sea.* United States Naval Institute, Annapolis, Maryland. 692 p.

Heizer, Robert F., and Theodora Kroeber, eds. 1979. *Ishi the last Yahi: A documentary history.* Univ. of California Press, Berkeley. 242 p.

Heizer, Robert F., and M. A. Whipple, eds. 1971. *The California Indians: A source book.* Univ. of California Press, Berkeley. 619 p.

Helm, June, ed. 1981. *Handbook of North American Indians—Subarctic.* Smithsonian Institution, Washington, D.C. 837 p.

Henige, David. 1990. Their numbers become thick: Native American historical demography as expiation. *In* Clifton. 1990. p. 169–191.

———. 1998. *Numbers from nowhere: The American Indian contact population debate.* Univ. of Oklahoma Press, Norman. 532 p.

Hershey, Robert Alan, and Richard Guest. 1994. Intellectual property rights and American Indian tribes. In *American Indian Relationships in a Modern Arizona Economy.* Sixty-fifth Arizona Town Hall. Oct. 30–Nov. 2. p. 173–180.

Hill, Edward E. 1974. *The Office of Indian Affairs, 1824–1880: Historical sketches.* Clearwater Publishing Co., Inc., New York. 246 p.

Hill, Edward E., comp. 1981. *Guide to records in the National Archives of the United States relating to American Indians.* U.S. Govt. Printing Office, Washington, D.C. 467 p.

Hill, H. W., ed. 1984. *The consolidated treaty series index, Vol. 3, 1852–1885.* Oceana Publications, Dobbs Ferry, N.J. p. 359, 413, 479.

Hill, Liz. 1999. BIA priorities: Troubled trust management, education. *Indian Country Today*, April 12–19.

Hirschfelder, Arlene, and Paulette Molin. 1992. *The encyclopedia of Native American religions.* Facts on File, New York. 367 p.

Hirschfelder, Arlene, and Martha Kriepe de Montaño. 1993. *The Native American almanac: A portrait of Native America Today.* Prentice Hall, New York. 341 p.

Hodge, Frederick Webb, ed. 1907. *Handbook of American Indians north of Mexico.* Smithsonian Institution, Bureau of Ethnology, Washington, D.C. Bulletin 30, Part 1, 972 p. and Part 2, 1221 p.

———. 1975. *Handbook of American Indians north of Mexico.* Rowan and Littlefield, Totowa, N.J. Part 1, 972 p. and Part 2, 1221 p.

Hoover Commission—Commission on Organization of the Executive Branch of the Government. 1949. *Indian Affairs: A Report to Congress.* U.S. Govt. Printing Office, Washington, D.C. 81 p.

Horsman, Reginald. 1988. United States Indian policies, 1776–1815. *In* Washburn. 1988. p. 29–39.

Hou Hawaiians v. State of Hawaii. 1985. 764 P.2d 623.

Houghton, Richard H., III. 1989. An argument for Indian status for Native Hawaiians—The discovery of a lost tribe. *American Indian Law Review* 14(1):1–55.

House Concurrent Resolution 108. 1953. 83rd Cong., 1st sess. 67 Stat. B132.

Howarth, Rea. 1999a. It is as bad as you thought. *American Indian Report.* Oct.

———. 1999b. BIA: Can it be fixed? *American Indian Report.* Oct.

———. 1999c. Second Helpings: As first-generation compacts expire, states reach for a bigger piece of the tribal gaming pie. In *American Indian Reeport.* Aug. 1999.

———. 2000. System clearly out of control: Document destruction and a coverup surface in the multi-million dollar trust fund case, as plaintiffs wonder when the government will admit its mistakes. In *American Indian Report.* Jan. 2000. p. 9–10.

Howe, Henry. 1851. *Historical collections of the great West. Vols. I & II.* Henry Howe. Cincinnati, Ohio. 440 p.

Hultkrantz, Ake. 1987. *Native religions of North America.* Harper Collins Publishers, New York. 144 p.

Iacopi, Robert L., ed. 1972. *Look to the mountain top.* Gousha Publications, San Jose, Calif. 121 p.

Indian Arts and Crafts Act. 1990. P.L. 101-644, 104 Stat. 4662, 25 USC Sec. 305.

Indian Arts and Crafts Board. 1991a. *Summary and text of Title I, Public Law 101-644.* U.S. Dept. of the Interior, Washington, D.C. 6 p.

———. 1991b. Fact sheet. U.S. Dept. of the Interior, Washington, D.C. 6 p.

Indian Child Welfare Act. 1978. P.L. 95-608, 92 Stat. 3069, 25 USC Sec. 1901 et seq.

Indian Citizenship Act. 1924. P.L. 68-233, 43 Stat. 253.

Indian Civil Rights Act. 1968. P.L. 90-284, 82 Stat. 73, 77-81.

Indian Depredation Act of 1891. 26 Stat. 851.

Indian Education Act of 1972. P.L. 92-318, 86 Stat. 235, 334-345. As amended.

Indian Education Act of 1988. P.L. 100-297, 102 Stat. 363. As amended.

Indian Gaming Regulatory Act. 1988. P.L. 100-497, 102 Stat. 2467.

Indian Health Amendments of 1992. P.L. 102-573, 25 U.S.C. 1601 et seq.

Indian Health Care Improvement Act. 1976. P.L. 94-437, 90 Stat. 1400. As amended. 25 USC Sec. 1601 et seq.

Indian Health Service. 1988. *Indian Health Service accomplishments: Fiscal year 1988.* Rockville, Md. 32 p.

———. 1991a. *Regional differences in Indian health: 1991.* Rockville, Md. 73 p.

———. 1991b. *Service area population estimates and projections 1980–2010.* Rockville, Md. 38 p.

———. 1991c. *Trends in Indian health: 1991.* Rockville, Md. 93 p.

———. 1992a. Fact sheet. Rockville, Md. 2 p.

———. 1992b. Personal communication. Public Information Office. Jan. 23.

———. 1997. *Trends in Indian health 1997.* Rockville, Md. 214 p.

———. 2000. www.ihs.gov (March 14).

Indian Law Enforcement Reform Act. 1990. P.L. 101-379, 104 Stat. 473, 42 USC 2991a.

Indian Removal Act of 1830. 4 Stat. 411.

Indian Reorganization Act. 1934. 48 Stat. 984, 25 USC 461 et seq.

Indian Self-Determination and Education Assistance Act. 1975. P.L. 93-638, 88 Stat. 2203, 25 USC Sec. 450–450n, 455–458e.

Institute for the Development of Indian Law. 1973. *A chronological list of treaties and agreements made by Indian tribes with the United States.* Washington, D.C. 34 p.

———. 1975. *Proceedings of the Great Peace Commission of 1867–1868.* Washington, D.C. 176 p.

International Indian Treaty Council. 1992. Press Release. San Francisco, Calif. (Mar.)

———. 2000. www.aimovement.org (March 3).

Jackson, Helen Hunt. 1886. *A century of dishonor: A sketch of the United States government's dealings with some of the Indian tribes.* Roberts Brothers, Boston. 514 p.

Jackson, Robert H. 1999. *Race, caste, and status: Indians in colonial Spanish America.* Univ. of New Mexico Press, Albuquerque. 151 p.

Jaumes, M. Annette, ed. 1992. *The state of Native America: Genocide, colonization, and resistance.* South End Press, Boston, Mass. 460 p.

Jennings, Francis. 1975. *The invasion of America: Indians, colonialism, and the cant of conquest.* W. W. Norton & Company, New York. 369 p.

―――. 1984. *The ambiguous Iroquois empire: The covenant chain confederation of Indian tribes with English colonies.* W. W. Norton & Company, New York. 438 p.

Jim, Rex Lee. 1994. *Dancing voices: Wisdom of the American Indian.* Peter Pauper Press, Inc., White Plains, N.Y. 64 p.

Johanson, Bruce E. 1982. *Forgotten founders: How the American Indian helped shape democracy.* Harvard Common Press, Boston. 167 p.

Johnson, Lyndon B. 1968. *Special message to the Congress on the problems of the American Indian: "The Forgotten American."* Public Papers of the President of the United States, p. 335–344. (Mar. 6.)

Johnson v. McIntosh. 1823. 21 U.S. 543.

Johnson, Michael. 1999. The native tribes of North America. Compendium Publishing, London. 256 p.

Johnson-O'Malley Act. 1934. 48 Stat. 596, 25 USC Sec. 452–454.

Johnson, Ralph W., and Berrie Martinis. 1995. Chief Justice Rehnquist and the Indian cases. *Public Land Law Review* 16:1–25.

Johnson, Steven L. 1977. *Guide to American Indian documents in the Congressional Serial Set: 1817–1899.* Clearwater Publ. Co., Inc., New York. 503 p.

Johnson, Troy, Joane Nagel, and Duane Champagne, eds. 1997. *American Indian activism: Alcatraz to the longest walk.* Univ. of Illinois Press, Urbana. 297 p.

Jones, Mike. 1991. Personal communication. Real Estate Office, Bureau of Indian Affairs, Washington, D.C. Dec. 6.

Josephy, Alvin M., Jr. 1968. *The Indian heritage of America.* Alfred A. Knopf, New York. 384 p.

―――. 1982. *Now that the buffalo's gone: A study of today's American Indians.* Alfred A. Knopf, New York. 300 p.

―――. 1989. *The Patriot Chiefs: A chronicle of American Indian resistance.* Penguin Books, New York. 364 p.

―――. 1994. *500 nations: An illustrated history of the North American Indian.* Alfred A. Knopf, New York. 468 p.

Josephy, Alvin M., ed. 1961. *The American Heritage book of Indians.* American Heritage Book Company, New York. 424 p.

———, ed. 1991. *America in 1492: The world of the Indian peoples before the arrival of Columbus.* Vintage Press, New York. 477 p.

Kappler, Charles J., ed. 1904. *Indian affairs: Laws and treaties, Vol. 2, Treaties.* U.S. Govt. Printing Office, Washington, D.C. 1099 p.

Katz, William Loren. 1996. *The Black West: A documentary and pictorial history of the African American role in the westward expansion of the United States.* Touchstone Books, New York. 348 p.

———. 1997. *Black Indians: A hidden heritage.* Aladdin Paperbacks, New York. 198 p.

Kawano, Kenji. 1990. *Warriors: Navajo code talkers.* Northland Publishing Company, Flagstaff, Ariz. 107 p.

Kee, Joe, Jr. 2000. Personal communication. Instructor of Navajo Language, Northern Arizona Univ. February 9.

Kehoe, Alice B. 1990. Primitivists and plastic medicine men. *In* Clifton. 1990. p. 193–209.

Kelley, Matt. 2000. U.S. reveals trust-fund fix delays. *The Albuquerque Journal,* March 3.

Kelly, Lawrence. 1988. United States Indian policies, 1900–1980. *In* Washburn. 1988. p. 66–80.

Kickingbird, Kirke. 1979. *Old problems—Present issues: Nine essays on American Indian law.* Institute for the Development of Indian Law, Washington, D.C. 22 p.

———. 1988. *Your rights as American Indians.* Institute for the Development of Indian Law, c/o Native American Legal Resources Center, School of Law, Univ. of Oklahoma, Oklahoma City. 22 p.

———. 1995. What's past is prologue: The status and contemporary relevance of American Indian treaties. *St. Thomas Law Review* 7(Summer): 603–629.

Kickingbird, Kirke, and Karen Ducheneaux. 1973. *One hundred million acres.* Macmillan Company, New York. 240 p.

Kickingbird, Kirke, Lynn Kickingbird, Charles Chibitty, and Curtis Berkey. 1977. *Indian sovereignty.* Inst. Devel. Indian Law. Washington, D.C. 49 p.

Kickingbird, Kirke, Lynn Kickingbird, Alexander Tallchief Skibine, and Charles Chibitty. 1980. *Indian treaties.* Inst. Devel. Indian Law. Washington, D.C. 90 p.

Kickingbird, Kirke, Alexander Tallchief Skibine, and Lynn Kickingbird. 1983. *Indian jurisdiction.* Institute for the Development of Indian Law, Washington, D.C. 122 p.

Kickingbird, Lynn, and Kirke Kickingbird. 1977. *Indians and the U.S. government.* Inst. Devel. Indian Law. Washington, D.C. 115 p.

Klein, Barry T., ed. 1997. *Reference encyclopedia of the American Indian.* Eighth edition. Todd Publications, West Nyack, N.Y. 735 p.

Klein, Laura F., and Lillian A. Ackerman. 1995. *Women and power in Native North America.* Univ. of Oklahoma Press, Norman. 294 p.

Krech, Shepard III. 1999. *The ecological Indian: Myth and history.* W. W. Norton & Company, New York. 318 p.

Kvasnicka, Robert M. 1988. United States Indian treaties. *In* Washburn. 1988. p. 195–201.

LaBarre, Weston. 1972. *The Ghost Dance: Origins of religion.* Waveland Press, Prospect Heights, Ill. 677 p.

———. 1989. *The peyote cult.* (5th ed.) Univ. of Oklahoma Press, Norman. 334 p.

LaDuke, Winona. 1999. *All our relations: Native struggles for land and life.* South End Press, Cambridge, Mass. 241 p.

Laenui, Poka. 1993. The rediscovery of Hawaiian sovereignty. *American Indian Culture and Research Journal* (17)1:79–101.

Lakota Times. 1991. Indians in media create resource clearinghouse. Dec. 24.

Lamphere, Louise. 1983. Southwestern ceremonialism. *In* Ortiz. 1983. p. 744–763.

Lantis, Margaret. 1984. Aleut. *In* Damas. 1984. p. 161–184.

Larabee, L.W., ed. 1961. *The papers of Benjamin Franklin.* Yale Univ. Press, New Haven, Conn. 4:114–121.

League of Women Voters. 1976. *Indian country.* League of Women Voters Education Fund, Washington, D.C. 120 p.

Leland, Donald. 1990. Liberty, equality, fraternity: Was the Indian really egalitarian? *In* Clifton. 1990. p. 145–167.

Leonard Peltier Defense Committee. 1991. Information Pamphlet. Lawrence Kans. Winter 1990–1991. 1 p.

———. 2000. www.freepeltier.org (March 22).

Letgers, Lyman H., and Fremont J. Lyden, eds. 1994. *American Indian policy: Self governance and economic development.* Greenwood Press, Westport, Conn. 228 p.

Leubben, Thomas E. 1980. *American Indian natural resources: Oil & gas.* Inst. Devel. Indian Law, Washington, D.C. 91 p.

Libby, Orin G., ed. 1998. *The Arikara narrative of Custer's campaign and the battle of the Little Bighorn.* Univ. of Oklahoma Press, Norman. 219 p.

Lick, Derek. 1991. Indians want reforms in U.S. recognition rules. In *Arizona Daily Star,* Oct. 23.

Littlebear, Richard. 2000. To save our languages, we must change our teaching methods. *Tribal College* XI(3):18–20 (Spring).

Little Eagle, Avis. 1991. Braves fans assault protesters. In *Lakota Times,* Oct. 30.

———. 1992. Lakota discuss exploitation of religion, preserving culture. In *Indian Country Today,* Nov. 6.

———. 1998. New twist to Bering Strait theory. *Indian Country Today,* June 8–15.

Little Thunder et al. v. State of South Dakota. 1975. 518 F.2d 1253.

Littman, Jonathan. 1991. Reservation industry not business as usual. *San Francisco Chronicle* article reprinted in *Arizona Daily Star,* Sept. 8.

Lone Wolf v. Hitchcock. 1903. 187 U.S. 553.

Lopach, James J., Margery Hunter Brown, and Richard L. Clow. 1990. *Tribal government today: Politics on Montana Indian reservations.* Westview Press, San Francisco. 193 p.

Lopez, Rebecca. 1999. Tribes seek trademark protection for sacred symbol. *Prescott Courier,* July 11.

Lowie, Robert H. 1954. *Indians of the Plains.* The Natural History Press, Garden City, N.Y. 258 p.

Luka, Jean, Esq. 2000. Acting Programming Director, Administration for Native Americans. Personal communication. Jan. 7.

Lyman, Stanley David. 1991. *Wounded Knee 1973: A personal account.* Univ. of Nebraska Press, Lincoln. 180 p.

Lynch, Donald F. 1990. Alaska. In *Academic American Encyclopedia.* Grolier Corporation, Danbury, Conn. Vol. 1, p. 240–247.

———. 1991. Alaska. In *Encyclopedia Americana.* Grolier Corporation, Danbury, Conn. Vol. 1, p. 457–473.

Lyng v. Northwest Indian Cemetery Protective Assn. 1988. 485 U.S. 439.

Lyons, Oren. 1993. Law, principle, and reality. *In* Samuels and Thompson. 1993. p. 209–215.

Lyons, Oren, John Mohawk, Vine Deloria, Jr., Laurence Hauptman, Howard Berman, Donald Grinde, Jr., Curtis Berkey, and Robert Venables. 1992.

Exiled in the land of the free: Democracy, Indian Nations, and the U.S. Constitution. Clear Light Publishers, Santa Fe, N.Mex. 414 p.

MacNeish, Richard S. 1971. Early man in the Andes. *Scientific American* 224(4): 36, 46

Mahon, John K. 1988. Indian-United States military situation, 1775–1848. *In* Washburn. 1988. p. 144–162.

Maine Indian Land Claims Settlement Act. 1980. P.L. 96-420, 94 Stat. 1785.

Mancall, Peter C. 1995. *Deadly medicine: Indians and alcohol in early America.* Cornell Univ. Press, Ithaca, N.Y. 268 p.

Maniaci, Jim. 2000. Navajos mobilize to get money from Washington. *The Gallup Independent*, March 11.

Martin, Phillip. 1984. Foreword. *In* Taylor. 1984. p. ix.

Martinez v. Southern Ute Tribe. 1957. 249 F.2d 915.

Mashpee Tribe v. New Seabury Corp. 1979. 592 F.2d 575.

Mason, W. Dale. 2000. *Indian gaming: Tribal sovereignty and American politics.* Univ. of Oklahoma Press, Norman. 320 p.

Matthiessen, Peter. 1991. *In the spirit of Crazy Horse.* Viking Penguin, New York. 645 p.

May, Philip A. 1994. The epidemiology of alcohol abuse among American Indians: The mythical and real properties. *American Indian Culture and Research Journal* 18(2):121–143.

May, Philip, and Mathew B. Smith. 1988. Some Navajo Indian opinions on alcohol abuse and prohibition: A survey and recommendations for policy. *Journal of Studies on Alcohol* 49:324–334.

McClain, S. 1994. *Navajo weapon.* Books Beyond Borders, Boulder, Colo. 304 p.

McClanahan v. Arizona State Tax Commission. 1973. 411 U.S. 164.

McCool, Daniel. 1987. *Command of the waters: Iron triangles, federal water development, and Indian water.* Univ. of Californai Press, Berkeley. 321 p.

———. 1993a. Indian water settlements: The prerequisites of successful negotiation. *Policy Studies Journal* 21(2):227–242.

———. 1993b. Intergovernmental conflict and Indian water rights: An assessment of negotiated settlements. *Journal of Federalism* 23(winter):85–101.

———. In press. Winters comes home to roost. *In* Miller, Char. *Fluid arguments: water in the American West.* Univ. of Arizona Press, Tucson.

McDermott, John D. 1998. *A guide to the Indian wars of the American West.* Univ. of Nebraska Press, Lincoln. 248 p.

McGaa, Ed (Eagle Man). 1992. *Rainbow tribe: Ordinary people journeying on the Red road*. Harper, San Francisco. 264 p.

McGuire, Thomas, William B. Lord, and Mary G. Wallace, eds. 1993. *Indian water in the new West*. Univ. of Arizona Press, Tucson. 241 p.

McLuhan, T.C. 1971. *Touch the earth: A self-portrait of Indian existence*. Promontory Press, New York. 185 p.

McNeley, James K. 1990. *A Navajo curriculum in the national context*. Paper presented at Conference on Native American Voices: Culture and Learning. Prescott College, Prescott, Ariz. Aug. 12 p.

McNickle, D'Arcy. 1973. *Native American tribalism: Indian survivals and renewals*. Oxford Univ. Press, New York. 190 p .

————. 1975. *They came here first*. Harper & Row, San Francisco. 325 p.

McNitt, Frank. 1972. *The Navajo wars: Military campaigns, slave raids, and reprisals*. Univ. of New Mexico Press, Albuquerque. 477 p.

Medicine, Beatrice. 1993. North American indigenous women and cultural domination. *American Indian Culture and Research Journal* 17(3):121–130.

Melmer, David. Campbell scolds Babbitt over special trustee. *Indian Country Today*, April 12–19.

Meriam Report. 1928. *The problem of Indian administration*. Inst. for Govt. Research, Washington, D.C. 872 p.

Merrill, Malcolm. 1994. American Indian relationships in a modern American economy. Arizona Town Hall, Phoenix. 208 p.

Merrion v. Jicarilla Apache Tribe. 1982. 455 U.S. 130.

Messenger, Phyllis Mauch. 1999. *The ethics of collecting cultural property*. Univ. of New Mexico Press, Albuquerque. 301 p.

Meyer, Michael A. 1984. *Special chronological list, special chronologies (A) Colonial and like treaties (B) Postal and telegraphic etc. agreements, Vol. 2*. Oceana Publications, Inc., Dobbs Ferry, New York. 425 p.

Meyer, Michael C., and William Sherman. 1991. *The course of Mexican history*. Oxford Univ. Press, New York. 718 p.

Michno, Gregory. 1994. *The mystery of E Troop: Custer's gray horse company at the Little Bighorn*. Mountain Press Publishing Company, Missoula, Mont. 349 p.

Middlekauf, Robert. 1982. The glorious cause: The American revolution, 1763–1789. Oxford Univ. Press, New York. 696 p.

Mihesuah, Devon. 1993. Suggested guidelines for institutions with scholars who conduct research on American Indians. *American Indian Culture and Research Journal* 17(3):131–139.

————. 1996. *American Indians: Stereotypes and realities*. Clarity International, Regina, Sask., Canada. 149 p.

————. 1998. *Natives and academics: Research and writing about American Indians*. Univ. of Nebraska Press, Lincoln. 213 p.

————, ed. 2000. *Repatriation reader: Who owns American Indian remains?* Univ. of Nebraska Press, Lincoln. 335 p.

Mistaken Chief, Duane, Sr. 2000. Using Blackfeet language to rediscover who we are. *Tribal College* XI(3):26–27 (Spring).

Moffitt, John F., and Santiago Sebastian. 1996. *O brave new world: The European invention of the American Indian*. Univ. of New Mexico Press, Albuquerque. 399 p.

Momaday, N. Scott. 1991. *The becoming of the Native: Man in America before Columbus*. In Josephy. 1991. p. 13–19.

Montana v. United States. 1982. 450 U.S. 544.

Montoya v. Bolack. 1962. 872 P.2d 387.

Montoya v. United States. 1901. 180 U.S. 261.

Mooney, James. 1928. *The aboriginal population of American north of Mexico*. Smithsonian Misc. Coll., Vol. 80, No. 7. Smithsonian Institution, Washington, D.C. 40 p.

Moore, John H. 1993. *The political economy of North American Indians*. Univ. of Oklahoma Press, Norman. 349 p.

Morgan, Lewis Henry. 1996. *League of the Iroquois*. Carol Publishing Group, Secaucus, N.J. 477 p.

Morton v. Mancari. 1974. 417 U.S. 535.

Moses, L. G. 1996. *Wild west shows and the images of American Indians, 1883–1933*. Univ. of New Mexico Press, Albuquerque. 364 p.

Moses, L. G., and Raymond Wilson, eds. 1985. *Indian lives: Essays on nineteenth- and twentieth-century Native American leaders*. Univ. of New Mexico Press, Albuquerque. 227 p.

Murr, Andrew. 1999. Who got here first? The war over the first Americans rages as science sifts through spear points—and shibboleths. *Newsweek*, Nov. 15.

Nabokov, Peter. 1991. *Native American testimony: A chronicle of Indian-White relations from prophecy to the present, 1492–1992*. Penguin Books, New York. 474 p.

Nagel, Joane. 1997. *American Indian ethnic renewal: Red power and the resurgence of identity and culture*. Oxford Univ. Press, New York. 298 p.

Nash, Philleo. 1988. Map. *In* Washburn. 1988. p. 274.

National Academy of Public Administration. 1999. *A study of management and administration: The Bureau of Indian Affairs.* Washington, D.C. 130 p.

National Archives and Records Administration. n.d. *Ratified Indian treaties, 1722–1869.* National Archives Microfilm M668. Washington, D.C.

National Congress of American Indians. 1976. *Treaties and trust responsibilities.* Major Policy Resolution Number One. Adopted Oct. 21.

———. 1991. *The 1990s: A new federalism on our terms.* Washington, D.C. 3 p.

———. 1992. Personal communication. Public Information Office. Apr. 1.

National Gambling Impact Study Act. 1996. P.L. 104-169.

National Gambling Impact Study Commission. 1999. www.ngisc.gov (Dec. 7).

———. 2000a. www.ngisc.gov/c-law (March 29).

———. 2000b. www.ngisc.gov/research/nagaming.

———. 2000c. www.ngisc.gov/reports/fullrpt.html.

National Geographic Society. 1991. 1491: America before Columbus. *National Geographic* 180(4):1–99. (Oct. issue)

National Indian Education Association. 1991. *Description and history of the NIEA.* Washington, D.C. 6 p.

National Indian Gaming Association. 2000. www.niga.org (March 26).

National Indian Gaming Commission. 1991. *Commission fees.* 56 Federal Register, No. 158. p. 56282.

———. 1992a. *25 CFR Part 502—Definitions under the Indian Gaming Regulatory Act; Rule.* Vol. 57 Federal Register No. 69, p. 12382. (Apr. 9)

———. 1992b. *25 CFR Parts 515, 519, 522, 523, 524, 556, 558—Service: approval of Class II and Class III gaming ordinances under the Indian Gaming Regulatory Act procedures; proposed rules and notice.* (July 8)

———. 1992c. *25 CFR Parts 571, et al.—Compliance and enforcement procedures under the Indian Gaming Regulatory Act: Proposed rule.* Vol. 57 Federal Register No. 132, p. 30584. (July 9)

———. 2000. www.nigc.gov (April 1).

National Indian Policy Center. 1991. Fact sheet. Washington, D.C. 1 p.

———. 1992. *Report to Congress: Recommendations for the establishment of a National Indian Policy Center.* Washington, D.C. 81 p.

National Indian Youth Council. 1991a. *Americans Before Columbus* 19(1):1–8.

———. 1991b. *The choice is yours.* Albuquerque, N.Mex. 1 p.

————. 1991c. Information pamphlet. Albuquerque, N.Mex. 1 p.

National Museum of the American Indian Act. 1989. P.L. 101-185, 103 Stat. 1336.

Native American Graves Protection and Repatriation Act. 1990. P.L. 101-106, 104 Stat. 3048.

Native American Journalists Association. 2000. www.naja.com (March 25).

Native American Languages Act. 1990. P.L. 101-477 (sec. 101), 104 Stat. 1154, 25 USC 2901.

Native American Programs Act. 1975. P.L. 93-644. 88 Stat. 2324, 42 USC 2991a.

Native American Rights Fund. 2000. www.narf.org (March 23).

Native Hawaiian Health Care Act. 1988. P.L. 100-579, 102 Stat. 2916, 42 USC 11701.

Native Hawaiians Study Commission Act. 1980. P.L. 96-565 (Title III), 94 Stat. 3324.

Native Village of Tyonek v. Puckett et al. 1992. U.S. Circuit Court of Appeals for the Ninth Circuit. No. 87-3569. (Jan. 13)

Navarro, Jay, Stan Wilson, Lawrence Berger, and Timothy Taylor. 1997. Substance abuse and spirituality: A program for Native American students. *American Journal of Health Behavior* 21(1)3–11.

Niehardt, John G. 1959. *Black Elk speaks.* Simon & Schuster, New York, 238 p.

Nelson Act. 1905. 33 Stat. 617.

Nevada v. United States. 1983. 463 U.S. 110.

Nez Perce Treaty. 1868. 15 Stat. 693.

Nichols, Roger L., ed. 1986. *The American Indian: Past and present.* Alfred A. Knopf, New York. 312 p.

Nielsen, Marianne O., and Robert A. Silverman, eds. 1996. *Native Americans, crime, and justice.* Westview Press, Boulder, Colo. 321 p.

Niethammer, Carolyn. 1977. *Daughters of the earth: The lives and legends of American Indian women.* Touchstone Books, New York. 279 p.

Nixon, Richard M. 1970. *Special message to the Congress on Indian affairs.* Public Papers of the President of the United States: Richard Nixon. p. 564–576. (July 8)

Noe, Winfried. 1998. *Native American astrology: The wisdom of the four winds.* Sterling Publishing Company, New York. 128 p.

Noriega, Jorge. 1992. American Indian education in the United States: Indoctrination for subordination to colonialism. *In* Jaimes. 1992. p. 371–402.

Norrell, Brenda. 1999. Challenges galvanize Indian country. *Indian Country Today.* Dec. 1. p. A-3.

O'Brien, Bill. 2000a. Tribes pledge unity in future dealings with the state. In *Traverse City Record-Eagle,* Traverse City, Mich. March 17.

———. 2000b. Three fires unite tribes. *Traverse City Record Eagle,* Traverse City, Mich., March 12.

O'Brien, Sharon. 1989. *American Indian tribal governments.* Univ. of Oklahoma Press, Norman. 349 p.

Office of Indian Education. 1991. OIE Information pamphlet. U.S. Dept. of Education, Washington, D.C. 4 p.

———. 2000. Telephone communication with Washington, D.C. staff, U.S. Department of Education. March 23.

Office of Subsistence Management. 2000. www.r7.fws.gov/asm/home. U.S. Fish and Wildlife Service, Anchorage, Alaska (907) 786-3888 (March 23).

Office of the Federal Register. 1990. *United States government manual 1990/91.* Supt. of Documents, U.S. Govt. Printing Office, Washington, D.C. 907 p.

Oklahoma Enabling Act. 1906. 34 Stat. 267.

Oklahoma Indian Affairs Commission. 1991. *Proceedings—Sovereignty symposium IV.* June 10–12. 675 p.

Oklahoma Organic Act. 1890. 26 Stat. 81.

Oklahoma Tax Commission v. Citizen Band Potawatomi Indian Tribe of Oklahoma. 1991. 111 S. Ct. 905.

Old Army Press. 1979. *Chronological list of actions, etc. with Indians from January 15, 1837, to January 1891.* Fort Collins, Colo. 79 p.

Oliphant v. Suquamish Tribe. 1978. 435 U.S. 191.

Oliver, Ethel Ross. 1988. *Journal of an Aleutian year.* Univ. of Washington Press, Seattle. 248 p.

Oregon v. Smith. 1990. 494 U.S. 872.

Organic Act—Alaska. 1884. 23 Stat. 24.

Ortiz, Alfonso, ed. 1979. *Handbook of North American Indians—Southwest. Vol. 9.* Smithsonian Institution, Washington, D.C. 701 p.

———. 1983. *Handbook of North American Indians—Southwest. Vol. 10.* Smithsonian Institution, Washington, D.C. 868 p.

Owen, Roger C., James J. F. Deetz, and Anthony D. Fisher. 1967. *The North American Indians: A sourcebook.* The Macmillan Company, New York. 752 p.

Oxford English Dictionary. 2nd ed. 1989. Oxford Univ. Press, New York.

Pace, Julie A., ed. 1992. Symposium: The Native American Graves Protection and Repatriation Act of 1990 and state repatriation-related legislation. *Arizona State Law Journal* 24(1).

Park, Charles. 1975. Enrollment: Procedures and consequences. *American Indian Law Review* 3:109–111.

Parker, Alan R. 1992. Personal communication. Director, National Indian Policy Center, Washington, D.C. March 24.

Parman, Donald L. 1978. The "big stick" in Indian affairs: The BAI-A-LIL-LE incident in 1909. *Arizona and the West* 20:342–360.

———. 2000. Personal communication. Professor of History, Purdue University, Ind. March 26.

Parry, Clive, ed. 1969. *The consolidated treaty series.* Oceana Publications, Inc., Dobbs Ferry, N.Y. 231 Vols.

Parsons Yazzie, Evangeline. 2000. Personal communication. Asst. Professor and Director, Navajo Language Program, Northern Arizona Univ., Flagstaff. Jan. 13.

Parsons Yazzie, Evangeline, and Jack Utter. 1998. *A time line of Navajo foreign affairs: 1540–1846.* Friends of the Navajo Treaty Project, Navajo Program, Northern Arizona Univ., Flagstaff. 27 p.

Pass, Gail. 2000. Personal communication. Administrative staff, Alaska Federation of Natives. March 24.

Patton, Phil. 2000. Zia Pueblo Indians seeking return of sun symbol. *The Arizona Republic*, Jan. 22.

Paul, Doris A. 1973. *The Navajo code talkers.* Dorrance Publishing Company, Pittsburg, Pa. 170 p.

People v. Woody. 1964. 394 P.2d 813.

Peyote Way Church of God, Inc. v. Thornburgh. 1991. 922 F.2d 1210.

Pevar, Stephen L. 1992. *The rights of Indians and tribes.* Southern Illinois Univ. Press, Carbondale. 335 p.

Pfefferbaum, Betty, Rennard Strickland, Everett R. Rhoades, and Rose L. Pfefferbaum. 1996. Learning how to heal: An analysis of the history, policy, and framework of Indian health care. *American Indian Law Review* 20:365–397.

Philip, Kenneth R. 1999. *Termination revisited: American Indians on the trail to self-determination, 1933–1953.* Univ. Nebraska Press, Lincoln. 247 p.

Pierpoint, Mary. 2000. Parole denied for Leonard Peltier. *Indian Country Today.* June 21.

Polakovic, Gary. 1999. Skeleton may be oldest in New World. In *Los Angeles Times*, April 11.

Porter, Kenneth W. 1996. *The Black Seminoles: History of a freedom-seeking people*. Univ. Press of Florida. 352 p.

Porter, Robert. 1998. (Quoted in) Landmark case revisited by Indian supreme court. *American Indian Report*, Dec., p. 28.

Price, H. Marcus III. 1991. *Disputing the dead: U.S. law on aboriginal remains and grave goods*. Univ. of Missouri Press Columbia. 136 p.

Price, John A. 1978. *Native studies: American and Canadian Indians*. McGraw-Hill Ryerson Ltd., Toronto. 309 p.

Prince v. Board of Education of Central Consolidated School District No. 22. 1975. 543 P.2d 1176. (N.Mex.)

Prucha, Francis Paul, S.J. 1977. *United States Indian policy: A critical bibliography*. Indiana Univ. Press, Bloomington. 54 p.

———. 1979. *The churches and the Indian schools: 1888–1912*. Univ. of Nebraska Press, Lincoln. 278 p.

———. 1981. *Indian policy in the United States: Historical essays*. Univ. of Nebraska Press, Lincoln. 272 p.

———. 1982. *Indian-white relations in the United States: A bibliography of works published 1975–1980*. Univ. of Nebraska Press, Lincoln. 179 p.

———. 1984. *The great father: The United States government and the American Indians. Vol. II*. Univ. of Nebraska Press, Lincoln. 1302 p.

———. 1985. *The Indians in American society: From the Revolutionary War to the present*. UCLA Press, Los Angeles. 127 p.

———. 1986. *The great father: The United States government and the American Indians* (abridged ed.). Univ. of Nebraska Press, Lincoln. 426 p.

———. 1990a. *Atlas of American Indian affairs*. Univ. of Nebraska Press, Lincoln. 191 p.

———. 1990b. *Documents of United States Indian policy*. Univ. of Nebraska Press, Lincoln. 338 p.

———. 1994. *American Indian treaties: A history of a political anomaly*. Univ. of California Press, Berkeley. 562 p.

Public Law 280. 1953. 67 Stat. 588.

Puyallup Tribe of Indians Settlement Act. 1989. P.L. 101-41, 103 Stat. 83.

Reid, John Phillip. 1970. *A law of blood*. New York Univ. Press, New York. 340 p.

Religious Freedom Restoration Act. 1993. 42 U.S.C. Secs. 2000bb-2000bb-4.

Republic News Service. 1999. Canada's 'iceman' could predate European era. *The Arizona Republic*, Aug. 25.

Reyhner, Jon, ed. 1992. *Teaching American Indian students*. Univ. of Oklahoma Press, Norman. 328 p.

———. 2000. A resource guide: Native American language renewal. *Tribal College* XI(3):42–45.

Reyhner, Jon, and Jeanne Eder. 1989. *A History of Indian education*. Eastern Montana College, Billings. 158 p.

Reynolds, Jerry. 1991. Border run drinking style reinforces old stereotypes. In *Lakota Times*, Oct. 2.

Rhoades, Everett R., John Hammond, Thomas K. Welty, Aaron Handler, and Robert W. Ambler. 1987. The Indian burden of illness and future health interventions. Public Health Reports, *Jour. U.S. Public Health Service* 102(4):361–368.

Rhoades, Everett R., Luana Reyes, and George D. Buzzard. 1987. The organization of health services for Indian people. Public Health Reports, *Jour. U.S. Public Health Service* 102(4):352–356.

Rice v. Cayetano. 2000. U.S. Supreme Court. No. 98-818. Decided Feb. 23.

Roessel, Ruth. 1981. *Women in Navajo society*. Navajo Resource Center, Rough Rock Demonstration School, Rough Rock, Ariz. 184 p.

Rogers, George W. 1990. Alaska. In *Colliers Encyclopedia*. Macmillan Education Company, New York. Vol. 1, p. 438–452.

Rollins, Peter C., and John E. O'Connor, eds. 1998. *Hollywood's Indian: The portrayal of the Native American in film*. Univ. of Kentucky Press, Lexington. 226 p.

Rolo, Mark Anthony. 1999a. Last Comanche code talker honored. *Indian Country Today*, Dec. 15.

———. 1999b. Under heavy fire, Gover insists he has support: Saginaw PR blitz blasts BIA leadership. In *Indian Country Today*. Sept. 6.

———. 2000a. Clinton wants extra $1.2 billion. In *Indian Country Today*. Feb. 9.

———. 2000b. Budget expected to receive bipartisan support. In *Indian Country Today*. Feb. 16.

———. 2000c. Gover selling a new and improving BIA. In *Indian Country Today*. Feb. 9.

Rosebud Sioux Tribe v. Knipe. 1977. 430 U.S. 585.

Rosenstiel, Annette. 1983. *Red & white: Indian views of the white man, 1492–1982*. Universe Books, New York. 192 p.

Rouse, Irving. 1992. *The Tainos: Rise and decline of the people who greeted Columbus.* Yale Univ. Press, New Haven, Conn. 211 p.

Royce, Charles C. 1899. *Indian land cessions in the United States.* Bureau of American Ethnology, Washington, D.C., 18th Annual Report, 1896–1897, Part 2. p. 521–997.

Russell, George L. 1991. *A map of American Indian history.* Thunderbird Enterprises, Phoenix, Ariz.

———. 1994. *American Indian digest: Facts about today's American Indians.* Thunderbird Enterprises, Phoenix, Ariz. 72 p.

———. 1998. *Reservation roster.* Russell Publications, Phoenix, Ariz. 28 p.

Samuels, Bruce, and Diane E. Thompson, eds. 1993. Native American struggle: Conquering the rule of law, a colloquium. *New York University Review of Law and Social Change.* p. 199–245.

Sanders, Douglas. 1985. *Aboriginal self-government in the United States.* Queen's University, Kingston, Ontario, Canada. 69 p.

Santa Clara Pueblo v. Martinez. 1978. 436 U.S. 49.

Savilla, Elmer. 1991. Yet another chapter in the saga of Peltier's case. In *Lakota Times,* Oct. 9.

Scheurkogel, Norma. 1992. Personal communication. International Indian Treaty Council, San Francisco. Mar. 27.

Schickel, Richard. 1975. Editorial comments. In *New York Times,* Feb. 9.

Schmid, Randolph E. 1998. Prehistoric maritime communities found: Peru sites yield evidence of group that harvested fish. In *The Arizona Republic,* Sept. 19.

Schroeder, Susan, ed. 1998. *Native resistance and the pax colonial in New Spain.* Univ. of Nebraska Press, Lincoln. 200 p.

Scott, Walter. 1991. *Walter Scott's personality parade.* Box 5573, Beverly Hills, Calif.

Seattle Times. 2000. U.S. seeks to extract DNA from Kennewick Man. In *The Arizona Republic,* Feb. 5.

Seldon, Ron. 2000. Massive education needed. In *Indian Country Today.* Sept. 13–20. p. B-4.

Seminole Nation v. United States. 1946. 315 U.S. 286.

Seminole Tribe of Florida v. Florida. 1996. 517 U.S. 44.

Seneca Nation Claims Settlement Act. 1990. P.L.101-503, 104 Stat. 1292.

Service, Elman R. 1963. *Profiles in ethnology.* Harper and Row, New York. 509 p.

Shoemaker, Nancy. 1999. *American Indian population recovery in the twentieth century.* Univ. of New Mexico Press, Albuquerque. 156 p.

Shorris, Earl. 1971. *The death of the Great Spirit.* Signet, New York. 205 p.

Shurts, John. 2000. *Indian reserved water rights: The* Winters *Doctrine in its social and legal context, 1880s–1930s.* Univ. of Oklahoma Press, Norman. 352 p.

Silverman, Jeff. 1991a. Personal communication. Public Information Office, Alaska Federation of Natives, Anchorage. Dec. 9.

———. 1991b. Personal communication. Public Information Office, Alaska Federation of Natives, Anchorage. Dec. 23.

Simard, Jean-Jacques. 1990. White ghost, red shadows: The reduction of North American Natives. *In* Clifton. 1990. p. 333–369.

Simmons, Janice. 1992. Personal communication. Public Affairs Staff, Bureau of Indian Affairs, Washington, D.C. Jan. 21.

Slotkin, James S. 1967. The peyote way. *In* Owen, Deetz, and Fisher. 1967. p. 648–654.

Slotkin, Richard. 1985. *The fatal environment: The myth of the frontier in the age of industrialization, 1800–1890.* Univ. of Oklahoma Press, Norman. 636 p.

Sly, Peter W. 1988. *Reserved water rights settlement manual.* Island Press, Covelo, Calif. 259 p.

Smith, Dean Howard. 2000. *Modern tribal development: paths to self-sufficiency and cultural integrity in Indian country.* Altamira Press of the Littlefield Publishing Group, Walnut Creek, Calif. 184 p.

Smith, James G.E. 1981. Western woods Cree. *In* Helm. 1981. p. 256–270.

Smith, Jane F., and Robert M. Knvasnicka, eds. 1981. *Indian-White relations: A persistent paradox.* Howard Univ. Press, Washington, D.C. 278 p.

Smith, Michael T. 1986. The history of Indian citizenship. *In* Nichols. 1986. p. 232–241.

Snyder Act. 1921. 42 Stat. 208.

Sockbeson, Henry. 1990. Repatriation Act protects Native burial remains and artifacts. Native American Rights Fund, *Legal Review* 16(1):1–4.

Sokolow, Gary. 1990. The future of gambling in Indian country. *American Indian Law Review* 15(1):151–183.

Spaeth, Nicholas J., Julie Wrend, and Clay Smith, eds. *American Indian law deskbook: Conference of the western Attorneys General.* Univ. Press of Colorado, Niwot. 466 p.

Special Committee on Investigations. 1989. *Final report and legislative recommendations*. Senate Select Committee on Indian Affairs, 101st Cong., 1st sess., Report 101-216. U.S. Govt. Printing Office, Washington, D.C. 238 p.

Spicer, Edward H. 1962. *Cycles of conquest: The impact of Spain, Mexico, and the United States on the Indians of the Southwest*. Univ. of Arizona Press, Tucson. 609 p.

———. 1969. *A short history of the Indians of the United States*. Van Nostrand Reinhold Co. New York. 319 p.

———. 1982. *The American Indian*. Belknap Press, Cambridge, Mass. 210 p.

Stago, Lula M. 1998. The identification and analysis of factors contributing to Navajo student dropout at Seba Dalkai school. Ed. D. dissertation, Northern Arizona Univ., Flagstaff. 278 p.

Stago, Phil, Jr. 2000. Former council member, White Mountain Apache Tribe. Personal communication. March 26.

Stallings, Laurence. 1963. *The doughboys*. Harper & Row, New York. 404 p.

Standing Bear, Luther. 1933. *Land of the spotted eagle*. Houghton Mifflin Co., New York. 259 p.

Standing Bear v. Crook. 1879. U.S. District Court for the District of Nebraska (25 F. Cas. 695, D.Neb., No. 14,891).

Stand Up For California. 2000. http://standup.quiknet.com/impact/ngisc_recommendations_summary.html (March 27).

Stanley, Dyanne. 1992. Personal communication. Public Information staff, International Indian Treaty Council, San Francisco. Mar. 26.

Stannard, David E. 1992. *American holocaust: Columbus and the conquest of the New World*. Oxford Univ. Press, New York. 358 p.

Starkey, Armstrong. 1998. *European and Native American warfare, 1675–1815*. Univ. of Oklahoma Press, Norman. 208 p.

State of Hawaii. 1991. Hawaii State Department of Business and Economic Development and Tourism. Personal communication with Documents Librarian. Sept. 17.

Stedman, Raymond W. 1982. *Shadows of the Indian: Stereotypes in American culture*. Univ. of Oklahoma Press, Norman. 282 p.

Steinmetz, George. 1992. *The preventable tragedy: Fetal alcohol syndrome*. National Geographic 181(2):36–39. (Feb. issue)

Stewart, Omer. 1987. *Peyote religion: A history*. Univ. of Oklahoma Press, Norman. 454 p.

———. 1991. Peyote and the law. *In* Vecsey. 1991. p. 44–62.

Stiffarm, Lenore A., and Phil Lane, Jr. 1992. The demography of Native North America: A question of American Indian survival. *In* Jaumes. 1992. p. 23–54.

Stillman, Pamela. 1991. State experts meet to warn of fetal alcohol problems. In *Lakota Times*, Nov. 13.

Stokes, Brian. 2000a. Congress considers new process for tribal recognition. *Indian Country Today*, May 31.

———. 2000b. Senate committee passes Hawaiian recognition bill. *Indian Country Today*, Sept. 27.

Strickland, Rennard. 1997. *Tonto's revenge.* Univ. of New Mexico Press, Albuquerque. 154 p.

———. 1998. Implementing the national policy of understanding, preserving, and safeguarding the heritage of Indian peoples and Native Hawaiians: Human rights, sacred objects, and cultural patrimony. *In* Carrillo. 1998. p. 198–204.

Sugden, John. 1997. *Tecumseh: A life.* Henry Holt and Company, New York. 492 p.

Sutton, Imre. 1985. *Irredeemable America: The Indians' estate and land claims.* Univ. of New Mexico Press, Albuquerque. 421 p.

Swanton, John R. 1969. *The Indian tribes of North America.* Smithsonian Institution Press, Washington, D.C. 726 p.

Swidler, Nina, Kurt E. Dongoske, Roger Anyon, and Alan S. Downer. 1997. *Native Americans and archaeologists: Stepping stones to common ground.* Altamira Press of the Littlefield Publishing Group, Walnut Creek, Calif. 298 p.

Swisher, Kareb Gayton, and John W. Tippeconnic III, eds. 1999. *Next steps: Research and practice to advance Indian education.* Eric Clearinghouse on Rural Education and Small Schools, Charleton, W.V. 317 p.

Szasz, Margaret Connell. 1999. *Education and the American Indian: The road to self-determination since 1928.* Univ. of New Mexico Press, Albuquerque. 326 p.

Szasz, Margaret Connell, and Carmelita Ryan. 1988. American Indian education. *In* Washburn. 1988. p. 284–300.

Tallman, Valerie. 1991. Native philosophy can overcome environmental racism, summit told. In *Lakota Times*, Nov. 13.

Taylor, Theodore W. 1984. *The Bureau of Indian Affairs.* Westview Press, Boulder, Colo. 220 p.

Teters, Charlene. 1991. Using Indian team names is cruel, racist. In *Arizona Daily Star*, Nov. 19.

Texas Band of Kickapoo Act. 1983. P.L. 97-429, 96 Stat. 2269.

Thomas, Cyrus. 1899. Introduction. *In* Royce. 1899. p. 527–647.

Thompson, William N. 1996. *Native American issues.* ABC-CLIO Publications, Santa Barbara, Calif. 293 p.

Thornton, Russell. 1987. *American Indian holocaust and survival: A population history since 1492.* Univ. of Oklahoma Press, Norman. 292 p.

Tibbles, Thomas Henry. 1972. *Standing Bear and the Ponca chiefs.* Univ. of Nebraska Press, Lincoln. 143 p.

Tiller, Veronica E. Velarde. 1996. *Tiller's guide to Indian country: Economic profiles of American Indian reservations.* BowArrow Publishing Company, Albuquerque, N.Mex. 698 p.

Time-Life Books. 1990. *The old West.* Prentice Hall Press, New York. 432 p.

Toledo v. Nobel-Sysco, Inc. 1986. 651 F.Supp. 483.

Trask, Mililani B. 1991a. Personal communication. Governor of the Sovereign Nation of Hawaii, 152-B Koula Street, Hilo, Hawaii 96720. Nov. 22.

———. 1991b. Historical and contemporary Hawaiian self-determination: A Native Hawaiian perspective. In *Arizona Journal of International and Comparative Law* 8(2):77–95.

———. 1992. Personal communication. Governor of the Sovereign Nation of Hawaii. Apr. 29.

Treaty of Dancing Rabbit Creek with the Choctaw Nation. 1830. 7 Stat. 333.

Treaty of Doak's Stand. 1820. 7 Stat. 210.

Treaty of Fort Laramie. 1868. 15 Stat. 635.

Treaty of Guadalupe Hidalgo. 1848. 9 Stat. 922 (1851).

Treaty with Russia. 1867. 15 Stat. 539.

Treaty with the Cherokees. 1817. 7 Stat. 156.

Treaty with the Makah. 1855. 12 Stat. 939.

Treaty with the Senecas, et al. 1867. 15 Stat. 517.

Treaty with the Wyandots. 1855. 10 Stat. 1159.

Tribally Controlled Schools Act. 1988. P.L. 100-297, 102 Stat. 385.

Trigger, Bruce G., and Wilcomb E. Washburn, eds. 1996. *The Cambridge history of the native peoples of North America. Vol. I: North America.* Cambridge Univ. Press, New York. 1104 p.

Trujillo, Michael H. 2000. Indian Health Service Introduction. www.ihs.gov/ AboutIHS/IHSintro.asp (March 14).

Tundra Times. 1991. *Alaska Native Claims Settlement Act: A scrapbook history.* Anchorage. 63 p.

Tyler, Lyman S. 1973. *A history of Indian policy.* Bureau of Indian Affairs, U.S. Dept. of the Interior. Washington, D.C. 328 p.

Tzu, Sun. 1991. *The art of war.* Shambala Publications. Boston, Mass. 114 p.

Underhill, Ruth. 1957. Religion among American Indians. *Annals of American Academy of Political and Social Sciences* 311:127–136.

———. 1965. *Red man's religion: Beliefs and practices of the Indians north of Mexico.* Univ. of Chicago Press, Chicago. 301 p.

———. 1974. Religion among American Indians. *In* Worton. 1974. p. 116–119.

Unger, Steven, ed. 1977. *The destruction of American Indian families.* Association on American Indian Affairs. 90 p.

United Effort Trust. 1979. *Federal/Indian trust relationship.* Washington, D.C. 2 p.

U.S. Bureau of the Census. 1991. *American Indian and Alaska Native areas: 1990.* Racial Stat. Branch, Population Div. Washington, D.C. 52 p. (June)

———. 1991. *1990 Census counts of American Indians, Eskimos, or Aleuts and American Indian and Alaska Native areas.* Racial Stat. Branch, Population Div. Washington, D.C. 16 p. (July)

———. 1991. Release CB91-229. 4 p. (July 5)

———. 1991. Release CB91-232.6 p. (July 11)

United States Commission on Civil Rights. 1918. *Indian tribes: A continuing quest for survival.* Supt. of Documents, U.S. Govt. Printing Office, Washington, D.C. 192 p.

United States Congress. 1964. *List of Indian treaties.* House Committee on Interior and Insular Affairs, 82nd Cong., 2nd sess., Comm. Print No. 30. Sept. 8.

U.S. Department of Commerce. 1974. *Federal and State Indian reservations and Indian trust areas.* U.S. Govt. Printing Office, Washington, D.C. 604 p.

U.S. Department of the Interior. 1894. *Indians taxed and not taxed.* U.S. Govt. Printing Office, Washington, D.C. 683 p.

———. 1931. Secretarial Order No. 494. Mar. 14.

United States Government Manual. 1997. *Ready and Forward.* U.S. Govt. Printing Office, Washington, D.C. 860 p.

U.S. Indian Claims Commission. 1978. Final report. U.S. Govt. Printing Office, Washington, D.C. 141 p.

U.S. Public Health Service. 1987. Public Health Reports 102(4):350–376.

———. 1998. 43 CFR 36.10 et seq.

U.S. v. Wheeler. 1978. 435 U.S. 313.

U.S. v. Winans. 1905. 198 U.S. 371.

Unrau, William E. 1985. Charles Curtis: The politics of allotment. *In* Moses and Wilson. 1985. p. 113–137.

Utley, Robert M. 1963. *The last days of the Sioux Nation.* Yale Univ. Press, New Haven. 314 p.

———. 1981a. *Frontiersmen in blue: The United States Army and the Indian, 1848–1865.* Univ. of Nebraska Press, Lincoln. 384 p.

———. 1981b. *The frontier Army: John Ford or Arthur Penn? In* Smith and Kvasnicka. 1981. p. 133–145.

———. 1984. *Indian Frontier of the American West, 1846–1890.* Univ. of New Mexico Press, Albuquerque. 325 p.

———. 1988. Indian-United States military situation, 1848–1891. In Washburn. 1988. p. 163–184.

———. 1993. *The lance and the shield: The life and times of Sitting Bull.* Ballantine Books, New York. 413 p.

Utley, Robert M., and Wilcomb E. Washburn. 1985. *Indian wars.* American Heritage Publishing Company, New York. 352 p.

Utter, Jack. 1991. *Wounded Knee & the ghost dance tragedy.* National Woodlands Publishing Co., Lake Ann, Mich. 29 p.

———. 1999. Tribal independence: A possible American model. *Native American Law Digest,* Sept. p. 5–10.

———. 2000. The Discovery Doctrine, the tribes, and the truth. Paper presented to the Federal Indian law session of the U.S. National Park Service and Canyon de Chelly Guides Association training seminar. Canyon de Chelly National Monument, Ariz. Feb. 11. 8 p.

Utter, Jack, Bob Valen, and Rita Cantu. 1989. Response to environmental despair, or—Invitation to a revolution. *Jour. Interpretation* 13(5):12–14.

Van Kamp, Preston P. 1998. *American Indian law review: 25th anniversary, 1973–1998.* Vol. 22. Univ. of Oklahoma College of Law, Norman. 661 p.

Vanwey, Kevin. 2000. Personal communication. Secretary, Indian Arts and Crafts Board, U.S. Department of the Interior, Washington, D.C. March 22.

Vaughn, Alden T. 1982. From white man to redskin: Changing Anglo-American perceptions of the American Indian. *American Historical Review* 87:917–953.

Vecsey, Christopher, ed. 1991. *Handbook of American Indian religious freedom.* Crossroad Publishing Co., New York. 180 p.

Verrill, A. Hyatt. 1927. *The American Indian. North, South, and Central America.* The New Home Library, New York. 485 p.

Vickers, Scott B. 1998. *Native American identities: From stereotype to archtype in art and literature.* Univ. of New Mexico Press, Albuquerque. 194 p.

Waldman, Carl. 1985. *Atlas of the North American Indian.* Facts on File, New York. 276 p.

―――. 2000. *Atlas of the North American Indian* (Rev. ed). Checkmark Books, New York. 385 p.

Waldron v. United States. 1905. 143 Fed. Repts. 413.

Walke, Roger. 1991. *Federal programs of assistance to Native Americans.* Senate Report 102-62. Senate Select Committee on Indian Affairs. U.S. Govt. Printing Office, Washington, D.C. 331 p.

Walker, Hans, Jr. 1989. *Federal Indian tax rules: A compilation of Internal Revenue Service rules relating to Indians.* 238 p.

Wall, Steve, and Harvey Arden. 1990. *Wisdom-keepers: Meetings with Native American spiritual Elders.* Beyond Words Publ., Hillsboro, Oreg. 128 p.

Wardwell, Lelia. 1991. *The Native American experience.* Facts on File, New York. 268 p.

Washburn, Wilcomb. 1973. *The American Indian and the United States: A documentary history.* Random House, New York. Vols. I–IV. 3119 p.

Washburn, Wilcomb, E., ed. 1988. *Handbook of North American Indians—History of Indian-white relations.* Smithsonian Institution, Washington, D.C. 838 p.

Washburn, Wilcomb E. 1975. *The assault on Indian tribalism: The General Allotment Law (Dawes Act) of 1887.* J. B. Lippincott Company, New York. 79 p.

Washington, George. 1783. Letter to James Duane. Sept. 7. Excerpted in Prucha. 1990. p. 1

Waterman, T. T. 1971. Ishi, the last Yahi. *In* Heizer and Whipple. 1971. p. 285–293.

Watkins, Joe. 2001. *Indigenous archaeology: American Indian values and scientific practice.* Altamira Press of the Littlefield Publishing Group, Walnut Grove, Calif. 224 p.

Weatherford, Jack. 1988. *Indian givers.* Fawcett Columbine, New York. 272 p.

―――. 1991. *Native roots: How the Indians enriched America.* Fawcett Columbine, New York. 310 p.

Weatherhead, L.R. 1980. What is an "Indian tribe?"—The question of tribal existence. *American Indian Law Review* 8:1–47.

Webb, George W. 1966. *Chronological list of engagements between the Regular Army of the United States and various tribes of hostile Indians which occurred during the years 1790–1898.* Argonaut Press, New York. 141 p.

Weber, David J. 1992. *The Spanish frontier in North America.* Yale Univ. Press, New Haven, Conn. 579 p.

White, Richard, and William Cronon. 1988. Ecological change and the Indian-white relation. *In* Washburn. 1988. p. 417–429.

White, Robert H. 1990. *Tribal assets: The rebirth of Native America.* Henry Holt and Company, New York. 291 p.

Wiley v. Keokuk. 1870. 6 Kansas 59.

Wilkins, David E. 1997. *American Indian sovereignty and the U.S. Supreme Court: The masking of justice.* Univ. of Texas Press, Austin, 403 p.

Wilkinson, Charles F. 1988. The idea of sovereignty: Native peoples, their lands, their dreams. *Legal Review of the Native American Rights Fund* 13(4): 1–11.

———. 1999. *Fire on the plateau: Conflict and endurance in the American Southwest.* Island Press, Covelo, Calif. 402 p.

Wilkinson, Charles F., and John M. Volkman. 1975. Judicial review of Indian treaty abrogation: "As long as the water flows and the grass grows upon the earth"—How long a time is that? 63 *California Law Review* 601.

Williams, Robert A., Jr. 1990a. *The American Indian in Western legal thought: The discourses of conquest.* Oxford Univ. Press, New York. 352 p.

———. 1990b. Gendered checks and balances: Understanding the legacy of white patriarchy in an American Indian cultural context. *Georgia Law Review* 24:1019.

———. 1991. Columbus Legacy: Law as an instrument of racial discrimination against indigenous peoples' rights of self-determination. *Arizona Journal of International and Comparative Law* 8(2):51–75.

———. 1996. "The people of the state where they are found are often their deadliest enemies:" The Indian side of the story of Indian rights and federalism. *Arizona Law Review* 38:981–997.

Williams v. United States. 1908. 207 U.S. 564.

Wills, Gary. 1991. "Native American" or "Pope"—let's use preferred names. In *Record-Eagle*, Traverse City, Mich., Sept. 30.

Wiminuche Band of Southern Ute Indians. 1913. Congressional ratification of 1911 agreement. P.L. 63-4, 38 Stat. 30.

Winik, Lyric Wallwork. 1999. There's a new generation with a different attitude. *Parade Magazine*, July 18 (cover story). p. 6–8.

Winters v. United States. 1908. 207 U.S. 564.

Woodhead, Henry, ed. 1992a. *The first Americans*. Time-Life Books, Alexandria, Va. 183 p.

———. 1992b. *The spirit world*. Time-Life Books, Alexandria, Va. 176 p.

———. 1993a. *The mighty chieftains*. Time-Life Books, Alexandria, Va. 184 p.

———. 1993b. *The way of the warrior*. Time-Life Books, Alexandria, Va. 184 p.

———. 1994. *War for the plains*. Time-Life Books, Alexandria, Va. 192 p.

———. 1995. *The woman's way*. Time-Life Books, Alexandria, Va. 184 p.

Wooster, Robert. 1995. *The military and United States Indian policy*. Univ. of Nebraska Press, Lincoln. 268 p.

Worcester, Donald E., ed. 1975. *Forked tongues and broken treaties*. The Caxton Printers, Ltd., Caldwell, Idaho. 470 p.

Worcester v. Georgia. 1832. 31 U.S. (6 Pet.) 515.

Workman, Bill. 1991. Indians aren't rushing to make tribal lands nuclear waste dumps. *San Francisco Chronicle*. Reprinted in *Arizona Daily Star*, Dec. 8.

Worl, Rosita. 1988. Alaska Natives today. In Fitzhugh, William W., and Aron Crowell. 1988. *Crossroads of continents: Cultures of Siberia and Alaska*. Smithsonian Institution Press, Washington, D.C. p. 319–325.

Worton, Stanley N. 1974. *The first Americans*. Hayden Book Co., Inc., Rochelle Park, N.J. 181 p.

Wrone, David R., and Russell S. Nelson, Jr., eds. 1973. *Who's the savage: A documentary history of the mistreatment of the native North Americans*. Fawcett Publications, Inc. Greenwich, Conn. 576 p.

Wunder, John R. 1994. *"Retained by the people:" A history of American Indians and the Bill of Rights*. Oxford Univ. Press, New York. 278 p.

Wutzke, Jeffrey. 1998. Dependent independence: Application of the Nunavut model to Native Hawaiian sovereignty and self-determination claims. In *American Indian Law Review* XXII(2):509–565.

Yakima Nation v. Brendale. 1989. 492 U.S. 408.

Yakima Nation Treaty. 1855. 12 Stat. 951.

Yavapai-Prescott Water Rights Settlement Act of 1994. P.L. 103-434, 108 Stat. 4526.

INDEX